Dog Training

4th Edition

by Wendy Volhard and Mary Ann Rombold Zeigenfuse, LVT

for dummies®

A Wiley Brand

Dog Training For Dummies®, 4th Edition

Published by: **John Wiley & Sons, Inc.**, 111 River Street, Hoboken, NJ 07030-5774, www.wiley.com

Copyright © 2020 by John Wiley & Sons, Inc., Hoboken, New Jersey

Published simultaneously in Canada

For general information on our other products and services, please contact our Customer Care Department within the U.S. at 877-762-2974, outside the U.S. at 317-572-3993, or fax 317-572-4002. For technical support, please visit www.wiley.com/techsupport.

Wiley publishes in a variety of print and electronic formats and by print-on-demand. Some material included with standard print versions of this book may not be included in e-books or in print-on-demand. If this book refers to media such as a CD or DVD that is not included in the version you purchased, you may download this material at http://booksupport.wiley.com. For more information about Wiley products, visit www.wiley.com.

Library of Congress Control Number: 2020932726

ISBN: 978-1-119-65682-1; ISBN 978-1-119-65684-5 (ebk); ISBN 978-1-119-65687-6 (ebk)

Manufactured in the United States of America

V421656_030920

Contents at a Glance

Table of Contents

Introduction

Both of us have had dogs of one kind or another since childhood.

Many years later we're still sharing what we have learned along the way. Every one of our dogs has been more of a teacher than a pupil, and we've discovered much more from our dogs than we could ever have hoped to teach them. This book is our attempt to pass on to you what our dogs have taught us.

Without help, few people can become proficient, much less an expert, in a given field. We certainly have had plenty of help. A well-trained dog is the result of education, more yours than your dog's. You need to know what makes a dog a dog, how he thinks, how he reacts, how he grows, how he expresses himself, what his needs are, and most important, why he does what he does. When you understand your dog fully, you can achieve a mutually rewarding relationship. A dog isn't a homogenous commodity. Each one is a unique individual, and in their differences lies the challenge.

As a dog trainer, every dog teaches you something. Most dog trainers you meet also show you something even if it's only how they communicate with the dogs with which they work. Communication is the key to all dog training. Without communication no training can take place. Dogs need to understand what you want, they need to know when you're pleased, and they need to know when you're finished and moving on. Play is a big part of training a dog. After all, training can be viewed as play as well as work, enjoyable either way.

Our goal in writing this book was to show how communication works and how you must communicate with your dog so both of you can learn the game of dog training. Enjoy as you read and put into practice all the information and advice in this book.

About This Book

We truly want this book to be a useful tool for you. And we don't want dog training to feel like a chore that you have to slog through step by step. So we've structured this book in such a way that you can jump in and out of the text as it interests you and applies to your situation. For instance, is your dog partially trained but needs to learn a few things? If so, consult the table of contents or index and go directly to the chapters you need.

Nor do we expect you to internalize every bit of information in this book. Throughout the text, we include reminders of key points and cross-references to more information about the topic at hand. Remember, dog training is fun! It isn't a series of tests that you have to pass — unless, of course, you and your dog enter the world of competitive events.

Because training starts the moment you bring your little bundle of fur home, we tell you about behavioral development and what to expect during the few weeks and months. We guide you with tips on training, tell you about up-to-date training equipment, and help you to establish a daily schedule. We devote a whole chapter to housetraining and crate training.

This fourth edition of *Dog Training For Dummies* is chock-full of new and revised exercises for you. In addition to a wide array of new photos, we've also

>> Reorganized many of the training exercises to make that more accessible and easier to follow

>> Updated exercises to reflect current training trends

>> Added exercises to make living with your dog easier and more fun from the start

>> Added new tricks so you and your dog can achieve the AKC Trick titles easily

>> Updated and revised Wendy's nutrition chapter with the most current information available

We consider our older dogs our friends as well and have included in this edition a chapter on keeping your old dog young. We offer exercises that can be used to limber up the old joints, tips on feeding, information on the latest supplements, and much more.

All in all, this is a practical book that we hope will make your relationship with Buddy the very best it can be.

Foolish Assumptions

In writing this book, we assume a few things about you:

» You have a dog or plan to get one.

» You want your dog to be well behaved — for his sake as well as yours.

» You're self-motivated and ready to make training a priority.

» You're looking for an inexpensive guide that gives you the freedom to train your dog what and when you want.

» You want to know more about training a dog.

No matter the amount of training experience you have, you can find this book helpful. Through our many years of working with a wide variety of dog breeds and personalities, we've picked up many tricks that are sure to prove useful even to experienced dog trainers.

Icons Used in This Book

To help you navigate your way through the text, we have included some highlights of important material, some hints, some cautions, and some true stories of success. This key information is marked with little pictures (or icons) in the margins. Here's what the icons tell you:

TIP

This icon draws your attention to ways to save time, money, energy, and your sanity.

WARNING

This icon raises a red flag; your safety or your dog's may be at risk. It also tells you about the don'ts of dog training. Proceed at your own risk!

REMEMBER

This icon directs you to information that's important to remember — key points that you want to focus on.

TECHNICAL STUFF

This icon highlights in-depth information that isn't critical for you to know but that can enhance your knowledge of dog training and make you a better teacher.

Where to Go from Here

The important thing about dog training is getting started *today*. The sooner you train your dog to behave the way you want him to, the sooner the two of you can live in peace together, and the more problems you can prevent down the road. So turn the page (or use the table of contents or index to get to the information you need the most) and get going! Your dog will thank you for it. You can also visit www.dummies.com and search for the "Dog Training For Dummies" Cheat Sheet for access to information you may need on a regular basis.

1

Setting the Stage for Successful Training

Discover what a well-trained dog looks like. Become aware of what your dog is learning from you at the time. Whether you know it or not, you're sometimes teaching your dog something and other times stopping him from doing something unwanted. Pick the six most important commands you want to teach your dog as the foundation of his training.

Look into your dog's personality and see how you affect everything he does and perceives through your body language and how you communicate with each other.

Find out what it takes to be the best dog trainer for your dog. Be aware of the other factors that surround your dog, such as his environment as well as those things born within your dog such as how he perceives the world.

Read about how your dog's nutrition and health affects his learning and retention of the training.

Know what you should buy to help you train your dog. A wide selection is available. Different things work better for different dogs.

Start on the right foot as you bring your new dog or puppy home, what to plan, and what to do first. Training doesn't end with Sit and Down but includes brushing fur and teeth and saving your house from destruction.

See what it takes to raise the best dog in the world, from birth to adolescence. All the critical periods of development can change your puppy for life, so learn what they're all about.

Chapter **1**

Dog Training: The Key to Your Dog's Safety and Your Sanity

S o you have a dog? Lucky you. You want to train your dog, right? Lucky dog. There is nothing that you can do to build a bond more quickly between you and your dog than training together, working as a team and spending time productively.

You want your dog to want to be with you, work for you, and then do it all again — for a treat, for praise, for play, because it's worth your dog's while. This chapter serves as a jumping-off point as you begin to develop your relationship with your dog. Training can be fun for you and for your dog. The results are what make all the time you put in training your dog worthwhile, but the journey of training is what can be so much fun — spending time with the dog who will become your best friend.

Someone once wrote: "All owners thinks they have the best dog in the world, and luckily they are all right." Hence, the role of the dog will be played by your dog, and we refer to him in this chapter and book as Buddy, your buddy, and for simplicity, Buddy is a he. Please insert your dog partner's name where necessary. We want your relationship with your dog to be a joy.

Understanding Why You're Training Buddy: To Do Something or Not to Do Something

Your dog is learning from the moment you meet each other, so you want to make sure you know what he's learning from you. Are you a pushover, a littermate, or the leader of the pack? You want your dog to see you as the pack leader, the coach. That means you set the rules, what games to play, when to eat, when to sleep, when to exercise, and when to train. Dogs don't know you're training them. All they know is you and he are spending time together, which is magical.

The important question when training your dog is this: Are you training your dog to *do* something or to *not do* something? The answer really can be both. You're teaching Buddy to be a good dog, to do this instead of doing that. To do something would be to sit here while you come in the door and greet your dog. To not do something would be don't jump up as you come in the door. Teaching your dog to sit while greeting you is so much more fun than teaching your dog to not jump up on you. As often as possible, you're going to teach Buddy what you *want* him to do rather than what you don't want him to do.

A BRIEF HISTORY OF DOGS

Dogs were originally bred for specific functions, such as guarding, herding, hauling, hunting, and so on. Before 1945, most dogs worked for a living, and many still do. The popularity of dogs as household pets is a relatively recent phenomenon, fueled in part by the heroic exploits of the dogs used in World War II as well as the fictional Rin Tin Tin and Lassie. The upshot of this popularity has been a demand for the family dog who is easy to train, good with children, a little bit protective, and relatively quiet. Even more fun are the dogs people love today in cartoons who are humanized such as Snoopy, Scooby Doo, Lady and the Tramp, and the list goes on. Dogs you own are real and need real guidance and training.

Identifying a Well-Trained Dog

A well-trained dog is a joy to have around. He's welcome almost anywhere because he behaves around people and other dogs. He knows how to stay, and he comes when called. He's a pleasure to take for a walk because he doesn't pull and can be let loose for a romp in the park. He can be taken on trips and family outings. He's a member of the family in every sense of the word. This is your goal for Buddy, to be a well-trained dog!

REMEMBER

The most important benefit of training your dog is safety: your safety, the safety of others, and your dog's own safety. A dog that listens and does what he's told rarely gets into trouble. Instead of being a slave to a leash or a line, a trained dog is a free dog — he can be trusted to stay when told, not to jump on people, to come when called, and to walk nicely with you.

For decades, we, Wendy and Mary Ann, have taught dog training classes, private lessons, seminars, and weeklong training camps. Working closely with veterinarians allows us to spend a lot of time doing behavior counseling with their clients. We ask people to tell us what a well-trained dog should look like and what they want to successfully train their dogs to do. They want a dog to be housetrained (Chapter 8 can help you with that task). Sadly more dogs are given up to shelters for failure to become house trained than any other issue. After that, in order of importance, a well-trained dog is one who

>> Doesn't jump on people

>> Doesn't pull on the leash

>> Does come when called

>> Doesn't beg at the table

>> Doesn't bother guests

Note that these requirements, with one exception, are expressed in the negative — that is, *dog*, don't do that. For purposes of training, we express these requirements in the positive — teach your dog exactly what you expect from him. Here's what the new list of requirements for a well-trained dog looks like:

>> Sit when I tell you. (Chapter 11 gives you the how-to.)

>> Walk on a loose leash. (Chapter 12 is your go-to.)

>> Come when called. (Chapter 10 explains how to teach the Come command.)

>> Go somewhere and chill out. (Head to Chapter 13 for more information.)

>> Lie down when I tell you and stay there. (Chapter 11 can help.)

The Sit and Down-Stay commands (see Figure 1-1) are the building blocks for a well-trained dog; if Buddy knows these commands and nothing else, you can still live with him. Of course, your Buddy may have some additional wrinkles that need ironing out, some of which are more matters of management than training. (Chapter 11 discusses these essential commands in greater detail.)

FIGURE 1-1: Well-trained dogs.

© John Wiley & Sons, Inc.

For instance, a favorite pastime of some dogs is raiding the garbage. Prevention is the cure here: put the garbage where your dog can't get to it. By moving the trash-can to a secured location, you're managing the environment that fixes the problem. By purchasing a trash container that can't be raided, again you're managing the environment and fixing Buddy's bad behavior. Management is much easier and more quickly successful than having to train an unwanted behavior. Of course, teaching the Leave It command and giving Buddy other things to occupy his attention is also great training. Management and training work hand in hand and together result in the best possible dog with whom you can live and be most proud.

For example, one of Wendy's Dachshunds learned to open the refrigerator by yanking on the towel Wendy kept draped through the door handle; therefore, the dog could help himself to anything he could reach. Prevention was the answer: Wendy removed the towel from the refrigerator handle.

WHAT IS AN UNTRAINED DOG?

The untrained dog has few privileges. When guests come to visit, he's locked away because he's too unruly. When the family sits down to eat, he's locked up or put outside because he begs at the table. He's never allowed off leash because he runs away and stays out for hours at a time. Nobody wants to take him for a walk because he pulls, and he never gets to go on family outings because he's a nuisance.

Dogs are social animals, and one of the cruelest forms of punishment is to deprive them of the opportunity to interact with family members on a regular basis. Isolating a dog from contact with humans is inhumane. Spending quality time with your dog by training him will make him the beloved pet he deserves to be.

Selecting a Training Model

You have many ways to train a dog, ranging from rather primitive to fairly sophisticated. Even technology has had its impact on dog training. For example, rather than fenced yards, people often now have invisible fences, which contain dogs within their confines by means of an electrical shock.

Our approach to training is for people who like their dogs and have them first and foremost as pets and companions or for people who want to like their dogs. Someone pointed this out us when she arrived for class. At that point she didn't like her dog but wanted to make her child happy by having a dog. Either way, we like your dog and want him to be the best possible dog and you to be the best possible trainer for him.

The training involves three phases:

» **The teaching phase:** In the *teaching phase,* the dog is taught specific commands in an area free of distractions so he can focus on his owner and can be successful.

» **The practicing phase:** When the dog reliably responds to the commands he has learned, distractions are introduced (we explain distractions in more detail in Chapter 10). As the dog progresses in this practice phase, the distractions become increasingly more difficult in order to simulate real-life situations.

» **The testing phase:** In the *testing phase,* the dog is expected to demonstrate that he's a well-mannered pet around other dogs and people.

REMEMBER

The ultimate object of any training is to have your dog respond reliably to your commands. Ideally, he responds to your first command. Telling your dog to do something only to have him ignore you is frustrating. Think of Buddy's response in terms of choices. Do you want to teach Buddy to think he has a choice of responding to you? You want a dog that understands — after you have taught him — that he must do what you tell him, no matter what is happening around him. A truly trained dog listens for your voice above all distractions.

Distractions do cause Buddy to struggle to hear your voice above other things as does the genetic influence of those things that Buddy was bred to do instinctively, that which is in harmony with his basic nature. Are all dogs the same to train or does the breed or mixture of breeds make a difference? Like people, dogs are individuals and have individual needs. Understanding breed characteristics and different teaching models helps to make the job of training that much easier.

First things first: Considering your dog's breed

Before you embark on your training program, consider what you want your dog to master, and then compare your answer to the task for which his breed was originally bred to do. Many people typically select their dogs based on appearance and without regard to breed-specific functions and behaviors. Whatever trait is in harmony with the breed of your dog is easier to teach or harder to break. For example, a Beagle uses his nose everywhere he goes. Teaching a Beagle to track or follow a scent is much easier than teaching a Greyhound to track. Greyhounds are bred to visualize movement rather than to sniff out prey.

Although most dogs can be trained to obey basic obedience commands, breed-specific traits determine the ease or difficulty with which they can be trained. You also need to consider other traits, such as energy levels and grooming needs. High-energy dogs must have outlets for all of that energy. Chapter 20 discusses problems that occur if your dog doesn't get the exercise he needs. After all, a tired dog is a happy dog, and a tired dog has a happy owner. As for grooming, brushing, bathing, and clipping of hair coats is time consuming and expensive if you hire a professional. For a dog to be healthy, the coat and skin needs to be cared for regularly. Chapter 6 discusses grooming.

REMEMBER

An excellent resource for breed-specific behavior and traits is *The Roger Caras Dog Book: A Complete Guide to Every AKC Breed*, by Roger Caras and Alton Anderson (M. Evans & Company). For each breed, the book lists on a scale from 1 to 10 the three characteristics you should pay attention to: the amount of coat care required, the amount of exercise required, and the suitability for urban/apartment life.

Training a dog: What are you really doing?

When training a dog you're either teaching him to do something (build a behavior) or not to do something (abstain from a behavior). For example, consider the Stay command. Are you teaching your dog to remain where he is or not to move from where he is? You can look at any command and ask this question. When training a dog, you're usually building a behavior. Look at Figure 1-2 to help understand.

FIGURE 1-2:
The difference between training to do something and training to stop an unwanted behavior.

	Action Build behavior	Abstention Eliminate behavior
+	Pos. reinforcement (add good)	Pos punishment (add bad)
–	Neg. reinforcement (avoid bad)	Neg punishment (remove good)

© John Wiley & Sons, Inc.

In the figure, the first column lists how to build a behavior. The second column lists how to abstain from a behavior. When talking about behavior in proper training terminology, *positive* means adding something, indicated with the plus sign (+), and *negative* means removing something, indicated with the minus sign (–). These two terms don't mean good and bad which is so often associated with positive and negative.

We need to define two other words in terms of behavior:

>> *Reinforcement* is used in the building of a behavior.

>> *Punishment* is used in the abstaining of a behavior.

An easy way to remember this distinction is that reinforcement of something makes it stronger or builds it, and punishment tends to stop something or abstains from something. These two sections examine reinforcement and punishment in more detail.

Reinforcement: Building a behavior

When training a dog, you want the dog to do something new and different. To do that, you need to motivate him by either giving him something he wants for doing the new task or getting him to avoid something he doesn't want for not doing it. Consider the following:

>> *Positive reinforcement (+)* is adding something the dog wants in order to encourage him to do something he wouldn't do on his own. For example, you want the dog to go upstairs, so you put a tiny treat on each step to induce the dog to go upstairs.

>> *Negative reinforcement (–)* is eliciting a behavior the dog wouldn't do on his own by making him avoid discomfort. The dog will do what is wanted because he wants to avoid the reinforcement from happening to him. For example, you want the dog to go upstairs, so someone gooses the dog's behind to get him to go upstairs to avoid the discomfort of the pinch. At the top of the stairs, you praise him because he went upstairs.

Which approach works best? It may depend on how hungry the dog is, how much he likes the treat being used, and something more interesting isn't going on around the corner, such as a BBQ. In the negative reinforcement approach, it may depend on how hard of a pinch is and if he doesn't mind the pinch versus the effort it takes to climb the stairs.

Training comes with so many variables. The BBQ next door is a distraction, which is why it's best to do early training when no distractions are around. The ability to climb the stairs or the difficulty of the task you're teaching plays a big part on how willing your dog is. Buddy may suffer the consequences instead of climbing the stairs or jumping into a pool if water is too scary. Make sure you break the task you're teaching into small parts to make it more easily understood and achievable.

You later can add distractions to the training after Buddy has learned the command. Distractions make the task more difficult for Buddy. When working with distractions, your dog needs to choose doing the task over being distracted. The object of distraction training is to train until your dog does the task no matter what is going on around him simply because you asked him to do so.

Punishment: Eliminating an unwanted behavior

When training a dog to stop doing an unwanted behavior, there should be a consequence. The consequence can be either adding something the dog doesn't want or removing something he does want. Consider the following:

>> **Positive punishment:** *Positive punishment* adds an unwanted consequence (+) at the start of the bad behavior just as it begins. For example, as soon as a counter-surfing dog sniffs the edge of the counter, you can shake a bottle half-filled with pennies at the dog as an unpleasant consequence. (*Oops:* If the dog is already on the counter or eating off the counter, using the bottle with

pennies is too late. The dog has been rewarded by getting the food off the counter. Because the Oops happened, the dog has learned to counter surf which is why it's an Oops.) To eliminate the bad behavior, you must add something that the dog doesn't want so he'll avoid the penny shaker and not counter-surf. When the bad behavior stops, you don't offer praise; you never want him to counter-surf, so don't praise him for his wishing he could still get up on the counter to eat.

>> **Negative punishment:** *Negative punishment* removes something (–) that the dog wanted because the dog behaved badly. For example, if a dog is jumping up on you when you come into the house, turn your back to the dog for a moment, removing your attention that he wants because he jumped up. Turn back toward him once more, and if he jumps again, spin around, removing your front, your facial expression, and your attention.

HOW TO MAKE YOUR DOG RING-WISE BY ACCIDENT!

The term *ring-wise* refers to a dog who won't perform in a show ring or in front of an audience or for friends. The dog becomes ring-wise because when a dog is performing in an obedience ring, the owner isn't permitted to use food to aid the dog to perform. Therefore, the dog won't perform in a ring after he has learned something because doing so isn't worth his while. Ring-wise is an unwanted label because dogs should perform whether there is food present or not.

Adding rewards or removing rewards, praising or not praising, and adding an unpleasant consequence or stopping an unwanted consequence all make the difference in the dog's learning.

When you use food all the time while training or practicing a behavior you're building, you're using positive reinforcements. When you stop using the food you normally use all of the time, you're using negative punishment because you're taking away what the dog wants. The dog will unlearn the trick or stop giving you the behavior under these conditions in front of an audience. In other words, he'll become ring-wise.

To avoid this problem, randomly use food. As he learns a behavior, you need to diminish his reliance on food. Instead of giving a treat every time, only give it every other or third time; skip a time once in a while and make it random. Buddy will learn to try harder to get the treat; he'll try to do the best for you and will remain focused on you as you continue to work. He'll learn that food comes if he keeps trying. Keep it fun, and Buddy will work always, even in front of an audience.

Identifying Six Basic Commands Every Dog Needs to Know

Every dog needs to know six basic commands: Sit, Down, Stay, Come, Heel, and Leave It. You can look at these as safety and sanity commands — your dog's safety and your sanity. Here's a look at each of these commands:

>> **The Sit command:** You use the Sit command (refer to Chapter 11) anytime you need your dog to control himself. You can use the command to teach your dog to do the following:

- Sit politely for petting instead of jumping on people

- Sit at the door instead of barging ahead of you

- Sit when you put his food dish on the floor instead of trying to grab it out of your hand

>> **The Down command:** You use the Down command (check out Chapter 11) when you want your dog to stay in one place for prolonged periods, such as when you're eating dinner or at the vet's office.

>> **The Come command:** You need to teach your dog the Come command (flip to Chapter 10) so you can call him when you take him for a hike, when he wants to chase a squirrel, or when it's time to come inside.

>> **The Stay command:** When you want to teach your dog to remain in place without moving, you teach him the Stay command (see Chapter 11).

>> **The Heel command:** Or the Let's Go command, depending on what you want, is when you want your dog to walk politely and not pull you on the leash (refer to Chapter 12).

>> **The Leave It command:** You teach your dog the Leave It command (head to Chapter 9) so he leaves stuff alone when you don't want him to have it.

Recognizing Factors that Influence Success

Of the many factors that influence success, you are the most important one. You're the one who decides how to approach training and what you want your dog to learn. Your dog is your responsibility and whatever your dog does — good or bad — is under your control.

Having a good relationship with your dog

The goal of training is to create a mutually rewarding relationship — you're happy and your dog is happy. To foster such a relationship, become aware of how many times you use your dog's name to change or control his behavior. Your dog's name isn't a command and certainly isn't a reprimand. His name is used to get his attention and is then followed by a command. See Chapter 9 for how to train Buddy to recognize his name.

REMEMBER

Stop nagging and learn to communicate with your dog through training. Focus on teaching Buddy what you want him to do rather than on what you don't want him to do. Above all, limit negative verbal communications, such as No," to emergencies. Repeatedly yelling "no" isn't the way to foster a good relationship. Instead of using "No," use a command that you've taught and actually means something. Too many people use "No," and therefore it means nothing.

A good relationship also requires spending quality time together. You can spend time with your dog by training, going for walks, playing ball, doing tricks, and so on. Chapter 17 provides some great ideas you can do with Buddy.

Owning a healthy dog

Your dog's health has an enormous influence on his training success. A dog who doesn't feel well won't learn well either. First and foremost, his health depends on what you feed him. You need to feed him a high-quality food that provides the nutrients he needs (see Chapter 4).

Your dog also needs an annual checkup by your veterinarian, preferably with bloodwork. Regular bathing and grooming are similarly important. If you live in an area where there are ticks, check him regularly. Deer ticks spread Lyme disease, which can have debilitating effects on your dog. Ticks, heartworms, and internal and external parasites need to be diagnosed and treated by your veterinarian.

Making training time a priority

One of the most common complaints for not training is: "I just don't have the time to train my dog!" First, look at training as a fun game — something you and your dog enjoy doing together. It shouldn't be a chore. Then identify the times during the day when you interact most with your dog.

Here are some times when you can take advantage of training opportunities:

>> **Feeding time:** If your dog is still a puppy, you feed him four, three and eventually two times a day. Each meal is a training opportunity — teach him to Sit and Stay before you put his dish down. Make him wait for a second or two, and then let him eat. You'll be surprised how quickly he catches on to this routine. You also can put the dish down first and follow the same procedure.

>> **When exiting and entering buildings:** If you have more than one dog, door manners are an absolute must. They're equally important for the single-dog household. It usually takes about 30 seconds for the dog to catch on that he's supposed to wait before you tell him it's okay to exit (or enter). It's a matter of consistency on your part until the behavior becomes automatic. Chapter 14 discusses door manners.

>> **While relaxing with your pooch:** You can teach the Leave It command while you're watching TV. Take a few treats to your favorite chair and have fun teaching the progressions to the exercise (refer to Chapter 9).

>> **During walks:** Every time you take your dog for a walk is a training opportunity to teach him to sit at the curb, to heel when passing other dogs, and to walk on a loose leash when walking beside you as you say "Let's go" and "Heel" (head to Chapter 12.)

All of these commands teach your dog to focus on you and look to you for direction — and they all happen as a part of your daily routine.

Oh, the Places You and Your Pooch Can Go: Beyond the Basics

Performance events for dogs date back to the early 1930s, and the first obedience trial under American Kennel Club (AKC) rules took place in 1936. The purpose of obedience trials, as stated in the AKC Obedience Regulations, is to "demonstrate the dog's ability to follow specified routines in the obedience ring and emphasize the usefulness of the purebred dog as a companion of man." Now AKC allows mixed breed dogs in all of their performance events, having a purebred isn't required to compete in AKC events. Following are some of the options you can explore if you want to take training to the next level. For all of the following, visit www.akc.org.

The Canine Good Citizen Certificate

In 1989, the AKC developed the popular Canine Good Citizen (CGC) test, a program for both purebred dogs and mixed breeds. The CGC test uses a series of exercises that demonstrate the dog's ability to behave in an acceptable manner in public. Its purpose is to show that the dog, as a companion for all people, can be a respected member of the community and can be trained and conditioned to always behave in the home, in public places, and in the presence of other dogs in a manner that reflects credit on the dog. (For more details on this test, go to Chapter 25.)

Now AKC has expanded the CGC to include the Urban and Farm and Advanced CGC tests. Your dog also can earn a Temperament Testing. AKC is just one of the National Dog Clubs though it is the largest and most well-known.

TIP

In many areas you can find classes to help you train your dog and prepare the two of you for the CGC.

AKC S.T.A.R. puppy program

The goal of the AKC S.T.A.R. Puppy program is similar to the Canine Good Citizen program, except that it's aimed at puppies. Just like the CGC program, the AKC S.T.A.R. Puppy program includes a *Responsible Dog Owner Pledge* as well as a basic training program in which puppies up to 1 year of age are eligible to participate. After you attend a basic training class locally, your puppy must take a test. Look on the internet for information on dog training in your area. When the puppy passes the test, he receives a certificate and a medal.

AKC tricks titles

AKC offers multiple titles for your dog as he learns and performs different levels of tricks. From Novice to Performer and Elite Performer and several in between. There is no limit to getting your dog to become a star and earn a title to prove it. See Chapter 17 to get you started.

More than training: Understanding how dogs help people

Man and dog have been together for a long time. It didn't take man long to recognize the dog's potential as a valuable helper. Originally, the dog's main jobs were guarding, hauling, herding, and hunting. Over time, more jobs were added to the canine's resume; now dogs perform an amazing variety of tasks. These tasks fall into four broad categories: service dogs, detection dogs, assistance dogs, and companion dogs.

For more information, visit the websites here for these organizations: Canine Companions for Independence (www.cci.org), Canine Assistants (www.canineassistants.org), Dogs for the Deaf (www.dogsforthedeaf.org), Assistance Dogs International, Inc. (www.assistancedogsinternational.org), Assistance Dogs of America, Inc. (www.adai.org), Guiding Eyes for the Blind (www.guidingeyes.org).

An Exercise to Get You and Your Pooch Started

Eager to get started with some training? We hope so! We begin with an exercise that shows you how to train your dog while you're feeding him. We chose this exercise because you're going to feed your dog two times a day (and even more frequently if he's a puppy), and each time you do so is a training opportunity. It's also a good exercise because the dog quickly figures out what is to his advantage, namely, he stays and he gets to eat. He'll also learn leadership while you work this exercise. Leadership means that you own the food and you're giving it to him, but only when you release him to the bowl. Leadership means you're the leader of the pack, the coach of the team, and your dog is the player.

TIP

If your dog is enthusiastic and bouncy, you'll have more success with this exercise when he's leashed rather than loose.

Follow these steps to successfully train your pooch Sit and Stay before eating:

1. **Prepare his meal as you normally do.**

2. **While your dog is wearing the leash and collar, pick up his leash with your left hand and hold it as close to his collar as is comfortable for you, but without any tension on his collar.**

3. **Pick up his dish with your right hand, say "Stay" and then put the dish on the floor.**

   When he makes a dive for the bowl, pull up and back on the leash and pick up the dish. He doesn't have to sit; he just isn't allowed to dive for the dish.

4. **Repeat Step 3 until he holds his position when you put the dish on the floor; see Figure 1-3.**

5. **After he's successful at maintaining his position, say "Okay" and let him eat in peace.**

   "Okay" is a release term to tell the dog he's now free to move. If you don't like "Okay," you can choose a term to your own liking, such as "You're free."

FIGURE 1-3: Teaching your dog the Stay command as a part of feeding him.

© John Wiley & Sons, Inc.

REMEMBER

As a general rule, it takes about three to five repetitions on the first try for the dog to get the message. *Avoid* the temptation to use negative communications, such a "No" or "Ah-Ah." Instead, use the leash to gently yet authoritatively control your dog. After several sessions, he'll more than likely sit on his own in anticipation of getting his meal.

Chapter **2**

Getting to Know Your Dog and How He Perceives the World

In this chapter, we discuss how your dog thinks. Discovering how your dog thinks isn't as complicated as it sounds. Knowing how to read your dog and how you impact his thoughts is what communication is all about. Not only do you want to know how your dog perceives the world, but you also want to see if you can change any misconceptions he may have.

To help you in understanding what motivates *your* dog, Wendy devised a Personality Profile. Each dog is an individual, and your training efforts need to take his personality into account to succeed with his training.

Determining What Motivates You and Your Dog

Motivation is defined as the reason one has for acting or behaving in a particular way. To help you understand motivation, look at Table 2-1 to see that humans and dogs have very similar motivations.

TABLE 2-1 ### Comparing Motivation with People and Dogs

People	Dogs
Money and what it buys	Toys/food
Love	Companionship
Success	Status
Competition	Territory

Dogs protect what they have and want what they need — food and shelter — just as people do. Dogs need companionship and seek it out, just as people do. Dogs live under a hierarchy and communicate their known position in the group or pack, the same as people do. And when it comes to self-preservation, dogs exhibit fight-or-flight behaviors, similar to how people do as well.

Dogs live by one basic rule: what's in it for me? If he thinks he'll benefit from something, he'll do it. If not, he won't. Chapter 1 examines positive and negative reinforcements. For example, a dog thinks, "Give me a reason for doing this, something I want, food" (obvious motivation) or "I'll do this to avoid something I don't like from happening" (motivating as an avoidance.) Positive reinforcement and negative reinforcement are based on the question, "What's in it for me?" That is, food or reward (positive reinforcement) versus removal of something uncomfortable (negative reinforcement.) Dogs reason this out and learn from it.

Being Aware of Your Dog's Body Language

Dogs communicate between themselves and between people. Although dogs have verbal communications, such as barks, whines, growls, and so on, they use body language all of the time like facial expressions, which includes the set of the eyes and the position of the whiskers, and how the ears are set, tail wags, and the elevation of the tail and head postures to name a few. Dogs also communicate through scent. For example, urine-marking behaviors and scent glands (anal glands) alert other dogs to dangers, and there are more that people can't even begin to understand.

People also use verbal and nonverbal communications. For dogs, body language is powerful; however for people, voice plays a bigger role than body language. When training, you need to learn what your dog's body is saying. Body language is the main way you and your dog communicate.

Recognizing Your Dog's Instinctive Behaviors

Your dog — and every other dog — is an individual animal that comes into the world with a specific grouping of genetically inherited, predetermined behaviors. How those behaviors are arranged, their intensity, and how many components of each are at work determine the dog's temperament, personality, and suitability for a task. Those behaviors also determine how the dog perceives the world.

Researchers have studied dog behavior and have made a list or catalog of all of the different forms of behaviors that dogs display. Researchers have divided those behaviors into four groups that benefit dog training and how humans communicate with their dogs. To give you a better understanding of your dog, we group instinctive behaviors into four drives:

>> Prey

>> Pack

>> Defense fight

>> Defense flight

Defense drive is divided into fight and flight because they're stimulated by the same factors yet are exhibited completely differently, one with fight behaviors and the other with flight behaviors.

These drives reflect instinctive behaviors that your dog has inherited and that are useful to you in teaching him what you want him to learn. Each one of these drives is governed by a basic trait. Not all dogs inherit all of these behaviors, but you'll see many parts of each of these drives in your dog.

The following sections break down these four drives in greater detail.

Prey drive

Prey drive includes those inherited behaviors associated with hunting, killing prey, and eating. The prey drive is activated by motion, sound, and smell. Behaviors associated with prey drive (see Figure 2-1) include the following:

>> Air scenting and tracking

>> Biting and killing

>> Carrying

>> Digging and burying

>> Eating

>> High-pitched barking

>> Jumping up and pulling down

>> Pouncing

>> Seeing, hearing, and smelling

>> Shaking an object

>> Stalking and chasing

>> Tearing and ripping apart

© John Wiley & Sons, Inc.

FIGURE 2-1: Dogs showing the chase, a typical prey-drive behavior.

CAN DOGS REASON?

As much as you want your dog to be able to reason, dogs can't reason in the sense that humans can. Dogs can, however, solve simple problems. By observing your dog, you learn his problem-solving techniques. Just watch him try to open the cupboard where the dog biscuits are kept. Or see how he works at trying to retrieve his favorite toy from under the couch. During your training, you'll also have the opportunity to see Buddy trying to work out what you're teaching him.

One of Wendy's favorite story involves a very smart English Springer Spaniel who had been left on her doorstep. The poor fellow had been so neglected that she didn't know he was a purebred Spaniel until after he visited the groomer. He became a delightful member of Wendy's family for many years. One day, the dog's ball rolled under the couch. He tried everything — looking under the couch, jumping on the backrest to look behind it, and going around to both sides. Nothing seemed to work. In disgust, he lifted his leg on the couch and walked away. He marked it as his and left.

REMEMBER

Typically, chasing is the most common part of prey behaviors. It's triggered when Buddy is chasing a moving object, such as a toy, cyclist, jogger, or car. Buddy also may shake and rip up soft toys or bury bones in the couch. Failure to recognize the strength of prey behaviors in dogs is the most common reason for so-called behavior problems. For managing prey drive behaviors, see Chapter 20.

Pack drive

Pack drive consists of behaviors associated with reproduction, being part of a group or pack, and being able to live by the rules. Dogs, like their distant ancestors the wolves, are social animals. To hunt prey that's mostly larger than themselves, wolves live in a pack. To ensure order, they adhere to a social hierarchy governed by strict rules of behavior. In dogs, this translates into an ability to be part of a group that includes humans in their pack and means a willingness to work with people as part of a team.

Pack drive is stimulated by rank order in the social hierarchy. Behaviors associated with this drive include the following:

>> Being able to breed and to be a good parent

>> Demonstrating behaviors associated with social interaction with people and other dogs, such as reading body language

>> Demonstrating reproductive behaviors, such as licking, mounting, washing ears, and all courting gestures

>> Exhibiting physical contact with people or other dogs

>> Playing with people or other dogs

REMEMBER

A dog with many of these behaviors follows you around the house, is happiest when with you, loves to be petted and groomed, and likes to work with you. (Check out Figure 2-2.) A dog with these behaviors may be unhappy when left alone too long, which is a feeling that can express itself in separation anxiety.

© John Wiley & Sons, Inc.

FIGURE 2-2:
A dog enjoying physical contact with a person, a typical pack drive behavior.

Defense drive, fight and flight

Defense drive is governed by survival and self-preservation and consists of both fight and flight behaviors. Defense drive is complex because the same stimulus that can make a dog appear aggressive (fight) can elicit avoidance (flight) behaviors, especially in a young dog.

Defense drive, fight

Fight behaviors aren't fully developed until the dog is sexually mature or about 2 years old. You may notice tendencies toward these behaviors at an earlier age, and life experiences determine their intensity. Behaviors associated with fight drive include the following:

>> Exhibiting hair (hackles) standing up from the shoulder forward

>> Growling at people or dogs when he feels his space is being violated (see Figure 2-3)

» Guarding food, toys, or territory against people and dogs

» Lying in front of doorways or cupboards and refusing to move

» Putting his head over another dog's shoulder

» Showing aversion to being petted or groomed

» Standing tall, weight forward on front legs, tail high, and staring at other dogs

» Standing his ground and not moving

WHOA! BUDDY'S GOT HIS HACKLES UP

Hackles refer to the fur along the dog's spine from the neck to the tip of his tail. When a dog is frightened or unsure and in defense fight, the fur literally stands up and away from his spine. In a young dog, it may happen frequently because the dog's life experiences are minimal. When he meets a new dog, for example, he may be unsure of whether that dog is friendly, so his hackles go up. A dog's whiskers also are a good indication of his insecurity; in a frightened dog, they're pulled back, flat along his face. His ears also are pulled back, his tail is tucked, and he cringes, lowering his body posture and averting his eyes. All in all, he'd rather be somewhere else, which is the defense fight.

On the flip side, when the hackles go up only from the neck to the shoulders, the dog is sure of himself. He's the boss, and he's ready to take on all comers. His ears are erect, his whiskers are forward, all his weight is on his front legs, his tail is held high, and he stands tall and makes direct eye contact. He's ready to rumble, which is defense fight.

Defense drive, flight

Flight behaviors demonstrate that the dog is unsure. Young dogs tend to exhibit more flight behaviors than older dogs. The following behaviors are associated with flight drive:

» Demonstrating a general lack of confidence

» Disliking being touched by strangers

» Exhibiting hair (hackles) that stands up the full length of the body, not just at the neck

» Flattening the body, with the tail tucked, when greeted by people or other dogs

» Hiding or running away from a new situation

» Urinating when being greeted by a stranger or the owner (submissive urinating)

Understanding how the drives affect training

Because dogs were originally bred for a particular function and not solely for appearance, you generally can predict the strength or weakness of the individual drives in the different breeds. For example, the northern breeds, such as Alaskan Malamutes and Siberian Huskies, were bred to pull sleds. They tend to be low in pack drive, and training them not to pull on the leash can be a bit of a chore. Herding dogs, such as Border Collies and Australian Shepherds, were bred to herd livestock under the direction of their master. Although high in prey drive, they also tend to be high in pack drive and should be relatively easy to train not to pull on the leash. The guarding breeds, such as the German Shepherd, Doberman, and Rottweiler, were bred to work closely with man, so they tend to be high in fight drive with a desire to protect family and property. They easily can be taught to walk on a leash. The Retrievers, which were bred to hunt with humans and retrieve the birds shot in the hunt, tend to be high in both prey and pack drive and generally love to retrieve. They, too, easily learn to walk on a leash.

Many of the behaviors for which dogs were bred, such as herding and hunting, are the very ones that get them into trouble today. These behaviors involve prey drive and result in chasing anything that moves. A guard dog may guard your home against intruders and protect your children, but those "intruders" may include the children's friends.

REMEMBER

Clearly, these are generalizations that don't apply to every dog of a particular breed. Today many dogs of different breeds were bred solely for appearance and without regard to function, so their original traits have become diluted.

Determining Your Dog's Personality Profile

To train Buddy, you need some insight into what's happening in his brain at any given moment. Here your powers of observation can help you. In many instances, Buddy's behavior is quite predictable based on what he has done in similar situations. You may be surprised at what you already know. You can almost see the wheels turning when he's about to chase a car, bicycle, or jogger. If you're observant, Buddy will give you just enough time to stop him.

However, you don't need to rely on observation alone. To help you understand how Buddy's mind works and, in turn, understand how to approach your dog's training, Wendy created the Volhards' Canine Personality Profile. The profile catalogs ten behaviors in each drive that influence a dog's responses and that are useful in training. The ten behaviors chosen are ones that most closely represent the dog's strengths in each of the drives. The profile doesn't pretend to include all behaviors seen in a dog nor does it interpret the complexity of their interaction. For example, what drive is Buddy in when he's sleeping? For purposes of training, it's not important. Although this Personality Profile is an admittedly crude tool for predicting Buddy's behavior, you'll find it surprisingly accurate.

The results of the profile can give you a better understanding of why Buddy is the way he is and the most successful way to train him. You can then make use of his strengths, avoid needless confusion, and greatly reduce training time.

REMEMBER

The profile or test is answered in a scale of 0 to 10 with 0 being never and 10 being always and every option in between. When completing the profile, keep in mind that it was devised for a house dog or pet with an enriched environment and perhaps even a little training, not a dog tied out in the yard or kept solely in a kennel — such dogs have fewer opportunities to express as many behaviors as a house dog. Answers should indicate behaviors Buddy would exhibit if he'd not already been trained to do otherwise. For example, before he was trained properly, did he jump on people to greet them or jump on the counter to steal food? Answer as he was before you trained him, so always or 10. Don't let your ego say otherwise. You want to know Buddy's true personality profile, his natural drive numbers. If you answer that he would never jump on someone because you worked hard teaching him not to, you aren't going to get accurate results in this test, so in this example you would choose 10 for always.

The possible answers and their corresponding point values are as follows:

>> Almost always — 10

>> Sometimes — 5 to 9

>> Hardly ever — 0 to 4

For example, if Buddy is a Beagle, the answer to the question "When presented with the opportunity, does your dog sniff the ground or air?" is probably "Almost always," giving him a score of 10.

You're now ready to find out who Buddy really is. You may not have had the chance to observe all these behaviors, in which case you leave the answer blank.

When presented with the opportunity, does your dog

1. Sniff the ground or air?   10   Yes

2. Get along with other dogs?   10

3. Stand his ground or show curiosity in strange objects or sounds?   10   Yes

4. Run away from new situations?   9   No

5. Get excited by moving objects, such as bikes or squirrels?   10   Yes

6. Get along with people?   10   Yes

7. Like to play tug-of-war games to win?   10   Yes

8. Hide behind you when he feels he can't cope?   8   ___

9. Stalk cats, other dogs, or things in the grass?   5   ___

10. Bark when left alone?   10   Ye

11. Bark or growl in a deep tone of voice?   0   ___

12. Act fearfully in unfamiliar situations?   2   ___

13. Bark in a high-pitched voice when excited?   10   ___

14. Solicit petting or like to snuggle with you?   10   Yes

15. Guard his territory?   ___

16. Tremble or whine when unsure?   0 _no_

17. Pounce on his toys?   10 ___

18. Like to be groomed?   2 ___

19. Guard his food or toys?   5 _yes_

20. Cower or turn upside down when reprimanded?   ___

21. Shake and "kill" his toys?   10 _yes_

22. Seek eye contact with you?   10 _yes_

23. Dislike being petted?   0 _no_

24. Act reluctant to come close to you when called?   5 _yes_

25. Steal food or garbage?   0 _no_

26. Follow you around like a shadow?   9 ___

27. Guard his owner(s)?   ___

28. Have difficulty standing still when groomed?   10 ___

29. Like to carry things in his mouth?   10 _yes_

30. Play a lot with other dogs?   10 _no_

31. Dislike being groomed or petted?   2 ___

32. Cower or cringe when a stranger bends over him?   0

33. Wolf down his food?   10 _yes_

34. Jump up to greet people?   10 _yes_

35. Like to fight other dogs?   0 ___

36. Urinate during greeting behavior?   0 _no_

37. Like to dig or bury things?   0 ___

38. Show reproductive behaviors, such as mounting other dogs?   0 _no_

39. Get picked on by older dogs as a young dog?   0 ___

40. Tend to bite when cornered?   0 ___

Score your answers by using Table 2-2.

After you've obtained the totals, enter them in the appropriate column of the "Profile at a Glance" shown in Figure 2-4. Simply shade in the columns to see your dog's profile at a glance.

Scoring the Profile

	Pack		Fight		Flight	
9. *5*	2. *10*		3. *10*		4. *9*	
13. *10*	6. *10*		7. *10*		8. *8*	
17. *10*	10. *10*		11. *0*		12. *2*	
21. *10*	14. *10*		15.		16. *0*	
25. *0*	18. *2*		19. *5*		20.	
29. *10*	22. *10*		23. *0*		24. *5*	
33. *10*	26. *9*		27.		28. *10*	
37. *0*	30. *10*		31. *2*		32. *0*	
Total Prey	34. *10*		35. *0*		36. *0*	
	38. *0*		39. *0*		40. *0*	
	Total Pack		**Total Fight**		**Total Flight**	

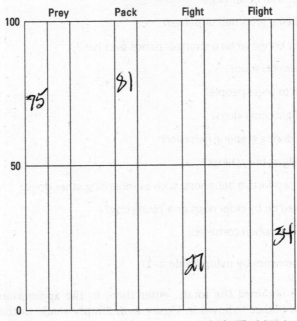

FIGURE 2-4: Your dog's Profile at a Glance.

Profile at a Glance

Prey — 75
Pack — 81
Fight — 27
Flight — 34

© John Wiley & Sons, Inc.

To make best use of the concept of drives in your training, you need to know what you want Buddy to do or stop doing. Usually, you want him to be in pack drive and he wants to be in prey. When you've mastered how to get Buddy out of prey and into pack, you have a well-trained dog. We discuss switching between drives later in the "Switching drives" section.

Deciding How You Want Buddy to Act

Before you can use the results of the profile in the preceding section, you need to look at what you want Buddy to do or — and this is often more important — stop doing. For example, when you walk Buddy on leash and want him to pay attention to you, he has to be in pack drive. If Buddy, on the other hand, wants to sniff, maybe follow a trail, or chase the neighbor's cat, he's in prey drive.

For most of what you want Buddy to do, such as the following, he needs to be in pack drive:

>> Come

>> Down

>> Sit

>> Stay

>> Walk on a loose leash

For most of what Buddy wants to do, such as the following, he's going to be in prey drive:

>> Chase a cat

>> Dig

>> Follow the trail of a rabbit

>> Retrieve a ball or stick

>> Sniff the grass

You can readily see that those times when you want him to behave that you have to convince Buddy to forget about being in prey drive. Dogs high in prey drive usually require quite a bit of training. A dog with high pack and low prey drive rarely needs extensive training. Such a dog doesn't do the following:

>> Chase bicycles, cars, children, or joggers

>> Chase cats or other animals

>> Chew your possessions

>> Pull on the leash

>> Roam from home

>> Steal food

In other words, he's a perfect pet.

Theoretically, Buddy doesn't need defense drive (fight) behaviors for what you want him to learn, but the absence of these behaviors has important ramifications. A very low defense-fight drive determines how Buddy has to be trained. For example, a Labrador, Bean, was low in defense drive. If anyone would lean over him, he would collapse on the floor and act as though he had been beaten. Katharina, a German Shepherd, on the other hand, who was high in fight-drive, would just look at you if you leaned over her, as though to say, "I'm good. What do you want?"

Training each dog required a different approach. With Bean, a check on his leash (a *check* is a quick tug on the leash that is like a snap back, quick and short) caused him literally to collapse — he didn't have enough fight behaviors to cope with the check. A slight tug on the leash or a quietly spoken command was sufficient to get him to ignore chasing a rabbit, switching him out of prey drive. Katharina, high in both prey drive and fight drive, required a firm check to convince her to override the prey drive and forget about the rabbit. The only difference between the two dogs was their score in fight drive on their Personality Profile. The high fight drive allows the dog to recover from the needed check that gets the dog out of prey drive, back into the desired pack drive. Refer to the following sections for the different profiles and how to deal with them.

REMEMBER

The beauty of the drives theory is that, if used correctly, it gives you the necessary insight to overcome areas when you and your dog are at odds with each other over appropriate behavior. A soft command may be enough for one dog to change the undesired behavior, whereas a firm check is required for another.

Bringing out drives

When you grill hamburgers on the barbecue, the aroma stimulates your appetite as well as everyone else's in the neighborhood. In effect, it brings out your prey drive. The smell becomes a cue. Incidentally, the smell also brings out Buddy's prey drive.

The following is a short list of cues that bring out each of the dog's major drives:

>> Prey drive is elicited by the use of motion (hand signals, running, swinging arms) a high-pitched tone of voice, the movement of an object of attraction (stick, ball, or food), smells, and the act of chasing or being chased.

>> Pack drive is elicited by calmly and quietly touching, praising and smiling, grooming, and playing and training while you stand up straight with an erect body posture.

>> Defense drive is elicited by your threatening body posture, such as leaning or hovering over the dog from either the front or the side, staring at the dog with direct eye contact (this is how people get bitten), leaning over and wagging a finger in the dog's face while chastising him, and checking the leash on the dog or using a harsh tone of voice.

Switching drives

Buddy can instantaneously switch from one drive to another. Picture this scene. Buddy is lying in front of the fireplace:

He's playing with his favorite toy. (He's in prey drive.)

The doorbell rings; he drops the toy, starts to bark, and goes to the door. (He's in defense-fight drive.)

You open the door; it's a neighbor, and Buddy goes to greet him. (He's in pack drive.)

He returns to play with his toy. (He's in prey drive.)

Buddy has switched drives from prey into defense, into pack, and back into prey. Dogs can switch from drive to drive willingly and freely. There are no limitations; he can go from drive to drive as he feels the need. Figure 2-5 shows how the arrows go back and forth between all of the drives.

During training, your task is to keep Buddy in the right drive and, if necessary, switch him from one drive to another. For example, say you're teaching Buddy to walk on a loose leash in the yard when a rabbit pops out of the hedge. He immediately spots it and runs to the end of the leash, straining and barking excitedly in a high-pitched voice. He's clearly in full-blown prey drive.

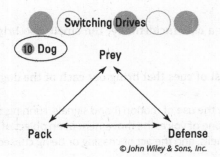

FIGURE 2-5:
How a dog can go between any drive as he chooses.

© John Wiley & Sons, Inc.

Now you need to get him back into pack drive where he needs to be to walk at your side. The only way you can do that is by going through defense drive. You can't, for example, show him a cookie in an effort to divert his attention from the rabbit. The rabbit is going to win out, unless you have a bigger rabbit. Look at Figure 2-6 to see how you must first take Buddy through the defense drive when switching Buddy from the prey drive into the pack drive.

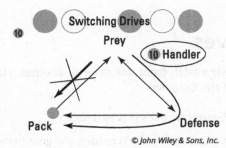

FIGURE 2-6:
Switching from defense drive into pack drive.

© John Wiley & Sons, Inc.

TIP

The precise manner in which you get Buddy back into pack drive depends on the strength of his defense drive. If he has a large number of defense (fight) behaviors, you can give him a firm check on the leash, which switches him out of prey drive into defense drive. Now you want him in pack drive, so touch him gently on the top of his head (don't pat), smile at him, and tell him how clever he is. Then continue to work on walking on a loose leash. If he's low in defense (fight) behaviors, a check may overpower him, and a voice communication such as "Let's Go" will be sufficient to get him out of prey drive into defense drive, after which you put him back into pack drive with praise and a smile.

REMEMBER

If your dog has few fight behaviors and a large number of flight behaviors, a check on the leash often is counterproductive. Body postures, such as bending over the dog or even using a deep tone of voice, usually are enough to elicit defense drive. By his response to your training — cowering, rolling upside down, not wanting to come to you for the training session — your dog will show you when you overpower him, thereby making his learning difficult, if not impossible. Use only enough defense–drive actions or communications as necessary to elicit defense drive in your dog. Every dog will be different depending on his Personality Profile.

Here are the basic rules for switching from one drive to another:

>> **From prey into pack:** You must go through defense drive by applying a defense-drive action such as using a firm voice or giving a check on the leash.

>> **From defense into pack:** Gently touch or smile at your dog, which is a pack-drive action. Stay still when you do it.

>> **From pack into prey:** Use an object (such as food) or motion, which is a prey-drive action.

REMEMBER

Understanding which drive Buddy needs to be in speeds up your training process. As you become aware of the impact your body stance and motions have on the drive that Buddy is in, you can deliver clear messages to him. Your body language becomes congruent with what you're trying to teach. Because Buddy is an astute observer of body motions, which is how dogs communicate with each other, he'll understand exactly what you want.

Applying drives to your training

After looking at your dog's Personality Profile (see the questionnaire earlier in the "Determining Your Dog's Personality Profile" section), you know the training techniques that work best and that are in harmony with your dog's drives. You now have the tools to tailor your training program to your dog. Here are the different categories your dog may be in:

>> **Defense-fight drive — more than 60:** A firm hand doesn't bother your dog much. Correct body posture isn't critical because your dog's high defense-fight drive numbers are very forgiving. Your tone of voice can be firm, but it should always be pleasant and nonthreatening.

>> **Defense-flight drive — more than 60:** Your dog won't respond to strong corrections. Correct body posture and a quiet, pleasant tone of voice are critical. Avoid using a harsh tone of voice or hovering — leaning over or toward your dog. Focus on still body postures and standing up straight with gentle handling.

>> **Prey drive — more than 60:** Your dog will respond well to a treat or toy during the teaching phase because of his high prey drive. A firm hand may be necessary, depending on the strength of his defense-fight drive, to suppress the prey drive when necessary, such as when chasing a cat or spotting a squirrel. A dog high in prey drive is easily motivated but is also easily distracted by motion or moving objects. Moving hand signals mean more to this

dog than commands. Focus on leaning backward with your body posture, using hand signals, and keeping your leash from dangling and swinging, so as not to confuse the dog. Any motion will put this dog into prey drive.

» **Prey drive — less than 40:** A dog low in prey drive probably isn't easily motivated by food or other objects, but he also isn't easily distracted by or interested in chasing moving objects. Use every prey drive your dog has and feed him before you need him in prey drive, such as when you want him to retrieve so he is in prey drive from the morsel of food. Use quiet verbal praise; you don't want a loud voice to flip him out of prey drive and into defense drive.

» **Pack drive — more than 60:** This dog responds readily to praise and physical affection. A dog high in pack drive likes to be with you and will respond with little guidance. The act of being together, training or playing together, will make this dog happy.

» **Pack drive — less than 40:** A dog low in pack drive probably doesn't care whether he spends much time with you. He likes to do his own thing and isn't easily motivated through pack-drive activities. Your best plan is to rely on prey drive in training. Low pack drive is usually breed-specific for dogs bred to work independently of man.

Consider some important hints to keep in mind when planning your training strategy:

» Dogs with a low defense-fight drive of less than 60 rarely get into trouble; in fact, they avoid it. Many young dogs without life experience fall into this category, and although their numbers may be quite low as pups, they may vary slightly with age. With a low fight-drive dog, a straight body posture is more important. Don't bend over; rather you need to squat down — as opposed to bending at the waist — to the dog's level especially when greeting him.

» Dogs who are high in prey or pack drive also are easily trained. Pay attention to the strengths of each drive. Dogs are happiest in the drive that they have the most of. Training should come more easily to them because most training needs both prey and pack drive. Review the switching behaviors you need to communicate with your dog in those two drives.

» If your dog is high in defense-fight drive, you need to work diligently on your leadership and control exercises and review them frequently. You want to be the pack leader with this dog. Bonding is great with a high defense-fight drive dog after he sees you as the coach of the team.

>> If your dog is high in prey drive, you also need to work on the leadership exercises to control him around doorways, objects, and similar distractions. A dog who is high in prey drive is distracted by everything — noise, motion, smells, and things near and far away. Life is distracting. Training is the key to all things.

>> If your dog is high in both prey and defense-fight drives, you have a dog that is alert and demanding, but with the defense-fight drive you have a dog with enough personality to work though the prey drive and distractions of life. This dog may be the dog you dreamed of, and he may want to do it all. Work on your leadership and training and how to switch between the drives.

Following are the nicknames for a few of the profiles. See if you can recognize your dog:

>> **The Couch Potato or some may say "The born perfect dog"— low prey, low pack, low defense fight:** This dog is difficult to motivate and probably doesn't need extensive training. He needs extra patience if training is attempted because he has few behaviors to work with. On the plus side, this dog is unlikely to get into trouble, doesn't disturb anyone, makes a good family pet, and doesn't mind being left alone for considerable periods of time.

>> **The Hunter — high prey, low pack, low defense flight:** This dog gives the appearance of having an extremely short attention span but is perfectly able to concentrate on what he finds interesting. Training requires channeling his energy to get him to do what you want. You need patience because you need to teach the dog through prey drive.

>> **The Gas Station Dog or Sentry Guard Dog — high prey, low pack, high defense fight:** This dog is independent and not easy to live with as a pet. Highly excited by movement, he may attack anything that comes within range. He doesn't care much about people or dogs and works well as a guard dog. Pack exercises, such as walking on a leash without pulling, need to be built up through his prey drive. Every dog is perfect for the task for which he was born. A sentry dog may not make a good family pet, but a good family pet wouldn't make a good sentry dog. Be practical when setting the goals that you have for the dog you have.

>> **The Runner — high prey, low pack, high defense-flight:** Easily startled and/or frightened, this dog needs quiet and reassuring handling. A dog with this profile isn't a good choice for children. Knowing what drives your dog and what personality he has would be wonderful to know before you get the dog, which would be an ideal situation. A dog with high defense flight can feel cornered easily. Always give this dog space and train with a calm, reassuring tone. Know what your plan is and don't get discouraged.

>> **The Shadow — low prey, high pack, and low defense fight:** This dog follows you around all day and is unlikely to get into trouble. He likes to be with you and isn't interested in chasing much of anything.

>> **Teacher's Pet — medium prey, pack, and defense fight:** This dog is easy to train and motivate, and mistakes on your part aren't critical. Teacher's Pet has a nice balance of drives. Figure 2-7 shows the graph for Teacher's Pet. Having medium drive in all the drives except defense-flight which is low, does give a personality that should be playful with people and other dogs. He should be able to handle most households and goals you might have for training a dog.

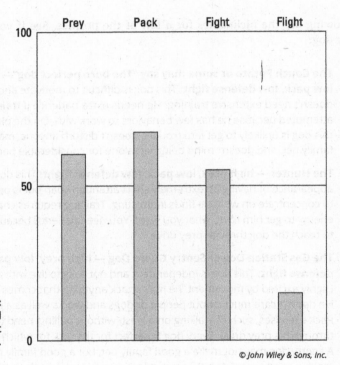

© John Wiley & Sons, Inc.

FIGURE 2-7:
A typical
Teacher's Pet
profile.

REMEMBER

The easiest dogs are balanced among all drives. No matter what you do, the dog seems to be able to figure out what you want. As we've mentioned, dogs are happiest in the drives in which they're highest. There are no bad dogs; there are only dogs best suited for one thing over another. By applying the principles of drives, you can turn your dog into a well-trained pet.

People frequently ask us, "Can you change a dog's drives — either reduce or enhance a particular drive?" In a few instances you can enhance a drive through training. For example, after you've taught a dog with few prey behaviors to retrieve, he'll be more inclined to participate in fetch games. As a general rule, however, you can't change a dog's drives. Your dog's personality is like the computer program you bought. Its personality is programed a certain way. Nature versus nurture does give you some room to build on your dog's drives. Through training and learning about drives you can communicate with your dog and training becomes more successful. By controlling your body language and keeping Buddy in the proper drive, you'll have more fun training him, and therefore you'll get the dog you want.

As Mary Ann says, "You get the dog you train, so train for the dog you want."

Remembering Who's Training Whom

Training is a two-way street: Buddy is just as involved in training you as you are in trying to train him. The trouble is that Buddy is already an expert at training you. He learned what he has to do to get what he wants from you and what is to his advantage and what isn't, and he'll do whatever he can to get what he wants. You, on the other hand, need to discover the skills of training him. Unintentional training is when you give into the training coming from Buddy. You must be aware into which drive your body language is switching Buddy. The tone of your voice, the tilt of your body, and the movements you make all put Buddy into a different drive.

One skill is figuring out how to recognize when you're inadvertently rewarding behaviors you may not want to reinforce. Begging at the dinner table is a good example. When Buddy begs at the table and you slip him some food, he's training you to feed him from the table. You need to ask yourself, "Is this a behavior I want to encourage?" If the answer is no, then stop doing it.

Consider two more examples of how your dog may be training you:

>> Buddy drops his ball in your lap while you're watching television, and you throw it for him.

>> Buddy nudges or paws your elbow when you're sitting on the couch, and you absentmindedly pet him. When he has had enough, he walks away.

Buddy has trained you well. Is there anything wrong with that? Not at all, as long as you can tell him to go lie down when you don't feel like throwing the ball or petting him.

ARE YOU SPOILING YOUR DOG?

We hope so. We certainly spoil ours. We take them for their daily walk, play ball in the backyard, do some training, and on weekends go for outings with friends and their dogs. Give your dog what he needs to get the dog you want and deserve. ***Remember:*** You get the dog you train, so train for the dog you want.

REMEMBER

Become aware of the interactions between the two of you and who initiates them — you or Buddy. One of the quickest ways to gain your dog's respect is to follow this simple rule: everything belongs to you, especially your attention, and Buddy has to earn what he wants. Buddy has to do something for you before you do something for him. Consider the following, for example:

>> Before he gets a meal, he needs to sit and wait until you give Okay that he may eat. (Chapter 1 gets you started with this exercise.)

>> When he comes to you for some petting, ask for a Sit, or any other behavior you have taught him, before you pet him.

>> If he comes and drops a ball in your lap, you decide when to play, not Buddy. If you don't want to play, just ignore him.

TIP

Each drive has joy associated with it. Prey drive has retrieving and jumping, pack drive has companionship and play, defense-fight drive has confidence and the ability for great bonding, and defense-flight drive has quiet and peace and security possible in it. Find the joy for your dog together and build on it.

Chapter **3**

Developing Training Savvy

Your dog's ability to learn and retain information — just like yours — is directly related to what goes on around him and how he feels. A noisy and distraction-filled environment makes it difficult for Buddy to concentrate on learning new commands. Strife in the household may cause Buddy to become frightened, irritable, and even aggressive, which can impede the learning process. Even what you feed your dog has an effect on his ability to learn.

How Buddy feels, both mentally and physically, influences his ability to learn. If he feels anxious, depressed, or stressed, learning and retention decrease in direct proportion to the degree of the dog's distress. If he's physically ill or in pain, he can't learn what you're trying to teach him. These observations are stating the obvious — just think how you'd react under similar circumstances. Yet, we must point out because some dog owners often seem to be oblivious to their effect on the dog's ability to learn.

As Buddy's teacher, you play a key role in his learning process — and not just because you're giving him the physical instruction. You also should create a positive training atmosphere that maximizes his chances for success by easing any stress that can get in the way. Some of that stress comes from within Buddy, and you can alleviate that part by tending to his unique emotional and physical needs. The rest comes from you, so be aware of what you bring to the table as a trainer. Setting realistic expectations and crafting a consistent training regimen go a long way toward creating a pleasant experience for both you and Buddy.

Managing the Dog Within

Even though some principal influences on your dog's ability to learn are under your control, some influences come from within your dog:

>> Breed-specific behaviors

>> Temperament

>> Mental sensitivity

>> Responses to visual stimuli

>> Sound sensitivity

>> Touch sensitivity

All these influences affect how the dog learns, what he finds difficult, and what comes almost naturally. For more information, head to Chapter 2 and take the Personality Profile of your dog. This profile examines all of these elements in great detail.

Breed-specific behaviors

Whether you have a designer dog, a dog of mixed origin, or a purebred, he comes with some specific behaviors, such as hunting or herding, among others. These behaviors, in turn, have been further refined. Some dogs hunt large game, others hunt small game, and yet others hunt birds. Some hunt close by, and others hunt far away. Some herd and guard, and others just herd; some were developed to herd cows, and others, sheep.

By studying the task or tasks for which a particular dog was bred, you can get a pretty good idea of what's going to be easy and difficult for your dog to learn. Most terriers, for example, are lively little dogs because they were bred to go after little furry things that live in holes in the ground. Shetland Sheepdogs like to round up kids, because they were bred to herd. Pointers are bred to stand on three legs, front leg raised to finger the game; Retrievers bring it back (see Figure 3-1); and Spaniels flush it. Each one has its own special talents.

FIGURE 3-1:
A Labrador
Retriever bred to
bring game
to hand.

Dog breeders of purebred dogs hardly ever select their breeding stock from working dogs these days. Instead, most dogs are bred to have correct ear or tail set or to have their eyes, faces, and bodies to look just so. Then there are the breeders who create designer dogs, such as Labradoodles, Goldendoodles, and Puggles, by purposefully breeding different breeds together. These dogs are very cute, but they have no predictable behavioral traits. The same is true of mixed breed dogs. However, you can begin to understand what makes your dog tick.

REMEMBER

Because most dogs were bred to work with or under the direction of man, these talents help with your training efforts. But sometimes the dog's instinct to do what he was bred for gets him into trouble. You may not want him hunting or herding or whatever, so you need to spend some of your training efforts redirecting these behaviors. Whenever you run into a roadblock in your training, ask yourself, "Is that what this dog was bred to do?" If not, it will take him more time to learn that particular exercise, and you'll need to be patient.

Temperament

Most people readily agree that good temperament is the most important quality for pets. Unfortunately, the explanation of exactly what good temperament often gets vague and elusive and sometimes contradictory. The official breed standard of most breeds makes a statement to the effect that the dog you're considering is loyal, loving, intelligent, good with children, and easy to train. If only that were true!

Simply defined, *temperament* is made up of the personality traits suitable for the job you want the dog to do. If you want your dog to be good with children and your dog has that personality trait, then he has good temperament. He may not do so well in other areas, such as guarding or herding, but that may not be what you were looking for.

Similarly vague and elusive have been attempts to define the dog's intelligence. Again, it goes back to function. We define a dog's *intelligence* as the ease with which he can be trained for the function the dog was bred.

You can better understand your dog's temperament if you have a sense of his drives (prey, pack, flight, and fight). The Personality Profile can help you discover your dog's strengths and limitations. You'll find which drive molds Buddy's behaviors.

REMEMBER

You need to recognize your dog's strengths and limitations because they have a profound influence on the ease or difficulty of teaching your dog a particular task. Circus trainers have an old saying: "Get the dog for the trick and not the trick for the dog." Exploit your dog's strengths.

Mental sensitivity

Dogs, like people, vary in their ability to deal with negative emotions. No matter how they cope, most dogs are keenly aware of your emotions. Moreover, the more you work with Buddy, the greater bond you'll develop. It may seem as though he can read your mind. Okay, he may not be able to read your mind, but he certainly senses your emotions. If you're feeling frustration, disappointment, or anger, Buddy can sense it.

REMEMBER

Because dogs are ill-equipped to deal with these emotions, they tend to become anxious and confused, which then slows or even prevents the learning process. Your job in training Buddy is to maintain an upbeat and patient attitude. As your dog's teacher, you must teach him what you want and don't want him to do. Without your guidance, your dog simply does what comes naturally to him — he's a dog! Blaming Buddy for what you perceive to be a shortcoming on his part doesn't help and undermines the very relationship you're trying to build.

Responses to visual stimuli

Saying that a dog responds to *visual stimuli* is a fancy way of saying that a dog responds to moving objects. For purposes of training, it relates to the dog's distractibility when faced with something that moves. This, too, varies from breed to breed and depends on the nature of the moving object. Consider a few examples:

>> Terriers are notoriously distractible. For example, a Yorkshire Terrier, although technically a member of the Toy Group, is convinced that he has to investigate every moving leaf or blade of grass. Although this behavior makes perfect sense to him because he is so low to the ground, it makes training him to pay attention a real challenge.

>> In the Hound Group, some breeds, such as Afghan Hounds, Borzois, and Salukis, called sight hounds, aren't much interested in objects close by. Instead, they focus on items far away. Other breeds, such as the Basset Hound, Beagle, and Bloodhound, are more stimulated by scents on the ground or in the air than by moving objects. Training a Beagle to walk on a loose leash while paying attention to you and not sniffing the ground can be a Herculean task.

>> The guarding breeds, such as the German Shepherd, Doberman Pinscher, and Rottweiler, were bred to survey their surroundings — to keep everything in sight, as it were. They, too, find it difficult and stressful to focus exclusively on you in the presence of distractions. Remember, their job is to be alert to what's going on around them.

>> The weavers of the Swiss Canton of Berne used the Bernese Mountain Dog as a draft dog, drawing milk carts to the marketplace. As a breed, moving objects don't usually excite these dogs. After all, it would hardly do for the little fellow to chase a cat with his wagon bouncing behind him.

>> The Newfoundland, an ordinarily sedate companion (see Figure 3-2), becomes a raving maniac near water with his instinctive desire to rescue any and all swimmers, totally disregarding the fact that he may not want or need to be rescued.

Sound sensitivity

Some dogs have a keener sense of hearing than others, to the point that loud noises literally hurt their ears. For example, Dachshund puppies can get quite upset when the vacuum cleaner is turned on. They're not afraid of the machine itself; they're just upset by the noise. They find it difficult to focus on lessons if a machine is running at the same time. Fear of thunder also can be the result of sound sensitivity.

REMEMBER

Under ordinary circumstances, sound sensitivity isn't a problem, but it can affect the dog's ability to concentrate in the presence of moderate to loud noises. A car backfiring can cause one dog to jump out of his skin, whereas it may only elicit a curious expression from another dog.

FIGURE 3-2:
The Newfoundland, a large breed, is a laid-back dog except around water.

© John Wiley & Sons, Inc.

Touch sensitivity – the adrenaline effect

A dog's threshold of discomfort depends on two things:

» His touch sensitivity

» What he's doing at the particular time

For purposes of training and for knowing what equipment to use, you need know Buddy's touch sensitivity. For example, when a dog doesn't readily respond to the training collar, he's all too quickly labeled as stubborn or stupid. But nothing could be further from the truth. The trainer has to select the right training equipment.

Discomfort thresholds tend to be breed specific. For example, a Labrador Retriever, who's supposed to be able to cover all manner of terrain as well as retrieve in ice-cold water, more than likely would have a high discomfort threshold. Shetland Sheepdogs tend to be quite touch sensitive and respond promptly to the training collar. What one dog hardly notices makes another one change his behavior. And therein lies the secret of which piece of training equipment to use.

Touch sensitivity isn't size related. Small dogs can have just as high a discomfort threshold as large dogs. Nor is touch sensitivity age related. A puppy doesn't start out as touch sensitive and become touch insensitive as he grows older. Some increase in insensitivity may arise, but it's insignificant. A dog's touch sensitivity, however, is affected by what he's doing. In hot pursuit of a rabbit, his discomfort threshold goes up, as it would during a fight. This phenomenon is referred to as the *adrenaline factor*. For example, consider if you're at a rock concert with loud music and dancing, a person might bump into you and you barely notice. Conversely if you're reading in a library and someone taps you on the shoulder, you might jump out of your skin. You're neither touch sensitive nor insensitive; your reaction is the adrenalin factor response.

REMEMBER

When you have an idea of Buddy's discomfort threshold, you know how to handle him and the type of training equipment you need. See Chapter 5 for more on training gear.

Stressing the Effects of Stress

Stress is a byproduct of daily life and can result from many factors — health, family, your job, the state of the economy, the state of the country, or even the state of the world. Even pleasurable experiences, such as taking a vacation, can be a source of stress.

Stress is a physiological, genetically predetermined reaction over which the individual, be it a dog or person, has no control. Stress is a natural part of everyone's daily lives and affects each person in different ways. Dogs are no different. Just like people, they experience stress. As your dog's teacher, you must recognize the circumstances that produce stress and its manifestations and know how to manage it.

REMEMBER

Your personal experiences with stress help you relate to what your dog is experiencing. Knowing how to identify the signs and symptoms isn't difficult when you know what you're looking for.

Understanding stress

In both dogs and people, stress is the body's response to any physical or mental demand put upon it. That response prepares the body to either fight or flee. Stress increases blood pressure, heart rate, breathing, and metabolism, and it triggers a marked increase in the blood supply to the arms and legs.

Stress takes its toll on the body, be it a person's or a dog's. When stressed, the body becomes chemically imbalanced. To deal with this imbalance, the body releases chemicals into the bloodstream in an attempt to rebalance itself. The reserve of these chemicals is limited; you can dip into it only so many times before it runs dry and the body loses its ability to rebalance. Prolonged periods of imbalance then result in neurotic behavior and the inability to function. When the body's ability to counteract stress has been maxed out, stress is then expressed in more than just physical ways: it manifests behaviorally and physically. This is as true for your dog as it is for you.

Mental and physical stress ranges from tolerable all the way to intolerable — that is, the inability to function. Your interest here lies with your dog's stress experienced during training, whether you're teaching a new exercise, practicing a familiar one, or administering a test, like the Canine Good Citizen test (see Chapter 25.) You need to be able to recognize the signs of stress and manage the stress your dog may experience.

REMEMBER

Stress is characterized as both positive and negative. When stress is *positive*, it manifests itself in increased activity; when it's *negative*, it results in decreased activity. The following list explains both:

>> **Help, I'm hyperactive!** So-called positive stress results in hyperactivity. Your dog may run around, not be able to stay still or slow down, not pay attention, bounce up and down, jump on you, whine, bark, mouth, get in front of you, anticipate commands, or not be able to learn. You may think your dog is just being silly and having fun, but he isn't. He's actually exhibiting coping behaviors for positive stress.

>> **Why am I so depressed?** So-called negative stress causes lethargy, with related behaviors such as lacking energy, being afraid, freezing, slinking behind you, running away, responding slowly to commands, showing little interest in exercise or training, or displaying an inability to learn. In new situations, Buddy gets behind you, seems tired and wants to lie down, or seems sluggish and disinterested. These aren't signs of relaxation; they're the coping behaviors for negative stress.

Recognizing the symptoms of stress

In dogs, signs of either form of stress — positive or negative — are muscle tremors; excessive panting and drooling; sweaty feet that leave tracks on dry, hard surfaces; dilated pupils; and, in extreme cases, urination, defecation (usually in the form of diarrhea), self-mutilation, and anxiety.

Anxiety is a state of apprehension and uneasiness. When anxiety is prolonged, two problems arise:

>> The dog's ability to learn and think is diminished and ultimately stops. It also can cause a panic attack.

>> Anxiety depresses the immune system, thereby increasing the dog's chances of becoming physically ill. The weakest link in the chain is attacked first. If the dog has structural flaws, such as weak *pasterns* (the region of foreleg between the wrist and digits), he may begin to limp or show signs of pain. Digestive upsets are another common reaction to stress.

REMEMBER

In and of itself, stress isn't bad or undesirable. A certain level of stress is vital for the development and healthy functioning of the body and its immune system. Only when stress has no behavioral outlet — when the dog is put in a no-win situation — is the burden of coping borne by the body. The immune system then starts to break down.

Origins of stress — intrinsic and extrinsic

Intrinsic sources of stress are inherited and come from within the dog. They include structure and health. Dogs vary in coping abilities and stress thresholds. Realistically, you can't do much to change your dog — for example, you can't train him to deal better with stress. But you can use stress-management techniques to mitigate its impact.

Extrinsic sources of stress come from outside the dog and are introduced externally. They range from the diet you feed your dog to the relationship you have with him. Extrinsic sources include the following:

>> Frustration and indecision on your part

>> Lack of adequate socialization

>> The dog's perception of his environment

>> Training location

>> Use of an appropriate training method

Fortunately, all these sources of stress are under your control (see the later section "Managing Your Dog's Environment").

Relating stress to learning

When you train Buddy, you can't prevent him from experiencing some stress, but you can keep the stress to a level at which he can still learn. If you find that your dog is overly stressed during a training session, stop the session. (One indicator of when Buddy has had enough is that he no longer takes a treat.) At that point, your dog's ability to learn is diminished, and neither of you will benefit from continuing.

What should you do? Don't think of training as a win-lose contest between you and your dog such as: "If I stop, Buddy will think he has won and he'll never do it for me." This line of thinking presumes that you and Buddy are adversaries, in some kind of a contest, or "You'll do it no matter what." Not exactly a teacher-student relationship!

Training Buddy has nothing to do with winning or losing, but with teaching. You can walk away from a training session at any time, whether or not you think you've been successful. When you see that no further learning is taking place, stop. If you don't and you insist on forcing the issue, you'll undermine both your dog's trust in you and the relationship you're trying to build.

TIP

Let Buddy rest for a few hours and try again. You'll find that the light bulb suddenly seems to turn on. By having taken a break at that point, you get *latent learning* — the process of giving the point a chance to work. Our advice is to quit training when you find yourself becoming irritable or when Buddy starts to show signs of stress.

Stress and distraction training

Prepare to be patient when you first introduce your dog to training with distractions. Naturally, Buddy is going to be distracted (that's the point!), but over time, he'll learn to respond correctly and ignore distractions. If you feel yourself becoming upset, it's time to take five.

REMEMBER

Try to make every new exercise or distraction a positive experience for your dog. A favorable introduction will have a positive long-term impact. The first impression leaves the most lasting impact. Whenever you introduce your dog to a new exercise or distraction, make it as pleasant and as stress free as possible so that it leaves a neutral, if not favorable, impression.

Managing stress

Become aware of how Buddy reacts to stress, positively or negatively, and the circumstances under which he stresses. Something you're doing, or even a location, may cause him stress.

Understand that Buddy has no control over his response to stress — he inherited this behavior — and that it's your job to manage it as best as you can. Through proper management, Buddy will become accustomed, with every successful repetition, to coping with new situations like a pro.

Managing Your Dog's Environment

Your dog has a keen perception of his environment. Continuous or frequent strife or friction in your household can have a negative impact on your dog's ability to learn. Many dogs also are adversely affected by excessive noise and activity and may develop behavior problems.

Look for the following signs that your dog has a negative perception of his environment:

>> Aggression

>> Aloofness

>> Hyperactivity

>> Irritability

>> Lethargy

Under these circumstances, learning is reduced — if it takes place at all — and your dog won't retain the lesson. However, if you have a keen perception of how your dog responds to his environment, you'll more easily attain your training goals. This section provides some tips on creating the best possible environment for learning.

Starting on the right foot

You've heard the saying "You don't get a second chance to make a first impression." You also know that the first impression leaves the most lasting impact. The stronger that impression, the longer it lasts.

TIP

Introductions to a dog's new experiences need to be as pleasant as possible. For example, Buddy's first visit to the vet needs to be a pleasant experience, or he'll have an unpleasant association with going to the vet. Ask the doctor to give him a dog treat before his examination and another treat at the end of the visit.

The importance of making a good first impression applies to your dog's training as well. A particularly traumatic or unpleasant first experience can literally ruin a dog for life. The object is to make your dog's first impression of training as pleasant as you can.

Recognizing your dog's social needs

Dogs are social animals that don't do well when isolated. For example, if you work outside the home, you may need to leave your dog alone at home. Then when you get home, your dog is terribly excited and wants to play and be with you. But you also may need to go out in the evening, leaving your dog alone again.

If you simply don't have the time to give your dog the attention he craves, consider a doggie daycare. Your dog will spend his day playing and interacting with other dogs and having a good time using his excess energy needs. A tired dog is a happy dog and has a happy owner. In addition to keeping Buddy entertained and amused, many doggie daycare facilities provide other services, such as bathing and grooming.

A potential downside of doggie daycare is that Buddy may think it's playtime whenever he meets another dog, making him difficult to control around other dogs. Other potential downsides are possible exposure to disease and parasites, trauma due to inexperienced handling by daycare personnel, and personal liability for Buddy's actions. If you're considering a doggie daycare, do your research first and visit the doggie daycare before you select one. Ask if the dogs get rest periods during the day. Also see how well the staff monitors the play time.

REMEMBER

As with any behavior, when it comes to exercise, your dog has a certain amount of energy. After Buddy has expended that energy, he is tired. If that energy isn't expended, it may redirect itself into barking, chewing, digging, house soiling, self-mutilation, and similar behaviors — clearly not what you have in mind for the well-trained pet. If your schedule doesn't allow for enough exercise for Buddy, look into doggie daycare or dog walkers in your area to help you.

Identifying your dog's emotional needs

Dogs have emotions. Here are some of them:

>> Anger

>> Apprehension

>> Depression

>> Fear

>> Happiness

>> Joy

>> Sadness

You can see your dog exhibit some of these emotions, such as joy and happiness, on a daily basis, but what about sadness and depression? Dogs react with the same emotions that people exhibit over the loss of a loved one, be it a family member or another dog.

REMEMBER

How can you tell whether your dog is experiencing any of these negative emotions? The answer is, pretty much the way you can tell with a person. If your dog mopes around the house, doesn't seem to enjoy activities he previously enjoyed, is lethargic, isn't particularly interested in food, and/or sleeps a lot, chances are, he's depressed. Under those circumstances, he may not feel much like training.

We frequently see dogs with anxiety, apprehension, and fear — behaviors that can be hereditary or situational. Whatever the cause, training such a dog requires a great deal of patience and an understanding of how difficult it is for him to learn. On the other hand, the rewards are significant because, through the structure of training, the dog's confidence increases, sometimes to the point at which these behaviors disappear altogether.

Feeding your dog's nutritional needs

The most important influence on your dog's ability to learn, and the one under your most immediate control, is what you feed him. Because feeding is so important, we devote Chapter 4 to this topic. Nutrition is the fuel that runs Buddy's engine. Poor fuel provides a poor performance, so understanding how to feed Buddy correctly avoids stressing his system by providing enough nutrients for it to work properly.

So many dog foods are on the market today that making the best choice for Buddy can be a bewildering task. Just as you do when buying food for yourself or your family, you need to look at the ingredients. Dogs are carnivores and need animal protein. Select a food that lists animal proteins, such as chicken, beef, or lamb, in the first three ingredients. Avoid foods containing a lot of grains. When it seems that more comes out of your dog's rear end than went into the front end, you can safely bet that the food contains more filler than protein.

Understanding the "You" Factor

Several factors influence how successful you'll be in turning your pet into a well-mannered companion. Some of these are under your direct control, and others come with your dog or come from his surrounding environment. We discuss the factors that are out of your control in the earlier sections in this chapter. Here in this section, we examine the factors that are under your direct control. A direct relationship exists between your awareness and understanding of the following factors and your success as your dog's teacher.

Knowing your expectations

Most people's expectations of their dogs vary. Some of these expectations are realistic; others aren't. You've heard people say, "My dog understands every word I say," and perhaps you think yours does as well. If it were as easy as that, you wouldn't need dog trainers or training books. Your words coupled with your body language aid your dog to be able to understand your words.

Sometimes your dog may seem to really understand what you say. Enough truth does exist to perpetuate this myth. Although dogs don't understand the words you use, they do understand tone of voice — and sometimes even your intent. Scientists have found that words used in the same tone of voice and inflection and with the same body motions allow a well-trained dog to learn to the capacity of a 2-year-old child.

Ask yourself these questions for a clearer picture of your expectations:

Are your expectations realistic?

Do you believe your dog obeys commands because he

>> Loves you?

>> Wants to please you?

>> Is grateful?

>> Has a sense of duty?

>> Feels a moral obligation?

We suspect that you answered yes to the first and second questions, became unsure at the third question, and then realized that we were leading you down a primrose path.

WARNING

If your approach to training is based on moral ideas regarding punishment, reward, obedience, duty, and the like, you're bound to handle the dog in the wrong way. No doubt your dog loves you, but he won't obey commands for that reason. Does he want to please you? Not exactly, but it sometimes seems like he does. What he's really doing is pleasing himself.

REMEMBER

Buddy is usually interested in only one thing: What's in it for me right now? Buddy certainly has no sense of duty or feeling of moral obligation. The sooner you discard beliefs like that, the quicker you'll come to terms with how to approach his education.

Are your expectations too low?

Do you believe your dog doesn't obey commands because he

>> Is stubborn?

>> Is hardheaded?

>> Is stupid?

>> Lies awake at night thinking of ways to aggravate you?

If you answered yes to any of these, you're guilty of *anthropomorphizing*, or attributing human characteristics and attributes to an animal. It's easy to do, but it doesn't help in your training.

Dogs aren't stubborn or hardheaded. To the contrary, they're quite smart when it comes to figuring out how to get their way. And they don't lie awake at night thinking of ways to aggravate you — they sleep, just like everybody else.

What should your expectations be?

So why does your dog obey your command? Usually for one of three reasons:

>> He wants something.

>> He thinks it's fun, like retrieving a ball.

>> He has been taught specific behaviors.

When he responds to a command for either the first or the second reason, he does it for himself; when he responds for the third reason, he does it for you. This distinction is important because it deals with reliability and safety. Ask yourself this question: if Buddy responds only because he wants something or because it's fun, will he respond when he doesn't want something or when it's no longer fun? The answer is obvious.

REMEMBER

The well-trained dog responds because he has been taught. This doesn't mean you and he can't have fun in the process; just make sure the end result is clearly understood. When you say "Come," there are no options, especially when his safety or the safety of others is involved.

Knowing your attitude

Look at the following situation: Buddy has taken himself for an unauthorized walk through the neighborhood. You're late for an appointment but don't want to leave Buddy out on the streets. You frantically call and call. Finally, Buddy makes an appearance, happily sauntering up to you. You, on the other hand, are fit to be tied, and you let him know your displeasure in no uncertain terms by giving him a thorough scolding. Ask yourself, "Is this the kind of greeting that will make Buddy want to come to me?" If the answer is no, then stop doing it, no matter what.

REMEMBER

Don't train your dog when you're irritable or tired. You want training to be a positive experience for your dog. If you ever get frustrated during training, stop and come back to it at another time. When you're frustrated, your communications consist of "No!" "Bad dog!" "How could you do this?" and "Get out and stay out!" You're unhappy, and Buddy is unhappy because you're unhappy. An unfriendly or hostile approach doesn't gain you his cooperation; it needlessly prolongs the teaching process. When you become frustrated or angry, Buddy becomes anxious and nervous and has difficulty learning. A better approach is to train Buddy when you're in a better frame of mind. You want training to be a positive experience for both of you.

One of the commands you want Buddy to master is to come when called. To be successful, remember this principle: whenever your dog comes to you, be nice to him. Don't do anything the *dog* perceives as unpleasant. No matter what he may have done, be pleasant and greet him with a kind word, a pat on the head, and a smile. Teach your dog to trust you by being a safe place for him. When he's with you, follows you, or comes to you, make him feel wanted.

You may ask, though, "How can I be nice to my dog when he brings me the remains of one of my brand-new shoes, or when he wants to jump on me with muddy paws, or when I just discovered an unwanted present on the carpet?" A dog's behavior can be utterly frustrating at times. What you must accept is that, at that moment in time, the dog doesn't understand that he did anything wrong. He understands only your anger — but not the reason for it. As difficult as it may be, you have to grin and bear it, lest you undermine the very relationship of mutual trust you're trying to achieve through training.

Being consistent with commands and tone of voice

If any magic is involved in training your dog, it's consistency. Your dog can't understand "sometimes," "maybe," "perhaps," or "only on Sundays." He can and does understand "yes" and "no." For example, you confuse your dog when you encourage him to jump up on you while you're wearing old clothes but then get angry with him when he joyfully plants muddy paws on your best suit.

Dogs often pick up consistent cues from unexpected sources. For example, before leaving for work, Mary always put Heidi in her crate. It wasn't long before Heidi went into her crate on her own when Mary was about to leave. "What a clever puppy," thought Mary. "She knows that I'm going to work."

Dogs often give the appearance of being able to read your mind. In actuality, by observing you and studying your habits, they learn to anticipate your actions. Because dogs communicate with each other through body language, they quickly become experts at reading yours.

What Heidi observed was that, immediately before leaving for work, Mary invariably put on her makeup and then crated her. Heidi's cue to go into her crate was seeing Mary putting on her makeup. Then one evening, before dinner guests were to arrive, Mary started "putting on her face." When Heidi immediately went into her crate, Mary realized the dog hadn't been reading her mind, but had learned the routine through observation.

REMEMBER

Consistency in training means handling your dog in a predictable and uniform manner. If more than one person is in the household, everyone needs to handle the dog in the same way. Otherwise, the dog becomes confused and unreliable in his responses.

TIP

Most dogs eventually ignore commands that don't lead to tangible consequences. When Buddy responds to a command, praise him. When he chooses not to respond to a command he has been taught, show him what you expected from him. Reinforce your command; don't repeat it over and over again.

So does this mean that you can never permit your puppy to jump up on you (or do some other sometimes permissible behavior)? Not at all. But you must teach him that he may do so only when you tell him it's okay. But beware that training a dog to make this distinction is more difficult than teaching him not to jump up at all. The more black-and-white you can make it, the easier it will be for Buddy to understand what you want.

Outlasting your dog — be persistent

Training your dog is a question of who is more persistent — you or your dog. Some things he can master quickly; others will take more time. If several tries don't bring success, be patient, remain calm, and try again.

How quickly your dog will learn a particular command depends on the extent to which the behavior you're trying to teach him is in harmony with the function for which he was bred.

For example, a Labrador Retriever, bred to retrieve game birds on land and in the water, will readily learn how to fetch a stick or a ball on command. On the other hand, an Afghan Hound, bred as a coursing hound that pursues its quarry by sight, may take many repetitions before he understands the command to fetch and then responds to it each and every time. A Shetland Sheepdog, bred to herd and guard livestock, will learn to walk on a loose leash more quickly than a Beagle, bred to hunt hares.

Knowing to avoid "no"

As of right now, eliminate the word "no" from your training vocabulary. All too often, *no* is the only command a dog hears, and he's expected to figure out what it means. No exercise or command in training is called "no."

You need to avoid negative communications like "no" with your dog because they undermine the relationship you're trying to build. Also, don't use your dog's name as a reprimand. And don't nag your dog by repeatedly using his name without telling him what you want him to do. If you find yourself in a situation where it's imperative to interrupt Buddy's behavior, use the word "stop" instead.

REMEMBER

Begin to focus on the way in which you communicate with Buddy. Does he perceive the interaction as positive or negative, pleasant or unpleasant, friendly or unfriendly? How many times do you use the word "no," and how many times do you say "Good dog" when interacting with him? If everything the dog does brings forth a stern "Don't do this," "Don't do that," or "No, bad dog" this negative communication will have a negative effect on your dog's motivation to work for you.

In dealing with your dog, ask yourself, "What exactly do I want Buddy to do or not to do?" Use a *do* command whenever possible so that you can praise your dog instead of reprimanding him. You'll notice a direct relationship between your dog's willingness to cooperate and your attitude. Get out of the blaming habit of assuming that Buddy's failure to respond is his fault. After all, *you* are his teacher! Your dog's conduct is a direct reflection of your teaching.

Does this mean you can never use the word "no"? Not exactly. In an emergency, you do what you must do. But remember, do so only when in dire need.

Repeating commands

In training, use your dog's name once *before* a command to get his attention, as in "Buddy, Come." The quickest way to teach your dog to ignore you is to use his name repeatedly — and raising your voice doesn't help, either. When trying to communicate with someone who doesn't understand English, shouting doesn't improve their understanding.

TIP

Get into the habit of giving a command once and in a normal tone of voice — a dog's hearing is 80 times better than yours. By repeating commands, you systematically teach your dog to ignore you, and changes in inflections from please to threats don't help. Most people are unaware of how many times they repeat a command. Give the command, and if your dog doesn't respond, show him exactly what you want him to do.

Giving a dog a short name or even changing his name can change his behavior as strange as that sounds. A student came to class once who had a rescue dog named Trouble. She worked with Trouble for a long time and made a very good show dog out of him. Her complaint was that he always looked downtrodden and unhappy. We suggested that she rename him — at first just when she worked him — and then gradually in his daily life. His name was changed to Puppy; he responded happily to his new name and perked right up. Hard to believe, but true. Saying your dog's name should elicit a tail wag and happy look from your dog (see Chapter 9 for the Name Recognition game). The power of words and how you feel when you say them comes through. If you use a negative name, you say it with a negative tone. A dog can react to that subtle tone. By changing the name Trouble to something more positive such as Puppy can change not only how you think about your dog but also how you react when you say it, which bleeds onto the dog as well. Words are powerful. Be as positive as you can be as often as you can be.

REMEMBER

When training your dog, think of teacher and student — with you being the teacher. As every teacher knows, learning is a process of successive approximation. Children aren't born knowing how to read and write; they learn these skills in small increments. Similarly, a dog learns commands in small increments, one step at a time. Repetition enforces that incremental learning.

Chapter **4**

Understanding the Vital Role That Nutrition and Health Play in Training

Your dog's behavior, training, happiness, health, longevity, and overall well-being are inextricably intertwined with what you feed him. Dogs, just like humans and all other animals, have specific nutritional requirements that need to be met. What your dog eats has a tremendous impact on his health and his trainability. Dogs' lifespans in the last few years have decreased and what Buddy is fed has so much to do with this.

This chapter helps you figure out what food is right for Buddy, including the different kinds of dog food on the market and our suggestions, common health issues and our solutions for dealing with them, your vet's role in your dog's health, when vaccines are necessary, and the expanding role of veterinary medicine into acupuncture, homeopathy, and chiropractic. We also explain when complementary medicine may be helpful for your dog, especially during the years when he's growing, being trained, and as he ages. Training a dog that isn't feeling well is frustrating for both you and your dog.

These last years have seen an explosion not only in the amount of dog foods on the market, but also in canine nutritional research. Did you know that now one in two dogs die of cancer worldwide? Many dogs also are dying from heart problems. What these two facts have in common is that both diseases are directly related to certain kinds of dog food.

We aren't trying to turn you into an expert on canine nutrition, but having a basic knowledge is important. What we are going to do is to tell you from our experience the best ways to feed your dog so he enjoys good health, longevity, and few visits to the veterinarian. If you do want to become an expert on feeding your dog, see *The Holistic Guide for a Healthy Dog*, 2nd Edition, by Wendy Volhard and Kerry Brown, DVM (Howell Book House). For additional information about any of the information in this chapter, go to www.volharddognutrition.com/. (All the dogs photographed in this book were and are fed from the options mentioned in this chapter.)

REMEMBER

When a dog's body is under stress — from poor health, vaccines, or poor nutrition — his brain doesn't have the ability to retain the information you're teaching. This explains why some dogs get stuck in their training and don't seem to progress.

Finding the Right Food for Buddy

Not all dog foods are alike; enormous quality differences exist between the different types. Since the massive recall in 2008 of dog foods containing contaminated ingredients from China (which killed thousands of cats and dogs), the market has exploded with different types of food. Dry, freeze-dried, frozen, raw, dehydrated, canned, semi-moist, and grain-free foods are available in a bewildering variety. With so many choices, trying to make an informed decision can become an overwhelming task. Here are the main choices:

>> **Kibble:** This type is the most popular way to feed your dog, but it has its disadvantages. Most kibble diets contain a lot of grains, but research has shown an increase in cancer in dogs with a large amount of grains in their diet. Grains are starch, which breaks down into sugar which in turn feeds cancer. Grain-free kibble diets are available on the market, but they too have their problems because they've been associated with heart disease in dogs.

REMEMBER

Even if the package says "complete and balanced," if kibble is your choice, then you must add a complete food supplement to the bowl of kibble to return all the nutrients that are cooked out during the heating process. Also adding some vegetables and raw meat can offset the lack of nutrients in these foods.

>> **Raw diet:** A totally *raw diet* is probably the best way to feed a dog. However, getting that diet properly balanced is difficult, which is why so many people shy away from it. You can buy at some pet stores, raw diets that are balanced, but they're inclined to be rather expensive. Some of them say they're balanced, but they aren't, so carefully read the labels.

>> **Dehydrated whole food base:** Our choice over the last 35 years has been to feed a *dehydrated whole food base* mix, which contains all the vitamins, fat, and minerals a dog needs. It's made from human-grade, nongenetically modified ingredients that are sourced in the United States. Each ingredient has been tested for molds and bacteria before it's mixed, during the mixing process, and before it's put into bags. To our knowledge, no other food produced has these built-in safeguards. We simply add a fresh, raw protein to it and some water to rehydrate the base mix, and it's done. And even better, the dogs love it. It's great for dog at all life stages: puppies, pregnant females, old dogs, and dogs in performance events.

Frozen, freeze dried, canned, dehydrated and semi moist are other choices you can make. The same rules apply: read the labels to make sure you're feeding a balanced product. If the food is processed (cooked) in any way, you have to add a whole food supplement to achieve balance. We recommend adding a supplement like Endurance.

REMEMBER

Good health starts in the gut, which contains different kinds of bacteria. The simple fact is that if bacteria is kept in balance, your dog will live a long and healthy life. Bad health, even small issues like reoccurring ear problems, dirty teeth, and bad breath, can be directly attributed to poor gut balance. To get Buddy's diet just right for him, you need to know the most common and most visible symptoms of nutritional deficiencies. Recognizing these deficiencies saves you a great deal of money in veterinary bills because you can make the necessary adjustments to his diet. The closer you are to a raw diet, the longer your dog will live.

If you want a really healthy dog like CJ (see Figure 4-1), we show you how to do it in the following sections.

Deciphering dog food labels

On the back of every dog food package is information that helps you decide which food is right for your dog. The information lists the ingredients in order of weight, in descending order. The package contains the guaranteed analysis for crude protein, fat, fiber, moisture, and often calcium, phosphorus, and magnesium ratios. The label also may state that the food is nutritionally complete or provides 100 percent nutrition for the dog. To make this claim, the food has to meet the nutrient requirements of the Association of American Feed Control Officers (AAFCO) — a guarantee that some form of testing, anywhere from two to six weeks, has been done on the product.

FIGURE 4-1:
A very
healthy dog.

© John Wiley & Sons, Inc.

By law, the heaviest and largest amount of whatever ingredient contained in the food has to be listed first. By looking at the list of ingredients, you can easily discover the protein's origin. For example, if the first five ingredients listed come from four grains, the majority of the protein in that food comes from grains. The more grains in a dog food, the cheaper it is to produce. We wonder what Buddy — the carnivore — thinks of such a food.

Make sure you carefully read the labels of the dogfood and do some research. Don't allow the visual on the package or the perception of certain ingredients determine your overall purchasing decision.

Look for a food that has two or three animal proteins in the first five ingredients — or better yet, one that lists animal protein as its first two or three ingredients. Check out foods that are listed for all growth stages or that are specifically designed for puppies. For more information of which are the best foods in each category, go to www.dogfoodadvisor.com. This site run by a well-respected nonprofit keeps a list of current recalls from manufacturers not only of dog food but dog treats as well.

Different types of meat have different levels of protein, with beef being low and chicken and fish being high in protein. Lamb is in the middle. Venison has the highest protein content and should be fed sparingly. Feeding Buddy a food too high in protein is as dangerous as feeding a diet too low in protein. Long-term use of a high-protein food can damage the kidneys. We recommend beef-based foods for most dogs as a maintenance diet, chicken-based food for dogs that have had surgery or are healing from some disease, and lamb-based food if your dog doesn't like beef. Fish-based foods are too high in protein for regular use and make the kidneys work too hard.

Most pet foods use similar formulas and are allowed to have no more than 1 percent salt in their formulas, which makes salt a convenient marker of quantity. Read the list of ingredients on the bag you're choosing and find salt. Anything that follows salt is basically found in minuscule amounts in the product. Those beautiful pictures on the bag of expensive ingredients, organic ingredients, and GMO-free ingredients actually fall almost 5 to 25 ingredients past the salt divider. The promise of cranberries, along with images of blueberries, apples, and duck, which took up more than half the front of the bag, was deliberately misleading. The reality was that the amount of those four ingredients together most likely equals the size of a single blueberry. If you want to give your pet cranberries, then go buy some that are fresh and locally grown and add them to your dog's food occasionally.

A dog food company also must list its name and address and give its telephone number, plus provide the date of manufacture, the weight of the product in the package, and the life stage for which the food is intended. The *life stage* can be puppy, maintenance, adult, performance, old age, or lite food for overweight dogs. Some breed-specific foods are now popular, including Labrador food, Dachshund food, and so on. Some foods are designed specifically for those dogs with health-related issues, such as hip dysplasia. Organic and natural kibbles also are available.

Evaluating Buddy's current food

Following is a quick checklist to help you determine whether Buddy is getting what he needs from the current food you're feeding. Note that for each item Buddy is the source of your information.

- ❑ He doesn't want to eat the food.
- ❑ He has large, voluminous stools that smell awful.
- ❑ He has gas.
- ❑ His teeth get dirty and brown.
- ❑ His breath smells.
- ❑ He burps a lot.
- ❑ He constantly sheds.
- ❑ He has a dull coat.
- ❑ He smells like a dog.
- ❑ He has frequent diarrhea or vomiting.
- ❑ He is prone to ear and skin infections.

- ❑ He has no energy or is hyperactive.
- ❑ He easily picks up fleas and ticks.
- ❑ He has to be wormed frequently.

REMEMBER

All these conditions happen occasionally with any dog — but only occasionally. When several of the items on the list occur frequently or continuously, you need to find out why.

Understanding the Nutrients Your Dog Needs

Since the 2008 pet food recall, pet owners have become more concerned about the ingredients in their pets' foods, and their demands for greater quality have been answered in the marketplace. The cliché "garbage in, garbage out" applies with terrifying validity.

Like yours, your dog's body consists of cells — a lot of them. Each cell needs 45 nutrients to function properly. The cells need the following nutrients:

- ➤➤ Protein
- ➤➤ Carbohydrates
- ➤➤ Fat
- ➤➤ Vitamins
- ➤➤ Minerals
- ➤➤ Water

TECHNICAL STUFF

All these nutrients need to be in the correct proportion for the necessary chemical reactions of digestion, absorption, transportation, and elimination to occur. If the cells are going to be able to continue to live, the exact composition of the body fluids that bathe the outside of the cells needs to be controlled from moment to moment, day by day, with no more than a few percentage points variation. So feeding a balanced diet daily is critical for Buddy's overall health. To find out whether the diet you're feeding is balanced, consider visiting your veterinarian for a blood test (chem screen and complete blood count). This blood test will reveal if Buddy is in balance.

REMEMBER

These preceding nutrients are the fuel that's converted into energy. Energy produces heat, and the amount of heat your dog produces determines his ability to control his body temperature. Everything your dog does, from running and playing to working and living a long and healthy life, is determined by the fuel you provide and the energy it produces.

The term *calorie* is used to measure energy in food. Optimally, every dog will eat the quantity of food he needs to meet his caloric needs. The food you feed must provide the appropriate amount of calories so your dog's body can

» Produce energy to grow correctly

» Maintain health during adulthood

» Reproduce

» Grow into a quality old age

In the following sections, we start off by discussing a puppy's special nutritional needs, and then we move on to the nutritional needs of all dogs during their adult life. For information on older dogs (8 years old and older), see Chapter 22.

Meeting puppy's nutritional needs

In contrast to humans, dogs grow *fast*. During the first 7 months of Buddy's life, his birth weight increases anywhere from 15 to 40 times, depending on his breed. By 1 year of age, his birth weight increases 60 times and his skeletal development is almost complete. For strength and proper growth to occur, he needs the right food. He also needs twice the amount of food as an adult while he's growing, especially during growth spurts. Nutritional deficiencies at an early age, even for short periods, can cause problems later on. Some of the larger breeds continue to grow until they're 4 years of age.

The most critical period for a puppy is between 2 and 7 months, which is the time of maximum growth. His little body is being severely stressed as his puppy teeth drop out and his adult teeth come in. His adult coat also comes in at this time. He's growing like a weed, and at the same time his body is being assaulted with vaccines. During this time of growth, Buddy needs the right food so that his immune system can cope with all these demands and onslaughts.

Puppy foods contain more protein than adult or maintenance foods. Manufacturers know that puppies need more protein for growth. Nonetheless, you still need to know the source of the protein — that is, animal or plant. These foods also have to be carefully balanced with calcium, phosphorus, and magnesium. If you choose carefully, you can select a food that's suitable for a growing puppy (see Figure 4-2) as well as for an adult dog.

FIGURE 4-2:
Choose a food
that can be fed to
all life stages.

© John Wiley & Sons, Inc.

REMEMBER

If you're raising a giant-breed puppy (one that will mature to weigh more than 75 pounds), your choices are limited because the dog food companies have conducted little to no research on how to successfully raise these larger dogs. The research that has been done was on dogs weighing 25 to 75 pounds at maturity. In many dog foods, the ratio of calcium, phosphorus, and magnesium is insufficient in relationship to the protein content. So you'll often hear breeders of these large dogs tell their puppy owners to buy adult foods for their pups to make them grow more slowly. But this is a double-edged sword. Pups of these breeds don't get the amount of protein they need to develop correctly, and this malnutrition often leads to structural problems early in life. Adding some fresh raw meat such as a quarter cup of ground beef and some broccoli twice a day for a 50-pound dog is a great way to improve kibble and prevent cancer.

After you've selected a food for young Buddy on the basis of its protein percentage, your job isn't quite done yet. You also have to check the items we discuss in the following sections, which apply to both puppies and adults.

Keeping your dog's diet rich in protein

Your dog is scientifically categorized as a carnivore by the shape of his teeth. He isn't a vegetarian. He needs meat to be healthy and to maintain his proper protein levels. His teeth are quite different from yours — they're made for ripping and tearing meat. Also, his digestion starts in his stomach, not in his mouth as does a human. All the enzymes in his system are geared toward breaking down meat and raw foods.

The dog food packages tell you how much protein is in a specific food. The amount of protein is important, but the source of that protein is even more important. The manufacturer has choices as to what kind of protein to put into the food.

The percentage of protein on the package generally is a combination of proteins found in plants or grains, such as corn, wheat, soy, and rice, plus an animal protein, such as chicken, beef, or lamb.

REMEMBER

The activity level of your dog is likely to correspond with the amount of animal protein he needs in his diet. The majority of the Working breeds, Sporting breeds, Toys, and Terriers need a higher level of animal protein in their diets. For instance, the busy little Jack Russell is apt to need more animal protein than a pooch that spends his time lying around the house.

ANIMAL PROTEIN: GETTING TO KNOW THE SIGNS OF DEFICIENCY AND EXCESS

The signs of a deficiency and an excess of protein (or any nutrient for that matter) are almost identical. In other words, both too much and too little protein have the same symptoms. When Buddy doesn't get enough protein or eats a food that's too high in animal protein, one or more of the following may occur:

- Aggression
- Chronic skin and/or ear infections
- Compromised reproductive system, heart, kidney, liver, bladder, and thyroid and adrenal glands
- Excessive shedding and poor, dull coat quality
- Gastrointestinal upsets, vomiting, or diarrhea
- Impaired ability to heal from wounds or surgery, such as spaying and neutering
- Kidney problems
- Lack of pigmentation
- Poor appetite
- Some kind of epilepsy or cancers
- Spinning or tail chasing
- Timidity
- Weakened immune system that can't properly tolerate vaccines

This is only a short list of the more common symptoms associated with animal protein deficiencies or excesses. That's why we suggest getting bloodwork done to make sure Buddy is in balance before changing his diet or adding supplements.

TECHNICAL STUFF

Amino acid is the name given to the building blocks of protein. When amino acids are heated, they're partially destroyed. All dry and canned commercial dog food is heated in the manufacturing process. So, commercial food contains protein that's chemically changed by heat and therefore deficient in amino acids. We show you how to compensate for that in the "Making choices as to how to feed Buddy" section later in this chapter. The freeze-dried, frozen, and dehydrated diets provide protein that's in a more natural form.

Going easy on the carbohydrates

Your dog needs the carbohydrates found in grains and most root vegetables for proper digestion. The digestive process first breaks down carbohydrates into starch and then into simple sugars and glucose, which are necessary for energy and proper functioning of the brain. Buddy also needs carbohydrates for stool formation and correct functioning of the thyroid gland.

Dogs don't need many carbohydrates to be healthy, however. A diet low in carbohydrates and high in protein is ideal. Oats, barley, wheat, and brown rice are carbohydrates that contain a lot of vitamins and minerals. They also contain protein and fat. Corn is a popular ingredient because of its low cost, but avoid foods that contain corn because those foods are lower quality. Many grain-free foods are on the market, and it's difficult to know whether they're in fact good for your dog. If you want to feed Buddy a grain-free food, make sure the protein is balanced out with enough root vegetables. Grain-free food has been associated with heart problems in dogs, so be careful and ask your vet to run bloodwork.

WARNING

Soy is another carbohydrate found in some of the cheaper foods. Soy is high in protein, but it binds other nutrients and makes them unavailable for absorption. We recommend that you stay away from dog foods containing soy.

Carbohydrates have to be broken down for the dog to be able to digest them. Dog food companies use a heat process to break them down, and therein lies a problem. The heat process destroys many of the vitamins and minerals contained in the carbohydrates. The question that immediately comes to mind is, "Where do dogs in the wild get the grains and vegetables they need?" The answer is from the intestines of their prey, all neatly predigested.

REMEMBER

If you feed raw vegetables to a dog that has only been fed dry kibble, chances are he won't be able to break them down and you'll see them in his stool. His stomach acid and digestive juices are too weak to digest them. If you want to introduce your dog to a healthier diet by adding fresh vegetables and meat, our suggestion is to first lightly cook them, and then over a week, cook them less and less until the fresh foods are eaten raw. If you still see vegetables in the stool, consider keeping Buddy on lightly cooked vegetables. Doing so allows his stomach acid to come back to the proper pH for digestion.

Knowing the value of fats — in moderation

Fat is either *saturated* or *polyunsaturated,* and your dog needs both. Saturated fat (omega-3) comes from animal sources, and polyunsaturated fat (omega-6) comes from vegetable sources. Together they supply the essential fatty acids (EFA) necessary to maintain good health. Look for a dog food that contains both animal and vegetable oils.

REMEMBER

In the manufacturing of the majority of kibbled dog foods, fat is sprayed on as the last ingredient. Fat makes the dog food palatable, like potato chips and French fries. This fat often is used by fast-food restaurants first and collected by the dog food manufacturer to spray onto dog food to make even poor-quality food taste good. Fat goes rancid quickly, which causes all sorts of health problems. Buy in small quantities and keep what you aren't using in the refrigerator. Don't leave opened kibble at room temperature. After it's exposed to air, kibble loses what little nutrients are left after cooking.

Saturated fat is used for energy. So, for dogs who get a great deal of exercise or participate in competitive events, the food they eat needs to contain 20 percent animal fat.

Not enough animal fat in your dog's diet can create:

>> Cell damage

>> Dry skin

>> Growth deficits

>> Heart problems

>> Lack of energy

On the other hand, too much animal fat in the diet creates:

>> Cancer of the colon and rectum

>> Mammary gland tumors

>> Obesity

Polyunsaturated fat is found in vegetable sources such as flaxseed oil, safflower oil, sunflower oil, wheat germ oil, olive oil, and corn oil. Your dog needs polyunsaturated fat for a healthy coat and skin. Lack of polyunsaturated fat in your dog's diet can cause

>> Coarse, dry coat

>> Extreme itching and scratching

>> Horny skin growths

>> Improper growth

>> Poor blood clotting

>> Skin lesions on the belly, on the inside of the back legs, and between the shoulder blades

>> Skin ulcerations and infections

>> Thickened areas of skin

REMEMBER

Linoleic acid is one of the three essential fatty acids that have to be provided daily in your dog's food. Safflower, sunflower, and flaxseed oil provide the best source of this acid and are the least allergenic. Flaxseed oil is fragile and can become rancid quickly if not stored correctly, however. These oils are better than corn oil or olive oil that contain only a tiny amount of linoleic acid. We advise refrigeration after the oil has been opened.

Ensuring that your dog's diet is fortified with vitamins and minerals

Your dog needs vitamins and minerals in his food to release the nutrients and enzymes from the ingested food so his body can break down food and absorb its nutrients.

We called dog food manufacturers that produce kibble to ask them about their source of vitamins and minerals and how they protected them against destruction from the heat process. We were astonished by their responses. They acknowledged awareness of the problem and said that to overcome it, they added more vitamins to the food to make up the difference. Of course, doing so is nonsense. If vitamins are destroyed by heat, it doesn't make any difference how much you put in the food. They'll still be destroyed.

We also discovered that most of the finished products weren't tested as to their vitamin and mineral content after being made. This lack of testing also applies to many of the raw and frozen diets in the marketplace. In other words, vitamins and minerals go into the food, but what actually reaches your dog seems as much a mystery to some of the manufacturers as it is to us.

Two types of vitamins exist:

>> **Water-soluble:** Vitamins B and C, which are water-soluble, are necessary for the breakdown of protein and many other chemical processes in the body. Any excess is filtered through the kidneys and urinated out between four to eight hours after ingestion. For this reason, these vitamins must be present in each meal.

>> **Fat-soluble:** Vitamins A, D, E, and K are fat-soluble and stored in the fatty tissues of the body and the liver.

Your dog needs both types of vitamins. Your dog's overall health is dependent on the availability of both vitamins and minerals in a usable form. So, you need to add these to any kind of commercial kibble, to canned food, and to some of the frozen and raw diets.

Minerals make up less than 2 percent of any formulated diet, and yet they're the most critical of nutrients. The minerals are needed to

>> Correctly compose body fluids

>> Form blood and bones

>> Promote a healthy nervous system

>> Function as coenzymes together with vitamins

Although your dog can manufacture some vitamins on his own, he isn't able to make minerals. As a result, you need to add them to his diet with a product like the balanced, all-in-one supplement, Endurance. Trying to supplement your dog's food by using individual vitamins and minerals isn't a good idea. To do supplement properly, you would need to have a lot of experience in clinical nutrition.

Vitamins and minerals begin to break down when you open a bag of dog food and expose the food to the elements. So make sure you close the food tightly and keep it away from light. Doing so helps to retain the quality of the contents. (Vitamins B and C are particularly sensitive to exposure.)

Don't forget to quench his thirst: Keeping fresh water around

Water is the most necessary ingredient for dogs. They need it on a daily basis. If a dog has adequate water, he can live for three weeks without food, but he can live only a few days without water. Your dog uses water for the digestive processes, for breaking down and absorbing nutrients, and for maintaining his body temperature. Water helps to transport toxic substances out of the body through the eliminative organs. Water also keeps the acid levels of the blood constant.

REMEMBER

Make sure your dog has access to fresh water in a clean bowl at all times. The exception is when the puppy is being housetrained. During that time, you need to limit access to water after 8 p.m. so the puppy can last through the night without having to go out. Use a heavy grade stainless steel or glass bowl — they keep the water fresh. Some ceramic bowls can leach lead out into the water.

REMEMBER

Do you know that the dog's drinking bowl is the third most germ-laden place in the house after the toilet bowl and the kitchen sink? Merely topping up the water level does nothing to control harmful bacteria or even toxins that can be lurking in the water. Not only are these bugs unpleasant, but also they can cause illness in people, especially those with weak immune systems. Wash your dog's bowl every day. Rinse them under running water and either hand-wash in hot soapy water or put them on the top rack of the dishwasher. Use a stainless steel or glass bowl for food and drink and stay away from plastics and ceramics.

The kind of food you feed Buddy determines how much water he needs. For example, kibble contains about 10 percent moisture, so your dog needs about a quart of water for every pound of food he eats. A dog fed only canned food, which is around 78 percent moisture, needs considerably less water. If fed raw foods, a dog may drink less than a cup of water a day because the food contains sufficient water.

If you store your dog's food in a container different than the original bag, wash the container when it empties and before you add a new bag of food to replace what was eaten.

Paying close attention to preservatives

Dog food manufacturers have choices on how to preserve the fat in food to prevent it from becoming rancid. They can use the chemicals BHA, BHT, ethoxyquin, or propyl gallate. If a fat is preserved with these chemicals, it has a long shelf life and isn't significantly affected by heat and light. Even so, many dog owners prefer not to feed these chemicals to their dogs, especially ethoxyquin, which has been associated with chronic degenerative diseases, allergies, arthritis, and shortened life spans to name a few.

A manufacturer also can use natural preservatives, such as vitamins C and E and rosemary extract. Vitamin E is listed on packages as *tocopherol*. Most of the newer foods use these natural preservatives. The downside to natural preservatives is a shorter shelf life — no more than three to four months (provided the food is stored in a cool, dark place around 40 degrees, refrigerated or frozen).

Making Choices about How to Feed Buddy

You have several options for feeding Buddy — from using commercial dry food (or beefing up a commercial kibble diet) to using the natural and raw diets to making your own. All the options have their pros and cons, so only you can decide which options is best for your lifestyle and comfort level. The following sections explain each option.

Feeding a dog twice a day is the most efficient way to feed him. And always be sure to have fresh water available to him. We suggest feeding at 7 a.m. and 6 to 7 p.m. Feeding earlier in the late afternoon or evening may be too much time between meals. As a result, some dogs vomit yellow bile first thing in the morning. If you have to feed earlier, give Buddy some small biscuits before bedtime.

Feeding Buddy commercial dry food

Your first option is, of course, feeding Buddy a commercial dry kibble diet that you buy at the pet store or grocery store. Dry kibble has been the staple of the dog food market, and now many of the natural or organic foods on the market are challenging it. You have a huge variety from which to choose, but be aware that the latest findings on feeding kibble only to your dogs. Research has shown a 50 percent rate of cancer in all dogs worldwide who eat dry kibble only. The carbohydrates in dry kibble break down in the body to sugar, which fuels cancer. Most dry and almost all prescription diets have more than 50 percent carbohydrates and therefore more than 50 percent sugar. Look for a food that has around 15 percent carbohydrates, which is ideal.

REMEMBER

If Buddy doesn't eat the amount recommended on the package for his weight, he's not getting the minimum daily requirement of known nutrients that are necessary on a daily basis for good health. If Buddy is turning up his nose at his food, we recommend you change his food to something he's more tempted to eat. If you can't find a dry kibble that works for him, try one of the other options in this chapter.

The most important information to know is that you have to choose a kibble that lists two to three meat-based ingredients (animal proteins) in the first five ingredients on the label (refer to the earlier section, "Deciphering dog food labels" for the basics of reading a label). This is true for dogs in all life stages, including overweight and less active dogs. You'll find foods that advertise "grain free," which isn't necessarily a good thing (see the earlier section "Going easy on the carbohydrates"). Select a food that contains some grain (preferably oats, barley, wheat, or brown rice or one that has a large number of root vegetables), up to 25 percent of the total ingredients.

REMEMBER

You want to choose a kibble that has 26 to 34 percent protein in it. When reading labels, you'll see the levels of protein for dry kibble vary from 16 to 47 percent. Some of the newer brands of kibble have far too much protein in them, and dog owners are now seeing the result of long-term feeding of this food in the form of kidney problems because the kidneys get overworked trying to break down the protein. Kibbles that are too low in protein, often advertised for senior or over-weight dogs, cause your dog to get fat, don't provide enough protein to rebuild cells and maintain health, supply too many grains, and often contain soy, which isn't digestible by dogs.

WARNING

Stay away from foods that contain corn, rye, soy, spinach, bell peppers, tomatoes, trans fats, soy oil, artificial coloring and preservatives, or genetically altered grains. These are cheap ingredients with little, if any, nutritional value. Some actually stop the digestive tract from working properly. Most of these items can't be digested and make Buddy's digestive tract work too hard for no benefit.

Offering beefed-up commercial dry food

If you want to continue feeding your dog a commercial, dry kibble diet or one of the grain-free kibbles, but you're concerned about the nutrients that he's getting, you can beef up that diet to give him what he needs. You can upgrade the diet in one of two ways: with an all-in-one supplement that contains all the food groups of protein, carbohydrates, vitamins, minerals, and oils or with a supplement plus fresh foods. We explain both options in the following sections.

Enhancing dry kibble with an all-in-one supplement

Feeding commercial kibble enhanced by an all-in-one supplement is the simplest method of adding the nutrients lost in the manufacturing of commercial cooked kibble. To apply this diet, choose a kibble according to our guidelines in the preceding section "Feeding Buddy commercial dry food" and then add a complete supplement to it. Follow the directions on the product as to how much to add.

TIP

The supplement we suggest is called Endurance. It has been clinically proven over many years and is dehydrated. It contains a small amount of liver, natural vitamins, minerals, herbs, dried fruit, fish oil, and ginger. It aids digestion by settling the stomach, reduces shedding, and increases vitality and longevity. Many police forces and professional trainers use it to keep their working dogs in good health.

Adding a supplement plus fresh foods to dry kibble

With this option, you add a supplement such as Endurance plus fresh meats and vegetables to commercial kibble. The quantities of the respective ingredients listed in this section are for a 50-pound dog. You can adjust this recipe according to your dog's weight. This option offers digestive enzymes contained in the raw foods, which aids digestion and cuts down the time the food is in the stomach. The University of Helsinki in Finland recently ran a study on the feeding of both raw food and kibble to see its effect on health, particularly cancer. The study showed that by adding fresh food to a dry kibble reduced the chance of cancer by 40 percent. Dogs fed only kibble showed cancer markers in their blood within 4 months of feeding.

REMEMBER

When calculating the amount for the weight of your dog, err on the side of too little, rather than too much. Some dogs eat more than their weight indicates, and some dogs eat less. Your dog's metabolism and the amount of daily exercise he gets determine the amount of food he needs. Use common sense and keep all ingredients in proportion.

To apply this diet, mix together the following ingredients and serve to your dog twice a day:

High-quality dry kibble (follow the directions on the package as to how much to feed).

¼ teaspoon Endurance plus 2 tablespoons of water to rehydrate the supplement.

¼ cup of ground beef (80 percent meat to 20 percent fat) lightly cooked for the first week, then cooked less and less over time until it's raw; rotate once a week with canned mackerel or cottage cheese; if your dog prefers chicken, serve it lightly cooked. However, chicken, because of the way the chickens are fed, is one of the most allergenic meats in the marketplace. Try to use organic chicken if you can.

2 tablespoons fresh vegetables (lightly cooked the first week, and then cooked less and less over time until they're raw).

For vegetables use carrots, parsnips, beets, sweet potatoes, broccoli, leeks, zucchini, squash, kale, cabbage, or any vegetable your dog likes. Chop the vegetables in a food processor or parboil them so it's easier for your dog to digest the cellulose. Whenever you can, use vegetables that are in season, because they have more nutrients. Vegetables that are shipped long distances contain fewer nutrients. For treats, try chopped carrots, broccoli, parsnips, rutabaga, lettuce, bananas, prunes, cucumbers, or any in-season fruit or vegetable that your dog likes.

WARNING

Stay away from those fruits and vegetables that are commonly sprayed many times with pesticides before they reach the marketplace — for example, apples, bell peppers, carrots, celery, cherries, grapes, kale, lettuce, nectarines, peaches, pears, or strawberries. If you can find organic versions, they should be safe. However, grapes and onions have been associated with gastric problems and even death in dogs that already have underlying disease states. As always, a small amount isn't harmful, but too much can make Buddy feel sick.

REMEMBER

Making major changes in Buddy's diet without keeping track of how these changes affect him isn't a wise idea. He may be out of balance nutritionally, which will have short- and long-term effects on his health. We recommend that you have a blood test done before making a dietary change and again six months later.

Trying a raw food or frozen diet

Our more than 40 years living with dogs have made it abundantly clear that feeding a balanced raw diet — which emulates what Buddy would eat in the wild — is the best and most efficient way to feed a dog. A correctly formulated raw diet provides all the known nutrients in a form the dog can quickly digest and turn into energy. Dogs fed this way tend to live longer and healthier lives than their counterparts who are fed commercial dry foods.

One-third of all dog food sold now in pet stores and some supermarkets is in the form of natural or raw diets, which include kibble with organic ingredients, frozen food, and dehydrated foods. Some of these foods are complete in themselves, but others suggest adding raw ingredients.

We have always felt that many disease states — including musculoskeletal disorders like hip dysplasia, skin diseases, and gastric upsets — certainly are exacerbated (if not actually caused by) poor nutrition. For more information on feeding raw diets, visit rawfed.com/myths/research.html.

Many natural and raw diets are available for you to choose from, but making the correct choice is even more difficult than comparing commercial dry foods. We apply the same criteria to the examination of natural and raw food diets as we do to commercial dry foods: Both need to be clinically tested and provide a balanced diet for a dog. Diets, especially homemade ones (raw or cooked), that don't meet these criteria can do more damage to your dog than dry dog food.

WARNING

Many of the new raw and frozen diets aren't balanced and haven't had any long-term clinical testing. Some even use ingredients that are known to be canine allergens. Some use indigestible vegetables, and some lack fiber and the correct ratio of nutrients. Other diets suggest feeding raw chicken wings or backs; that sounds easy enough, but it's hardly a balanced diet. Just because a food's ingredients are advertised as human grade, organic, or whatever doesn't mean they're good for your dog. So, clearly you must be cautious when choosing your dog's raw or frozen diet. Write to the manufacturer and ask how many years of clinical testing have been done on a particular diet. You'll be surprised by the answers. Generally testing is done over a six-week period with dogs in a laboratory. One raw food we like is Dr. B's Longevity food available at www.drbslongevity.com/. Formulated by an integrative veterinarian, it has medicinal mushrooms, vegetables, and raw meat. If dogs have difficulty eating after surgery, they usually like this food.

So are any of the available raw or frozen diets balanced? Of course. Just be vigilant in choosing the correct one for your dog. Read the label to make sure they're complete. If they aren't, read the guidelines as to what you should add to make them complete. Long-term feeding of an unbalanced diet can create a battery of new health problems not seen before in dogs.

TIP

Before changing Buddy's diet, we recommend that you take him to the vet for a baseline blood test. After Buddy has been on his new diet program for six months, have the vet perform another blood test and compare it to the previous one. The follow-up blood test will tell you whether his new diet is an improvement and whether he's in nutritional balance.

A dog's digestive system isn't the same as a human's — it's much shorter and food is processed more quickly. The dog's stomach acid is extremely strong, and in a healthy dog, this acid kills any bacteria that enter it. A sick dog, or a dog switching over to a raw diet from a kibble diet, needs a transition diet to rebuild that stomach acid to the point where it can deal with either E. coli or salmonella.

REMEMBER

Feeding raw meat or raw chicken to a dog can cause digestive upsets if the meat contains high levels of bacteria in the form of E. coli or salmonella. Although a dog that has been fed raw foods for a long time can easily deal with both of these bacteria, a sick dog or a dog just being transferred over to a raw diet may experience digestive problems. We suggest you buy your meat or chicken from a reliable supermarket where the products are for human consumption.

After you follow the transition diet (see the later section "Transferring Buddy to his new diet"), you need to use a simple method of killing bacteria the first time uncooked meat is used. To do so, put the meat or chicken into a sieve in the sink, pour boiling water over it, and cool it before feeding. Doing so kills the bacteria. After taking this step for a couple of weeks, the stomach acid will be strong enough to deal with the bacteria without problems, and you can introduce the raw meat.

Making your own food: Wendy's Natural Diet

Making one's own dog food is hardly a new idea. Every dog alive today can trace its ancestry back to dogs that were raised on homemade diets. The dog food industry, in comparison to dogs themselves, is young — maybe 70 to 80 years old — although canned meat for dogs was sold at the turn of the 20th century. Originally, the commercial foods were made to supplement a homemade diet.

REMEMBER

A homemade diet allows you to tailor make it for your dog's nutritional needs, and it's ideal for all dogs. The drawback to this type of feeding is that gather all the ingredients and make the food.

Many, but not all, present-day dogs are the beneficiaries of poor breeding practices, a lack of understanding of genetics on the part of many breeders, and 30 years of overvaccination and poor nutrition. Because of poor genetics (whether pure bred or a mixed breed), many can't thrive on commercially prepared rations. They exhibit disease states, which often are mistaken for allergies. These disease states can be deficiency diseases caused by feeding cereal-based foods or foods where the fat has turned rancid. Making the food from scratch or taking advantage of the new clinically tested food called Rescue formulated for these dogs is a viable, available option for these dogs. Check out www.volharddognutrition.com for more information.

Wendy started making her own dog food almost 40 years ago. Based on the pioneering work of Juliette de Bairacli Levy and the National Science Foundation's guidelines for dog food, her homemade diet was a 12-year labor of love to get the balance required. The results were amazing, as seen by Pavi, a Newfoundland who competed in both agility and obedience competitions until he was almost 12 years old. He garnered more than 20 titles. You can see Pavi in competition in Figure 4-3. The diet increases health and longevity, contains a lot of moisture in the natural ingredients, and produces more manageable stools. Plus dogs love to eat it. Wendy is still seeing great results today with the newer dehydrated versions of the food. See the next section for more information.

For more information on raising your dog holistically, transferring to a purely Natural Diet, making the diet and storing it, as well as a list of suppliers for ingredients, go to www.volharddognutrition.com. You also can look to the *Holistic Guide for a Healthy Dog*, 2nd Edition, by Wendy Volhard and Kerry Brown, DVM (Howell Book House).

TIP

The easiest way to travel with homemade or NDF2 diets is to make the required number of meals and freeze them in portion-control plastic bags. Keep the bags in a cooler, adding ice every day. You can travel safely up to 10 days using this method of packing the food.

FIGURE 4-3:
Pavi, an
11-year-old
Newfoundland,
in Agility
competition.

Using the Natural Diet Foundation (NDF2)

The Natural Diet Foundation, or NDF2, is a dehydrated version of the original homemade Natural Diet. It came about because so many professional dog people asked me to come up with a diet to which they only needed to add one ingredient. These are busy people who train dogs for a living and travel a lot, so they don't have time to shop around for fresh ingredients for their dog food. They all wanted the benefits of feeding naturally but didn't have the time to do it. They also wanted to stay with this diet that had been clinically proven over so many years rather than experimenting with many of the new diets on the market.

So, 20 years ago Wendy worked out the NDF2 diet, which is essentially the same as the original diet but in a dehydrated form. The only ingredients you have to add are meat and water. It has been an amazing success story, and she's now seeing 16-year-old dogs, raised from puppies on this food, who are in incredible health and whose structure is outstanding — a necessary trait for dogs being worked or shown.

NDF2 contains all the non-meat ingredients your dog needs for a healthy, vigorous, and long life. It's made every two weeks in small batches with whole human-grade foods and herbs that come from the United States. Overall, this recipe has been clinically tested for more than 40 years. It's a food for all life-stages, from puppies to older dogs. It's also hypoallergenic and contains no genetically modified products.

Transferring Buddy to his new diet

When changing from dry kibbled foods to a higher-grade kibble and supplemented diet as those suggested earlier in the chapter, you must give your dog's system time to get used to the new ingredients. Your dog's intestinal tract needs about 6 to 11 days to be fully able to break down and digest a new diet.

When switching Buddy to a diet that is supplemented with raw foods, use the following transition diet. The transition diet allows time for the internal bacteria to adjust to a change in diet. (Transitioning your dog to a completely raw diet requires a different process. Refer to the earlier section, "Trying a raw food or frozen diet" for more information.)

Here's how to transition your dog to a supplemented dog food diet:

> **Day 1:** Add a small amount of your new food to each of Buddy's meals.
>
> **Day 2:** Double the amount you fed on Day 1 of the new food and decrease Buddy's old diet by the same amount.
>
> **Days 3 through 6:** Gradually increase the new diet and decrease the old diet until you have changed him over completely.

REMEMBER

If at any time Buddy has loose stools, his digestive system needs more time to adjust to his new food.

After your dog has been introduced to the new additions in his diet for a couple of weeks, it's time to introduce bones. Once or twice a week, give your dog a bone as a special treat. They love beef (soup) bones, raw chicken neck, chicken feet, and the tips off chicken wings. If you're not sure about how long these items have been in the supermarket case, douse them with boiling water to kill any bacteria before feeding. One of the benefits of feeding bones is that your dog will have beautiful, pearly white teeth.

When you give your dog a bone, leave him alone (but not unattended) — dogs can get possessive about their bones. It's a special treat, and he wants to be in a place to relax and enjoy it. His crate is the perfect place. It also contains any soggy mess associated with gnawing on his bone. Give Buddy an hour or so to enjoy his bone and then pick it up and refrigerate it and give it to him the next day. Too much marrow in the bone's center may be a little rich for some dogs to digest all at once.

WARNING

Feeding Buddy too many bones can give him constipation and hard, chalky stools. Only give your dog bones that can't splinter. We recommend you feed bones no more than twice a week.

WHAT ABOUT TABLE SCRAPS?

There's nothing wrong with adding table scraps to Buddy's food, provided they don't exceed 10 percent of his total diet. Many dogs love leftover salad, meat scraps, and veggies. However, you do need to avoid certain foods, particularly those with a high sugar count, such as chocolate (which can be poisonous) and highly salted foods. Also avoid giving raw spinach, an ingredient that is found in so many of the newer raw food diets. It contains oxalic acid that binds calcium and some minerals from being absorbed by the body. Avoid peppers, which are part of the deadly nightshade family, and can be allergenic. Processed human foods also aren't recommended for dogs.

Sizing up supplements

The reality is that if you're feeding correctly, you rarely need supplements of any kind. The nutrients should be in the food; they shouldn't have to be added as extras at high prices. The number of supplements available tells you a lot about the quality of the food on the market. If you're adding a lot of supplements to Buddy's food, it's time to think of changing to a balanced food that contains these ingredients.

REMEMBER

You occasionally do need supplements. We've sorted through the thousands of products on the shelves and can recommend some that are known to work (we've used them ourselves, and our students have had good results as well). We mention a few supplements in the following health section, and we go into more detail regarding the supplements we recommend in Chapter 22, which focuses on older dogs. As dogs get older, they need supplementation.

Exploring Common Health Issues That Affect Behavior and Training

A dog that's fed correctly and given enough exercise and mental stimulation rarely exhibits behavior problems. He deals well with stress, hardly ever gets sick, and keeps his youthful characteristics into his teens. Also, a dog who's fed properly and is in good health, ages well and has few to no gray hairs. In fact, it's often difficult to tell this dog's age.

When your dog doesn't feel quite right, he won't act quite right. When he doesn't feel well, he doesn't have the ability to learn or retain information. Training him can be perplexing because you've properly taught a sequence of an exercise and yet he shows no knowledge of what you've taught him. Not feeling well can manifest itself in many ways, but you as his owner, know he isn't acting as he did before. In the following sections we provide information on some common health issues that affect behavior and training. We also discuss some supplements that may help Buddy feel better. Checking with his veterinarian is also a wise decision if you notice something unusual.

REMEMBER

Prevention is the best policy when it comes to your dog's health. Here are some things you can do to prevent health problems later on and have a long and happy training career with Buddy:

>> **Visit your veterinarian annually.** When you take Buddy to the vet, choose to have titers done (rather than vaccinations) to see Buddy's level of protection against parvovirus, distemper, and Lyme disease. (We explain what titers are in the later section "Looking at the problems with overvaccinating.") At the same time, ask your vet to perform blood work (a chem scan, a complete blood count, and a thyroid [T4]) to see whether Buddy is in nutritional balance and whether all his organ systems are working properly. Signs of problems can show on bloodwork long before physical manifestations appear.

REMEMBER

Take Buddy on his birthday for his checkup the first thing in the morning for his blood test. For accurate results Buddy needs to have fasted overnight on a 12-hour fast. Subsequent testing over the next years, always taken at the same time of day, allows you to see how Buddy's body is aging. Take in a fecal sample at least twice a year.

>> **Provide an arthritis formula if necessary.** If your puppy's structure isn't perfect or if he's in performance events of any kind, consider using an arthritis formula as a preventative. In the past, these products have been used after the dog was diagnosed with arthritis. Since then, however, research has shown that when structural problems become obvious in the young dog, the use of these products can be helpful in preventing arthritis later in life.

The product we have recommended for years is called Myristin. We have used Myristin successfully with clients' dogs who were experiencing cruciate ligament problems as well as loose shoulders, loose hock joints, poor hips, and so on. This product works for 90 percent of dogs. The other 10 percent requires a different form of supplement. We recommend System Saver, which is an anti-inflammatory and works to build up the immune system. See www.volharddognutrition.com for more information on these products.

>> **Keep his teeth healthy.** Dirty teeth can cause harmful bacteria buildup resulting in gingivitis, loose teeth, and bacterial infection of the gums. The bacteria drain into the system via the stomach and can, over a period of time, cause heart ailments. Clean teeth also prevent doggy breath. To keep teeth clean, feed the correct diet with bones a couple of days a week. Or you can

clean Buddy's teeth with a toothbrush and dog toothpaste or cleaning gel. We recommend Petzlife products, available through www.petzlife.com. See Chapter 22 for more information.

>> **Choose an appropriate food for your dog.** Feeding the correct food helps to prevent internal and external parasites. External parasites, like fleas and ticks, are less likely to be attracted to a dog who's fed correctly, because his skin has a correct pH that deters external parasites. The acid/alkaline balance of his digestive tract makes a poor environment for internal worms to survive. Check out the earlier section "Making Choices about How to Feed Buddy" for more information.

Here comes that needle again: Examining vaccination issues

Giving vaccines is a necessary part of owning a dog. Depending on what part of the United States or Canada you live can play a role in which vaccines your vet suggest. Here are some of the more common vaccines:

>> **Bordatella:** Also known as *kennel cough,* many boarding kennels require this vaccine before they'll accept a dog, although the vaccine is a regional thing.

>> **Distemper:** This is a core vaccine.

>> **Hepatitis:** This also is a core vaccine.

>> **Leptospirosis:** This one isn't advised unless of a local outbreak.

>> **Lyme disease:** We don't advise this vaccine because it has too many side effects.

>> **Parvovirus:** This is a core vaccine.

>> **Rabies:** Every county in the United States has a rabies vaccine requirement. The rabies vaccine is the only mandatory one.

Except for rabies these vaccines are voluntary. Just make sure your veterinarian doesn't give multiple vaccines at the same time. Whether you vaccinate your dog is your choice. If you choose, you can refuse them and/or ask for titers instead. This way you can make an informed decision.

Vaccines can disrupt a training program for your dog by making him feel unwell for a few days after they have been given. Sometimes vaccines interrupt the ability of the dog to do scent work like tracking or scent articles in obedience competition. The effects can last from three weeks to nine months. Some breeds of dogs have adverse reactions to vaccines and can experience swollen joints (as Great Danes can do with the rabies vaccine), some temporary paralysis (such as German Shepherds and Rottweilers from the parvovirus vaccine), seizures (such as Labradors from the rabies vaccine), and so on. Make a wise decision for you and your dog after you have researched all the facts.

TIP

To help you make a decision as to what is correct for your dog, check out *What Vets Don't Tell You About Vaccines* by Catherine O'Driscoll (Abbeywood Publishing). She did a worldwide study of vaccines and reports of the long-term effects of overvaccinating. She charts diseases associated with overvaccinating and quotes the noted authorities in the United States, including Jean Dodds, DVM, and Ronald Schultz, MD, DVM, of the University of Wisconsin, on the current vaccine protocols recommended. For more information on O'Driscoll and her research, visit www.canine-health-concern.org.uk.

Looking at the problems with overvaccinating

During the past 30 years, dog owners have seen a steady increase in the number of vaccinations that dogs receive each year. Sadly, instead of improving the dogs' health and longevity, the practice has frequently had the opposite effect.

Overvaccinating has created unintended and undesirable reactions to vaccinations, which result in *vaccinosis,* the term used to describe those undesirable reactions. The reactions can range from none to constant ear infections, licking feet, skin problems, paralysis, and even death. And they may occur as a result of one vaccine, several vaccines given at the same time, or repeated vaccinations given in a relatively short time frame.

WARNING

Too many vaccinations too close together can cause a puppy's immune system to break down and can result in serious health problems. We aren't against vaccinations, but we're against random, repetitive, routine, and completely unnecessary vaccinations. Thank goodness in the last few years, vaccine protocols have changed and most up-to-date veterinarians are using vaccines more sparingly.

For instance, one of our students who had a young 16-week-old Newfoundland puppy took her dog to the veterinarian for booster vaccinations. The puppy received eight vaccinations all at the same time including rabies. By the time she got home her dog was completely paralyzed and after 4 months of treatment ranging from acupuncture, homeopathy, and ozone, the paralysis, although improved had not enabled her to walk and she had to be put down. Veterinary medicine had nothing to offer. Some breeds of dogs are prone to vaccine reactions. If this happens to your dog, ask your veterinarian for a certificate that exempts that dog from further shots.

Search online for your breed of dog and find out if your dog is prone to vaccination reactions.

Where do annual booster shots fit into this picture? Actually, they don't. According to Kirk's *Current Veterinary Therapy* XI-205 (W.B. Saunders Co.) — the textbook used for many years by veterinary schools — no scientific basis or immunological reason necessitates annual revaccinations. Immunity to viruses can last for many years — even for a dog's lifetime.

REMEMBER

When your dog already carries the antibodies against a particular virus, a revaccination can wreak havoc with his immune system. The many adverse reactions to unnecessary vaccinations have caused breeders, dog owners, and vets to begin questioning the need for boosters and to become more cautious in the way vaccines are administered. By law, your dog only needs a rabies vaccination and the rabies booster only every three years. Don't ever give your dog a rabies shot before he's 6 months of age.

Some breeds of dogs have extreme — even fatal — reactions to vaccines. Others develop odd behaviors and reactions such as the following:

>> Aggression

>> Anaphylactic shock

>> Anxiety or fear

>> Epilepsy and other seizure disorders

>> Excessive licking

>> Insomnia

>> Separation anxiety

>> Snapping at imaginary flies

>> Swelling of the whole body, cutting off air supply

WARNING

A rabies vaccine given in conjunction with other vaccines can be responsible for aggression, epilepsy, and other seizure disorders. Labradors seems to be especially vulnerable.

How do you know if your dog will have a reaction to a vaccine? You don't, and that's the problem. Fortunately, you don't have to take the chance. When you take Buddy in for his annual checkup, a titer test, a blood test that tells you whether Buddy has *antibodies* (or resistance) to the diseases for which he's already been vaccinated. If he has a high *titer*, or level of antibodies, to the disease, you don't need to have him revaccinated. Titering is becoming a more acceptable alternative to revaccinations. (Refer to the next section for information on whether businesses accept titering in place of revaccination.) Titer your dog in late spring or early summer when the viruses are active. Titering in the winter doesn't give you the correct information.

Whether you're rescuing a dog from the local humane society, adopting an "off-the-track" Greyhound, or buying a puppy from a pet store, be aware that the dog will probably have been vaccinated before you get him. Humane societies usually give you the dates when your rescue dog was vaccinated. Taking him to your veterinarian for a once-over health check is a good idea, but don't vaccinate again. Either titer the dog in the next six months or wait another year and titer before vaccinating, if necessary. However, remember that if your dog has reacted in the past to vaccination, the next time he's vaccinated, the reaction will be worse. So be careful! See how to deal with adverse reactions in the later section "Quelling fear, anxiety, and other conditions with homeopathy."

Vaccinating for boarding or schooling

Sometimes you have to vaccinate your dog. Many boarding kennels, obedience schools, and dog parks, for example, require proof of vaccination. However, titers are becoming more acceptable with these businesses and schools. The Pet Care Services Association (formerly known as the American Boarding Kennel Association) considers titers acceptable. Before you board your dog at a member kennel, ask about titers.

TIP

Before you vaccinate, call any facilities to which you may take your dog. If you do need to vaccinate, remember that it takes your dog three weeks to build immunity.

Because not everything's cut and dried in this world, suppose that Buddy is one of those dogs who have adverse side effects from vaccinations, and as a result, you adamantly refuse to vaccinate him. But now you can't find a boarding kennel that will honor your wishes. What then? Well, you're going to have to find someone to come in and dog sit for you while you're away. If you can't find a reliable local pet sitter, try Pet Sitters International (www.petsit.com), which is an international organization that has trained pet sitters in most areas of the United States and Canada. The local obedience organization also may be able to help you.

WARNING

Vaccinating a healthy dog stresses his immune system, whether or not you see a reaction. Boarding a dog also is stressful — even at the nicest boarding kennels. Under stress, Buddy is vulnerable to picking up disease. It can affect his training and his ability to handle stress especially at dog shows. If you have to vaccinate, do it at least three weeks before kenneling.

Using flea and tick medications

Flea and tick medications can affect Buddy's health and behavior in numerous ways. After using them, Buddy can become lethargic or limp or he can vomit or have loose stools, seizures, and reoccurring skin problems.

In fact, any time you use chemicals with Buddy, you're running the risk of side effects. Your goal is to raise him without using anything but natural products. Some medications can affect the balance of bacteria in the gut. It takes about three weeks after finishing the medication for the gut flora to be re-established. To fasten the process, you can use a tablespoon of fermented veggies (such as sauerkraut) in his food twice a day for a 50-pound dog. For a toy breed, use just a teaspoon.

Ask yourself if you need to use flea and tick medications at all. If you live in the southern part of the United States, you probably need to use some form of prevention. Here are three lines of defense other than the traditional flea and tick medications:

>> **Make sure your dog eats a proper diet.** A proper diet is a deterrent because the skin's pH isn't attractive to parasites.

>> **Use an herbal spray that doesn't have unwanted side effects.** We recommend Wondercide available online. This product is all natural and also protects your pet from mosquitoes, which in turn protects them from heartworm.

>> **Make your own natural solution.** Mix a solution of apple cider vinegar and water (half and half), put into a spray bottle, and spray Buddy before he goes for his walks or to the dog park. This deterrent is effective, and you get used to the side effect of having Buddy smell like salad dressing.

Uncovering the rise in doggy hypothyroidism

Providing poor nutrition, overvaccinating, and neutering or spaying a puppy too early can cause a disease called hypothyroidism or suppression of the thyroid gland. *Hypothyroidism* refers to an underactive thyroid, which causes physical as well as behavioral abnormalities. Successfully training a dog who has hypothyroidism is difficult. When a dog has hypothyroidism, his ability to learn and retain information is severely curtailed. This lack of learning ability is frustrating for both dog and handler. Very few veterinarians have that much knowledge about this disease, which is perhaps the most common disease in dogs.

Rarely seen until the 1970s, this condition has become more prevalent because the way of managing dogs has changed in the last 50 years. Less homemade or raw diets and overvaccination is mainly the cause. More than 50 percent of young dogs today show some signs of hypothyroidism. As the dog ages, the percentage increases. When you take Buddy for his yearly checkup, have your veterinarian add a thyroid test to his blood draw.

TECHNICAL STUFF

The thyroid gland is part of the endocrine gland system. This system not only controls many of the hormones in the body, but it also controls the brain's ability to deal with stress. It certainly affects his behavior. In a study done at the University of Southampton in England, it was found that more than 50 percent of dogs turned over to a humane society because of aggression problems were suffering from hypothyroidism.

The physical manifestations of hypothyroidism can show from as young as 5 months of age onward. This disease is most commonly diagnosed at around 4 years of age, but dogs 8 years and older also have hypothyroidism, which correlates to the aging process. Dogs with this disease may show the following signs:

>> Heart disorders

>> Lack of control over body temperature — the dog is either too cold or too hot under otherwise normal conditions

>> Oily, smelly, scaly skin and blackened skin on the belly and under the arms

>> Some kinds of paralysis

>> Seizures

>> Thinning of the hair on each side of the body, usually around the rib cage and shoulders, on the tail and inside the back legs (see Figure 4-4)

>> Unexplained weight gain (see Figure 4-5)

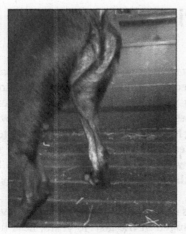

FIGURE 4-4:
Thinning hair due to hypothyroidism.

© John Wiley & Sons, Inc.

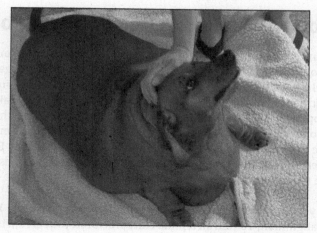

FIGURE 4-5:
Obesity due to
hypothyroidism.

Behavioral manifestations of hypothyroidism may include

» Unexplained aggression toward people or other dogs

» Being picked on by other dogs

» Difficulty learning

» Fear and anxiety, including separation anxiety and fear of thunderstorms

» *Lick granulomas,* where the dog licks constantly at one spot, usually on a leg, and goes down to the bone

» Obsessive-compulsive behavior, such as spinning and extreme hyperactivity

» Overreaction to stressful situations

» Self-mutilation

TIP

How can you tell if Buddy has a thyroid-related problem? If he's exhibiting any of the physical signs or behaviors listed in this section, make an appointment with your vet as soon as possible. This condition often is overlooked by veterinarians as was the case shown in Figure 4-4. If you want to reassure yourself that Buddy doesn't have hypothyroidism, ask your vet to do a blood test and ask for a complete thyroid panel. The results can tell you whether Buddy needs medication. All laboratory reports indicate a low and high normal reading for each test done. High readings are uncommon in adult dogs. Low normal readings need to be supplemented with a low dose of thyroid medication.

The bone crusher: "Oh, my aching back"

Performance events, especially agility, are athletic activities for a dog. So you really shouldn't be surprised that various parts of performing dogs' bodies may go out of whack. After all, human athletes have troubles all the time. Because the dogs' performances are affected, many competitors routinely take their dogs in for chiropractic adjustments. Agility competitors have found that it can shave seconds off a dogs' performance if he is in perfect alignment. It makes sense — if the spine is straight, the dog can move more quickly and easily. Even if your dog isn't a performing dog, remember that simply playing ball or Frisbee with Buddy can have the same effect as performance events.

TIP

To keep your dog in tip-top shape, have a chiropractor examine him. Buddy may need an alignment. To find an animal chiropractor in your area, visit the American Holistic Veterinary Medical Associations website at www.ahvma.org.

Quelling fear, anxiety, and other conditions with homeopathy

Many dogs experience fear or anxiety under different conditions. For example, anxiety can occur when Buddy

» Encounters situations that he perceives as stressful

» Goes on a trip away from home

» Has a reaction to a vaccine

» Senses and experiences thunderstorms

» Visits the vet

We've been quite successful in dealing with this sort of anxiety with homeopathic remedies. We even carry a small homeopathic emergency kit with us wherever we go, just in case. (We also provide information on anxiety and handling other special situations in Chapter 21.)

Homeopathy relies on the energy of natural substances, which come from plants or minerals. Homeopathic remedies come in pellet, granular, or liquid form. Popular until the discovery of antibiotics in 1928 but used almost exclusively after 1942, homeopathy fell out of favor during the middle of the 20th century. Today, it's enjoying resurgence all over the world, and many vets in Europe are trained both in traditional medicine and homeopathy.

REMEMBER

Because the homeopathic remedies are so diluted, they're safe to use and don't cause side effects. You can find many of these remedies in large supermarkets and health food stores. We suggest the potency of 30c. These remedies most often come in pellet form, and one dose is three pellets fed 15 minutes before or after food.

The following list includes a few common homeopathic remedies and the problems they treat. We find these remedies helpful and use them frequently.

>> **Aconite:** Fright, anxiety, and fear of thunderstorms

>> **Apis:** Bee stings and any shiny swellings

>> **Arnica:** Bruising from falls and dog bites and recuperation from any operation

>> **Belladonna:** Heat stroke, hot, red ears, and hot spots

>> **Carbo Veg:** Bloating or gas (settles the stomach if used 15 minutes before eating)

>> **Chamomilla:** Vomiting of yellow bile and teething problems

>> **Ferrum Phos:** Stops bleeding

>> **Hydrophobinum (or Lyssin):** Reactions to rabies vaccine

>> **Hypericum:** Stops pain to nerve endings after injury or operations

>> **Ignatia:** Grief, insecurity, stress, or sadness

>> **Ledum:** Tick, insect, or spider bites

>> **Nux Vomica:** Any kind of poisoning; recuperation after anesthesia

>> **Phosphorus:** Sound sensitivity

>> **Rescue Remedy:** Use for stress or trauma. (We always carry it when we travel with our dogs.) Bach Flower Remedy comes in liquid form.

>> **Rhus Tox (poison ivy):** Rheumatism and itchy, oozing rashes

>> **Sulphur:** Skin conditions and mange

>> **Thuja:** Reactions to core vaccines (distemper, parvovirus, and so on)

TIP

Many holistic veterinarians are trained in homeopathy, and you probably can find one in your area without difficulty. To find a holistic vet go to the American Holistic Veterinary Medical Association's website at www.ahvma.org/find-a-holistic-veterinarian.

Treating chronic conditions with acupuncture

Many vets today use acupuncture for a variety of chronic conditions. Acupuncture specializes in putting the body back into balance. Among its many applications, acupuncture is particularly effective with allergies, skin disorders, ear problems, incontinence in old dogs, and the aches and pains that come with age. It also can be effective for structural problems and chronic diseases of major organs, such as the heart, kidneys, liver, lungs, and stomach.

TIP

We advise seeking the help of an acupuncture veterinarian for dogs who are in performance events and for those who are middle-aged or older. Treatments can make an older dog feel like a puppy again. To find a veterinarian in your area who's trained in acupuncture, contact the American Holistic Veterinary Medical Association's website at www.ahvma.org.

collars

» **Taking advantage of training treats**

» **Checking out other supplies, including harnesses and electronic devices**

Chapter **5**

Gearing Up for Training Success

og training is no different from any other activity — you need the right equipment for the job. Many choices are available to you, and in this chapter, we address the factors that determine what training equipment to use under what circumstances.

Just because it's a collar or a leash doesn't mean you can use it to train your dog. Chapter 1 discusses how a mother dog teaches her puppies to stop doing something she doesn't want them to do. She uses a *correction*, something the puppies perceive as unpleasant, to get them to stop. This unpleasant experience teaches the puppies responsibility for their own behavior. A puppy says to himself, "If I use my teeth on Mommy, I'll get nailed. If I don't, mommy will lick my face." So puppy chooses not to use his teeth on Mommy. That, at any rate, is the gist of the puppy's thought process.

Teaching your dog responsibility for his own behavior is the key to training. Therefore, the dog must perceive the correction as unpleasant so he can avoid it. If he doesn't perceive the correction as unpleasant, he has nothing to avoid, and the objectionable behavior continues. Therein lies the importance of the correct training equipment.

As a general rule, a correction with a collar and leash is used to deal with unde-sired behaviors the dog does on his own, such as chasing a cat. Treats are used to teach the desired behaviors that the dog wouldn't do on his own, such as sitting on command. This chapter focuses on just what you need to help you prepare for training so you and Buddy are successful.

Choosing the Right Training Leash and Collar

The type of training collar and leash you need depends on a number of factors, including the following:

>> Your dog's Personality Profile (see Chapter 2)

>> Your dog's touch sensitivity or threshold of discomfort

>> Your dog's size and weight in relation to your size and weight

>> The equipment's effectiveness

>> Your dog's safety

>> Your aptitude for training your dog

REMEMBER

Training isn't a matter of strength but finesse. For you, Buddy's teacher, it doesn't have to be a heavy aerobic workout. Also, in selecting training equipment, keep in mind the circumstances. A dog's *touch sensitivity,* or threshold of discomfort, increases proportionally with the interest the dog has in what appeals to him (see Chapter 2 for more information about understanding your dog's mind). For exam-ple, when you train Buddy in your backyard, where he has fewer distractions, a buckle collar may be sufficient to get him to respond. When he's out in the real world and wants to chase a squirrel or another dog, you may need to use a training collar to get him to listen to the command given.

We provide info to help you choose the best leash and collar in the following sections.

Deciding on a leash

Leashes come in an assortment of styles, materials, widths, and lengths. The fol-lowing are the most common materials:

REMEMBER

>> **Cotton web:** Cotton web leashes are readily available in pet stores and through catalogs and websites, and they come in a variety of colors (see Figure 5-1). We get ours from Handcraft Collars (www.handcraftcollars.com).

>> A good training leash is a 6-foot cotton web leash — it's easy on the hands, easily manipulated, and just the right length. It's also the most economical. For the average-size or larger dog, such as a Labrador, a cotton web leash that's ⅝-inch wide is ideal. For toy dogs, such as a Yorkshire Terrier, a leash that's ¼-inch wide is a good choice.

>> **Nylon:** A nylon leash is another good one for training. Looking a lot like the cotton web leash, the nylon type also is economical and can be easily manipulated, which is an important factor for the training method in this book. However, nylon isn't as easy on your hands as cotton web, especially with larger dogs.

>> **Leather:** Leather leashes also are quite popular, although they're more expensive than cotton web and nylon leashes. They're usually bulkier than cotton web or nylon but don't readily lend themselves to the approach to training described in this book.

>> **Chain:** Chain leashes are cheap but are noisy and awkward. Chain leashes often are used with large dogs, but they're heavy, unwieldy, and hard on the hands. For example, if you wanted to fold the leash neatly into one hand or the other, as required by the training techniques in this book, you wouldn't be able to do so without considerable discomfort. It's definitely not a leash you should use for training Buddy.

>> **Flexi leashes:** They aren't good training leashes because the purpose of the flexi is to allow the dog to pull the leash out of the apparatus that you hold. The flexi is also clumsy to hold and because the length of the leash varies as you use it, the dog isn't taught consistent distances from you as you walk.

FIGURE 5-1:
Cotton web leash.

© John Wiley & Sons, Inc.

Selecting a collar

Collars come in a dazzling assortment of styles, colors, and materials. When training your dog, you need two types of collars:

>> **A training collar:** The purpose of a training collar is for you to be able to guide your dog when he's on leash and, if necessary, to check your dog. (A *check* is a crisp tug on the leash, followed by an immediate release of tension.) A check is used mainly for *abstention training,* which is when you want your dog to stop doing something that he wants to do, such as chasing a cat or a jogger. (See Chapter 1 for more on abstention training.) The check creates an unpleasant experience for the dog, which he can avoid by stopping the unwanted behavior (similar to a mother dog snapping at a puppy). Several different types of training collars are available, which we discuss later in this section.

>> **A buckle collar:** When not training, your dog should wear a buckle collar with ID tags attached. The collar can be leather, nylon, or cotton web. Buckle collars come in an assortment of colors and styles and are made of fabric or leather. Collars made of fabric usually have plastic clasps; the leather ones usually have metal clasps. If your dog weighs more than 50 pounds and hasn't yet been trained, you're better off using a leather collar with a metal clasp — a plastic clasp may break when your dog lunges after a cyclist or other moving object.

Buckle collars aren't meant to be used for training or walking because they don't allow for communication between you and your dog. Your dog can really pull and lean into a buckle collar, which can pull you off your feet. Train your dog first before leashing him to a buckle collar. Buckle collars are ideal for holding your dog's identification.

REMEMBER

You must use these two types of collars correctly. Remove the training collar when you aren't training your dog or when you can't supervise him. And don't try to use a buckle collar to train. For the untrained dog, buckle collars are virtually useless. Picture yourself trying to hang on as a fully-grown Rottweiler decides to take off after a cat. Trying to control that dog with a buckle collar would definitely be a heavy aerobic workout.

We discuss the advantages and disadvantages of different training collars in the following sections.

Nylon snap-around collars

The *snap-around collar* (refer to Figure 5-2 for an example) is the first-choice collar because of its effectiveness and versatility. It works well with dogs of all sizes with an average discomfort threshold. For dogs with high discomfort thresholds, consider the pinch collar (see the next section). The attention of the dog is the only reason to use any collar and leash while training. The best way to get your dog's attention is by a quick check or tug on the leash and collar, just enough for your dog to look at you to see what you want or need. The nylon snap-around collar has a metal clasp that enables you to fasten the collar around the dog's neck. That way, you can fit the collar high on your dog's neck where you have the most control.

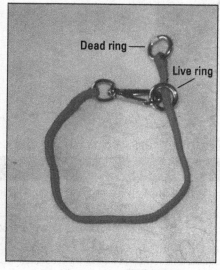

FIGURE 5-2:
The floating ring is the live ring and the stationary ring is the dead ring.

TIP

A snap-around collar should fit high on your dog's neck, just below his ears, as snug as a turtleneck sweater or neck-tie, for maximum control (see Figure 5-3). To get a good fit, measure the circumference of your dog's neck directly behind his ears with a tape-measure or a piece of string that you can then measure with a ruler.

The placement of the snap-around collar is the secret to its success. It works similarly to a slip collar that we discuss in the "Slip-on collars, chain or nylon" section, but because those fall to the shoulders, they aren't an effective means to communicate with your dog. The snap-around collar lays at the top of the neck, above the trachea or throat, so they're safe to use and move the focus of your dog to you when you give a quick check on the collar. It's amazing how well these collars work to get your dog's attention when fitted properly. Your dog's attention is what you need more than anything. Your dog's joy to work with you is what you want, which you can get with the correct equipment and the success they provide.

Table 5-1 presents some advantages and disadvantages to a snap-around collar.

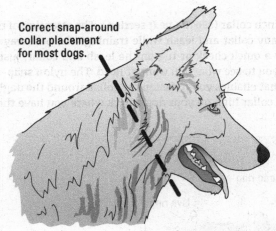

Correct snap-around collar placement for most dogs.

FIGURE 5-3:
Correct snap-around collar placement.

© John Wiley & Sons, Inc.

TABLE 5-1   **Pros and Cons of Nylon Snap-Around Collars**

Advantages	Disadvantages
Fairly inexpensive.	A puppy will grow out of it quickly, and you may need to purchase others.
Can be fitted exactly to your dog's neck.	Not as easy to put on as a slip-on collar.
Very effective.	
Quite safe.	
When fitted to right behind the ears, there is no pressure on the trachea since the collar rests above where a buckle collar would rest.	

Some dogs don't respond to a check on a snap-around collar — that is, the check doesn't create an unpleasant experience for the dog and doesn't change his behavior. The dog may be touch-insensitive and have a high discomfort threshold. Or, the dog's size and weight in relation to your size and weight may be such that he doesn't feel your check. Or the dog is so light or small and has high prey drive so that he can't recognize the collar check when he's in full prey-drive mode. (See Chapter 2 for more about drives.) When your dog is in full prey drive, you may need to consider a pinch collar.

REMEMBER

Take the training collar off your dog when he isn't being trained and whenever he isn't under your direct supervision so he doesn't accidentally get it caught on something that could choke him. Also, don't attach any tags to the training collar. When you're not training your dog, use a buckle collar to which you've attached his tags.

The best source for snap-around collars is Handcraft Collars because of the quality and durability. The collars from Handcraft come in half-inch increments.

Pinch or prong collars

The names *pinch collar* and *prong collar* describe the same piece of equipment. *Pinch* refers to the effect it has on the dog, and *prong* refers to its appearance. For old-time trainers, the pinch collar was the only collar to use for training. A pinch collar certainly is an effective and efficient training tool (see Figure 5-4). The pinch collar is also wonderful when you can't or don't want to apply too much pressure to the collar. A slight check with a pinch collar is enough to get your dog's attention. Those who use one for the first time often refer to it as power steering. We jokingly call it the *religious collar* because it makes an instant convert out of the dog.

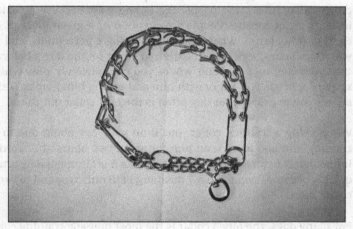

FIGURE 5-4:
A pinch collar.

© John Wiley & Sons, Inc.

According to many certified animal chiropractors, the pinch collar is generally the safest training collar because it doesn't require much force or pressure on your dog's neck or trachea. Therefore, the pinch collar doesn't cause vertebrae or neck. The pinch collar is also an effective training collar for strong, rambunctious dogs with a high prey drive. Table 5-2 offers some of the highlights and lowlights of using the pinch collar.

Pinch collars come in four sizes: large, medium, small, and micro. We've never used or recommended the large size, because it appears to have been made for elephants. For a large, strong, and rambunctious dog, the medium size is more than adequate. For Golden Retriever–sized or smaller dogs, the small size is sufficient. For toy dogs, use the micro version, which are harder to find in a local pet store. You can find them on Amazon.

TABLE 5-2   **Pros and Cons of Pinch Collars**

Advantages	Disadvantages
Readily available in pet stores and through catalogs.	Looks like a medieval instrument of torture.
Very effective.	Twice as expensive as a snap-around collar.
Can be fit to the exact size of the dog's neck.	
Very safe — it's self-limiting in that it constricts very little and it doesn't put pressure on the trachea. Therefore it's perfect for snub nose dogs or Brachiocephalic dogs such as Pugs and Bulldogs.	

REMEMBER

Any collar or piece of training equipment can be misused or abused. The intent of the user is the key to achieving a harmonious relationship through training. The pinch collar rubs some people the wrong way, because it looks like a medieval instrument of torture. People's perception of a given piece of equipment, however, is immaterial. What counts is the dog's perception, and your dog will tell you. Does your check have the desired effect on the dog's behavior? Are you putting your dog in a position where you can sincerely praise him for the correct response, or are you angry with him and calling him names? Using the collar that allows you to praise your dog often is the best collar out there.

TIP

When using a training collar, put it on your dog about one to two hours before training him and leave it on him for about two hours afterwards. If you put it on immediately before training and then take it off immediately after you finish, he'll quickly become "collar wise," meaning he'll only respond to commands when the collar is on.

For many dogs, the pinch collar is the most humane training collar, especially if it saves them from a one-way trip to a shelter. The pinch collar isn't the right solution for every training problem or for every dog, but it's the right solution under certain circumstances and is often referred to as a life-saver.

If you decide to use a pinch collar, it should sit right behind the ears, just like a snap-around collar does. Simply expand or contract the collar by adding or removing links, respectively.

Slip-on collars, chain or nylon

A *slip-on collar*, also called a *choke* or *choker collar*, usually made of chain or fabric, is one that slips over the dog's head. Because such a collar needs to fit over the dog's head, it has the tendency to slide down the dog's neck when on the dog. The strongest part of a dog's body is where the neck joins the shoulder blades. The farther the collar slides down the neck, the more difficult controlling the dog becomes and the less effective the collar is as a training tool.

CLARA'S STORY

When we met Clara, she was in her mid-60s. She lived in a large house outside of town, fairly isolated, although she could see some of her neighbors. We discovered that Clara had had a number of dogs during her life and after her last dog died, had acquired a German Shepherd puppy. Clara felt that she needed a dog that would protect her. She named the puppy Ursa. Whenever we talked, Clara would expound on Ursa's virtues — how sweet she was, how easy she was to train, how well she played with the grandchildren, and how many tricks she'd learned.

As time went by, we found out more about Clara. She'd had back surgery with steel rods implanted, and she frequently had to wear a neck brace. She then told us that she had put Ursa on a pinch collar to walk her. Clara said, "She just got too strong for me. Every time we went for a walk, she would sniff the ground where the deer had been and she would pull so hard that I didn't think I could hold her. So, I put her on a pinch collar to control her and now, after two weeks, I can walk her on her regular collar and she no longer pulls me off my feet. Without the pinch collar to help me, who knows what I would have done. I even thought that I might have to give her up, a thought I couldn't bear. Who knows what would have happened to her?"

Now when we meet Clara, she often has Ursa with her, and according to Clara, the dog is a saint. She said, "Instead of being frustrated and angry with her, I tell her what a good girl she is. I'm happy, and she is happy."

WARNING

Slip-on collars, when improperly used, pose a danger to your dog's trachea and spine. Avoid them! Animal chiropractors have made observations of spinal misalignment caused by this collar. Because slip-on collars aren't effective and have a poor safety record, we recommend you save your money and get something that works, such as the nylon snap-around collar or the pinch collar.

Readying a Reward: Treats Are Your Training Buddies

Other than your ingenuity and intellect (and the proper equipment), treats are another powerful training tool you can use. Treats are most effective when Buddy is hungry rather than after he has just eaten a meal. Fortunately, most dogs are food motivated.

You can use treats in one of two ways:

>> **As a reward for a desired response:** When you use a treat as a reward, you keep the treat hidden from the dog, so he doesn't know whether he's going to get it. For example, you say "Down," and Buddy lies down. He may get a treat, or he may not.

When conditioning your dog to a particular command, the treat needs to *immediately* follow the desired behavior so the dog understands that he's being rewarded for that particular response. Don't fumble around for a treat and give it to him when he's offering a different behavior. If you're teaching Buddy to sit on command and he gets up just as you give him the treat, you're rewarding Buddy for getting up, not a result you wanted at all.

>> **As a lure or inducement to obtain a desired response:** When you use a treat as a lure, the treat is in the open. You can use it to entice the dog to obey a particular command, such as lie down, and when he does, he gets the treat. When a treat is used in this way, it's within the dog's control whether he gets the treat or not.

REMEMBER

Because you're going to use treats both as a reward and as an inducement, you need to decide where to carry them. Some people use fanny packs, some a trouser pocket, and still others a shirt pocket. All these options are fine so long as you can reach them quickly to reward the desired response. Having a few in the palm of your hand when working on a particular exercise isn't a bad idea. The key is to use the treat *before* the dog does something else you don't intend to reward. If you can't get to the treat quickly, Buddy may do something you don't want to reward — and you'll have lost the moment to reinforce the appropriate behavior. A good habit is having some treats with you at all times.

In the following sections, we discuss the ideal treats best for training as well as what to do when your dog isn't excited about food treats.

Picking the ideal tasty treat

A great treat is a dry treat that you can keep in a pocket for easy reach. When you use something moist or soggy that needs to be carried in a plastic bag, by the time you fish it out to give to your dog he has forgotten what it's for. Many dry and semi-dry treats are available. To maintain your dog's health, avoid treats high in salt or sugar. Experiment to find out what your dog likes and responds to. Trying to train a dog with treats he doesn't like is pointless.

TIP

The ideal treat is dry and no bigger than ¼ inch (even smaller for toy dogs). The bigger the treat, the longer it takes Buddy to consume it, which will break his concentration from what you're teaching him. A favorite that is available on www.volharddognutrition.com are called Elec-tro-bytes, which are dry, small, can be broken in small pieces for puppies or toy dogs, and don't make your pocket smell for days afterwards. They provide valuable replacement nutrition for working dogs or dogs being trained.

Dogs also like carrots, broccoli, almost any kind of fruit, and cheese (low-sodium string cheese). For a selection of dog treats, check out a pet store. Make sure you choose a treat with very few ingredients and preservatives and one that provides good nutrition for your dog.

WARNING

Not all human food is safe for dogs. For example, the chemical agents found in chocolate that make it good and tasty to people are harmful for dogs. So keep chocolate away from Buddy. Also avoid macadamia nuts and onions, which can cause abdominal pain and nausea. Grapes and raisins and candy that contains xylitol as a sugar substitute can cause liver failure, and seizures; xylitol is deadly to dogs. Always check the ingredient list of your sugar-free candies and gums before bringing them into your home or car where your dog can get access to them.

Opting for toys when food treats don't work

Some dogs don't respond as well to treats as they do to other objects, such as balls, Frisbees, large stones, or sticks. In that case, use whatever turns your dog on — as long as it doesn't become a hindrance in your training. Your Buddy also may respond to verbal praise or petting as a motivator. You also can use a clicker (see Chapter 1).

For example, Katharina, a German Shepherd wouldn't take treats in training. She would, however, respond to a stick or a toy, so that's what was used with great success and joy to Katharina. Instead of using a food reward after each exercise or release, her owner who carried a stick in her back pocked threw a stick for her to retrieve to Katharina's delight.

Considering Other Equipment You Can Use

A variety of options are available to control dogs. More than likely you're familiar with some of them; others may be new to you. Some are training tools and others are management tools. The difference between the two is that a training tool teaches the dog to assume the responsibility for his behavior, whereas a management tool doesn't; it simply manages the dog's behavior. For example, a crate is a management tool — it controls the dog's movements.

We mention these tools to familiarize you to them. Some dog owners have successfully used them in special circumstances. We list them here solely to provide you with information of the options available to you.

Using head halters

The *head halter* (see Figure 5-5), such as the popular Gentle Leader, is an adaptation from the head halters used for horses. It works on the premise that where the dog's head goes, eventually the rest of the body will automatically follow.

FIGURE 5-5:
A head halter.

© John Wiley & Sons, Inc.

Whereas the pinch collar looks downright menacing, the head halter looks quite inviting and user-friendly. Interestingly, your dog's reaction (and he's the one that counts) is likely to be quite the opposite. He'll readily accept a pinch collar, but many vigorously and vociferously object to the head halter, at least initially. Many dogs don't like anything on their face, and such a dog will most likely try to rub it off and even look like a fish on a line, trying to get it off. You can use food to distract him if your dog starts such behavior, and you should be ready for this reaction. Play, feed, walk, distract your dog until he doesn't mind the head halter.

The following list describes the principal advantages of the head halter after your dog has learned to accept the effect it has on him:

>> **It's calming and tranquilizing.** This collar is helpful with nervous, timid, shy, or hyperactive dogs.

>> **It's equalizing.** A head halter helps smaller handlers with larger dogs, senior citizens, and handicapped handlers control their dogs.

>> **It's helpful with muzzling.** This collar helps with inappropriate sniffing behavior, whining or barking, some forms of aggression, and play biting or nibbling.

>> **It's readily available at pet stores.** You also can find these halters on the Internet by searching for them with your favorite browser.

Table 5-3 provides some additional advantages of the head halter as well as some disadvantages.

TABLE 5-3   **Pros and Cons of the Head Halter**

Advantages	Disadvantages
Readily available in pet stores and online.	Greatest potential for serious damage to your dog's neck if you yank on the leash while he is wearing a head halter.
Not very expensive.	Transition tool only.
Minimum strength required to use it.	The dog doesn't learn to accept responsibility for his behavior. When the halter is removed, the dog often reverts to previous behavior.

WARNING

Because this halter controls the head, a strong pull by the dog or the owner can do serious damage to the dog's neck. In this regard, it isn't quite the same principle as the head halter for horses. Because most people are smaller than horses, the halter is used to control the horse's head from below. In contrast, most people are taller than their dogs, and any pull or tug is going to be upward and, at times, simultaneously to the side. Tugging the dog's neck in this way creates great potential for injury. In relation to a person, a horse's neck also is correspondingly stronger than a dog's. The halter can and often does have a depressing effect on the dog. The irony here is that this highly marketable tool has great potential for damage, while the torturous-looking pinch collar is the safest.

Going for a body harness

Body harnesses, which are attached around the chest and back of a dog, are perfectly fine for dogs who don't pull or for small dogs whose pulling isn't terribly objectionable. But for a medium-sized or large dog that pulls, harnesses aren't a good idea because you give up the control you're trying to achieve. The dog literally leans into the harness and happily drags you wherever he wants to go. Harnesses are effective if your dog has a neck injury. Veterinary technicians and veterinarians often say a dog who arrives at a veterinary clinic for veterinary care will need a muzzle because a dog who pulls on a harness hasn't had the leadership lessons learned, where the owner is the leader and the dog is not. Harnesses allow the dog to think he is setting all of the rules by pulling his owner.

REMEMBER

Another option for a dog that pulls is a harness often referred to as a *nonpulling harness* or a harness for easy walking (see Figure 5-6). These harnesses are specifically designed to control pulling by applying pressure to calming points under the armpits when the dog pulls. Non-Pull harnesses are a management tool (not a training tool) for dogs with delicate necks, such as sight hounds, and for dogs who have experienced a neck injury. You can order one online or buy one at your local pet store and see if it works for you and your dog.

FIGURE 5-6:
A dog in a nonpulling harness.

© John Wiley & Sons, Inc.

Exploring electronic and other training and management equipment

Electricity has long been used to contain livestock (mainly cattle) as well as horses. Its application to dogs as a training tool and for containment purposes is of more recent origin. Electronic devices became popular with the training of sporting dogs to retrieve birds their owners had shot. The owners needed to be able to control their dogs over distances up to half a mile. Since that time, the concept of controlling the dog through the use of electricity has spawned the many devices that we describe in this section.

REMEMBER

Today's electronic devices don't pose much of a risk for the dog, and we aren't aware of any instances when a device's failure has injured a dog. The main risk to the dog is an owner's lack of knowledge of how to use a particular device properly.

A trainer is an individual who has knowledge of all these training devices and knows when and how to use them when the situation arises. For the beginner or impatient owner without education in a device's proper application, it's far too easy to use the device incorrectly. For example, a remote-trainer is frequently used as a means of punishment rather than a teaching tool. A remote trainer isn't meant as punishment, but rather it's used to put pressure on a dog to change his behavior.

Electric fences

Many housing developments have covenants against fences. That's a problem when you have a dog you want to keep confined. Tying a dog out on a line, except for brief periods, isn't a humane option.

Never fear, technology is here, and the *electric fence* (or *invisible fence*) is the answer. Here's how the system works: a wire is buried around the boundary of the area in which the dog is to be contained. Initially, the area is marked with little flags to provide the dog with a clear visual stimulus. The dog wears a collar that's designed to vibrate or beep when the dog approaches the boundary. When the dog gets too close, he receives a shock. The intensity of the shock can be adjusted. After the dog has learned to respect the location of the boundary, the flags are removed.

Electric fences are best for neighborhoods that don't allow fences and in farm communities where the dog needs to be prevented from visiting the neighbor, who is worried about the dog bothering his livestock.

WARNING

All in all, the system works well for the majority of dogs, but it isn't foolproof. Here are a few of the problems you may encounter:

>> It doesn't keep other dogs or animals out of the fenced area because they aren't connected to the system. If you have a female dog that isn't spayed, you could run into a problem when she's in season and an unaltered male comes to visit with breeding on his mind. It can't keep children out of your yard either.

>> Some dogs, in a state of high excitement, will "burn" through the fence. Then they find themselves on the outside of the fence and are afraid to come back in — or they may simply run off.

>> Some dogs develop aggressive tendencies toward people on the other side of the boundary.

>> Some dogs quickly become "collar wise" and disregard the fence when not wearing the collar. Should that happen, he needs to wear the collar every time you let him out.

>> Costs of the systems vary and depend on the size of the enclosure. The least expensive systems are found in pet stores, but in this situation, the owner must learn how to use them. A more expensive option is to use a company that installs the fence and sends a trainer who does the initial training of the dog and instructs the owner on how to use it.

As a result of these problems, you need to keep an eye on Buddy when he's out in the yard. Don't leave him for prolonged periods without supervision.

Shock collars or remote training collars

A *shock collar* is a buckle collar with a small box attached. The side of the collar that faces the dog has two small prongs that fit snugly against the dog's neck. The handler has a hand-held controller with settings that go from low to high electrical stimulation. Therefore it's considered a *remote collar* because you have a device to activate the collar when the dog is away from you. The euphemisms for this type of collar are the *e-collar* and the *remote trainer*. The word "shock" is often replaced with "stimulation." In simple terms, the electrical stimulation replaces the check on the collar with a leash. Remote trainers are most successful for controlling dogs at a distance.

REMEMBER

We don't recommend that beginners use these collars without training on the use of the collar first. Shock collar use requires knowledge of training and dogs. When used incorrectly, these collars can severely traumatize a dog. Seek a professional trainer if you're considering such a collar. If you insist on using any kind of electronic collar, try it out on yourself first so you know what it feels like to your dog. Whatever you do, don't point the controller at your dog or wave it at him in a threatening motion — he'll associate the stimulation with you, and that's not what you want. Keep the controller out of your dog's sight.

TECHNICAL STUFF

This collar's origins date back to the 1960s, when they were primarily used for gun dogs. They gave the trainer the ability to communicate with the dog over long distances. The main problems with the early collars were their unreliability and their limitations in terms of controlling the amount of stimulation — even at the lowest setting, the shock administered was needlessly intense.

Enormous quality differences exist within the different makes of remote trainers — essentially, you get what you pay for. The three features influencing the price of a remote-trainer are use of rechargeable versus replaceable batteries, range, and flexibility. The more sophisticated collars provide the most flexibility in adjusting the intensity of the stimulation, its length, and its range (up to 1 mile). Of course, these high-end collars are the most expensive, ranging from

$200 to $500. They may include a tone feature, to which some dogs respond without the need for stimulation.

Generally, such collars aren't carried in retail stores and are only available online. The following are some of the manufacturers of these collars: Dogtra, Innotek, PetSafe, and Tri-Tronics. You can purchase the products at the manufacturers' websites or at www.gundogsonline.com or www.amazon.com.

Vibration collars

The *vibration collar* works much the same as a remote trainer or shock collar (see the preceding section), but it relies mainly on vibration (rather than electric stimulation) at different levels of intensity to communicate with the dog. The vibration is more annoying than unpleasant, but for many dogs it's just as effective as a remote trainer.

The vibration collar works well with deaf dogs. Cost varies from $30 to $150. They're available from www.amazon.com.

Bark collars

To deal with excessive barking, you have several different *bark collars* to choose from. Your options are a mild shock, a mechanism that sprays a liquid (usually citronella), vibration, or ultrasound (a loud noise only the dog can hear). The collars use either a microphone or vibration to set the collar off. The more sophisticated ones use both to prevent loud noises or the barking of another dog from setting off the collar. They range in price from $30 to $60 and are available from the manufacturers listed in the preceding section. There are also features that increase in intensity if the dog continues to bark but resets back to the lowest level one if the dog is quiet for a period. With more features, the cost does increase also. These can be very effective tools, but they should be introduced to your dog while you're home, so you can help the dog to be quiet which will stop the stimulation of the collar. Your dog needs to learn how to shut off the stimulation that is to stop barking. If the collar were to surprise the dog for the first time and the dog hasn't learned how to turn off the stimulation, he could continue to vocalize unknowingly, and you'd have lost the opportunity for initial training.

TIP

If Buddy is an uncontrollable barker, you may want to consider a bark collar — it's a lot cheaper than being evicted.

LOCATING YOUR RUNAWAY WITH A GPS COLLAR

The latest entries into the e-collar arsenal are GPS tracking and locator collars. You use these collars to locate your pet if he has run away or been stolen. You can even look at a map online that shows you the exact location of your pet. They're fun if you have a lot of property to see where your dog has gone during his romp on your land. While such collars can locate your pet, training is another option to teach your dog to come when called. GPS is a tool, but shouldn't become a daily need. These collars are getting more affordable all the time.

Citronella collars

Citronella collars are used as bark collars (as noted in the preceding section), but they're also used to deter chasing. When activated by the owner, the collar emits a puff of citronella in the direction of the dog's nose. For example, if a dog chases a car, just before he gets there the owner presses the button and the dog gets a whiff of citronella. The expectation is that the dog considers the puff of citronella unpleasant enough to stop chasing things. Although not an electronic device, it works on the same principle. Because electric collars aren't allowed in England, for example, Citronella collars are the collar of choice there instead of the electric collars.

TECHNICAL STUFF

In a 1996 study at the Animal Behavior Clinic of Cornell University Veterinary School, the citronella collar was found to be more effective to control nuisance barking than the electric bark collar.

Prices range from $45 to $60, and they come in scented and unscented versions. Both are available through www.amazon.com.

Scat-mats

Don't want your dog taking his daily nap on your favorite armchair or couch while you're at work? The *scat-mat*, with which you cover that coveted piece of furniture, may be your answer. When Buddy jumps on it, the scat-mat gives him a slightly unpleasant shock, which will stop him from jumping on the furniture. The mat also can be used to prevent Buddy from entering another room in the house. No special collar is required.

The customary sizes of scat-mats are 30 inches long by 16 inches wide or 48 inches long by 20 inches wide. They can be extended by plugging two together. They're either battery powered or can be plugged into a wall outlet. You can find scat-mats at most of the larger pet stores for $10 to $75, depending on the size.

Indoor-containment systems

Do you want to stop Buddy from counter surfing or jumping on the kitchen table? If so, consider buying an indoor containment system. It consists of a 6-inch disc and a collar for your dog. You place the disc in the center of the countertop or table, and then you adjust the setting for intensity and the distance you want Buddy to stay away. When Buddy gets too close, he receives a mild shock.

The system is battery operated and prevents a dog from jumping on counters or coffee tables. It works on the same principle as the invisible fence (see the earlier section on this product). These systems are carried by most pet store chains, and they generally cost around $40.

For instance, dear friends of ours acquired an English Staffordshire Bullterrier. Meigs is the most adorable butterball on four legs — one solid muscle with incredible leaping ability. He's affectionately referred to as "a sack of cement on four pogo sticks." Even as a puppy he exhibited aspirations of ascending the coffee table. As early as 9 months of age, he was able to jump on the kitchen table from a dead standstill. Very cute, but hardly acceptable. The indoor containment system took care of it. You can teach Leave It, but of course you need to be present to reinforce that command. With indoor-containment systems and scat-mats, you don't need to be present for them to work.

The Pet Convincer

The Pet Convincer is a powerful substitute to yelling or screaming at your dog to control unwanted behaviors. Although the Pet Convincer is a shortcut to patient training, it's nevertheless an effective deterrent to those behaviors dog owners find most annoying and most difficult to deal with: for example, when Buddy goes ballistic when someone comes to the door, when he can't be dissuaded from jumping on people, when he barks incessantly, and so on. It also can be used when taking your dog for a walk. It can protect your dog from being bothered by another dog. It also works well for joggers and cyclists to ward off potentially unfriendly dogs.

This hand-held device, powered by a replaceable CO_2 cartridge, releases a blast of air. The blast of air, whose intensity is controlled with a trigger, is intended to stop the undesirable behavior. The noise of the blast acts as a deterrent. No doubt it will work better than screaming at the dog. It also provides a good chance the "correction" will carry over to the next time the dog encounters the problematic situation, such as someone coming to the door. You can purchase this product at www.petconvincer.com for $35.

This training tool should never be used in an enclosed space, such as a car. When triggered, make sure it's directed away from the dog's face.

Ultrasonic handheld devices

Many types of handheld remotes emit an ultrasonic tone to the dog, and they're viewed as deterrents to the dog's behavior. Some of them work on some issues with some dogs. These devices are relatively inexpensive, but they aren't always effective. There are many claims to them and some do work. They work similarly to the previously described Pet Convincer, but instead of a blast of air, they emit an ultrasonic tone that's unpleasant to the dog's ears. Mainly the device is a distracter to the dog and can help redirect your dog's behavior if you're there to help work on the desired alternate behavior. Training specific alternative behaviors is what the most effective tool is, always, either with a remote device or not.

New toys and tools are developed every year. Some have great uses and others aren't effective training tools. Use your commonsense and read about them before spending your money on them. If you choose to use them, enjoy your dog and the new technology.

2

Performing Puppy Preliminaries

Be as prepared as you can be when you bring your puppy home, including having the necessary supplies such as a crate, food, collar and leash, and toys.

Get your puppy used to using a collar and leash so you can be successful in starting your training plan.

Comprehend more about your puppy's developmental periods to help you understand his physical, behavioral, and emotional needs. You'll be amazed at how quickly he learns.

» Introducing your puppy to his new home

» Laying the groundwork for training

» Grooming your puppy

» Looking at health issues that interfere with training

Chapter **6**

Bringing Your Puppy Home: What You Need to Know

You're getting a new dog! Congratulations! Everyone you know is going to be jealous. Excitement abounds. While anticipating your new puppy's arrival, you've probably thought about the day-to-day care this new family member will need. You may even have made a list of necessities to purchase: food and water bowls, a leash, grooming aids, and so on. But the necessities don't stop there. You also need to think about laying the groundwork for training. Everything you do from now on teaches your puppy to be the perfect pet you have always wanted.

Teaching your puppy is about more than getting a response to a command; it's also about raising a dog you can live with and take anywhere and who can be a joy as a companion for many years. This chapter guides you through the first weeks and shows how your training relationship starts on day one.

Preparing for Puppy's Arrival

A little advance preparation for the exciting day makes your puppy's homecoming go smoothly. Before Buddy comes home, you need to gather the following (see Figure 6-1):

>> A crate and crate pad

>> The food you intend to feed and the dishes you're going to use

>> A collar and leash

>> Toys

FIGURE 6-1: Items you need before your puppy comes home.

You can get almost everything you need at a pet supply store, whether in person or online. Ordering online makes for convenient shopping, but you may prefer to check out your options at a local pet store.

In the following sections, we provide info on each of the items you need to gather before welcoming puppy into your home.

Puppy's home at home: Readying a crate

The idea of putting your dog in a crate may seem like a form of punishment. Humans often see confinement as punishment, but dogs see crates as their bedroom inside of your home. A crate serves as a den and a place of comfort, safety, security, and warmth. Puppies, as well as many adult dogs, sleep and hang out in a crate most of the day, and many prefer the comfort of their den. For your peace of mind, as well as your puppy's, get a crate — your dog's home within a home. We show you why having a crate is important and how to use one and set it up in the following sections.

Understanding the advantages of a crate

Consider a few of the many advantages to crate training your dog:

>> **A crate is a babysitter.** When you're busy and can't keep an eye on Buddy but want to make sure he doesn't get into trouble, you can put him in his crate. You can relax, and so can he. In other words, it's similar to a playpen for a toddler.

>> **A crate helps Buddy begin housetraining.** Using a crate is ideal for getting Buddy on a schedule for housetraining (see Chapter 8). Dogs don't want to soil their bed, so a proper-sized crate teaches them to hold their elimination.

>> **A crate prepares him for being crated at the vet's office.** Few dogs are fortunate enough to go through life without ever having to be hospitalized. Buddy's first experience with a crate shouldn't be in a cage or crate at the veterinary hospital — the added stress from being crated for the first time can slow his recovery. This stress isn't necessary if you train your dog to be comfortable in a crate at home. Veterinary technicians and staff are so grateful when a dog happily goes into a cage or kennel at the vet hospital, showing that the dog will be comfortable there while hospitalized.

>> **A crate helps with bed rest.** Crate training pays off when you need to keep your dog quiet and calm, such as after being altered or after an injury. Remember his crate is his secure place inside your home.

>> **A crate makes driving safer.** Driving any distance, even around the block, with your dog loose in the car is tempting fate. An emergency stop could fling your pet around the car like a pinball. Having Buddy in a crate protects you and him. Slamming on the brakes going 35 miles an hour causes a loose dog to move as a 400-pound projectile possibly causing fatal damage to the dog and/or others.

>> **A crate relaxes him on vacation.** Taking your well-trained dog with you on vacation is fun. His crate is his home away from home, and you can safely leave him in a hotel room knowing that he won't be unhappy or stressed — and that he won't tear up the room. Also a surprise visit from housekeeping won't allow Buddy to sneak out the door because he'll be safely crated.

>> **A crate gives Buddy his own special place.** It's a place where he can get away from the hustle and bustle of family life and hide out when kids (or other pets) become too much for him.

Selecting the best crate for your puppy

Get a crate that's big enough to accommodate your puppy when he becomes an adult dog. Select one that's large enough for your dog to turn around, stand up, or lie down in comfortably (as Figure 6-2 shows).

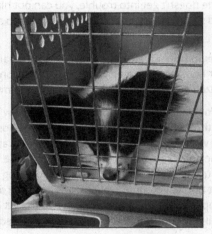

FIGURE 6-2:
A crate is a comfy den for your dog.

© John Wiley & Sons, Inc.

TIP

If you expect that your puppy will become a much bigger adult dog, buy a crate that comes with a divider that enables you to increase the size of the crate as he grows. The most versatile crates have two doors, one on the side and one at the end. You'll appreciate this flexibility, especially when you need to move the crate from room to room.

If you plan to travel with your dog, get a crate that collapses easily and is portable so you can take it with you. Or consider investing in a second crate for the car. Lugging a crate from the house to the car and back again quickly gets old.

The two main types of crates are as follows:

>> **Solid-sided crates:** Often referred to as an *airline crate,* this type (see Figure 6-3) is the most comfortable for your dog. Your dog prefers a solid-sided crate because it gives him the security he wants and needs. The crate is confining like a den would be, and remember that dogs are den animals.

FIGURE 6-3:
A solid-sided crate.

© John Wiley & Sons, Inc.

>> **Wire crates:** Wire crates are collapsible and easy to transport, but they don't provide the security that solid crates do. The wire crate in Figure 6-4 shows the dog in the crate for purposes of our discussion so you can see inside the crate. The wired crate forces the dog out in the open and can make the pup feel exposed. People aren't den animals so people often think wire crates are better due to the openness, but it's actually the opposite — the solid crate offers much more calmness and security.

Both types need a crate pad — you don't want your growing puppy or adult dog to constantly be on a hard surface because it's tough on joints. Get a crate pad with a removable cover that you can clean in the washing machine. Toss a blanket into the crate to keep Buddy warm.

REMEMBER

Make sure the size of the crate fits the size of your dog. The crate should only be large enough for Buddy to stand up, turn around, and lie down. The crate is a bed to sleep in, not exercise in.

FIGURE 6-4:
A wire crate
forces a dog to
be exposed.

Positioning the crate in your home

Establish an area where your puppy will spend the majority of his time — a place where he won't feel isolated from his new family. The kitchen, family room, or whatever room is most used in the house (but still contains a quiet area) is an ideal place where Buddy can eat and take frequent naps.

Another option for a crate location is in your bedroom. When a new puppy is crated in your room, he's aware of your scent and hears your breathing. You set a good example for sleep, and nighttime counts as quality bonding time for you and your puppy. Dogs are pack animals and want to be with their pack. Sleeping together, dog in his crate, you in your bed, counts as social time. Later, you may not need the crate at night, but for a puppy's chewing stages and the housetraining period, a crate is an essential tool.

REMEMBER

Make sure Buddy's crate is available to him when he wants to nap or take some time out. He'll use it on his own, so make sure he always has access to it. Depending on where it is, your dog will spend much of his sleeping time in his crate.

WARNING

Never use your dog's crate as a form of punishment. If you do, he'll begin to dislike the crate, and it will lose its usefulness to you. You don't want Buddy to develop negative feelings about his crate. You want him to like his private den.

ALTERNATIVES TO TRAVEL CRATES

The safest way to transport your dog in a vehicle is in his crate. A loose dog in a car is a danger to you and your dog — keeping Buddy in a crate protects both of you. For some vehicles, such as sedans, crates are too large or cumbersome. One solution is a harness designed for dogs that is secured by the seatbelt, not unlike a car seat for a child (check out the accompanying figure of a dog wearing a seat belt). A dog can ride comfortably on the rear seat, either sitting up or lying down.

In a station wagon or SUV, another alternative is a dog barrier that separates the cargo area from the main cabin. Talk to your car dealer about this option.

Puppy's menu: Selecting a proper diet and set of dishes

Choosing a food for your growing puppy isn't easy — a lot of choices are available. We recommend the Natural Diet Foundation, or NDF2; you can find the details in Chapter 4 and at www.volharddognutrition.com. The NDF2 is one of the easiest methods of feeding a high-quality diet, which is important for your puppy's growth and health. What you feed your puppy will determine the ease or difficulty you'll have in training Buddy. The better the diet, the easier it is to train him.

REMEMBER

After you settle on a diet for Buddy, be sure to pick out a set of dishes — one for food and one for water. Try to avoid brightly painted or cute ceramic dog dishes. Many companies use lead in the manufacturing process of these dishes; over time the lead can leach into the food in the dish. Stick with stainless-steel dishes instead. They come in various sizes and are easy to keep clean. These dishes will last your puppy a lifetime.

Puppy's everyday collar, ID, and leash: Preparing Buddy to go outside

When you're getting ready to bring home Buddy, you need the following items to keep him safe and speak for you if he gets away, such as identification:

>> **Everyday collar:** For your puppy's everyday collar, you need a flat, fabric, adjustable buckle collar that can be made bigger as he grows. This collar holds your dog's identification tags.

>> **ID tags:** Tags should have a good contact number for you, phone number, and address. If you find a dog from around the corner, a quick walk can return him to the rightful owner. Tags should be strong enough to hold up to wear and small enough not to catch on furniture or fencing.

>> **Leash:** Get a 6-foot-long soft fabric leash for training and walking.

Puppy's toys: Playing with Buddy

Toys are a wonderful way to amuse Buddy for hours at a time and keep him from chewing your possessions. They also can be used in training for dogs that aren't that interested in food. You need a variety of them, including the following:

>> **Several large plush toys:** Puppies love to play with soft toys and carry them around. However, avoid stuffed animal toys if you have a puppy who likes to rip and tear them apart. They often contain stuffing and squeakers that puppies consider edible. Also beware of the following:

- Toys with hard eyes or studs that your puppy will pull off — and can swallow.

- Toys that resemble shoes or your clothes. It's difficult for a puppy to understand the difference between his toys and your stuff.

>> **Interactive toys:** Interactive toys are great for puppies because they teach as they amuse. The puppy will need to figure out how to get the treat, and it gives him something to work on that provides a reward at the end. Such toys are especially important when a puppy is teething. Here are some options:

- **Hard rubber toys:** The Kong Company specializes in hard rubber toys that can be filled with treats or frozen yogurt to keep dogs occupied. Kong toys come in different sizes, colors, and strengths. The colors identify the strength of the toy; black is virtually indestructible and is the favorite retrieving toy of most retrievers who love holding things in their mouths at all times.

- **Softer treat holders:** Some interactive toys come in different shapes and sizes and can be stuffed with treats. Some puppies prefer them to the harder toys because they're made of a softer rubber compound. Visit your local pet store to see all the different varieties.

- **The Buster Cube:** This toy can be the all-time favorite of many dogs who love to dig and root. You put some treats inside the cube and watch your dog go at it. Dogs learn how to roll the cube so treats randomly fall out. Note that on a hardwood floor, the cube is a bit noisy. The Buster Cube is made of cleanable, high-impact plastic. The Small Cube measures 3⅛ inches square, and the Large Cube is 4½ inches square.

>> **Chew bones:** Gumma bones or natural bones from the butcher can be fabulous chewing toys for your puppy. When picking out real bones, the long bones are much better than the knuckles.

WARNING

Never give a cooked bone to a dog because it can splinter and cause problems. Stay away from steak bones or bones that are cut into a circle such as a ham bone because they're easily caught in Buddy's lower jaw.

TIP

Some toys cost a fortune to buy new, but you often can buy them for a fraction of the original cost at your local thrift store. Make sure they're cleaned and disinfected after you get the used toys home.

Bringing Puppy Home — Now What?

You've brought your bundle of fur home, so now what do you do? First off you need to get him acclimated to his new home and surroundings, including introducing him to any children or resident pets. You also need to get his potty habits started and find a good place for him to sleep. We show you how to do all of this in Chapter 8.

Adding a puppy or living with a dog is life changing. Living with a dog is time consuming and can be expensive, but it's worth every penny you spend. Living and loving a dog adds so much to your life, fun, exercise, and companionship. When you bring him home, help him get used to his new surroundings and his new life. These sections address what areas to focus on.

Getting your puppy used to his collar and leash

Prior to starting your training, Buddy will need to get used to wearing his buckle collar. Put this collar on Buddy after his nap, take him outside to relieve himself, and let him eat with his collar on. At first he may scratch at it, because he isn't used to having something around his neck. As he gets used to wearing his collar, the scratching will stop.

After he's comfortable with his collar, introduce Buddy to his leash. Attach the leash to his collar and let him drag it around the room. You need to keep an eye on him so the leash doesn't get entangled. Don't pick up the leash just yet.

REMEMBER

When he's comfortable with the leash tagging along behind him, your next step is to get Buddy used to walking on leash while you're holding it. At this age, if you try to get your puppy away from home using your leash, he may resist. He doesn't want to leave home, and you'll wind up dragging him, giving him a negative feeling about his leash. Instead, pick him up and carry him a short distance from the house. At that point, he'll happily lead you back. After several repetitions he'll get used to his leash. Make it fun for your puppy and give him the occasional treat to motivate him to keep moving.

When you're ready to start doing some training with your puppy, you have to put the snap-around collar on him. We use the collars and leashes from www.handcraftcollars.com, a site that offers high-quality products that last a long time. A snap-around collar is measured to fit high on your dog's neck, away from any pressure on the trachea. To put the collar on, start with you and your dog facing each other. Then hold the collar with the rings in your right hand (all the "Rs" together, ring, ring, and right hand).

1. **Attach your leash to the stationary ring before you get started.**

    Check out Figure 6-5-d to see where to attach your leash. It's helpful to attach the leash before you put the collar on. Therefore the floating ring is left for the hook on the collar in Step 4.

2. **Take the two rings in your right hand with the sewn-on ring and the floating ring together in your right hand, facing your dog.**

See Figure 6-5-a.

3. **Place the collar under your dog's neck and bring the ends up to the top of his neck, directly behind the ears.**

REMEMBER

Figure 6-5-b shows the proper placement of the collar in this step. When you begin to put on the collar, the dog flexes his neck muscles, expanding the circumference of the neck by as much as a half inch, creating the impression that the collar is much tighter than it actually is (similar to the effect produced by a horse taking in air as it's being saddled).

4. **Attach the clasp to the floating ring.**

The smooth side of the clasp needs to be next to the dog's skin. See Figure 6-5-c to see what this step should look like.

You're good to go! Make sure the collar is right behind your dog's ears and high on the neck. This is where it's most effective.

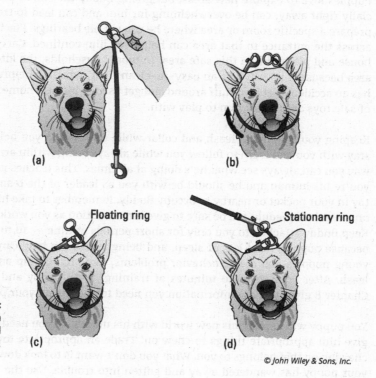

(a)

(b)

Floating ring

Stationary ring

FIGURE 6-5:
How to put on a snap-around collar.

(c)

(d)

© John Wiley & Sons, Inc.

TIP

After you get the collar on your dog, you may get the impression that it's much too tight and that you can barely get it around Buddy's neck. We suggest that after the first time you put the collar on, you wait for five minutes. After the dog has relaxed, you then can test for correct snugness. You need to be able to slip two fingers between the collar and your dog's neck (one finger if you have a toy dog). If your fingers won't fit, the collar is too tight; if you can get three or more fingers through, the collar is too loose. One way to make the collar smaller is to tie a knot in it and then attach it as you normally would.

REMEMBER

Before reaching 16 weeks of age, you puppy will follow you wherever you go. This tendency provides you with endless training opportunities. Although he won't understand what you're saying to him, you can use this behavior to teach him the Touch command (see Chapter 9), which is an effective foundation for future training.

Getting Buddy situated in his new home

Puppies love to explore new areas, but giving Buddy the run of the house, especially right away, can be overwhelming for him and can lead to trouble. Instead, prepare a specific room or area where he can get his bearings. Placing a baby gate across the entrance to that area can help keep him confined. Carry him into the house and place him in this safe area. In most households, the kitchen is a good area because it usually has an easy-to-clean floor, which is helpful when puppy has an accident. Let him sniff around and get used to his new home. Scatter plenty of safe toys around for him to play with.

Keeping your puppy on leash and collar while attached to you helps your puppy stay with you and learn to follow you while always being within arm's reach. This way you can always see what he's doing at all times. This teaches your puppy that you're his human and he should be with you as leader of the team. Keep a chew toy in your pocket or nearby to occupy Buddy. Remember to take him out to potty on a regular schedule and be sure to give him attention as you work and train him. Keep Buddy attached to you only for short periods of time — 10 to 30 minutes — because puppies need lots of sleep, and being awake too long can overstimulate young puppies and create behavior problems, like jumping up and chewing the leash. After your 10 to 30 minutes of training, potty puppy and let him sleep. Chapter 8 gives you the information you need to potty train your puppy.

You puppy will explore his new world with his mouth, so you need to be nearby to give him appropriate things to chew on. Trade an appropriate toy for what he's chewing on that belongs to you. What you don't want is to look down and find that your puppy has wandered away and gotten into trouble. Use the leash and baby gates to keep him in the same room as you. These steps can be inconvenient, but you only need to do them for a short time. They'll lead to a lifetime of a dog that is trustworthy in the house.

REMEMBER

The more activity the puppy has, the more he'll need to relieve himself. Confining him to an area at first will greatly aid in his housetraining. Being attentive to your dog's potty habits must always be foremost in your mind. (See more about potty training in Chapter 8.)

The first time you feed your puppy, place his food in his crate to introduce him to his den and establish the idea that the crate is where good things happen (see the earlier section "Puppy's home at home: Readying a crate"). Leave the door open when you feed him initially until he learns that the crate or den is his. Later you may not need to feed him in a crate, but when you bring him home, using the crate to feed him adds one more reason for him to love being in his crate.

Introducing puppies and kids

Teaching dogs and children to coexist can go well or badly depending on the boundaries you set. Although small children generally can get along well with dogs — especially if their parents are comfortable around dogs — parents do need to make the effort to teach their children how to interact correctly with the puppy. Remember the following:

>> Parents must be watchful that children don't pinch, pull fur, twist ears, fall on, or chase the puppy.

>> Parents need to monitor interactions between the children and the puppy. Children tend to run, squeal, and wear loose clothing, all of which incite the puppy's prey drive and encourage nipping. It's a parent's responsibility to keep children from overstimulating the new puppy.

>> Parents should teach the children to be calm around the puppy and to pet Buddy gently.

>> Parents must stop young children from carrying the puppy, because they may drop him. Until children are completely stable and steady while walking, they shouldn't carry a puppy.

>> Parents must be responsible for training the puppy and then include the kids after the puppy has learned a lesson; the responsibility of training must fall on an adult or teenager, not young children. While training a dog, children are seen as littermates rather than authority figures. Usually 11-year-old kids can handle training a dog who isn't challenging the child's authority.

Tolerance for playing with children varies within and among breeds. Early exposure also is a factor. Dogs between the ages of 7 and 12 weeks that are exposed to well-behaved children generally get along well with kids. The most important thing a parent can teach the child is to respect the puppy, thereby fostering a harmonious relationship.

Parents do both the child and the dog a favor if they insist that children keep their hands at their sides or cross them across their chest when around puppies or dogs they don't know. Children are inclined to lift up their arms when greeting a puppy, which encourages the puppy to jump. Of course, children also must be taught that they should *never* go up to a strange dog and try to pet him. Only after permission is sought from the owner is approaching and petting a dog acceptable. Figure 6-6 shows how a dog and child can be great friends.

FIGURE 6-6:
A harmonious relationship, a boy and his dog.

A safe place where the dog can retreat and not be bothered by a child is essential. When Buddy has had enough play and tries to hide under the bed, don't try and pull him out. The dog is looking for a safe place and rest away from the kids. Listen to your dog and give him a break from all activity.

Meeting resident pets

When you already have a dog and Buddy is a new addition to your household, you need to stage the introduction. You can't assume that the resident dog will automatically accept Buddy.

REMEMBER

Introduce a new family member to an older dog by first placing them both on leash. The best approach is to take the older dog outside to the front of the house, which is neutral territory. Then carry the puppy from the car to the front and let the two meet on leash. Let your older dog sniff the puppy from top to toe but only after the initial introductions and a short walk. Puppies at this age often turn upside down and pee. In dog language this is a sign of great respect. A short walk on leash is always a good idea after a quick sniff when introducing your new puppy to an existing pet. The walk distracts everyone and gives the dogs something to do instead of waiting for a possible altercation.

When the older dog has satisfied his curiosity, let him invite the puppy into the house. You need to keep an eye on the interaction between the two. Above all, make as much fuss over the older dog as you do over the puppy. You don't want to create the impression that he's being replaced. If the introduction goes badly, alternate between crating the resident dog and the puppy until they get used to each other.

Introducing a new dog to an existing cat in the household requires a small crate for the cat. After all, your new dog may not know what a cat is, so you need to allow the dog and cat to sniff each other and to keep the cat from running off. Running away triggers the chase instinct in the dog, which is never a good idea. By giving them a couple evenings of hanging out together, cat in crate, dog not in crate, you allow them to get used to each other. You can also help redirect the dog away from the crate if he gets too curious.

Tending to his potty needs

Housetraining your puppy can be a challenge, but it needn't be a nightmare. We devote Chapter 8 to the topic, so flip ahead for expert advice on establishing a schedule.

REMEMBER

Here's what you need to keep in mind when you bring your puppy home:

>> Establish a toilet area in your yard and take Buddy there after he wakes up, shortly after he eats or drinks, and after he has played or chewed.

>> When you see Buddy sniffing and circling, take note! He's letting you know that he's looking for a place to go. When you see this behavior, take him out to his toilet area so he doesn't have an accident in the house.

>> After 8 p.m., remove his water dish so he has a better chance of lasting through the night without needing to potty.

Deciding where your puppy should sleep

We can't stress enough how important sleep is for your growing puppy. After all, he's a baby and needs lots of sleep to grow properly, digest his food, and stay calm. Puppies that don't get enough sleep often get overstimulated and bite at hands, have more accidents, and get whiny. Establish a schedule in which your puppy is crated in a quiet place for a couple hours after morning playtime and again after subsequent play periods during the day.

TIP

If he gets whiny when you crate him, put a few small treats into one of the Kong toys. Playing with these toys will use up the excess energy and help him fall asleep quickly.

At night, you have some choices for where your puppy will spend his sleeping time. Puppies hate to be alone, so if you isolate the puppy from you, the first week or so he will scream louder and louder until you can't stand it any longer. He's preprogrammed to do so; he's telling his mother that he's lost and to come find him. We suggest you set his crate in your bedroom and close to you when you first get him.

The best idea is to have a crate by the side of your bed, using it as a bedside table. Put the puppy in the crate when you go to bed, and he'll be happy to snuggle down knowing you're close by. If he gets anxious, you can put your fingers through the crate to reassure him that you're there and he isn't alone. Having a soft, stuffed toy in his crate also helps.

If your puppy is part of a multidog household, you can leave all the animals together in the same sleeping area so the puppy has company. Make sure the crate has a soft blanket and large soft toy in it so the puppy stays warm.

Starting Buddy's Education

Puppies love to learn, and they'll learn with or without you. Naturally, you want to teach Buddy what you want him to learn. Puppies will retain for a lifetime the lessons they learn between 7 and 12 weeks of age. At this age, Buddy is still easy to physically control. The older he gets and the larger he grows, the more difficult the task becomes — and the more unpleasant it gets for your dog. The best time to start is now. In the following sections, we show you the most important exercises to start with when educating your puppy.

REMEMBER

Name Recognition is a great first lesson. Chapter 9 gives you instructions on how to teach this fabulous game. As obvious as it seems, an amazing number of dogs don't respond to their names. Training by giving a command to dog who doesn't respond to his name has little chance for success.

REMEMBER

Furthermore, having a veterinary chiropractor look at your puppy during his first year of life to make sure that everything is in order is a good idea. Vigorous play, especially with other dogs, can cause all manner of misalignments, which can then interfere with proper growth. To find one near you, go to www.ahvma.org/find-a-holistic-veterinarian where chiropractic veterinarians are listed by state.

Training for grooming

You can do much of the routine care a dog needs yourself without having to lay out a small fortune for someone else to do it for you. Examples are brushing, bathing, trimming nails, cleaning ears, and brushing teeth. If you start the grooming training when Buddy first comes home, he'll accept it and you'll have a puppy that you can groom for the rest of his life. Start now while Buddy is small; this way you can manage to pick him up and put him on a table. The most successful time to introduce grooming is after your puppy has had a playtime or has exercised.

The equipment you need for grooming depends on the kind of dog you have, because the type of dog you have dictates generally how much grooming he needs. Even shorthaired dogs require some brushing. Regular grooming saves on vacuuming and keeps his coat and skin healthy.

TIP

For more information on how to make your puppy look his best, see *Dog Grooming For Dummies* by Margaret H. Bonham (John Wiley & Sons, Inc.).

Brushing your puppy

Instead of trying to groom Buddy with both of you struggling on the floor, start by putting him on a table. Grooming on a table is comfortable for you and has a calming effect on your dog. If you have a longhaired breed, he'll need to get used to spending a lot of time on a table. If you have a large-breed dog, you may need the assistance of a family member to get him on the table. Outside tables such as picnic tables work well too, so find the perfect spot to use as your grooming area.

Any solid table will do, but you need to place a towel on it to prevent the puppy from slipping. Lift Buddy onto the table and give him a treat. Gently stroke him all over his body. When he relaxes on the table, bring out your soft-bristle brush and let him smell it. Put a treat on the table, and when he's occupied with it, gently brush his body, mimicking what you did when you stroked him. (Figure 6-7 shows how to groom a puppy.) Give a treat each time you brush another body part. Doing so will keep him occupied, so he won't try to play with the brush. If you follow this routine daily, Buddy will look forward to his grooming sessions.

FIGURE 6-7:
Grooming a
puppy on a table.

© John Wiley & Sons, Inc.

Even if your puppy is shorthaired, you need to brush him at least once a week, if not more. Brushing is essential in stimulating the skin; it keeps the skin healthy by bringing blood to the surface. Short hair is more difficult to vacuum up than long hair.

When a pup reaches 3 to 5 months, he'll start to lose his puppy coat. The puppy coat usually starts to fall out on the tail, up the spine, and then each side of his body. Before it sheds, his coat gets dull; the fur is dead and is making room for the adult coat to come in. Keeping puppy brushed helps keep dog fur off the floor and your clothes.

Bathing your puppy

Even in the best of households, puppies get into things that smell. Dogs love to investigate new smells by rolling in them. No one wants to spend time with a smelly puppy, so Buddy needs to learn to be bathed.

REMEMBER

Various opinions exist concerning how often a dog should be bathed. The simple answer is that you should give Buddy a bath when he smells like a dog or has rolled in something stinky. Heaven forbid he should have an encounter with a skunk. Many methods can neutralize skunk oils. Here is the most common de-skunking mixture:

1. Mix 1 quart of hydrogen peroxide, ½ cup of baking soda, and 1 teaspoon of liquid dish soap.

2. Pour the mixture on a dry dog and then rub it in.

3. **Allow it to sit for a few minutes and then rinse.**

4. **Repeat if necessary and follow up with a normal wash with your dog's regular shampoo.**

You can use the bathtub or the shower, or you can bathe him outside, weather permitting (see Figure 6-8). When you first put Buddy into the bathtub or shower, let him calm down before you turn on the water. When you finally turn it on, go slowly and let him look at it. (The water should be quite warm but not hot.) If you're using a sprayer, spray away from him first so he can get used to the sound and sight of the spray. Then, starting at his neck and shoulders, wet his body down to his back legs and tail. Continually tell him what a good boy he is. Keep your voice light and encouraging.

FIGURE 6-8: Bathing your puppy.

© John Wiley & Sons, Inc.

TIP

If your puppy is too bouncy, put a collar on him so you can control him with one hand. Or have a family member hold him by the collar while you bathe him.

After you wet the puppy, rub dog shampoo all over and lather his coat. (A good choice of shampoo is a coconut oil–based shampoo that has the correct pH for puppy skin and doesn't take the oil out of his coat.) Avoid Buddy's head; bathe only from the neck down. You don't want to get water in his eyes or ears; doing so will scare him. Rinse him carefully, making sure no soap is left in the fur; rinse him twice so you're sure he is truly soap free. Lift puppy out of the sink or shower and put him on the same towel-covered table you're using for grooming. With a treat held just above his nose, make him sit and then gently rub him dry with a towel as in Figure 6-9. While he's on the table, you can wash his face with a wet facecloth, but be sure to stay away from his eyes. After his bath, keep him in a warm area until he's completely dry.

FIGURE 6-9:
Drying puppy
after a bath.

Trimming nails

Your puppy's nails need trimming when you can hear him coming on a hardwood floor. Trimming his nails isn't as difficult as it sounds. First, get him accustomed to having his nails touched. To do so, wait until he's relaxed and then play with his feet, touching each nail.

After your puppy gets used to having his nails and toes touched, put Buddy on the table you're using to groom. Place him in a position in which he's comfortable, whether that be sitting or lying down. Using a dog nail clipper, cut just the tip of one nail. Chances are, your puppy will squeak, not so much out of discomfort, but because it's a new experience. Give him a treat. When he's comfortable with having one nail done, try doing just one foot this first session. Remember to clip the little dewclaws on the side of his front legs. Do one foot a day for four days, and you'll have all the nails trimmed.

You also can use a grinder, such as a Dremel tool, to grind his nails or to smooth out the edges after you've trimmed them. This type of tool makes quite a bit of noise, so it pays off to spend a little time letting Buddy see the grinder and smell it when it's turned off and when it's turned on without using it on his nails. Some puppies are sound sensitive, so we don't suggest using it for these pups. Have Buddy lie down on the grooming table, treats between his paws, and just try one nail at a time. Over a few days you can get all the nails done.

TIP

You may need a family member or friend to help you hold the puppy sufficiently still so you can clip his nails.

Cleaning ears

Part of your weekly grooming needs include cleaning your puppy's ears. Prick-eared dogs, such as German Shepherds or Corgis, don't need ear cleaning as frequently as floppy-eared dogs, who seem to vacuum up dirt with their hanging ears. The earflaps of drop-eared dogs need weekly cleaning.

To get started, get Buddy to sit or lie down on the grooming table and gently play with his ears. Lift up the ear flaps on the floppy-eared dog or stroke the prick ear before you start to clean them. Give Buddy a treat and tell him what a good boy he is.

When you and Buddy are both ready to start cleaning, combine in a spray bottle a mixture of half apple cider vinegar and half water. Spray a small amount onto a cotton ball and gently clean the part of the ear that you can see. If you don't know what you're doing, going farther into the ear canal is dangerous — leave that deep cleaning to your vet on Buddy's annual health exam or more frequently if Buddy has problems or his ears start to smell bad.

Cleaning the pearly whites

Buddy's mouth is the gateway to his overall health. First, get him used to his mouth being handled. Gently lift his lips on each side of his mouth and touch his teeth. At first, most puppies fight having their mouths handled. But be patient; Buddy will get used to the feeling.

With Buddy on the grooming table, put your arm around his neck and shoulders. After he's comfortably positioned, lift his lips on each side. Praise him for allowing you to look at his teeth on both sides of his head. Then you're ready to wet a cotton ball with warm water and gently wipe his teeth. Give him a treat. By following this process, you're training Buddy to accept his mouth and teeth being touched. You can also wrap one of your fingers with an old nylon stocking and rub his teeth with your wrapped finger, which is good for massaging his gums as well as his teeth.

As he grows older and is no longer a puppy, you can introduce a soft toothbrush, which should be used weekly when he's an adult. A human toothbrush is suitable, but a dog toothpaste (which is flavored for his palate) makes the process more enjoyable for Buddy.

REMEMBER

Training Buddy to accept this routine is one of the most important things you can do for him, because as an adult, Buddy's teeth can get coated with tartar that will inflame his gums. Gum disease produces bacteria that have been implicated in heart disease, stroke, and some cancers.

Cleaning the eyes

Keep your puppy's eyes clean and wiped out if matter collects in them. Usually a damp cloth to wipe his face off should be efficient. Eyes are a common place for dust or seeds to collect in the lower eye lids. A stream of contact eye saline can be enough to flush any debris from his eyes. Contact lens saline is rather cheap and a good thing to have in your medicine closet for such a need.

Spaying and neutering

The latest research has revealed that spaying/neutering a puppy at too young of an age has serious long-term side-effects on structure. Puppies and young dogs need the hormones that the reproductive glands produce for them to grow properly. Research recommends that the puppy be fully grown before you take him to the veterinarian for this surgery. Wait if you can until your puppy is at least 2 years old to avoid long-term side-effects from early spay/neutering. It's interesting that the United States is the only country where it's recommended to neuter young dogs. Research has disproven that neutering stops aggression and other behavioral problems.

Solving Perplexing Puppy Problems

Here are some of the more commonly asked questions in puppy classes about health conditions that interfere with housetraining and training in general:

» **My puppy pees small amounts frequently even though I take him outside regularly.** The stress of leaving his mother and littermates along with a long journey to his new home can cause a puppy to get an infection called *cystitis,* which is an inflammation of the bladder, making the puppy think he needs to urinate frequently. What you see is puppy straining and producing a few drops of urine. Don't ignore this symptom and think it will get better — it won't. Cystitis can wreak havoc with your housetraining efforts, so be sure to make an appointment with your veterinarian.

» **My puppy doesn't want to eat his food.** Find out what Buddy's previous owner or breeder fed the puppy before he left home. Try to get some of that food and see if merely the change in diet has affected his appetite. Also take a look at Chapter 4 for dietary suggestions.

A puppy on medication may have an upset tummy and not feel like eating. Try feeding small meals often. If your puppy is on certain antibiotics, the lack of appetite generally disappears after the medication is stopped. If all else fails, you can drop goat's milk or full fat organic yogurt mixed with honey (a half cup of goat's milk or yogurt to 1 teaspoon honey) into the side of his mouth with an eyedropper, to get him going. After he starts to eat, he'll generally continue. Stop training until he feels better.

When a puppy is teething (anywhere from 4 to 6 months, depending on the breed), his mouth gets sore. Food can get stuck in the teeth, so you'll often see puppy running his face along the floor or against the couch. Gently put your index finger into the puppy's mouth to clear out anything that's stuck. Provide lots of toys and bones to gnaw on during this teething period. Buddy needs to chew to loosen the baby teeth. If he has baby teeth that aren't coming out, an occurrence that's common, take him to your veterinarian. Again, stop training until your puppy feels better.

>> **My puppy needs to take pills, and I don't know how to give them.** As a matter of course, teach your puppy to take food off a spoon. Put a little of his favorite food on the end of a teaspoon and encourage him to eat it. At first he'll want to lick it off, but after several repetitions, he'll open his mouth. You can then scrape the food onto the back of his front teeth. Do this on a regular basis as a training exercise, and your puppy will readily take food from a spoon.

Now when you need to give him a pill, you can hide it in some food on the spoon and he'll willingly take it. You can put the pill into peanut butter, butter, sour cream, yogurt, meat, or anything your dog likes.

>> **My puppy eats stools when outside.** Various causes are attributed to this habit, but it's usually a sign that the food you're feeding your puppy isn't suitable for him. Pups eat stools to get undigested nutrients they're lacking in their own food. One way to stop the behavior is to keep the yard picked up. You also may want to take a look at the feeding suggestions in Chapter 4. Adding digestive enzymes can help.

TIP

Some dogs are partial to horse poop or cat poop. This behavior is objectionable to you, but it won't do Buddy any harm. With the Leave It command in Chapter 9, you should be able to stop it.

>> **My puppy constantly bites me when I handle him.** When the puppy mouths you too hard, yell "Ouch" in a loud tone of voice. Then distract the puppy with a toy. In most instances, it takes only a couple times for the puppy to catch on that this mouthing isn't acceptable behavior. Some puppies are more persistent than others, in which case you may need to take Buddy gently by the scruff of the neck and lift his front paws off the ground.

>> **Should I worm my puppy frequently?** Don't worm your puppy without first taking a fecal sample to your veterinarian to be tested. If your puppy has worms, your veterinarian will give you the appropriate medicine for that particular worm. Stay away from wormers in supermarkets or pet stores. Having your puppy ingest too many chemicals at a young age is dangerous, upsets his stomach, and makes him feel unwell. If you do find that he has worms and isn't feeling well, stop training until he feels better.

» **Is it safe to use flea and tick products with my puppy?** Wendy recommends a product called Wondercide, which is totally natural and safe for your puppy and adult dog. Besides fleas and ticks, it also protects your dog against mosquitoes. This company also has a product to treat your garden. Your veterinarian will give you her recommendations for flea and tick controls as well as heartworm preventions. Make an educated choice to keep your puppy healthy.

REMEMBER

Ticks can carry Lyme disease. If you live in an area where ticks are prevalent, be vigilant with your puppy, especially in wooded areas. The most common symptoms of Lyme disease include muscle aches and fatigue. Use a flea comb to look for ticks after your walks in grass and fields. Flea combs have very small teeth that are close together, and you should be able to examine your dog for any ticks that he may have picked up by combing him with a flea comb.

Chapter **7**

Surviving Your Puppy's Critical Growth Periods

Everyone wants a super puppy, one that's well behaved and listens to every word you say — a Lassie. Of course, heredity plays a role, but so does early upbringing and environment. From birth until maturity, your dog goes through a number of developmental, critical periods. The many scientists and behaviorists who've studied dog behavior over the last century have made important discoveries about a puppy's developmental periods and how they relate to his ability to grow into a well-adjusted pet. What happens or doesn't happen during these periods has a lasting effect on how your dog turns out, his ability to learn, his outlook on life, his behavior, and how he responds to your efforts to train him.

In this chapter, we explain the developmental periods your pooch will go through and how to begin training him according to the stage he's in. We also discuss how spaying and neutering can affect your dog and his trainability.

Understanding Your Puppy's Early Development

Puppies go through distinct critical periods in the first 12 weeks of life. What happens during this time influences not only their temperament but also their health and overall development. In the following sections, we discuss each of the puppy periods your pet will go through so you can begin training him appropriately.

Birth to 7 weeks: the Canine Socialization Period

The first puppy period is from birth to 49 days. During this time, the puppy needs his mother and the interaction with his littermates. He also needs to have interaction with humans. All these interactions are important because they lay the foundation for the puppy's future with his human family and what he may encounter as he grows.

WARNING

Be wary of obtaining a puppy who has been taken away from his mother prior to 7 weeks of age, because it not only deprives the puppy of important behavioral lessons but also can affect the puppy's future health. For example, the puppy obtains antibodies to many diseases by feeding from his mother. Every sip of milk is like a vaccine that protects the puppy for many weeks after he leaves the litter and is placed in his new home.

Between 3 to 7 weeks of age, the mother teaches her puppies basic doggy manners. She communicates to the puppies what's acceptable and what's unacceptable behavior. For instance, after the puppies' teeth have come in, nursing them becomes a painful experience, so she teaches them to take it easy. She does whatever it takes, such as growling, snarling, and even snapping, and she continues this lesson throughout the weaning process when she wants the puppies to leave her alone. After just a few repetitions, the puppies get the message and respond to a mere look or a curled lip from mother. The puppy learns dog language — or lip reading, as we call it — and bite inhibition, an important lesson for when he goes home with his new human family and a new mother to listen to. During the mother dog's training, the puppy will learn that there is an authority figure and what that authority looks like. These lessons will transfer to you more easily because of what the mother dog has taught her puppies. Without these lessons, by leaving the litter too young, the puppies will not recognize authority and they will think they are the center of the universe. This is very unfortunate for the new owners or you.

Besides learning from their mothers, puppies also learn from each other. While playing, tempers may flare because one puppy bites another too hard. The puppies discover from these exchanges what it feels like to be bitten and, at the same time, to inhibit biting during play. (See Figure 7-1.)

Photograph by Jane Kelso

FIGURE 7-1:
Puppies discover valuable lessons while playing.

REMEMBER

Puppies separated from their canine families before they've had the opportunity for these experiences with mother and littermates tend to identify more with humans than with other dogs. To simplify, they don't know they're dogs, and they tend to have their own set of problems, such as the following:

>> Aggression toward other dogs

>> Difficulty with housetraining

>> Separation anxiety

>> Excessive barking

>> Mouthing and biting their owners

>> Nervousness

>> An unhealthy attachment to humans

At about the 49th day of life, when the puppy's brain is neurologically complete, that special attachment between the dog and his new human owner, called *bonding*, takes place. Bonding is one of the reasons that the 49th day is the ideal time for puppies to leave the nest for their new homes.

WARNING

Bonding to people becomes increasingly difficult the longer a puppy remains with his mother or littermates. The dog also becomes more difficult to train. In addition, with delay, the puppy has the potential to experience built-in behavior problems, such as the following:

>> The pup may grow up being too dog oriented.

>> The pup probably won't care much about people.

>> The pup may be difficult to teach to accept responsibility for his own behavior.

>> The pup may be more difficult to train, including housetraining.

Getting to know everyone: Weeks 7–12 the Human Socialization Period

Your dog is a social animal. To become an acceptable pet, the pup needs to interact with you and your family as well as with other humans and dogs during the 7th through 12th weeks of life. If denied these opportunities, your dog's behavior around other people or dogs may be unpredictable — your dog may be fearful or perhaps even aggressive. For example, unless regularly exposed to children during this period, a dog may be uncomfortable or untrustworthy around them.

TIP

Socializing your puppy is critical if you want him to become a friendly adult dog. When your puppy is developing, expose him to as many different people as possible, including children and older people of all shapes, sexes, and sizes. Let him meet new dogs, too. Introduce him too to different surfaces — grass, carpet, wood floors, sidewalks, gravel, and so on. These early experiences will pay off big time when your dog grows up.

Your puppy needs the chance to meet and have positive experiences with those persons and activities that will play a role in his life. The following are just a few examples:

>> You're a relative who has visiting kids occasionally come by: Have your puppy meet children as often as you can.

>> You live by yourself but have friends that visit you: Make an effort to let your puppy meet other people, particularly members of the opposite sex.

>> You plan to take your dog on family outings or vacations: Introduce riding in a car.

You can set up all these encounters by taking him to the local park. Most people love to meet puppies. And he can get used to the ride on the way there!

A common way for people to greet a puppy or an adult dog is to pat it on top of the head, just as they do with children. Puppies and adult dogs don't like this form of greeting any better than kids do. Patting a dog on the head encourages jumping, the very behavior most owners don't want. Instead, stand up straight or kneel down, and then greet the puppy with a smile and a hello. Put the palm of your hand on his chest and calmly stroke it in a massaging motion. Doing so will calm him. When meeting a puppy or dog for the first time, slowly put the palm of your hand toward him and let him smell you.

Socialization with other dogs is equally important to socialization with humans and should be the norm rather than the exception. Puppies learn from other dogs but can only do so if they have a chance to spend time with them. Make it a point of introducing your young dog to other puppies and adult dogs on a regular basis. Many communities now have dog parks where dogs can interact and play together. If you plan to take your puppy to obedience class or dog shows or to use him in a breeding program, he definitely needs to have the chance to interact with other dogs (see Chapter 18). Time spent now is well worth the effort — it will build his confidence and make your job training him that much easier.

Socialization is important for Buddy at this time, but so is training him. Begin training your puppy as soon as you get him. The puppy will learn whether you teach him or not, so you may as well teach him what he needs to know. Start teaching the exercises listed in Part 3. At this age it's much easier to physically manipulate the puppy than after he has grown into an unruly teenager.

TIP

During this development period your puppy will follow your every footstep. Encourage this behavior by rewarding the puppy with an occasional treat, some petting, or a kind word. Taking advantage of your puppy's willingness to follow will make teaching the Come command that much easier (head to Chapter 10 for more details on this command).

Suddenly he's afraid: Weeks 8–12 the Fear Imprint Period

Weeks 8 through 12 are called the *fear imprint period*. During this period, any painful or particularly frightening experience leaves a more lasting impression on your pup than if it occurred at any other time in his life. If the experience is sufficiently traumatic, it could literally change your puppy's life.

TIP

During the fear imprint period, avoid exposing the puppy to traumatic experiences. When you need to take your puppy to the veterinarian, have the doctor give him a treat before, during, and after the examination to make the visit a pleasant experience. Although you need to stay away from stressful situations, do continue to train your puppy in a positive and nonpunitive way.

REMEMBER

During the first year's growth, you may see fear reactions at other times. Don't respond by dragging your puppy to the object that caused the fear. On the other hand, don't pet or reassure the dog either — you may create the impression that you approve of this fearful behavior. Rather, distract the puppy with a toy or a treat to get his mind off whatever scared him and go on to something pleasant. Practice some of the commands you've already taught him so he can focus on a positive experience. After a short time — sometimes up to two weeks — the fearful behavior will disappear.

Now he wants to leave home: Beyond 12 weeks: "Been there, done that"

Sometime between 4 and 8 months, your puppy begins to realize that there's a big, wide world out there. Up to now, every time you called, Buddy probably willingly came to you. But now he may prefer to wander off and investigate alone. Buddy is maturing and cutting the apron strings, which is normal. He's not being spiteful or disobedient; he's just becoming an adolescent.

While he's going through this phase, make sure you keep Buddy on a leash or in a confined area until he has learned to come when called. Otherwise, not coming when called becomes a pattern — annoying to you and dangerous to Buddy. If calling Buddy over and over again becomes a habit, breaking it will become difficult; prevention is the best cure. Teaching your dog to come when called (before he has developed the habit of running away) is easy. Practice calling him in the house, out in the yard, and at random times. Have a treat in your pocket to reinforce the behavior you want. (For more on teaching the Come command, check out Chapter 10.)

TIP

When you need to gather a wandering Buddy, don't, under any circumstances, play the game of chasing him. Instead, call his name in an excited tone of voice. If that doesn't work, run the other way and get Buddy to chase you. You also can kneel on the ground and pretend you've found something extremely interesting, hoping Buddy's curiosity brings him to you. If you have to, approach him slowly in an upright position, using a nonthreatening tone of voice until you can calmly take hold of his collar.

Your puppy also goes through teething during this period and needs to chew anything and everything. This chewing behavior is a physical need. Puppies have the irritating habit of going for shoes left out. If one of your favorite shoes is demolished, keep your cool. Look at it as a lesson for you to put your possessions out of reach. Scolding Buddy won't stop the need to chew, but it may cause him to fear and mistrust you.

Your job is to provide acceptable outlets for this need, such as chew bones and toys. Real dog bones from the butcher are some of dogs' favorites chew bones. A dog can't easily break them and they provide hours of entertainment. They also keep your dog's teeth clean. Kong toys (www.kongcompany.com) are another favorite, especially the hard rubber ones that are virtually indestructible and can be stuffed with peanut butter or yogurt They come in different sizes appropriate to the size of your dog and can keep most dogs busy for hours. Just be sure they're large enough that he can't accidentally swallow one.

WARNING

Stay away from soft and fuzzy toys. Chances are, your dog will destroy them and may ingest a part of them. Rawhide chew toys can be dangerous because they're often treated with chemicals and can become soft and gooey while chewing; therefore, the dog can swallow them and get them stuck in his intestines. If you do provide these toys for your pet, be sure to supervise him so he doesn't ingest pieces.

When Buddy is going through this stage, you may want to consider crating him when he's left alone. Doing so keeps him and your possessions safe, and both of you will be happy. Crating him during this growth spurt helps with his house-training, too. With all the chewing he does during his teething, accidents sometimes happen (chewing stimulates bowel movements in puppies). See Chapter 8 for more on housetraining.

The Terrible Twos: Managing the Adolescent from 4 Months to 2 Years

The adolescent stage of your dog's life, depending on the breed, takes place anywhere from 4 months to 2 years and culminates in sexual maturity. Generally, the smaller the dog, the sooner he matures. Larger dogs enter (and end) adolescence later in life.

Adolescence is a time when your cute little puppy can turn into a teenage monster. He starts to lose his baby teeth and his soft, fuzzy puppy coat. He goes through growth spurts and looks gangly either up in the rear or down in front; he's entering an ugly-duckling stage.

REMEMBER

Depending on the size of the dog, he achieves 40 to 70 percent of adult growth by the time he's 7 months old. If you haven't done so already, you'd better start training now, before the dog gets so big that you can't manage him. As Buddy begins to mature, he starts to display some puzzling behaviors as well as some perfectly normal but objectionable ones.

Because adolescence can be such a tricky time in a pup's life (and yours!), in the following sections, we provide some information to help make the transition as smooth as possible.

Surviving the juvenile flakies

The term *juvenile flakies* most accurately describes what's technically known as a second fear imprint period (refer to the earlier section "Suddenly he's afraid: Weeks 8–12" for more information on this period). Juvenile flakies are apprehension or fear behaviors that usually are short lived. They're caused by temporary calcium deficiencies and hormone development related to a puppy's periodic growth spurts.

REMEMBER

The timing of this event (or events) isn't as clearly defined as it is with the first fear imprint period, and it coincides with growth spurts; hence, it may occur more than once as the dog matures. Even though he may have been outgoing and confident before, your puppy now may be reluctant to approach someone or something new and unfamiliar. He also may suddenly be afraid of familiar people and things.

BEING PATIENT WITH THE FLAKIES

One day, when Wendy's Dachshund, Manfred, was 6 months old, he came into the kitchen after having been outside in the yard. There he noticed on the floor, near his water bowl, a brown paper grocery bag. He flattened, looked as though he'd seen a ghost, and tried to run back out into the yard.

If Manfred was going through a growth spurt at this time, which is normal at 6 months, he could've been experiencing a temporary calcium deficiency, which in turn would produce his fear reaction.

He'd seen brown paper grocery bags many times before, but this one was going to get him. Wendy reminded herself that he was going through the flakies and ignored the behavior. A few hours later, the behavior disappeared.

If you happen to observe a similar situation with your puppy, don't try to drag him up to the object in an effort to "teach" the puppy to accept it. If you make a big deal out of it, you create the impression that he has a good reason to be afraid of whatever triggered the reaction. Leave the puppy alone, ignore the behavior, and it will pass.

TECHNICAL STUFF

Fear of the new or unfamiliar is rooted in evolution. In a wild pack, after the pups become 8 to 10 months of age, they're allowed to go on a hunt. The first lesson they have to learn is to stay with the pack; if they wander off, they may get lost or into trouble. Apprehension or fear of the familiar also is caused by growth spurts. At this point in a puppy's life, hormones start to surge. Hormones can affect the calcium uptake in the body, and, coupled with growth, can be a difficult time for the growing puppy.

Blame it on the hormones: Understanding how hormones affect behavior

During the period from 4 months to a year, the male puppy's hormones surge to four times his adult level, and this surge can have important effects on his behavior. You usually can tell when he's entering this phase. The most obvious sign is that he stops listening to you. He also may try to dominate other dogs in the household or ones he meets outside. Fortunately, after this enormous surge, his hormones ultimately return to normal.

REMEMBER

Hormones drive behavior, which means that the intensity of behaviors increases in direct proportion to the amount of hormones coursing through his system.

TIP

Doing leadership exercises and training your puppy at this age is definitely a good idea. When Buddy experiences a surge of hormones during training, do some heeling or retrieving to get him back into the proper frame of mind.

A SAD FACT OF LIFE

The majority of dogs in animal shelters are delivered to those shelters at around 8 months of age, when they're no longer "cute" and have "stopped listening." Millions of dogs are surrendered annually because their owners didn't want to spend 10 to 15 minutes a day training them when they were young.

Although female puppies going through puberty may show similar traits, more often they show greater dependency on their owners. They follow their owners around, looking at them constantly, as if to say, "Something is happening to my body, but I don't know what. Tell me what to do." However, keep in mind that females are just as apt to show mounting behavior as males.

REMEMBER

During this time the necessity for training and protection increases. The freedom that the male puppy had before now becomes limited. The better trained he is, the easier this transition will be, but it requires a real commitment on your part. The female, in turn, needs to be protected during her heat cycle, which usually occurs every 6 months and lasts around 21 days. Her attraction is so potent that you may discover unwanted suitors around your house, some of whom may have come from miles away.

Meeting the mature adult when your dog finally grows up

No matter how much you wish that cute little puppy could remain as is, your pup is going to grow up. It happens anywhere from 1 to 4 years, depending on the breed. Smaller breeds will mature faster than larger breeds. If you trained Buddy as a younger dog, he'll now become the perfect pet you always wanted. Figure 7-2 shows a pup on the way to adulthood.

FIGURE 7-2:
Yes, your pup will grow up.

© John Wiley & Sons, Inc.

Spaying or Neutering to Help with Behavior and Training

Unless you intend to exhibit your dog in dog shows to get a championship or to breed the dog, you need to seriously consider neutering or spaying. However, current research shows that neutering too early affects structure as the dog ages. The correct age to think about neutering your dog is after the growth plates are intact, somewhere between 18 months and 3 years.

When an intact male becomes aware of a female in season anywhere in the immediate area, chances are he'll be oblivious to any commands you have taught him. View such situations as training opportunities — to remind Buddy that you still expect him to obey. After all, what better distraction is there? If you find you have difficulty controlling Buddy under such circumstances, see Chapter 5 for information on training equipment and Chapter 3 for more on the *adrenaline effect*. The *adrenaline effect* is when whatever your dog is doing affects his ability to "hear" you. A beagle pursuing a rabbit will not hear you call him. But a beagle in the house at dinner time will hear you every time you call. What equipment is needed to aid your call with each example is affected also. No leash or collar is needed inside at dinner time, yet a training collar and long leash is a must when Buddy is running after a rabbit outside.

In the following sections, we show you both the pros and cons of spaying or neutering your pooch, including the effect the procedures have on your pet.

Heeding the advantages

For both males and females, the advantages of altering your pet generally outweigh the disadvantages. For the male, the advantages of altering include the following:

>> Keeps him calm and less stressed around a female in season

>> Reduces the tendency to roam

>> Diminishes mounting behavior

>> Makes training easier

>> Helps to prevent marking behavior in the house

In short, he'll be easier to live with and easier to train. Neutering also curbs the urge to roam or run away. So if the front door is left open by accident, he won't go miles to find a female in season.

TECHNICAL STUFF

It isn't true that dogs that have been altered lose their protective instincts — it depends on the age when the dog was altered. Generally, dogs altered after a year of age retain their protective instincts.

If you spay your female, she, too, will stay closer to home. Perhaps even more important are these benefits:

>> You won't have to deal with the mess that goes with having her in season.

>> You won't have to worry about unwanted visitors camping on your property and lifting a leg against any vertical surface.

>> You won't have to worry about accidental puppies, which are next to impossible to place in good homes.

Finally, and most important in the context of training, she'll be more even-keeled, a distinct benefit.

Acknowledging the disadvantages

Altering changes the hormone level in a dog's body. Some dogs that are altered develop hormonal deficiencies that can produce arthritis and bone disease and can affect joint and bladder function. Researchers have specifically evaluated the effect on clinical orthopedic disease (hip dysplasia, elbow dysplasia, and cranial cruciate ligament disease), neoplasia (lymphosarcoma, mast cell tumor, osteosarcoma, hemangiosarcoma, and mammary cancer), urinary incontinence, and pyometra, according to studies stated in *AKC Canine Health Foundation* (February 2019).

The most common deficiency seen is hypothyroidism. It's thought that around 70 percent of all pure-bred dogs have hypothyroidism. Detected in dogs as young as 6 months of age and all the way up to the age of 8 and beyond, hypothyroidism requires a special blood test for diagnosis.

Hypothyroidism can cause these problems:

>> Dull, oily, thinning, and smelly coats

>> Increased shedding

>> Separation anxiety

>> Skin problems

>> A tendency to gain weight

REMEMBER

Regardless of these disadvantages, we recommend altering a dog that isn't going to be bred simply because altered dogs are so much easier to live with. However, remember, spaying or neutering too early also causes long-term problems. See the preceding section for the advantages of altering.

Knowing when to spay or neuter

If you decide to alter your dog, think about having the surgery after 18 months of age for both sexes.

TO BREED OR NOT TO BREED YOUR DOG? THAT'S THE QUESTION

Don't even contemplate breeding your dog unless

- Your dog is purebred and registered.

- You didn't get your dog from an animal shelter or pet store.

- You have at least a three-generation pedigree for your dog.

- Your dog has at least four titled dogs, such as conformation or working titles, in the last three generations.

- Your dog is certified free of genetic disorders applicable to the breed.

- Your dog conforms to the standard for its breed.

- Your dog has a stable temperament.

The correct reason to breed dogs is to better the breed. Breeding should never be done because it sounds fun or you want to make money. That always backfires. Health certificates, C-sections, vaccines, and health guarantees are all part of a good breeding program. Not to forget, feeding and nursing care of the mother dog and puppies is also very expensive. You should have potential puppy homes lined up before you breed, too; at least half of the puppies you expect should be lined up with forever homes before you decide to breed your dog.

Breeding dogs for the purpose of exposing your children to the miracle of birth is *not* a good idea. The world already has enough dogs that don't have homes, and finding homes for your puppies will be much more difficult than you think, if not impossible. Rent a DVD or look on YouTube if you want your children to understand the birthing process.

Depending on the breed and size of the female, she'll go into her first season any time after 7 months of age. For a Yorkshire Terrier, it's apt to be sooner, and for a giant breed, it's likely to be later, sometimes as late as 18 months of age.

If you want a dog to show more adult behaviors and take more responsibility — like being a protector or guard dog, training for competitive events, or working for a living — think about altering males or females between 18 months and 2 years of age.

REMEMBER

A dog that hasn't been neutered until after a year of age, or a female that has gone through two seasons, is generally easier to train for competitive events such as obedience or agility trials. Dogs have become fully grown by that time, are emotionally mature, have learned more adult behaviors, and can accept more responsibility.

3

Tackling Training Basics

Familiarize yourself with the few simple steps to potty training your dog. The most important part is your part and the role you play in the process. Discover how to successfully housetrain your dog; a few weeks of being inconvenienced gives you a dog trained for a lifetime plus a clean and soil-free home.

Train your dog to come to you when he's called. Before you can do that, he first needs to learn his name and what you mean for him to do when you say that name.

Teach you dog to go away from you on command, another important concept. Most people have never thought how useful this command can be.

Train Buddy on the fundamentals for all dogs — Sit, Lay Down, and Stay. Nothing can be simpler when you have a plan.

Teach Buddy how to walk politely beside you, which is the No. 1 behavior most people want from their dogs.

Instruct your dog to go to his bed, a dog bed nearby where he can lay and hang out with the family.

Make your home as safe as possible for your dog. Safety begins with openings to the outside such as doors and gates. Teaching your dog to not bolt out an opening can save his life.

Check out some common doggie do's and don'ts that every dog owner needs to know.

» Becoming housetrained requires three things to know

» Setting up a feeding and elimination schedule

» Dealing with accidents

» Exploring an alternative to crate training

Chapter **8**

The Ins and Outs of Housetraining

As with any training, some dogs catch on more readily to housetraining than others. As a general rule, most dogs don't present a problem, provided that you do your part. To speed along the process, we strongly recommend that you use a crate or similar means of confinement.

Dogs consider crates their dens. Because dogs are den animals, dens give dogs the feeling of safety, coziness, security, and comfort. A crate is your dog's bedroom inside of your house. A crate is also his home away from home when you travel, and it provides safety for both of you when he's with you in the car. The closest comparison to leaving your untrained dog in a crate would be as if you were told to go back to bed for a few hours and then promised evening entertainment when everybody returned home later. Sounds good, doesn't it? And here's a book (chew bone) in case you wake up and need something to occupy your attention.

Crates ideally are solid airline-type crates rather than open wire crates. The solid sides add to the den feeling and concept whereas a wire crate forces the dog to be out in the open and can actually cause him more stress. Humans may view a solid, dark crate as prison, but not to a dog who is instinctively a den animal. Confinement is security to a dog. Most puppies look for spots to nap under such as the coffee table or behind the furniture. Dogs are trying to reproduce the den environment. A solid crate works wonders as a den.

This chapter covers the keys to successful housetraining:

>> Appropriately using a crate or X-pen

>> Setting a schedule for feeding and exercising and sticking to that schedule even on weekends — at least until your dog is housetrained and mature

>> Practicing vigilance, consistency, and patience until your dog is trained

REMEMBER

If you've obtained an adult dog from a shelter or other source, he may not be housetrained. The rules for housetraining an adult dog are the same as for a puppy, but the process likely will go much more quickly. The adult dog's ability to control elimination is obviously much better than a puppy's. The things you must watch for are surface preferences and the ability to hold elimination. Dogs who have lived outdoors all their lives may never eliminate in the house because of grass and dirt preferences. But they also may eliminate at will, because they never had to hold it before, ever. This chapter offers advice for all tendencies.

Helping Buddy Get Used to His Crate

No matter whether Buddy is a puppy or a new adult dog you adopted, crate training Buddy provides peace of mind for you and a safe place for your dog when he needs some peace and quiet and wants to get away from the hubbub of family life.

To help get Buddy comfortable with his crate, follow these steps:

1. **Set up the crate in the family room and leave it open, which allows Buddy to investigate it.**

   Bring a container of treats over and plan to spend some play time around the crate.

2. **To get him to go inside, toss a treat or two in the crate and allow Buddy to reach in and eat them.**

   You may need to have the treats land just inside the door but gradually have them land farther toward the back. Allow him to eat the treats and come out on his own. Don't shut the door yet.

3. **To help him accept the door being shut, toss another treat into the crate and slowly swing the door shut, but don't latch it; just praise him for being inside and eating his treat.**

Open the crate door and say "Okay" as your release word and let him come out. At this point introduce a command for getting in the crate. You can use any command you want but be consistent. Here are a few good choices:

- Get in

- Kennel up

- Crate crate

4. **To train not coming out until you've given permission, say "Get in" as you toss a cookie in the crate.**

Doing so introduces the concept that you own the crate and the door of the crate, and therefore the passage through the door is yours, too. Hence, Buddy won't come charging out of his crate but rather politely will wait for your command to exit.

5. **Swing the door closed, but hold onto the door because you won't be latching it just yet.**

When Buddy is at the door, slightly open the crate an inch and then close it again. The visual pressure, not actual pressure of the door coming closed again toward Buddy, will stop any forward motion out of the crate.

The point is not to allow Buddy to burst out of his crate. He should politely wait for you to say "Okay" as his release word to exit the crate. As you continue to practice, slightly opening the crate, then closing it again, he'll start to respect the opening and even look up at you instead of inching out of the door. Smile and say "Okay." This command will let him out of the crate, and you can praise him.

REMEMBER

You also can feed Buddy in the crate to make the crate experience even more positive. Place his bowl in front of the crate and let him eat. The next time you feed him, place the food just inside the crate. With every successive meal, put the bowl farther inside the crate until it's at the far end. Leave the door open as he eats, because feeding him in the crate with the door open is just one more way of teaching Buddy how wonderful his crate is. Plus if you have more than one dog, feeding him in the crate gives him a place to eat without worrying about protecting his food dish. Take a look at Figure 8-1 to see a dog enjoying a meal in his crate.

TIP

Be sure to give Buddy something to occupy his attention when you leave. Interactive toys stuffed with treats or a Kong with treats inside are a wonderful way to distract him should he be awake during his time in the crate. Usually he'll sleep, learning your routine, while you're gone.

Balance crate time with energy outlets because exercise, training, walks, and so on are important to burn off the energy that he has, especially if he has spent a lot of time in his crate while you're away.

FIGURE 8-1:
Feeding a puppy
in a crate.

© John Wiley & Sons, Inc.

REMEMBER

How long can you ultimately leave Buddy in his crate unattended? That depends on your dog and your schedule. Adult dogs can stay in a crate for up to four to six hours. Puppies can't last that long, though. Over the course of a 24-hour period, puppies need to eliminate more frequently than adult dogs. A puppy's ability to control elimination increases with age, at the rate of about one hour per month starting the count at 2 months of age. Until he's 6 months of age, don't expect a puppy to last for more than four hours during the day without needing to eliminate. When sleeping, most puppies can last through the night.

Training a Dog to Eliminate Outside

The following sections examine the three factors that are crucial for Buddy to know when you're training him to eliminate outside. Buddy needs to know when to hold it and when to go, plus he needs to know you'll be trustworthy to allow him outside often enough to allow him to eliminate when he needs to go. These are the big three factors that teach a dog to be housetrained.

Hold elimination when inside the house

When training Buddy to eliminate outside, the most important lesson is that he understands he needs to hold elimination when he's inside the house. Go here but not there is a huge concept. It can be taught early in the whelping box with the mother dog and the breeder, but not all dogs have that early training opportunity. So it's up to you now.

When you're home and Buddy is awake and with you, keep him confined in the room with you. A properly trained puppy who learned that there is one place to live in and one place to potty in will wander off to a different area to eliminate. Even though holding it is the goal, the fact that he knows to go to a lesser-used area of the house or room is proper knowledge in which you can capitalize. Keep him close to you so you can watch him and make sure he doesn't slip out to eliminate. You also can close the door to the room you're in with your puppy or you can use a baby gate to close off the room.

After you have your puppy home or you get Buddy as an older dog, a crate is the best tool to teach him to hold his elimination. Refer to the "Helping Buddy Get Used to His Crate" section earlier in this chapter. When you aren't able to supervise Buddy or when you're leaving the house, the baby sitter is the crate. Buddy will sleep while you're gone, which is the goal. When you return, take him outside to eliminate.

REMEMBER

The leash is another great device to help you teach a puppy or new dog to hold elimination. Use the leash inside the house as an umbilical cord to keep him tethered to you until you've established a routine with Buddy and you can read his need to eliminate. If he's on leash, he'll never be more than 6 feet away from you and you can monitor his need to eliminate.

TAG-TEAM TRAINING WITH MOTHER DOG

We always say there is no better dog trainer than another dog, and the best trainer is the mother dog. Allow her to teach her lessons to her litter.

If Buddy is a puppy, do everything you can to see how he was raised while still with his litter. Even as early as only a few weeks old, while still with the mother dog in the whelping box, puppies learn that there are two places in their lives:

- One where they sleep, eat, and play

- One where they potty

These areas aren't the same place. The mother dog will usually try to set this distinction if given the opportunity.

The area where the puppies are raised should be large enough for the number of puppies in the litter and the breed that they're to allow for two areas. The litter should stay together at least until 7 weeks, longer in some cases. Your new puppy has a lot to learn from his mother dog as well as socialization from his littermates.

TIP

When you keep your new dog on a leash tethered to you, keep a chew bone handy to offer something correct to chew on rather than unwittingly allowing him to find something of yours to destroy. Doing so is another benefit of using the leash to train your dog inside of the home.

Know why he's outside — to eliminate

Teaching your dog why you're both outside is super important to eliminate. Why are you both outside? Look at it from your dog's point of view:

>> **Inside:** Your attention is about 95 percent on your life, working on your computer, watching TV, reading, talking, sleeping, whatever you like to do, whereas 5 percent of your attention is on your dog. What is he up to? Oh, he's sleeping or chewing on a bone. What a good dog. You don't want to interrupt him.

>> **Outside:** This is the reverse. Five percent of your attention is on your life: your yard or the weather and 95 percent of your attention is on your dog, playing together, sniffing the grass, walking around interacting, and so on. The dog is having fun enjoying all of your attention, but then he eliminates and you go back inside where you go back to your life. In other words, the dog's fun ends.

If you were the dog, what would you have learned? The fun ends when you eliminate, so don't eliminate if you're having fun outside with your owner. Of course, that's the last thing you want him to learn, but indeed that's the lesson you accidently taught.

REMEMBER

To train your dog to eliminate when he's outside, you need to reverse these percentages. When you're outside with your dog, watch him and don't ignore him. Avoid the temptation to play with him. Instead quietly stroll around to encourage him to sniff and then eliminate. Eliminating first is the most important thing you want to teach your dog — hurry up and go potty. When he does eliminate, then the fun can start. Praise, play, chase, treat, pick him up if possible, and make a huge party out of his elimination. Then and only then should you go back inside — after the party. Or even then and only then should you start your walk with him. The walk is the party, and the elimination is the purpose of going outside. Dogs love to take walks. If you walk first, you're teaching your dog never to potty on a walk, because when you potty, the walk ends. Always look at it from your dog's perspective.

Make sure you go outside with him to eliminate, no matter whether your yard is fenced or the weather is bad. Dogs are pack animals and love being with people. If you put your dog outside, most dogs will sit by the door waiting for you to open the door to come out and join them until trained to do otherwise. Dogs don't just empty because they're outside. During the housetraining process, you need to know when your dog is empty and when he isn't, when he actually went potty and when he hasn't. If he hasn't eliminated and you let him in the house, he'll empty inside because he truly does need to eliminate and was holding it, waiting for you to come out and join him. Go outside with him every time and keep track if he has gone or not. As your dog becomes trained and trustworthy, going outside won't need to be the case forever. You may be inconvenienced during this time of his training, but you'll eventually have a fully trustworthy and trained dog for the rest of his life.

Prove to Buddy that you're trustworthy to take him outside

Buddy needs to trust you'll take him outside so he can take care of business. You being trustworthy can be the hardest part because you need to be attentive. Mary Ann recommends a kitchen timer or the alarm app on your phone. You need to actually be reminded to take your dog outside often enough.

Most dogs quickly learn to hold elimination for eight hours at night and then another eight hours while you're work and they're in the crate (as soon as they're old enough to hold it that long), but they can't then hold it for another eight hours while you're home and the household is active.

When you're home and Buddy has access to water and activity, his metabolism will speed up, producing urine and the need to have a bowel movement. That's when the alarm is important. When Buddy is new to you and you're home and all are awake, take him out every 45 minutes because small bladders need emptied often. As we already mentioned, the night time is different and Buddy will learn to hold it longer, sooner, because all is quiet and his metabolism slows.

As Buddy gets older, you can keep adding 15 minutes a week to your timer, but don't be too quick to make it more than 90 minutes when everyone is home and the puppy is active. You can always adjust it, but having that alarm can help you remember to take him outside.

Special care is required when it's raining or is cold because many dogs, particularly those with short hair, don't like to go out in the wet any more than you do. Make sure your puppy actually eliminates before you bring him back into the house. If not, it will be as if you have a loaded puppy walking around in your house. Take him out again and keep him on leash in the house if necessary or even return him to his crate if you can't watch him. He has to go, even if it's raining. You don't want to find eliminations in your house, so be alert.

REMEMBER

Housetraining can be inconvenient, but if you use your crate, baby gate, leash, and timer, you can do it in no time. Just be diligent and consistent. A few months of being inconvenienced will give you a lifetime of a housetrained dog you can trust.

Establishing a Regular Feeding and Elimination Schedule

Being diligent with Buddy's feeding schedule and his ensuing elimination schedule will make housetraining go much smoother. Keep the following schedule in mind:

>> **From 7 weeks to 4 months of age:** Puppies need to be fed four times a day. Set a time to feed the puppy that's convenient for you, and aim to feed at the same time every day. Depending on your schedule, you may establish a comfortable routine of feeding at 7 a.m., noon, 5 p.m., and 9 p.m. This schedule works well if you go to bed around 11 p.m. and can take the puppy out before you retire for the night. Adjust the schedule to the time you normally get up in the morning.

>> **From 4 to 7 months:** Three daily meals are appropriate. From then on, feed twice a day. Feeding frequent small meals keeps your puppy calm, helps him grow evenly, and controls the time when he relieves himself. Also give your puppy a dog biscuit before bedtime to help him sleep through the night.

>> **Older than 7 months:** For many adult dogs, feeding two meals a day is best because it satisfies hunger through the day. Historically some people choose to feed once a day, so talk to your veterinarian to help you decide what is best for you and your dog.

REMEMBER

Feed the right amount. Loose stools are a sign of overfeeding; straining and dry stools are signs of underfeeding or a poor diet. Be sure to keep Buddy's diet constant and feed the same kind of food at every meal. Abrupt changes in food may cause digestive upsets that won't help your housetraining efforts. See Chapter 4 for more feeding options.

WARNING

For the sake of convenience, you may be tempted to put Buddy's meal in a large bowl and leave it for him to nibble on as he sees fit, a practice called *self-feeding.* Although self-feeding is convenient for you, for purposes of housetraining, don't do it. You won't be able to keep track of when and how much Buddy eats. You won't be able to time his intake with his need to eliminate. Don't prolong mealtimes, either: After ten minutes, pick up the dish and put it away. Feeding meals is healthier for your dog, and it helps you know his eating habits. You need to know if he goes off his food when he is sick.

REMEMBER

Have fresh water available at all times during the day when Buddy is outside of the crate. Two hours before your bedtime, remove his water dish so he can last through the night without having to make a trip outside. As an adult, most dogs won't drink at night. So not having water in the bedroom is a practice that can continue into adulthood.

If you're following a regular feeding routine, you're promoting a regular elimination routine, too. Puppies' biological clocks are astonishingly consistent. A puppy usually has a bowel movement several times a day and urinates perhaps six to eight times. Same goes for an adult — dogs will eat, then eliminate. Dogs will drink, then eliminate shortly thereafter. Dogs are routine animals and will hold it to specific times if your routine is consistent enough; they'll become comfortable with the same routine themselves.

Take Buddy to his toilet area after waking up, shortly after eating or drinking, and after he has played or chewed. Of course, you need to be aware of his unique elimination needs, too. Some puppies need to eliminate more than once in a relatively short period of time. In fact, it isn't uncommon for a dog to eliminate first thing in the morning and then again about a half hour later, because of his metabolism speeding up after the long night of rest and quiet. You'll discover your dog's routine by being aware and by being an active part of the solution.

An easy way to become aware of Buddy's elimination routine is by keeping a notebook or chart each time he goes potty. When you see your puppy sniffing and circling, take note! He's letting you know that he's looking for a place to go. Take him out to his toilet area so he doesn't have an accident in the house.

Designating a Regular Toilet Area

No matter whether you live in a house or an apartment, you need to start by selecting a toilet area in your yard, along a path, or in a park. Always take Buddy to that spot when you want him to eliminate. The designated place shouldn't be too far from the house. Walk directly to that area and then ignore him until he has eliminated.

If you and Buddy live in an apartment or condo, you probably have to jump through a variety of hoops, including taking elevators and stairs, to take out Buddy. Moreover, if you're mobility impaired, going outside with Buddy may be a real challenge.

The easiest way to housetrain an apartment or condo dog is to first follow the regiment by using a crate. If you're using a pee pad and tray (available at pet stores or online) in the apartment or condo, take him to the tray, just as you would take him outside. Usually pee pads aren't recommended unless you have a tiny toy breed. Even then, going outside is so much better, but pee pads and trays can work for you, if you aren't able to take Buddy out of your apartment (see Figure 8-2 for an example of a potty tray). When training to a potty tray, do the same thing as was discussed in the previous section. Take Buddy to the potty tray just as you'd take him outside. Keep a timer going to remind yourself to direct him to his potty tray so you don't let too much time go by without taking him to his pee pad.

FIGURE 8-2:
A potty tray to hold pee pads.

BALTO: AN EXAMPLE OF A STAR HOUSETRAINING PUPIL

First thing in the morning, Robert takes his 12-week-old Yorkie puppy, Balto, out of his crate and straight outside to his toilet area. Fifteen minutes after Balto's morning meal, Robert takes him out again. Robert then crates Balto and leaves for work.

On his lunch break, Robert goes home to let Balto out to relieve himself, and he plays with him for a few minutes. He then feeds Balto and, just to make sure, takes him out once more. For the afternoon, Robert crates Balto again until he returns. When he gets home, he walks and feeds Balto and allows him to spend the rest of the evening in the house where Robert can keep an eye on him and train him. This is an important part of the day for Robert because Balto needs lots of socialization and Robert gives Balto all he needs. Before bedtime, Robert takes Balto to his toilet area one more time and then crates him for the night in the room where Robert sleeps.

When Balto turns 7 months old, Robert will drop the noontime feeding. From that age on, most dogs need to go out only immediately upon waking (or soon afterward) in the morning, once during the late afternoon, a few times in the evening, and once again before bedtime.

REMEMBER

No matter where you live — in the city, in a neighborhood, or in the country — you also need to pick up after your dog. Even in your own yard, unless you have oodles of land, you need to pick up after him, for obvious sanitary reasons. And don't let him do his business in a neighbor's yard; to have good neighbors, you need to be a good neighbor.

TIP

You also may want to teach Buddy a command, such as Hurry Up, so you can speed up the process when necessary. Time the command to just before he starts and then lavishly praise when he has finished. After several repetitions, Buddy will associate the command with having to eliminate. The Hurry Up command is useful when you're traveling with Buddy, and it gets him used to eliminating on leash.

When Accidents Happen — Knowing What to Do

No matter how conscientious and vigilant you are, your puppy will have accidents. Housetraining accidents may be simple mistakes or may indicate a physical problem. The key to remember is that, as a general rule, dogs want to be clean. Also remember that accidents are just that — accidents. Your dog didn't do it on purpose. The following sections give you tips on what to do when accidents happen.

Avoiding punishment

When Buddy has an accident in the house, don't call him to you to punish him. It's too late. If you do punish your dog under these circumstances, it won't help your housetraining efforts, and you'll make him wary of wanting to come to you (thus hampering his learning of the Come command).

A popular misconception is that the dog knows "what he did" because he looks "guilty." Absolutely not true! He has that look because, from prior experience, he knows that when you happen to come across a mess, you get mad at him. He has learned to associate a mess with your response. He hasn't made — and can't make — the connection between the urge that caused the mess and your anger. Discipline after the fact is the quickest way to undermine the relationship you're trying to build with your dog.

Dogs are smart, but they don't associate what happened some time ago with belated consequences. When you come home from work and yell at your dog for having an accident in the living room, all you're doing is letting him know that you're upset on your return home. This reaction will cause undue stress on Buddy as he worries about your return home each day.

TIP

Instead, change the freedom you've given too early to Buddy and return to using the crate, not as a punishment, but as a training tool, to teach him to hold elimination longer. You can also go back to shortening the length of time you're gone. As soon as you stop using the crate, you can still come home at lunch to allow for an extra outing for elimination. Be fair and kind to your dog; remember you're a big part of your dog's success.

Dealing with the accidents

Depending on the situation, you should handle accidents in different ways. Consider the following:

>> **When you come upon a belated accident:** Keep calm and put your dog out of sight so he can't watch you clean up (seeing you clean up attracts him to the spot). Refer to the next section for more on cleaning.

>> **When you catch your dog in the act:** If you see Buddy squatting in the living room, sharply call his name and clap your hands. If he stops, take him to his toilet area. If he doesn't, let him finish and don't get mad. Don't try to drag him out, because that will make your clean-up job that much more difficult. Until your puppy is reliable, don't let him have the run of the house unsupervised.

Regressions in housetraining do occur. Regressions after 7 months of age may be a sign that your dog is ill. If accidents persist, take him to your vet for a checkup.

TIP

When traveling with your dogs, make it a point to keep to the regular feeding schedule and exercise routine as closely as possible to the same routine you have at home. Sticking to customary daily rhythm prevents digestive upsets that can lead to accidents.

Cleaning accidents

To adequately clean an area used by mistake inside, use an enzymatic cleaner to neutralize any urine odor. All sorts are available on the market. Buy one that neutralizes as it cleans. Soak up any urine with paper towels or a rag before you clean. Then saturate the full extent of the area with your cleaner and soak it up again.

Having a good rug shampooer is a good idea. Dogs will often have accidents or illness during their lifetime, and shampooers are wonderful appliances to clean up diarrhea, vomit, mud, or spills that you also make, especially that red wine.

Using an Exercise Pen for Housetraining

Although a puppy can last in his crate for the night when he's asleep, you can't leave a puppy in his crate for purposes of housetraining for longer than four hours at a time during the day. Your puppy will soil his crate, which definitely isn't a habit you want to establish.

If your schedule doesn't allow you to keep an eye on Buddy during the day or come home to let the puppy out in time, the alternative is an exercise pen, or X-pen. An X-pen (see Figure 8-3) is intelligent confinement and uses the same principle as a crate, except that it's bigger and has no top. An X-pen also can be used outdoors.

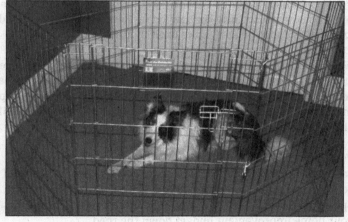

FIGURE 8-3: An X-pen is another form of containment.

© John Wiley & Sons, Inc.

First, you need to acquire an X-pen that's appropriate for the size of your dog. For a dog the size of a Labrador, the X-pen needs to be 10 square feet. For a smaller dog, 6 square feet should be plenty. Set up the X-pen where the puppy will be confined during your absence. If your dog is a super athlete who either climbs over or jumps out of the X-pen, you need to cover the pen with a piece of plywood or pegboard.

To get your dog comfortable in his X-pen, follow the same procedure as you did when introducing him to his crate (see "Helping Buddy Get Used to His Crate," earlier in this chapter). When Buddy is feeling at home in the X-pen and you're ready to leave him for the day, cover one-third of the area with pee pads. Buddy will get the hint and eliminate on the pee pads. Cover one-third of the remaining area with a blanket, adding some interactive toys or a biscuit. Finally, leave one-third uncovered.

As he gets older and his ability to control the elimination process improves, gradually reduce the area covered with pee pads until you can remove it altogether. Because a dog's natural desire is to keep his den clean, the process should be completed by the time he is 6 months of age.

Leave while he's occupied with his toys or the biscuit. Don't make a big deal out of leaving — simply leave.

Some people try to rig up confinement areas by blocking off parts of a room. Theoretically, doing so works, but it does permit Buddy to chew the baseboard, corners of cabinets, or anything else he can get his teeth on. You may want to confine your dog to part of a room with baby gates. This option works well for some people and some dogs, but remember, confinement in a small room allows access to the room and potential destruction to the room. Lots of chew toys are a must! Dogs have a second chewing stage around 9 months of age. That's when the adult back teeth set into the jaw bone. Keep your dog confined until older than 12 months, but to be safe, crate until 18 months of age.

WARNING

Whatever barrier you decide to try, don't use an accordion-type gate — he could stick his head through it and possibly strangle himself. Also, leaving a dog on a concrete surface isn't a good idea. Something about concrete impedes housetraining; many dogs don't understand why it can't be used as a toilet area. Concrete also wreaks havoc on the elbows of large breeds.

TIP

You'll find that, in the long run, your least expensive option — as is so often the case — is the right way from the start. Don't be penny-wise and pound-foolish by scrimping on the essentials at the risk of jeopardizing more expensive items. Splurging for an X-pen or a good solid crate now will probably save you money on your home improvement budget down the road.

DOING YOUR DOODY

Being a good dog neighbor means not letting Buddy deface the property of others, including eliminating in their yards. When Buddy's got to go, use only areas specifically designed for dog elimination. Even diehard dog lovers object to other dogs leaving their droppings on their lawn, the streets, and similar unsuitable areas. They also object to having their shrubbery or other vertical objects on their property doused by Buddy when he lifts his leg. If Buddy must potty in someone's yard, you need to be ready for poop-scooping duty. Always carry a bag to pick up after your dog. After all, part of responsible dog ownership is cleaning up after him. Don't let Buddy become the curse of your neighborhood. Do unto others . . . .

Chapter **9**

Focusing on Some Basic Training Commands

S tarting to train the basics is when the fun really begins. Training requires Buddy's focus on you, and he needs to know a few basic words that lead to all future training. This chapter covers getting Buddy to focus on you and how you can praise him for his work while he's working and after he's released. The relationship you have with Buddy is already starting to develop and as you continue to work together as a team, you'll be the coach and Buddy will be the team player.

Training for Attention: Praise Versus Petting

To train your dog you must have his attention. Without it, you can't teach him anything. How to get his attention requires a leash and some good food, a big smile on your face, and lots of nice words of praise from you.

Easier said than done, right? A great way to get his attention is to decipher between giving praise and petting and how you can incorporate praise into your training plan.

Understanding the difference between the two

As you continue training your dog, a very important distinction is between praise and petting. Keep the following in mind to help:

>> **Praise** is happy words said with a smile, which makes your dog's tail wag and him look at you. In other words, you *say* praise. Your dog responds with a wiggle and a look, which means he's working or doing what you asked him to do. You give praise while Buddy is doing a command you gave him.

>> **Petting** is *touching* your dog and massaging his ears, head, or body. You pet after he is done working and you've released him from his command with an "Okay" release word. Petting is the party you have after you say the release word.

Petting in general is distracting to your dog and can change the dynamics between the two of you. You don't want to be seen as working for him, being his massage therapist because you're petting him. Instead by using verbal praise while he's working for you, it's pleasing to your dog and something for which strives.

For example, you command Sit and help him get into a sitting position. You then *verbally praise* him and get your dog to wag his tail and look at you, pleased with himself. Then you say "Okay" and move your dog out of his sitting position by stepping forward, petting and partying with him, and giving him a massage and rubdown.

REMEMBER

You give praise while he works. You pet after he's done doing each command.

Using Okay to release from work

Every command must have an end command. For example, "Buddy, do this" until you're released with the Okay command. This is the basis for all training used in this book. You teach Buddy who is in charge with this concept, such as "Here is what Down means, now hold the position until you're released with the Okay command.

Teaching Okay is easy. Just follow these steps:

1. **Standing next to your dog on leash, say "Okay" in an excited, happy voice and take a few forward steps.**

   Reach for your dog and start petting him, which we call: partying with your dog.

2. **Repeat and review.**

You can also use a treat at the same time to help motivate his enthusiasm. The important part of this command is to make Okay all about you and your dog. Saying Okay is fun because you play together for a bit. The work is over, and now you've released Buddy. Always step forward a few steps, moving your dog out of position and connect with him by petting him. Party with your dog.

Practice getting your dog's attention

As you practice the Okay release word, Buddy's focus on you is the end result of that exercise. You want your dog's attention to train him. Buddy needs to be attentive to you and try to understand what you're asking of him. By starting with praise and petting and the Okay release word, you're well on your way to gaining Buddy's attention and joy of working together as a team.

You can help get your dog's attention with food after the release word, but use it wisely. You should never try and find a dog's mouth or to chase him down to eat a treat. If he doesn't care about a treat, forget it and don't chase him to give him the food, this would be rewarding his non-attention to you.

The best way to offer a treat is in your open hand with the treat laying in your palm or on your fingers. Figure 9-1 shows the correct way to offer a treat to your dog. The open hand allows your dog to gently take the treat from you without biting it out of your fingers.

Using the Yes command

Practice giving a treat with a Yes command. The word *yes* means perfection — the moment your dog is absolutely correct when learning a new lesson. You say "Yes," which means a treat is soon to follow. Practice this routine a dozen times until your dog looks for the treat after you say "Yes." Such practice prepares your dog for future training. To do so, follow these steps:

1. **Look at your dog, and when he looks at you, say "Yes" and give him a treat.**

2. **Say "Okay" to release him and pet him.**

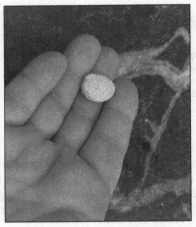

FIGURE 9-1:
Offer your dog a treat with an open hand.

© John Wiley & Sons, Inc.

3. **Stand still again and wait for him to look at you; when he does, say "Yes" and give him a treat.**

4. **Release with "Okay" and pet him.**

Practicing Name Recognition

You have probably said your dog's name a thousand times a day in the past. Now it's important that you're aware that his name is a command. His name means: "Look at me, move toward me, and see what I want you to do. Basically stop what you're doing and come to me." For a dog to know his name is a crucial lesson. Your dog's name means something, so don't say it and expect nothing from your dog. Show him what you want. Don't keep saying it over and over again. Rather, teach him that when you say his name, he's supposed to come to you and look at you.

REMEMBER

He should love his name and get excited when he hears it. Always use his name as a good thing and never as a precursor to punishment.

These sections explain how you can teach your dog his name.

Sequence 1: Having Buddy move toward you when he hears his name

The purpose of this step is for him to look at you and move in. Follow these steps:

1. **With Buddy on leash, walk around.**

   Don't let Buddy notice you. Move slowly around.

2. **Say "Buddy" and start walking backward while reeling in the leash.**

   As you walk backward and you reel in the leash, he'll start moving toward you.

3. **Say "Yes" and offer him a treat while you praise him.**

4. **Say "Okay" and pet him.**

5. **Repeat.**

After he has mastered this first sequence, add a freebie response to the treat. *Freebie* means that you don't actually use a verbal command yet, but by moving your hand with the treat in it you get a freebie response. More than likely you'll get a response from the dog that you want. By moving the treat upward as Buddy gets to the treat, he'll look up at your hand and he may sit. This is the freebie: getting a Sit yet not giving a command for it.

REMEMBER

Here you're concentrating on teaching Buddy what you expect from him when you say his name. You want him to immediately come toward you and ideally sit when he arrives. The important thing at this moment in his training is for him to learn to come when you use his name.

Now repeat the previous sequence with the freebie added at the end of Step 3. Praise him whether he sits or not. See if you get the freebie sit, without a sit command. Say "Okay," pet him, and repeat.

Sequence 2: Adding Come after his name

The steps in this sequence add the command that he's already doing, moving in to you after you say his name. Fundamentally you always want the individual whose name you say to bring his attention to you. This is true of your dog as well. Follow these steps:

1. **With Buddy on leash, walk around.**

   Don't let Buddy notice you. Move slowly around.

2. **Say "Buddy, Come" and start walking backward while reeling in the leash.**

3. **When he comes, say "Yes" and offer him a treat, lifting the treat slightly as he gets close to your hand.**

4. **Praise him whether he sits or not.**

   See if you get the freebee sit, without a Sit command.

5. **Say "Okay" and pet him.**

Praise him whether he's sitting or no.

6. **Repeat.**

Sequence 3: Making Sit mandatory

After he gets good at the name game, it's time to make the Sit a requirement and not just a freebie. Do Steps 1 and 2 the same. Then add the following:

1. **Say "Sit" and offer him a treat slightly lifting the treat as he gets close to your hand.**

2. **Say "Yes" as he sits.**

Help him, if necessary, by lifting his collar with one hand and tucking his tail with the other hand.

TIP

3. **Say "Okay" and pet him.**

4. **Repeat.**

Well done. Practice until it becomes second nature for you and your dog.

Teaching Your Dog the Touch Command

Touch is an easy command to teach that Buddy should know and understand for many reasons. The purpose of the Touch game is that your dog should move toward you, look at you, and allow you to touch him. Never should your dog avoid your touch. Use the Touch" command anytime you want your dog to move with you and/or toward you. Just follow the sequences in these sections to teach your dog this command.

Sequence 1: Getting Buddy to move toward you

The steps in this sequence get Buddy to move toward you:

1. **Put a treat in the palm of your hand snuggly between two of your fingers and have your hand flat like a plate as in Figure 9-2.**

2. **Show your palm to your dog a few inches from his nose, so he has to step toward it.**

   Your hand holding a treat between the fingers is referred to as *being loaded*. Don't move your hand toward your dog. Make sure your dog has to move toward your hand.

3. **Say "Touch."**

4. **As your dog moves toward your hand to get the treat, say "Yes" and allow him to get the treat from between your fingers.**

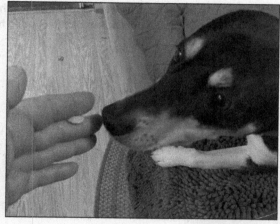

FIGURE 9-2: Offer the treat between two fingers with your hand flat.

© John Wiley & Sons, Inc.

Sequence 2: Increasing the distance Buddy needs to move toward you

This sequence increases the space that Buddy must move toward you:

1. **Hold your loaded hand a few feet not just inches, from your dog and say "Touch."**

   Your dog now has to walk to your hand to get the treat.

2. **Say "Yes" and allow him to get the treat from between your fingers.**

3. **Release with "Okay" and praise.**

Sequence 3: Not offering treat in the flat Touch hand

In this sequence, you don't have any treat in your Touch hand.

1. **With a few treats in your other hand, hold the treats ready to use close to your waist, as if that hand were a cup and then offer your free empty hand, flat like a plate as before (see Figure 9-3).**

2. **Say "Touch" and make sure your dog moves toward your hand, not you toward the dog.**

3. **When he noses your empty hand, say "Yes" and then with that hand, the touched hand, reach up and take a treat out of the cupped hand.**

4. **Give the treat to your dog and say "Okay."**

5. **Repeat over and over again.**

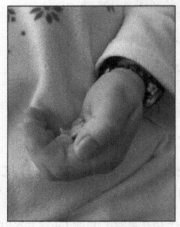

FIGURE 9-3:
Hold the treats in your other hand as if it were a cup of treats.

© John Wiley & Sons, Inc.

Sequence 4: Moving the touch hand in different positions

In the steps of this sequence you move around and your hand moves around. Buddy comes to your hand when you say "Touch."

1. **Repeat sequence 3, but you move around now and back up between each repetition.**

REMEMBER

2. **Move your hand, held flat like a plate, and hold it in different positions, higher or lower, to one side or the other.**

   Make sure your dog always moves toward your hand on the Touch command and touches your palm before he gets the Yes praise word and then a treat. Always reach up into the other hand held as a cup with treats and pick one out and give to your dog.

3. **Release and repeat.**

   See Figure 9-4 for an example.

FIGURE 9-4:
Your dog moves to your hand any time you give the Touch command.

© John Wiley & Sons, Inc.

Sequence 5: Mixing up the hand you offer

Here you mix up the hand you offer to Buddy, and you skip giving the treat every time:

1. **Alternate between your left and right hand as the Touch hand.**

   Buddy should come to either hand offered to him. You can keep backing up or moving along beside him, but each time you say "Touch," he should nose the hand that is offered to him.

2. **Say "Yes, good dog."**

   Do two in a row and then give a treat. Advance to three in a row and then give a treat. Make it lots of fun by smiling and praising and randomly giving him a treat.

Greeting with the Hello Command

No matter how many people you ask, having a dog not jump up on them seems to be the most desired behavior. The easiest way to teach this behavior is to teach it as a default behavior. This means your dog should automatically go into a sitting position as soon as someone looks down at him and reaches for him in a greeting manner. To get this behavior, teach Buddy to go into a sitting position when someone reaches for him and says, "Hello," which allows that person to pet him without Buddy jumping up. Buddy will learn the only way to get someone's attention will be to sit at her feet, not by jumping on her.

In essence, you have two commands that tell your dog to sit:

>> Sit, which we discuss in Chapter 11

>> Hello, which means to sit and to allow this person to touch you while you keep your bottom on the ground.

These sections break down the Hello command in easy steps.

Sequence 1: Focusing on the treat

You're going to use the dog's focus on the treat to get him into the sitting position. Stick to these steps:

1. **With Buddy standing, offer him a treat by stepping into him and leaning toward him, lift the treat over his nose and up, and say "Hello."**

   You want his nose to come up and look up over his head slightly. Your action gets him to look up and back. As you offer him the treat and lift it up and slightly over his head, step and lean into him and he should sit. The Hello command signals him to sit for the cookie.

2. **As he sits, say "Yes" and give him the treat and praise him verbally.**

3. **Say "Okay," back up, and release him as he gets up.**

Sequence 2: Greeting and praising

Here before you release him, you want to touch him on his head and praise. Steps 1–3 are the same as Sequence 1, but you add touching the top of his head as he eats his treat at the end of Step 2:

1. **With Buddy standing, offer him a treat by stepping into him and leaning toward him, lift the treat over his nose and up and say "Hello."**

2. **As he sits, say "Yes" and give him the treat and praise him verbally while you touch the top of his head as he eats his treat.**

3. **Say "Okay," back up, and release him as he gets up.**

Sequence 3: Training Buddy to hold the sitting position longer

This sequence is the same as sequence 2 except that the Sit should last longer and longer before you release him.

1. **With Buddy standing, offer him a treat by stepping into him and leaning toward him, lift the treat over his nose and up, say "Hello."**

2. **As he sits, say "Yes" and give him the treat and praise him verbally while you touch the top of his head as he eats his treat for a few more seconds each repetition.**

3. **Because you're probably leaning over him as you hand Buddy the treat, stand up straight while he eats his treat.**

   Buddy must hold the sitting position longer and longer.

REMEMBER

   If he gets up before you say "Okay," put him back into the sitting position. The Sit should have been 5 to 10 seconds, but he's working and shouldn't get up until you release him. Putting him back into the Sit requires you to pull up slightly on the collar and tuck his tail back into the sitting position.

4. **Say "Okay," back up, and release him as he gets up.**

REMEMBER

   We don't recommend you give him another treat to get him to sit again. If you do that, you'd be rewarding him for getting up, which isn't your intention. Rather you want him to realize the oops to his actions. He must learn to not get up until you release him.

Sequence 4: Having a friend help

To advance teaching the Hello command, ask someone else like a family member or a close friend to help. Show that person what you want her to do, such as lift up the treat over Buddy's head, stepping toward the dog, and so on. Pet Buddy's head and then stand up straight and release Buddy. By showing your friend what you want her to do, you're reviewing the exercise for Buddy. The review is always a good idea when someone acts as you and gets Buddy to cooperate. Reviews are something you should always practice and reinforce with Buddy. When someone bends over your dog's head and says, "Hello," Buddy should always sit and allow that person to pet his head. After all, a polite dog is a pleasure to be around.

Leave It: Getting Your Dog to Leave Stuff Alone

The Leave It command means: "Back off what you're looking at." It can be something gross on the ground or something you may have dropped and you don't want your dog to get, such as a pill or food that isn't safe for him. It can even be a cat or another dog on a walk. Leave It means not only to look away from what you're looking at, but also look at me. That command is important, fun, and easy to teach.

Before you start you need to remember a few important rules:

>> Never give a treat after you've said, "Leave it," without giving the permission word for your dog to take the treat, which is "Okay."

"Yes" means perfection for the sequence you're working on. So in sequence 1, you say "Yes" when your dog pulls his head away from the treat. In sequence 2, you say "Yes" when he looks at you, rather than when he pulls his head away.

You want more from the dog at that point, so watch your dog and read carefully to make sure you know what perfection is at each point.

>> Keep the sessions short — no more than five minutes at a time — and follow the steps in these sections (you can either sit or stand.)

Sequence 1: Introducing Leave It

The purpose of the steps in this sequence is to acknowledge that looking away is what you want Buddy to do. Follow these steps:

1. **Hold your hand pressed against your leg and with your palm facing up, show Buddy the treat.**

2. **When he goes for it, say "Leave it" while you close your hand into a fist.**

    You can turn your fist so that your palm now faces down if Buddy starts to paw at your hand for the treat.

3. **Observe your dog's reaction.**

He may stare fixedly at the back of your hand, he may try to get to the treat by nuzzling or nibbling your hand, or he may start barking. Ignore all these behaviors and don't repeat the command. You're looking for the first break in his attention away from your hand. Most dogs at this point either look to the right, to the left, or back up.

4. **The instant Buddy breaks his attention away from your hand, say "Yes" as the moment of perfection praise; then say "Okay" as the permission word and give him a treat.**

REMEMBER

Always give the Okay word for him to take the treat from you. Okay is the command that gives Buddy permission to eat the treat after the "Leave It" command.

The most difficult part of teaching this exercise is for you to remain silent and not to repeat the command. Be patient and wait for the correct response. Then say "Yes," praise him, release him, and reward him with the treat.

5. **Keep practicing this sequence until your dog is really good about backing off your fist for the Leave It command and praise.**

Sequence 2: Looking at you

This sequence teaches Buddy that you reward him with a treat by looking at you — and not at your hand. Follow these steps:

1. **Do Steps 1–3 from Sequence 1.**

You now want more from Buddy, and the Yes perfect moment won't be when he backs off the food hand, but rather when he makes eye contact with you.

2. **When he looks at you, say "Yes" and then praise him.**

To get him to look at you, praise him verbally for backing off your hand. You then can say "Yes" when he looks at you.

TIP

3. **After Buddy moves his head away, but he hasn't looked at you yet, reopen your hand to show the treat.**

Doing so makes it even clearer that Buddy must leave the treat when you say "Leave it." If he goes for the treat, shut your fist again, but don't pull your hand away. Just leave it against your leg. Keep closing your hand if he moves toward the treat, reopen your hand if he pulls away, and praise him. Don't let him get the treat even though it's right under his nose. Simply close your fist again.

4. **To get the treat from you, Buddy must look at you while the treat is still visible in your hand.**

When he does look at you, remember to say "Yes." Then pick up the treat, say "Okay" and give him the treat.

REMEMBER

If he goes back to your hand, make a fist and stop praising. When he backs off again, open your hand and praise him. You're waiting for him to look at you now. This step is important. The trick to helping him to look at you is the praise you verbally give him for not going toward the treat.

Sequence 3: Moving the treat from your hand to the floor

The purpose of the steps in this sequence is to get Buddy to understand that anything might become a Leave It command. Follow these steps:

1. **Sitting or kneeling comfortably on the floor, show Buddy a treat, put it on the floor, and cover it with your hand.**

2. **When his attention is on your hand or he tries to get to the treat, say "Leave it."**

3. **When he backs off your hand, uncover the treat and praise him quietly, but wait for him to look at you before you give him the "Yes" command and then the "Okay" release word.**

Don't release him directly to the treat on the floor but rather pick it up and then say "Okay" and let him have it. This detail can help Buddy understand that when he's told the Leave It command for something on the floor, he doesn't get it, ever. When something is bouncing across the floor and Buddy is in hot pursuit of it, the Leave It command means, "No, you don't get that unless I hand it to you. Ever."

Sequence 4: "Leaving" a dropped food item

The purpose of the steps in this sequence is that even a dropped food item, bouncing across the floor isn't to be had if you say "Leave It." Follow these steps:

1. **Put Buddy on leash and stand next to him; neatly fold the leash into your left hand, and hold your hand as close to his collar as is comfortable without tension on the leash.**

You need to make sure that the amount of slack in the leash is short enough that his mouth can't reach the floor.

2. **Hold the treat in your right hand, show it to Buddy, casually drop it, and say "Leave it."**

If he responds, praise him, pick up the treat, and from your pocket give him a different treat, not the one you told him to leave alone, with the "Okay" permission word.

If he goes for the treat, pull straight back on the leash, pick up the treat, and try again. Give the command immediately after letting go of the treat and before he wants to make a dive for it. Repeat until he obeys the command.

Test Buddy's response by taking off the leash, dropping a container of food, and saying, "Leave it." If he makes a dive for it, he's telling you that he needs more work on leash. If needed, practice more repetitions on leash.

Sequence 5: "Leaving" a found item on the ground outside

The purpose of the steps in this sequence are to insure that Buddy will leave anything he is looking at, no matter where you are or what it is. Follow these steps:

1. **Go outside and drop four or five pieces of food in the area where you're taking Buddy for his big test.**

Use a food item in the grass or on the ground that's readily visible to you such as some crackers or a few kernels of popcorn or cheese puffs.

2. **Put some of your regular treats in your pocket, and then walk Buddy on leash in the area where you left the food.**

3. **As soon as his nose goes to the food, say "Leave it."**

If he responds, praise enthusiastically, pick up the treat, and reward him with a different treat from your pocket. (Don't reward Buddy with the object he was told to leave alone.) If he doesn't leave it, check straight back on the leash.

If Buddy manages to snag a treat, your response is too slow. Practice walking around the food-contaminated area until he ignores the food on command.

REMEMBER
4. **Repeat until he ignores the food on command.**

Buddy should now know and respond to the Leave It command reliably. Test him off leash to see whether he has mastered this command or needs more work. You may need to review it with him periodically on leash.

TIP

If your dog is anything like most any other dog, he won't be far when you're in the kitchen preparing a meal. His presence there is a wonderful training opportunity. Casually drop a piece of food on the floor — maybe a small piece of bread or cheese, a little broccoli or carrot, or anything else he likes. When he tries to nab it, say "Leave it." If he does, pick up the food and reward him with something else. If he does nab the food, consider it a freebie and put Buddy on leash and try again.

Understanding other uses for Leave It

Teaching Buddy a reliable response to this command also transfers to other situations, such as chasing a cat and guarding a cabinet or dish. You also can use this command for excessive barking. Remember to reward correct responses with praise and a treat.

This command can save your dog's life if he's really reliable. Things you drop, such as medications or some foods, can potentially cause liver damage or kidney failure. Things you come across on walks can also be dangerous and potential life hazards, such as rotten food or other suspicious unknown things. More importantly, this command reinforces your leadership that you own all things.

Chapter **10**

Coming and Going: Two Essential Commands to Teach Buddy

Most everyone recognizes that having a dog who comes is valuable. Equally valuable is to have a dog who goes where you direct him to go. Run ahead toward the house, the car, or an arriving friend are just a few examples. Furthermore, helping Buddy understand he needs to leave you and go with someone is also useful. This chapter works on both the Come and Go commands and the leadership needed to train them both.

Understanding the Importance of Leadership: Okay Is the Word

To get your dog to leave something he's looking at or sniffing, you must have his respect. To gain a dog's respect you need to make sure your dog sees you as the pack leader, coach of the team, the mom, the dad. Use whatever word you feel best defines your relationship with your dog. Just remember more than anything you aren't a littermate or a sibling. *You* are in charge. You decide what your teammate does, when he does it, where he does it, and for how long he does it. This is leadership.

For example, if you say "Down," you expect your dog to down right there, no matter what is going on around him, and you expect your dog to hold the Down position for as long as it takes until you say "Okay," releasing him from that position. You are the leader.

DOWN AND HEEL ARE ESSENTIAL TO COME

An elderly farmer once contacted me (Mary Ann). I don't know why the farmer seemed elderly, but it was probably because what he was saying depicted a stubborn old man. He worked independently, so he wasn't used to being told what to do. He also had land, lots of land, where his dog didn't need to be on leash, but the dog needed to come when called.

One day this farmer called me.

"My dog won't come when I call him," the farmer said. "He'll never need to be on leash. I only need him to come when I call him, and I don't need to teach him any of those newfangled commands like Down or Heel. I just want him to come. All else will be fine after that."

"I understand what you're saying," I said. "But what you need to understand is that the very first thing we must teach your dog is to Down on command and to Heel precisely by your side."

In frustration, he grumbled at me and said something about me not getting what he was saying. "I just want to teach him to come when I call him," he said.

Again I agreed. "I understand you. You're right;" I continued. Down and Heel have nothing to do with the Come command, but *they have everything to do with the dog's coming.*"

He seemed to get what I was saying. In the end, the farmer taught his dog how to do a Down until he was released and to walk by his side when told to do so. The farmer and dog worked on the Come command and coming around distractions, and his dog became a champ at coming and watching the farmer while the two of them worked together all day on the farm.

The Down, Sit, Stand, Stay, and Heel exercises are all considered to be leadership exercises, and each one can help get you to the point where your dog will listen to each and every command you say and therefore come when called, which this chapter focuses on. Although this chapter is about coming and going, we discuss leadership first. The command that teaches leadership and is therefore, in our opinion, the most important command we teach, is the release word: "Okay," which means "Buddy, hold the position until you're released from it."

Follow these steps to teach the Okay release word; here is an example using any command.

1. **Say "Sit," "Good dog," or any other command you want to reinforce and praise while Buddy is doing the said command.**

   If Buddy gets up before you give the release word, replace him back into the Sit or whatever command without repeating the command.

2. **Say "Okay," play, and party with him.**

   The Okay release word is crucial for clear leadership coming from you. (See Chapter 11 for the Sit and Down command.)

Heel is the other leadership exercise. Heeling is walking with your dog while your dog is beside you walking on a loose leash. Heeling is a great leadership exercise because you decide where you walk, how fast or slow you walk, and which way you go. In other words, you're the leader of the pack. You set the pace and the direction. Refer to Chapter 12 for the Heel command.

Teaching Your Dog to Come When Called

Come is one of the most important commands for safety, which the dog learns. The truth is, "If you don't have a dog that comes . . . one day you won't have a dog!" That's why this book is full of different ways to teach your dog to come: Name Recognition, Recall, Touch. Every command you teach your dog helps him want to be with you and helps him come when called. The following sections focus on the actual way you can teach your dog to come when you call him and some important points to remember when using the Come command.

Teaching Buddy the Recall Game

Before you teach Buddy how to come, Buddy needs to master Name Recognition and Touch, which we discuss in Chapter 9. When you're ready to teach Come, follow these steps.

REMEMBER

You must do these exercises so you're sure your dog understands what Come means. When you say, "Buddy, Come," there must be no doubt that he *knows* what you expect of him. If he doesn't come when called, you need to be sure it isn't because he doesn't know what the command means, but rather because he couldn't hear you over the distractions of life.

Here's how to play the Recall Game and teach your dog the Come command. You'll need a partner because you'll be playing this game with another person. Refer to Figure 10-1.

FIGURE 10-1: Learning Come with the Recall Game.

© John Wiley & Sons, Inc.

1. **With Buddy on leash, hold the handle of the leash with your partner holding Buddy by the collar; say "Buddy, Come" and use the leash to guide him to you.**

   At this point your partner holding the collar lets go of Buddy. Avoid the temptation to reach for your dog. The next step is very important. Make sure both of you have treats easily accessible in your pocket. You'll need one at a time.

2. **When Buddy comes to you, show him the treat when he arrives while putting your hand through his collar, and only then give him the treat, pet him, and praise him enthusiastically.**

   You can — and should — pet Buddy when he reaches you so that coming to you is a pleasant experience. This situation is different from teaching the Sit or Down commands in Chapter 11 when you want him to remain in place and petting him would cause him to get up.

3. **Hold onto Buddy's collar and pass the leash to your partner, who says, "Buddy, Come," puts her hand through the collar while showing him the treat, gives the treat, and praises him.**

Keep holding Buddy after you call him until your partner calls him again. Back and forth. One of you is the leash person and then the holder of the dog.

Keep working on this exercise until your dog responds on his own to being called and no longer needs to be guided in with the leash.

4. **Repeat the exercise with Buddy off leash, gradually increasing the distance between you and your partner to 12 feet.**

Remember to keep showing Buddy the treat as you reach for his collar. Doing so is crucial for him to come all of the way in and being touched and taken by the collar.

5. **Have your partner hold Buddy by the collar while you go into another room and then call your dog.**

Keep in mind all of the tips about showing the treat before touching his collar and holding onto him until the next person calls.

6. **When he finds you, put your hand through the collar, give him a treat, and praise him.**

If he can't find you, *slowly* go to him, take him by the collar, and bring him to the spot where you called. Reward and praise.

7. **Have your partner go into another room and then call Buddy.**

8. **Repeat the exercise until Buddy doesn't hesitate in finding you or your partner in any room of the house.**

Add stairs and a second floor if you have one. Only go halfway up or down the staircase so Buddy learns that area is part of the playing field.

9. **Take Buddy outside to a confined area, such as a fenced yard, tennis court, park, or school yard, and repeat all of the steps there.**

Now you can practice alone. With Buddy on leash, take him for a walk. Let him sniff around, and when he isn't paying any attention to you, call him. When he gets to you, give him a treat and make a big fuss over him. If he doesn't come, firmly tug on the leash toward you, backing away as you call and then reward and praise him. Repeat until he comes to you every time you call him. After Buddy is trained, you don't have to reward him with a treat every time, but do so randomly.

You can add a whistle to the Recall Game or reteach the game using a whistle, especially if Buddy has accidently learned to ignore your calls. Blow the whistle and then say "Buddy, Come." Do everything else the same except add the whistle to your call.

TIP

Remembering what's important when you use the Come command

The Come command is arguably one of the most important commands you teach your dog. When you train your dog with the Come command, keep the following points in mind.

Exercise, exercise, exercise

Many dogs don't come when called because they don't get enough exercise. At every chance they get, they run off and make the most of this unexpected freedom by staying out for hours at a time. One of our mottos in life is: "A tired dog has happy owners," or "A tired dog is a happy dog." Either way, everyone is happy when the dog gets enough exercise. The problem though is *you* don't get to decide how much enough exercise is.

For instance, exercise requirements between a Border Collie and a Basset Hound are huge. A Border Collie can work all day and needs to do so or it will be a crazed lunatic looking for an outlet for all of that energy. On the other hand, a Basset Hound is happy hanging out all day sharing the sofa and taking short walks; that's plenty. If you're a Basset Hound person and you get a Border Collie, you need to figure out what enough exercise is for your dog or more than likely your dog will develop behavior problems. But if you throw the Frisbee for an hour, walk or jog for several miles, and do agility every night, your Border Collie will be the best-mannered, well-titled dog that has no issues, and you'll be proud. You and your Border Collie will both be happy. Enough exercise for every dog will be different.

REMEMBER

Consider what your dog was bred to do, and that background tells you how much exercise he needs. Just putting Buddy out in the backyard isn't good enough. You have to participate. Dogs are social animals.

When your dog comes to you, be nice to him

One of the quickest ways to teach your dog not to come to you when called is to call him to punish him or to do something the dog perceives as unpleasant. Most dogs consider it unpleasant to be called when their owners are leaving them alone in the house. In these circumstances, go and get Buddy instead of calling him to you. If you're still crating your young dog, call him to you for a treat or a special reward that goes in the crate with him and then release him and continue getting ready for your day. Calling him to you and releasing him several times before you actually leave for the day is great practice and won't make your departure seem so bad. Review going in the crate and releasing him from the crate multiple times a day. (Chapter 14 discusses how to use the Crate command.)

Another example of teaching your dog *not* to come is taking him for a run in the park and calling him to you when it's time to go home. Repeating this sequence several times teaches the dog that the party is over once called. Soon he may become reluctant to return to you when called because he isn't ready to end the fun. You can prevent this kind of unintentional training by calling him to you several times during his outing, sometimes giving him a treat and other times offering just a word of praise. Then let him romp again. Ending the fun is punishment for your dog, so calling him to you and ending the fun will result in a dog who doesn't come when called.

Teach Buddy the Come command as soon as you get him

Start right away. But remember, sometime between 4 and 8 months of age a puppy begins to realize there's a big, wide world out there (see Chapter 7). While he's going through this stage, keep him on leash so he doesn't learn that he can ignore you when you call him.

Dog training centers often get calls about training when dogs hit 8 months. What used to be a dog that always came when called is now a dog who ignores you. To the dog you've become boring. Using a leash to counteract that trend during this short period of time avoids the unintentional training you don't want. Unintentional training is when you accidently teach the opposite of what you expect to be teaching. You may think, "Buddy used to come, so let me call him again. Maybe he didn't hear me, so I'll call him again one more call and surely he'll come." In this case what you're really teaching him is you don't mean what you're commanding and you don't have any control when he is off leash, which is the last thing you want your dog to think about you. Instead, keep your dog on the leash for a while; you're simply stepping back to reinforce your previous training.

When in doubt, keep him on leash

Find out how to anticipate when your dog is likely not to come. You may be tempting fate by trying to call him after he has spotted a cat, another dog, or a jogger. Of course, sometimes you'll goof and let him go just as another dog appears out of nowhere. Refer to the next section for how to deal with distractions.

TIP

Resist the urge to make a complete fool of yourself by bellowing "Come" a million times. The more often you holler "Come," the quicker your dog learns he can ignore you when he's off leash. Instead, patiently go to him and put him on leash. Don't get angry with him after you've caught him, or you'll make him afraid of you, and he'll run away from you when you try to call him the next time.

Touch his collar before you reward

Touching his collar prevents him from developing the annoying habit of playing "Catch me if you can" — coming toward you and then dancing around you, just out of reach. Teach him to let you touch his collar before you offer him a treat or praise.

Training Your Dog to Handle Distractions

The following sections break up distractions into three degrees or levels. As the degrees go up, the distractions seem harder, although that may not be totally true. For example, if you have a ball-crazy dog versus a dog that doesn't ever want to retrieve something, the ball distraction isn't equal in difficulty to each dog. If your dog is a person-crazy dog that never met a stranger versus a one-person dog that never wants to be with anyone except you, then a person walking by and saying "Hi" isn't much of a difficulty. Know your dog when you choose your distractions.

Assuming you've done the training for Come, you're ready to call your dog around a distraction. We do suggest you work through the easier distractions first before moving to the more difficult distractions. For the purpose of this discussion, we refer to these distractions as first, second, and third degree.

Teaching Come with first-degree distractions

First-degree distractions are things in the nearby area but not relating directly to the dog. Examples include going to the park, going to the neighborhood convenient store and training outside, and working in a new location from where you usually train. To handle these distractions, follow these steps:

1. **Put your dog on leash and start down the street for a walk; when your dog sees something that interests him, such as someone walking on the other side of the road, set yourself up to call your dog by backing up to the end of your leash and keeping it slightly loose and say "Buddy, Come" and wait a second to see if he turns and comes.**

   If he does, really lay on the praise and party hardily. If he doesn't come, give a quick check on the leash and back up a little to encourage him to move toward you.

REMEMBER

A *check* on the leash is when you have a loose leash and you quickly snap it tight for a half second and then let it go slack again. This check should bring your dog's attention around to you. When he does have his attention focused on you, praise enthusiastically, squat down, and welcome him into your arms for a party of praise.

2. **Repeat calling Buddy several times on your walk until no matter what he's looking at, he always turns and comes to you or he gets a check on the leash, followed by praise and a party.**

   If Buddy needs more training, revisit the Recall Game from earlier in this chapter.

3. **In a fenced area, let your dog off leash and call, "Buddy, Come."**

   Allow him to become involved in a smell in the grass or a tree. Keep the distance between you and him no more than 10 feet apart. After you call him, praise him enthusiastically and reward his success if he responds. If he doesn't, don't call him again no matter ho. Buddy heard you, but he chose to ignore you. Instead, slowly walk up to him and firmly take him by his collar under his chin and trot backward to the spot where you called him. Then praise him and reward him even though you helped him be successful.

TIP

If your dog is a small dog, instead of bending over him so far to reach for the collar and backing up, walk up to him and put the leash on him, so you can be standing up while backing up and bringing him to where you called him. Doing so is important because too much bending over is difficult for a small dog because your body language is too defensive. Your small dog will respond better to you standing and reeling him in.

Teaching Come with second-degree distractions

Second-degree distractions are things that related directly to the dog. Examples include when people stop and talk to you while out and about or want to see your dog. People coming and going right beside your dog working is really distracting. Someone calling commands to your dog, but *without* using your dog's name is fair as a distraction.

The distracter using your dog's name isn't fair. She having her say "Down" while your dog is sitting is a second-degree distraction; your dog shouldn't go down, but rather stay seated because that's the command you left him under. You've said, "Sit," to your dog and not released him from that Sit. Your dog should hold that position no matter what goes on around him.

To teach Buddy to deal with second-degree distractions, have a friend help you work on them and follow these steps:

1. **Start with Buddy on leash and put him in a Sit-Stay if you've not trained the Stay command (refer to Chapter 11 for this command).**

   Use a secured area, such as a fenced yard, if you have one available. If you don't have a secured area, use a longer leash or put two leashes together so you can be farther than 6 feet away. If Buddy hasn't perfected the Stay, simply have him mill around on the long leash.

2. **Ask your friend to talk to your dog but not to touch him and not to use his name.**

   When your friend says something like "Here, puppy, puppy," and looks inviting, this is a second-degree distraction.

3. **After your friend has talked to Buddy, you should call him, "Buddy, Come."**

   Buddy has a choice now: come to you or go to your friend. If he comes to you, praise him, give him a treat, and party hard. If he goes to your friend, reel him into you and then praise him for coming, even though you helped him to be successful.

4. **Repeat the steps on leash a couple of times, and after Buddy has been successful at this level of distraction, move to off leash.**

   You want to handle the off-leash distraction if your dog goes to your friend the same way as if Buddy were on leash. Go to him, take him by the collar, and back up to where you called and then praise and reward.

5. **Repeat these steps until your dog comes to you, even with your friend talking to him.**

Teaching Come with third-degree distractions

Third-degree distractions are things being offered to your dog, such as a toy or food while he is working for you. For example, if your dog is in a Sit and someone offers a cookie and says "Down," that distraction is third degree. If you throw a Frisbee next to your dog in a Stay, it also would be a third-degree distraction.

To teach Buddy how to deal with third-degree distractions, stick to these steps:

1. **With your friend sitting on the ground, have her offer Buddy a treat.**

   Make sure the treat is small enough that she can hide it in her hand. She can use a container with a lid loosely placed on it if Buddy is too distracted by the food. You can have the lid loose. You don't want the dog to actually get any of the food from your friend, but you want the dog to think he might get some food. Hope springs eternal.

2. **On leash, you and Buddy walk up to the friend offering the treat.**

   Your friend doesn't give Buddy the treat. Let Buddy interact with the food and your friend while you quietly back up to the end of the leash.

3. **Say "Buddy, Come" and then wait one second.**

   If Buddy doesn't turn and come to you immediately, back up and check the leash. Even if you had to help, praise Buddy enthusiastically and give him a treat of your own.

4. **Repeat the third-degree distractions on leash until Buddy readily turns and comes each time you call him away from the food and your friend.**

   After you've had success on leash, you can try it off leash just as in the second-degree section. If Buddy goes for the food or your friend, walk up to him and take him by the collar (or reattach the leash), back up, and bring him with you. Praise him as if he bypassed your friend.

REMEMBER

A friend can offer a treat to your dog anytime, but when she's doing so while you're saying, "Buddy, Come," Buddy should come to you and not take the treat from your friend, which is a very important part of distraction training. You calling Buddy to come is the most important command that your dog must comply to immediately. He must ignore a friend with food, a bunny running in the field, or a car on the road. Come can mean life and death if he doesn't always come when called.

Doing all of these repetitions on and off leash around distractions can really pay off. After all, you want your dog to come to you no matter what.

Focusing on the Opposite of Come — Go

A command that few people think to teach their dogs is Go, which is quite useful in several ways: Get up into the car or Go. Go with the person taking your dog away from you at the veterinary office or Go. Get the ball the dog didn't see you throw or Go. At the park, send your dog out to play with other dogs or Go. When training alone and you want to practice the Come command, send your dog out so you can then call him to you. These sections explain the sequences to train this command.

Sequence 1: Teaching a target

Here, you want to teach Buddy to focus on a target such as a lid from a container you have saved like a butter lid. You can even use a plastic plate; just make sure that it's nonbreakable.

1. **Set the target on the ground in front of your feet and put your dog on your left and have your left hand in your dog's collar.**

   You want to teach your dog that the target is a place to find a treat.

2. **Place a treat on the target at your feet and then let go of the collar and with your left hand, point to the target, and release Buddy to the target with the Go command.**

   Use your left hand to point to the target (as in Figure 10-2). The best way to point or signal to the target is always use the hand closest to the dog, so with Buddy on your left, use your left arm. Use your whole hand as a flat paddle swinging toward the target with one large sweeping motion.

3. **Say "Go" and let Buddy eat the treat.**

   Walk up to the target if Buddy doesn't realize it's loaded. Say "Okay" and praise him.

4. **Do this sequence several times; remain close to the target, just in front your feet.**

FIGURE 10-2:
Use a hand signal for Go.

© John Wiley & Sons, Inc.

Sequence 2: Add Come after the release

This sequence advances the Go command to include Come. Just follow these steps:

1. **Hold Buddy with your left hand and load the target with your right hand.**

    Together with Buddy, step over the target and turn to face the target, still holding Buddy by the collar. You should be about a foot from the target. Take your hand out of Buddy's collar and use your signal to command Buddy's attention to the target as you say "Go." Buddy should go to the target and eat the treat.

2. **Say "Okay" and back up saying "Come."**

    Encourage Buddy to return to you. You have him on leash, so you can reel him into you.

3. **Repeat this sequence until you no longer need to help Buddy find the target.**

Sequence 3: Increase the distance to the target

Now you're ready to move farther away from the target with each successful repetition. Sequence 3 is a great exercise to work both Go and Come. Even better, dogs love to run and play with you, so your dog gets to run away from you to the target and the Go command and then gets to run toward you with the Come command. Here are the steps:

1. **Starting at 2 feet from the target, say "Go" and signal Buddy.**

    Always release with Okay after he has eaten the loaded treat and call Buddy back to you with Come.

2. **Load the target and repeat at 4 feet away.**

    Step over the target with Buddy holding onto the leash instead of the collar.

3. **Point and signal to the target, and say "Go."**

4. **Say "Come" to call Buddy back.**

    When Buddy gets to you, praise and release him with "Okay."

5. **Reload the target but set it up 2 feet farther away from the target each time.**

You can easily work at 10 feet still on leash; simply follow along with Buddy because your leash is only 6 feet long. Eventually when you're working Buddy off leash, you can put the target farther away up to 20 feet. Buddy must always go with the Go command directly to the target and return to you with the Come command. If not, you have progressed too rapidly, so decrease the distance of the target as a review.

Chapter **11**

Mastering Some Fundamentals: Sit, Down, and Stay

For the most part, basic training is about teaching Buddy to do something you want him to do when he's doing something else. A great example is the Come command, which we discuss in Chapter 10. This chapter focuses on teaching your dog a few new commands that are a foreign language to him, including Sit, Down, and Stay. A good example is when he sits, a position that Buddy does often on his own, but now you use the Sit command. You want Buddy to know that when you say "Sit" or any command, you want him to respond immediately the first time you say the command.

Understanding Why Sit Is So Important

The Sit command gives you a wonderfully easy way to control Buddy when you need it most. It's also one of the basic commands that you and your dog can quickly accomplish. In fact, the Sit is one of the most useful exercises you can teach Buddy. You can use it for all of these things:

>> When you walk in the street and stop at the curb or a traffic light

>> When you meet a neighbor and want to catch up on local news

>> Before Buddy goes up and down stairs

>> Before he goes through doors

>> When he is loose to make him stop

>> When guests arrive and you don't want Buddy to jump on them

REMEMBER

As your dog demonstrates that he has mastered sitting on command, start to reward the desired response with food every other time. Finally, reward him on a *random* basis — every now and then give him a treat after he sits on command. A random reward is the most powerful reinforcement of what your dog has learned. It's based on the premise that "if you work really well, you'll get a treat, so keep working harder." To make the random reward work, all you have to do is randomly give a treat, never after each and every command. Also, not every other time either, which would be a fixed pattern that your dog will learn to anticipate.

When Buddy wants to greet you by jumping up, tell him "Sit." When he does, praise him, scratch him *under* the chin (dogs don't like being patted on the head especially if they're high in defense-fight drive, see Chapter 2), and then release him. Following this simple method consistently, you can change your dog's greeting behavior from trying to jump on you to sitting to being petted. (Chapter 9 introduces the Hello command instead of Sit for politely greeting guests.)

Introducing Down and Its Commands

The Down command is a very important command, similar to Sit. The Down represents a submissive position to a dog. For a dog to willingly comply to the first Down command and go into that position completely is the sign of a well-trained dog and a sign of respect to the leader who is the person who gave the command. Dog trainers often argue which command is the most important for a dog to know. There will always be a group that chose Down to be that command.

The Down exercise is divided into three parts:

>> **The Down:** This obedience command means "lie down here and now" and should be taught in each of your daily training sessions. We explain how to teach it in the next section, "Training Your Dog Sit and Down Sequentially."

>> **The Long Down:** This exercise is taught for impulse control, holding a Down position for 30 minutes. You can teach this exercise as soon as you bring puppy or dog home. It's designed to teach Buddy that you're in charge in a nonthreatening way. Dogs taught this exercise right from the start fit into the family routine and train much more easily. We suggest teaching it in the evening when your dog is tired or your puppy is just about to go to sleep. (A tired dog is more easily trained to be still for 30 minutes than a hyperactive, energized dog.) We explain how to teach this command in the "Warming Up with the Long-Down Exercise," later in this chapter.

>> **Go Lie Down or Go to your Bed:** This is a natural extension of Down. This exercise is used when you sit down for dinner or any time you don't want to interact with the dog. Chapter 13 discusses this command.

Training Your Dog Sit and Down Simultaneously

As you teach Buddy the commands in this chapter: Sit and Down, there are two techniques. The first is a place-and-show sequence, and the second is a luring sequence. The place-and-show technique is taught first because you want to teach Buddy how to hold his position until he's released. If you start with the luring technique first, you won't be able to replace him into position without giving another lure. Here are the two techniques with the following sections spelling them out in more detail. The example is for the Sit.

>> **Placing and showing:** With this technique (Sequence 1), you place Buddy into a sitting position and label it "Sit" by tucking his tail under his hind legs with one hand while you hold his chest still with the other hand. You then hold him in the Sit position while you praise him. Then you release him with a happy Okay release word and play with him for a few seconds while you continue to pet him.

>> **Luring:** The *luring style* (Sequence 3) lifts a treat or cookie, and if the dog is interested in the treat, the dog will follow it into a different position. For Sit, raise the treat up and back over your dog's head slowly while he sniffs it, and the action of moving the cookie lures him into a sitting position.

Teach the Sit with place and show first and then do it with a lure. Here are the full sequences in detail. The same pattern goes for the Down command, so you can teach them simultaneously.

Sequence 1: Placing and showing

Using the place-and-show method as the first sequence for Sit and Down is critical because of the release word (Okay) and the concept of training Buddy to comply when you want him to obey. When you teach this method to sit on command and remain until you release him, if Buddy moves or gets up before you release him, you simply stop praising him and replace him back into the sitting position. Then after you've placed him back into the sitting position, you resume praising him only while he's sitting. Then you say "Okay" and get him to move while you play with him a few seconds.

REMEMBER

With Buddy standing next to you on your left side, you can either kneel next to him, sit in a chair next to him, or put Buddy on a table or garden wall if he's small enough. Training a small dog on an elevated surface is useful because you don't want to bend over him. Chapter 2 explains how your body language affects your dog's interpretation of what you're saying or doing. Follow these steps:

1. Put your right hand on Buddy's chest and your left hand on his shoulder blades; slide your left hand down his back and around his tail and tuck his knees as you keep your right hand on his chest, folding him into the sitting position.

2. Say "Sit" as you hold him in the sitting position and you verbally praise him for a few seconds.

3. Say "Okay" and start to pet him as you release him from the sitting position.

4. Do this sequence several times in a row and for several days in a row.

Sequence 2: Adding the Down

In the steps in this sequence as you place and show Buddy how to sit, you add the Down command before the release word. In other words, you string the three commands in a row: Sit, Down, and then Okay:

1. With Buddy in the Sit position next to your left side, reach over him with your left arm as if you're putting your arm around his shoulders.

2. Lift both of his front legs by the elbows by placing each one of your open palms under the elbows into a begging position and lift and lower him into a Down position as you say "Down" as Figure 11-1 shows.

3. **Praise him while he's still in the Down position and then say "Okay" and start to pet him.**

4. **Do this sequence several times in a row, for several days in a row.**

   Do both the Sit and the Down together along with the Okay release. Buddy must hold each position for a few seconds before you do the next command. Sit, praise, and pause. Down, praise, and pause. Okay and release.

FIGURE 11-1: Gently lowering your dog into the Down position.

© John Wiley & Sons, Inc.

Sequence 3: Luring into the Down

When you use the luring style to teach Buddy the Down position and he moves or gets up before you release him, don't give him another treat to get him back into the Down position, which would be rewarding him for getting up. Rewarding Buddy for getting up without being released is the last thing you want him to think you're doing. This is why you teach the luring sequence after the place-and-show sequence. If Buddy gets up himself without being released by you, you'll then immediately revert to the place-and-show sequence and return him to the

Sit position, resume praising him until you actually do release him with "Okay." Follow these steps:

1. **With Buddy in a sitting position (see sequence one) on your left side, place your left hand on his shoulders, take a small enticing treat in your right hand, and present it to his nose.**

2. **Slowly lower the treat from his nose to the floor directly in front of his feet, moving slowly and say "Down."**

   As Buddy follows the lowered treat with his nose, he'll fold himself into a Down position.

3. **Give him the treat and praise him, but don't release him.**

   If he gets up, lower him back into the Down as in sequence 2. Because you haven't released him, he should hold the Down position.

Sequence 4: Luring into the Sit

When you use the lure to move between the Down and the Sit commands, you must be ready to reposition or replace Buddy into the correct position if he changes his position without a different command from you or a release from you. Using the lure is easy but can be tempting to grab another treat if your dog moves out of the commanded position. Always reinforce the command after you've used a lure by reverting to Sequence 1:

1. **While Buddy is in the Down position, keep your left hand gently on his shoulders as you praise him quietly, reach for a treat with your right hand, and then move your left hand to the collar between his ears.**

2. **Present the treat with your right hand at Buddy's nose and slowly raise the cookie up and back in a 45-degree angle over and above his head; gently lift his collar if necessary as your right hand lifts the treat up and over his head and say "Sit."**

   When Buddy is up in a sitting position, let him eat the treat that he followed up.

3. **Hold him still with your left hand still in his collar and praise him softly and then say "Okay," release him, and play with him for a few seconds.**

4. **Repeat Sequence 3 and 4 together several times in a row for several days in a row.**

   Buddy should hold each position for a few seconds before you do the next command the same as you did.

TIP

Vary the time between the Sit and the Down commands, but remember he must hold each position until you release him. You want your dog to comply because he was commanded to do so, not because he learned a pattern of Down, Sit, Down, Sit in sequence. If he gets out of any of the positions, go back to Sequence 1.

Sequence 5: Adding collar pressure

The steps in this sequence introduce collar pressure in the presence of food, so upward collar pressure for Sit and downward collar pressure for Down won't be a problem for Buddy:

1. Place Buddy into a Sit in front of you.

You can be kneeling in front of him, you can be in a chair, or you can place Buddy on a table as in Sequence 1.

2. Put your left hand fingers in his collar under his chin while you hold a treat in front of his nose with your right hand.

3. As you lower the cookie with your right hand, press the collar toward Buddy's chest and down at the same time with your left hand in his collar.

By applying pressing toward Buddy, he should fold into a Down, and because the cookie is there helping his head lower, he should go right down.

4. Say "Down" simultaneously and let him eat the treat.

Don't release him yet.

5. While Buddy is in the Down position, reach for another cookie in your right hand and put your left hand in his collar between his ears.

6. Lift Buddy by the collar into the "Sit" as you raise the cookie from his nose up and over his head as you did in Sequence 4.

7. Say "Sit" simultaneously and give him the cookie and praise him.

8. Say "Okay" and release him.

9. Practice several times in a row for several days in a row.

REMEMBER

The Sit and Down are two of the most important commands that prove your dog sees you as the leader of the pack, the mom, the dad, the coach of the team. Practice makes perfect, and perfect practice makes perfect.

Sequence 6: Foregoing the treat

The last sequence of teaching the "Sit" and "Down" commands together only uses the collar pressure if necessary and no food. You need only use the collar pressure if Buddy doesn't follow the command the first time you give it. Buddy should wear the leash in these steps:

1. **Place Buddy in a Sit as in Sequence 1.**

Be close enough to reach out and touch your dog.

2. **Say "Down."**

Buddy should start to go down. If he doesn't, reach and take his collar from under his chin and apply slight pressure in his collar back, down and toward him. He has felt this type of pressure many times, but this time you didn't start with your finger in the collar before you gave the command, plus you don't have a treat in your other hand. Buddy should respond because of all of the practice you have done. If not, apply the pressure and praise him for going Down even though you helped.

3. **Practice doing more repetitions and in different locations.**

Dogs learn well in one location. Practicing in different locations is extremely important and is the first step of distraction training.

4. **With Buddy in the Down position, stand up with the slack leash in your hand, and say "Sit."**

If Buddy doesn't sit, use the leash to apply a slight amount of upward pressure on the collar, which lifts Buddy into the sitting position. Release with Okay and party together.

Warming Up with the Long-Down Exercise

One of the best impulse control exercises is the Long Down. Practice the Long Down exercise under the following conditions to start, and then you can use this exercise anytime:

>> When your dog is tired

>> After he has been exercised

>> When interruptions are unlikely

>> When you aren't tired or frustrated

If the situation allows it, you can watch television or read, as long as you don't move during the first two weeks of training this exercise. Stick to this schedule:

>> **Week 1:** Three times during the course of a week, practice the Long Down for 30 minutes at a time as follows:

1. **Sit on the floor beside your dog.**

2. **Say "Down" and place him in the Down position.**

   This is the only time you say the command during the 30 minutes, no matter how many times he gets up and you put him back. This exercise is not about teaching Buddy how to down on command but rather that you decide what he does and when and where. You are the leader of the team.

3. **If he gets up, put him back without saying anything.**

4. **Keep your hands off of him when he's Down, other than to replace him back into the Down position if he gets up.**

5. **Stay still.**

6. **After 30 minutes, release him, even if he has fallen asleep.**

   Well done. Even if Buddy gets up every 5 seconds, keep putting him back; this is a crucial leadership exercise, and you're doing a great job if you put him back each time he gets up.

TIP

As a general rule, the more bouncy the dog, the more frequently he'll try to get up and the more important this exercise becomes. Just remain calm, and each time he tries to get up place him back in the Down position. If your dog is particularly bouncy, put him on leash and kneel on the leash so your hands are free to put him back.

Some dogs cooperate relatively quickly, whereas others need more time. If your dog is in the latter group, your first experience with the Long Down (and his) will be the most challenging, and you'll be quite busy putting Buddy back into the Down position. As he catches on to the idea and gradually accepts the procedure, each successive repetition will go more easily.

>> **Week 2:** Practice three 30-minute Downs while you sit in a chair such as a kitchen chair next to your dog.

>> **Week 3:** Practice three 30-minute Downs while you sit across the room from your dog. Start with Buddy 3 to 4 feet in front of you, the second time 10 feet in front of you, and then the third time on the other side of the room.

>> **Week 4:** Practice three 30-minute Downs while you move about the room but stay within sight of your dog. You can be cooking or cleaning or simply walking around the room occasionally.

REMEMBER

After Week 4, practice a Long Down at least once a month; you can be working at home or simply relaxing while you do it. Either way, Buddy needs to be in a Down position within sight of you, but not necessarily near you. If he ever gets up, simply go back to him and replace him into the Down. Don't try to direct him from a distance, which only will break down his belief that you can control him from a distance. Go to him, put your finger in his collar, and return him to the Down position. No command is necessary because you've already given him the command.

Staying in Place: Sit-Stay and Down-Stay

You have two positions choices when giving the Stay command to Buddy. First give Buddy the position command and make sure he takes that position. Then give him the Stay command while he's in the correct position. Always release Buddy from the Stay with the Okay release word when you're done:

>> **Sit-Stay:** This command is used for relatively short periods.

>> **Down-Stay:** This command is for longer periods and is taught as a safety exercise to get Buddy to stop wherever he is and stay there. For example, suppose Buddy gets loose and finds himself on the other side of the road. He sees you and is just about to cross the road when a car comes. You need a way to get him to stay on the other side of the street until the car has passed by.

When working on Stay, no matter what position, you can use these three Ds to make the Stay more solid and reliable:

>> **Duration:** This is how long you do the Stay. Work on duration first before the next two Ds.

>> **Distance:** How far away from Buddy you practice the Stay is next important. After you successfully have worked on length of time, do Stays longer and longer and then practice on moving farther away from your dog, but go back to shorter periods to help him be successful.

>> **Distractions:** The third D stands for distractions, which includes what's going on around that makes Buddy concentrate on maintaining the Stay. Working with distractions such as the ones we mention in Chapter 10 include a person talking to him, another dog, or you eating. No matter the distraction, Buddy needs to remain in the Stay.

The following sections explain how you can add these two Stay commands to your dog's repertoire.

REMEMBER

After Buddy understands what you want, alternate between the Sit-Stay and Down-Stay every other day. Whether you start with Buddy in the Sit position or the Down position when you say Stay, he should remain in that position. If not, replace him back into the starting position and continue working on the length of time you're having Buddy stay.

Teaching the Sit-Stay

The Sit-Stay is one of the most useful exercises you can teach. When you have guests, when your doorbell rings and Buddy rushes barking to the door, when you want Buddy not to dash through open doors, the Sit-Stay exercise is what keeps Buddy safe. It's also useful for stair manners and for stopping him from jumping out of the car when the door is opened (we discuss door and stair manners in Chapter 14). Overall, use this command when you want your dog to remain quietly in one spot.

To teach the Sit-Stay, Buddy needs his training collar and his 6-foot training leash (see Chapter 5 if you need to pick one). Before you proceed to another step while teaching the command, make sure Buddy is solid on the previous one. Here are the steps to follow:

1. **With your dog on your left side, place your dog's collar high on his neck, directly behind his ears; neatly fold half of your leash accordion-style into your left hand, and place it against your belly button, allowing 3 feet of slack.**

2. **With Buddy sitting, say "Stay," and take a step out directly in front of your sitting dog and turn and face each other.**

3. **Count to ten, return to Buddy's side, pause for a few seconds, and then release with "Okay," taking several steps forward as you release him from his sitting position.**

   The Okay release word needs to actually move him from the sitting position. That's why you must move forward after you say "Okay."

TIP

While doing the Sit-Stay and you see that Buddy's attention is drifting, he's probably about to move. You can tell that your dog is thinking about moving when he starts to look around and begins to focus on something other than you. Any time you see that lack of attention, reinforce the Stay command by taking a step toward your dog with your right foot and with your right hand bring the leash straight up to a point directly above his head (refer to Figure 11-2).

FIGURE 11-2:
Reinforce the
Sit-Stay.

4. **Bring back your right foot and right hand to their original position without repeating the Stay command, count to 30 and pivot back to your dog's right side, pause for a few seconds, and then praise and release with "Okay" while you move forward a few steps taking Buddy with you.**

   Doing so guarantees that Buddy releases from the Stay position.

   You can then add the three Ds:

5. **Increase the duration and work on longer and longer Stays as your dog is learning to Sit-Stay.**

6. **After Buddy is successful with duration, start to add distance in small increments when you practice.**

   Say "Stay" and then place yourself 3 feet in front of your dog, keeping your left hand at your belly button and your right hand at your side, palm open, facing your dog. Put him back if you think he is about to move or if he does change positions.

7. **After Buddy is successful with distance, start adding distractions to your Sit-Stay practice.**

   Repeat over the course of several training sessions until your dog is steady on this exercise and practice on a regular basis. See Chapter 10 for the different levels of distractions.

8. **Buddy is ready to practice off leash, so take off his leash and put it in your pocket.**

Start close to him again and always keep your attention on him. If he moves or changes position, slowly go to him and put him back into the Sit, but don't repeat Sit or Stay. You aren't starting over again; you're fixing the command you were working on. Then release him with "Okay."

TIP

Until you read the signs that Buddy is thinking about moving, chances are you'll be late reading his intentions. When that happens, without saying anything, put him back to the spot where he was supposed to stay, stand in front of him, count to ten, return to his side, pause for a few seconds, and release him with "Okay."

Teaching the Down-Stay

The object of the Down-Stay command is for your dog to remain in a comfortable position for a long period of time. That's where the Down-Stay command comes in — the theory being that the dog is least likely to move in the Down position. Just as the Sit-Stay command in the previous section, you work through the Stay sequentially.

1. **With your dog on your left side, give Buddy the Down command beside you.**

Review the Down command from earlier in this chapter.

2. **Say "Stay," and take a step out directly in front of your downed dog and turn and face each other.**

3. **Count to ten, return to Buddy's side, pause for a few seconds, and then release with "Okay," taking several steps forward as you release him from his Down position.**

Your Okay release word needs to actually move him from the Down. That's why you must move forward after you say "Okay."

TIP

While doing the Down-Stay and you see that Buddy's attention is drifting, he's probably about to move. Any time you see that lack of attention, reinforce the Stay command by taking a step toward your dog with your right foot and with your left hand reach for his collar under his chin and apply just enough pressure down and toward his chest to return him to the Down position.

4. **Stand back up without repeating the Stay command, count to 30 and pivot back to your dog's right side, pause for a few seconds, and then praise and release with "Okay" while you move forward a few steps taking Buddy with you.**

Doing so guarantees that Buddy releases from the Stay position.

You can then add the three Ds:

5. **Increase the duration and work on longer and longer Stays as your dog is learning to Down-Stay.**

6. **After Buddy is successful with duration, start to add distance in small increments when you practice.**

Say "Stay" and then place yourself 3 feet in front of your dog, keeping your left hand at your belly button and your right hand at your side, palm open, facing your dog. Put him back if you think he is about to move or if he does change positions.

7. **After Buddy is successful with distance, start adding distractions to your Down-Stay practice.**

Repeat over the course of several training sessions until your dog is steady on this exercise and practice on a regular basis. See Chapter 10 for the different levels of distractions.

8. **Buddy is ready to practice off leash, so take off his leash and put it in your pocket.**

Start close to him again and always keep your attention on him. If he moves or changes position, slowly go to him and put him back into the Down, but don't repeat Down or Stay. You aren't starting over again; you're fixing the command you were working on. Then release him with "Okay."

TIP

Until you read the signs that Buddy is thinking about moving, chances are you'll be late reading his intentions. When that happens, without saying anything, put him back to the spot where he was supposed to stay, stand in front of him, count to ten, return to his side, pause for a few seconds, and release him with "Okay.

Chapter 12

Going for a Pleasant Walk

Taking your dog for a nice, long walk is music for your soul and good exercise for both of you — or it should be when you both know how to walk together. Teaching Buddy to walk on a loose leash makes your strolls a pleasure rather than a chore.

In this chapter, we provide you with everything you need to know in order to take a pleasant walk or romp in the park, including how to end Buddy's pulling and how to get him familiar with distractions.

Using the Right Leash and Collar When Walking Your Dog

Studies show that people who regularly walk their dogs get more exercise than those who go to the gym. What could be more fun than sharing that exercise routine with Buddy? Sometimes Buddy may pull. To end the pulling, you need to teach Buddy to walk on a loose leash. For that job, you need the right equipment. The sole purpose of using any equipment at all is to communicate between you and your dog. The leash and collar need to provide a means for you to get Buddy's attention that causes him to look at you and therefore gives you a reason to praise him. It's really as simple as that.

REMEMBER

The best way to get that attention is a quick check on the leash and collar. A *check* is a snappy pull on the leash that starts with no pressure and ends with no pressure. The shorter the pressure lasts, the better a check it is. Repeating the check or checking twice is better than pulling so hard and long on the leash that you end up simply dragging each other. It takes two to cause the leash to become tight — you pulling and the dog pulling on each end at the same time.

Different collars provide different results. The collar you need depends on the drives of your dog (see Chapter 2 for more information on drives). For example, a high prey drive usually needs more of a check than a high pack drive. Thus, having the right leash for walking is imperative. No matter how much of a check you need or provide, your dog's attention should be brought around to you and you must praise him for looking at you. If the collar you're using isn't bringing your dog's attention back to you when you give a quick, snappy check on the leash and collar, then you need to try another type of collar. Chapter 5 discusses the basics about your choices. The following focuses on selecting a leash and collar for walking:

>> **Snap-around collar:** The best choice is a snap-around collar, which is similar to a slip collar except it has a snap that allows the collar to snap around Buddy's neck, right behind his ears, instead of being so large as to go over his head. When fitted snugly behind a dog's ears at the top of his neck, this collar is effective because a check won't hit his trachea, and the check will be more of a guide to bring the dog's attention around to the owner.

>> **Web leash:** For a leash, our preference is a six-foot cotton web leash when walking with your dog. It's light yet strong, comfortable to hold, and easily folds up when you want a shorter length or want to put it in your pocket.

>> **Buckle collars:** They stay the same size all of the time, whether you're checking the collar or not and no matter if your dog is pulling or not. Most dogs can quickly ignore this collar. If anything, it becomes a nagging collar providing little to no results. Plus because a buckle collar is a collar that your dog might wear all of the time with identification on it, it most likely rests too low on his neck, which is where Buddy has a lot of muscle, and his trachea would get too much pressure if you were to yank on a buckle collar too much.

>> **Prong collars:** When used correctly, prong collars are effective and humane because they provide a quick check with little effort other than just enough to bring Buddy's attention immediately back to you. If held too tightly instead of loosely, though, when a check is needed, a dog can ignore a prong collar. Prong collars are used when your dog isn't responding well enough to just a snap-around collar. Often referred to as *power steering* because when used correctly, well fitted high on the neck and with little effort on the leash, the prong collar is an amazing tool to achieve focus from your dog.

TIP

Here are a few reasons you may want to consider using a prong collar:

● When you have a small dog with a lot of prey drive. The extra power steering allows for hardly any pull on the leash to get your dog's attention.

● When you have a large, strong dog and you don't want to use so much effort to get your dog's attention.

● When you aren't very steady on your feet and you want your dog to quickly respond to a quick tug on the leash.

A friend who uses two hearing aids equates a prong collar to a hearing aid for the dog.

REMEMBER

Dogs pull on a leash because they're more interested in the sights and scents in their environment than in you. Your job is to teach Buddy to become aware of your existence at the other end of the leash and to respect your presence. Praising him when he looks at you and rewarding him with your joyful praise makes the walks fun for Buddy too.

Taking a Pleasure Walk with Your Dog

The No.1 rule to walking your dog is that it's *Buddy's* responsibility to pay attention to you, not the other way around. Even though he may be several feet away from you eagerly pursuing a scent, he must be aware of where you are, never straining on the end of the leash but adjusting his speed to your pace and direction. He doesn't need to pay 100 percent attention to you — but he must be aware of you. A *pleasure walk* is fun for both you and your dog. It allows your dog to sniff as long as he's nearby and pacing himself to your pace and direction. It's like two friends enjoying each other's company.

REMEMBER

To teach Buddy to walk nicely with you, you need his collar and his leash. Take Buddy to an area that's familiar to him with no distractions; your backyard or a quiet street are good places. The command to use for a pleasure walk is Let's Go.

The following sections help you teach Buddy how to go on a pleasure walk.

Using a clock face to train your dog to walk

Imagine that you're standing inside the center of the clockface, which can help you train your dog. Figure 12-1 helps you prepare to train your dog to take a pleasure walk.

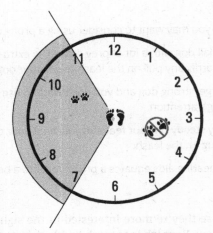

FIGURE 12-1:
Use this clockface
to train your
dog to walk.

The following breaks down Figure 12-1:

>> **You are in the center of the clock facing in the direction you are to walk.**

>> **The 12 is in front of you.** This area belongs to you — the team leader — and not Buddy. As a result, the 12 spot is off-limits to Buddy.

>> **The 6 is directly behind you.** You can't see it, so the 6 is off-limits to Buddy because you want to be able to see him without turning completely around.

>> **The 11 on the clockface is slightly to your left, and moving down to the left you pass the other numbers until you come to the 7.** This zone is Buddy's zone to start. The 7 to 11 on your left side is where you want Buddy to walk with you on a pleasure walk. For a pleasure walk to be pleasant, Buddy shouldn't wind the leash around you, so he needs to stay to one side of you as you walk.

Why do dogs walk on the left of all dog trainers? They traditionally do because people used to lead their horses on their right, and people might have carried their hunting weapons on their right.

>> **The 3 is on your right.** Just to orient you, this is the no-dog zone.

>> **The 9 is on your left.** This is the Heel position (refer to the following section, "Teaching Buddy How to Heel at Your Side" for more information).

TECHNICAL STUFF

The leash is 6-feet long, so the clockface or Buddy's zone must be smaller than the leash is long. Therefore, Buddy can never go outside the 5-foot zone of 7 to 11 on the clockface. You must know exactly where you want Buddy to be in order to teach him where he should be. If you aren't specific in your own mind, how will Buddy learn his place to walk with you?

Training the pleasure walk

Follow these steps when you're training your dog to go on a pleasure walk:

1. **Know Buddy's zone on the clockface and start in the 7-11 area (refer to the previous section for clarification).**

2. **Hold the leash loosely with both hands.**

Place your right hand directly above your left hand, and make a fist around the leash with half of the leash folded in your hands and the rest hanging loosely between you and Buddy. Hold the leash with both hands as though it were a baseball bat. Plant both hands firmly against your belt buckle or waist. Figure 12-2 shows you how this should look.

FIGURE 12-2:
How to
hold a leash.

© John Wiley & Sons, Inc.

3. **Say "Let's go" and start walking.**

Make sure Buddy is on your left, inside his zone when you start. As you walk, keep an eye on where Buddy is walking. If he is in the 7-11 zone and less than a few feet away from you, great and keep walking. If Buddy moves too far out in front or anywhere other than the 7-11 zone, check the leash back to you quickly, bringing Buddy back into his zone and immediately praise him for being back in his zone. Keep walking. Use the bring-back check while you keep walking.

4. **Change your direction as you walk.**

The clockface changes with you, but Buddy's zone is still on your left even though you're now walking in a different direction. Buddy needs to learn that you determine his zone. Everything is in relationship to you. Say "Let's go" as you make a turn to give Buddy a reason to look your way. Practicing in your yard makes it easier to vary your direction because there aren't sidewalks to restrict your direction as you walk.

REMEMBER

If Buddy decides to stop and sniff within his zone, that's fine; you can stop too. After all, it's a pleasure walk for both of you. When you're ready to move on, say "Let's go" and start walking again making sure Buddy is in his zone.

REMEMBER

The trick to a pleasure walk is that you walk where you want to go, as fast as you want to get there, while Buddy hangs out on your left on a loose leash. If he needs reminding where his zone is because he left the zone, check him back into his zone and praise him for being back. The praise after the bring-back is vital to the communication that you're teaching Buddy how to walk nicely on a walk.

TIP

The first few times you practice using the leash to keep Buddy in his 7-11 zone, you'll likely be a little late — Buddy will already be leaning into his collar. If so, extend your elbows a tiny bit to give the leash some looseness before you give a quick check on the leash. Concentrate on Buddy and figure out how to anticipate when you're about to make a turn.

5. **Practice this sequence over the course of several sessions until Buddy responds reliably to the Let's Go command.**

    Keep the sessions short — no more than five to ten minutes to start. Make it fun. Eventually you'll be walking around the block and then for a few miles a day. Buddy should always be in his zone of the clockface.

    As Buddy gets better with your pleasure walk, you can shrink his zone on the clockface. Whatever zone you choose is fine as long as you communicate the change to Buddy by being consistent as you bring him back with a check and praise him afterwards. For example, change or shrink his zone to be 8-10 on the clockface.

Teaching Buddy How to Heel at Your Side

Heeling is ideal when you cross the street, pass another pedestrian, or walk through a marketplace. Heeling is a controlled walk with Buddy directly at your side, moving smoothly together as one, whereas a pleasure walk is pleasant on a loose leash with Buddy freer to move at your side.

By teaching Buddy how to go on a pleasure walk in the preceding section, you're ultimately starting the process of teaching Buddy how to heel. The distinction is Buddy's location. The Heel position is on your left at 9 o'clock with Buddy walking with full attention with his ears in line with the seam on your pants, walking at the same pace and in the same direction as you. While heeling, Buddy learns to stop and sit at your side when you stop walking. (Chapter 18 briefly describes the heeling patterns in a competition.)

As you practice and teach Buddy to heel, make your sessions short. If you're taking a walk around the block, make the majority of the walk be a pleasure walk and interrupt the walk with short sessions of heeling for a few yards or so, and then release with Okay and go back to your pleasure walk. The following steps help you teach Buddy how to heel:

1. **Put Buddy on his training collar and leash, start with him on your left side, and throw the handle of the leash across your chest and over your right shoulder.**

   Your hands should be loosely funneled around the leash in front of you. When needed, you'll be able to take the leash in your hands by squeezing your hands shut around the leash and bringing Buddy back to the Heel position if he should leave his 9 o'clock spot as you walk.

2. **Say "Buddy, Heel."**

   By saying his name before the Heel command, Buddy should look up at you. By saying "Buddy, Heel" before you step off to walk, he'll be ready to move with you, not after you start to walk.

3. **Praise Buddy as he's moving nicely with you.**

   Do so as you walk with Buddy at your left side, still at 9 o'clock on the clockface. If he leaves your side, check him back to your left side by taking hold of the leash with your hands that are circled around the leash across your chest. The check brings him back to your left side as you continue to walk and praise him enthusiastically. Repeat this sequence as you walk around your yard, house, or sidewalk.

4. **Add a change of direction by turning around and going the other way by turning away from Buddy or to the right.**

   Say his name before you turn around so he looks at you and sees that you're turning. Praise him in the new direction as he remains by your side. Repeat turning around, always to the right and saying his name first. Also take hold of the leash as you turn to help keep Buddy with you.

5. **Add a change of pace, such as walk faster or slower, and then back to a normal pace for you.**

   You don't need to give a command to Buddy as you change your pace; simply use your leash to keep him with you and praise when he's beside you. Make sure Buddy learns to change his pace to match your pace, not the other way around.

6. **To end the exercise, say "Okay" and then release by running five steps straight forward and end by partying with Buddy.**

   Start again with Buddy on your left, leash over your shoulder, and say "Buddy, Heel." Release after a few yards by saying, "Okay" and then start over.

The other option instead of releasing is to teach Buddy to automatically sit at your side when you stop, which means that Buddy notices that you're stopping and then sits directly beside you in the Heel position. Initially there is nothing *automatic* about sitting in Heel position because you're helping him where to sit and how, but eventually Buddy should stop and sit when you stop and he is on the Heel command.

TIP

To teach the Automatic Sit, before you stop walking, take hold of the leash with your right hand, close to the top of Buddy's head, and lift the leash up slightly as your left hand tucks his tail under his hind legs as you say "Sit." Praise him for any attempt at a sit in the beginning and then release him.

As you practice the Automatic Sit, you and he will get better at this, and the Sit should happen squarely at your side in the Heel position. Saying "Sit" each time you ask for the Automatic Sit helps Buddy know what you expect from him when you stop. Eventually saying "Sit" won't be necessary, and as you stop and lift the leash slightly, he'll automatically sit.

Adding Distractions

As you practice the Heel command, do so in a distraction-free environment. As you and Buddy get good at heeling, you're ready to teach Buddy that it's his responsibility to pay attention to you while you say "Heel." You use the Heel command when you need more control, usually around distractions such as the marketplace, kids on bikes, other pedestrians, and so on.

Training with distractions

Follow these steps when incorporating distractions during teaching Heel:

1. **Start your session, still without distractions, by reviewing his response to heel with two or three about-turns.**

2. **Say Buddy's name as you make your turn.**

   The first several tries, Buddy will likely experience a tug on the leash before he turns to follow you. After several turns, however, he'll catch on and respond to your turn. When he does, praise lavishly and stop for that session. Review this sequence for several sessions.

3. **When he's comfortable with the routine and follows you without hesitation when you make a turn, you can move on to introducing distractions.**

   For this sequence, you need a distracter — a family member or anyone willing to stand still long enough. The distracter's job is just that: to distract Buddy with any object that may interest him. Food usually works. Of course, the distracter doesn't let Buddy obtain the object, because doing so would defeat the purpose of the exercise. Figure 12-3 shows a distracter at work.

FIGURE 12-3: Heeling with distraction.

© John Wiley & Sons, Inc.

   The distracter holds the object — for these purposes you can assume that it's food — close to his body, without waving it about or talking to Buddy. Because this is a new exercise for Buddy, you start at the beginning: You reintroduce the Heel command.

4. **From a distance of about 10 feet, say "Heel" toward the distracter.**

   When Buddy is aware of the food held by the distracter, say "Heel" again and do an about-turn. If Buddy fails to respond, he'll experience a tug on the leash because of the natural force of the turn at the distracter. Repeat the procedure until Buddy responds by following you on command and no tug occurs. When he remains with you, praise lavishly and end the session.

At your next session, review the same sequence; when Buddy responds correctly and end the session with lots of praise. Eventually follow the same sequence but eliminate saying "Heel" during the distraction and the about-turn because avoiding the distraction is the lesson Buddy has learned.

REMEMBER

Buddy should now have a pretty good idea of what to do while heeling and avoiding distractions, so you're ready to take him to new places. Chances are, on a walk in the park, you'll meet a number of new distractions, including other dogs. Exposing Buddy to a variety of new circumstances is a wonderful teaching opportunity. Practice in those settings both the Let's Go and Heel commands, and alternate between the two different commands.

The Heel command is more precise, and Buddy should avoid all distractions while you use it. Let's Go is less precise. While Buddy is on the Let's Go command, as long as he doesn't pull you toward a distraction, he's able to be beside you showing interest in something other than you for a few seconds. Buddy should never be allowed to stop being aware of where you are at all times.

To find out if Buddy has learned his lessons, try the ultimate tests. Go to a secure location, your fenced back yard, a fenced ball field, or fenced tennis court.

Try this first test: Buddy isn't beside you when you command him, he should join you since you said, "Let's Go."

1. **Go into the fenced area and remove his leash.**

2. **Let Buddy wander around a bit and then say "Heel."**

3. **Turn your back toward him and walk away.**

   If he comes to you, enthusiastically praise. If not, do a little more practicing. Praise him for joining you in your walk around the fenced area. The Heel command means, "Come with me. We are going." When Buddy comes to you and moves on with you, well done. Praise Buddy for being such a great friend.

Try this second test: Buddy starts sitting next to you. He should get up and move with you because you said, "Let's go."

1. **Go into the fenced area and sit Buddy next to you and then remove his leash.**

2. **While he sits there, pet him on his head to put him into pack drive (see Chapter 2 about drives).**

3. **Smile and say "Let's go," and then start walking; Buddy should move with you.**

Give the Buddy, Heel command off leash and start to walk forward. Praise him as he moves with you. Don't go more than a few steps the first time. Say "Okay" to release and have a big party together. What a great dog Buddy has become.

If he doesn't move with you, you need more practice on leash. The best way to teach a dog to work off leash is on leash. If you step off saying, "Buddy, Heel," and he doesn't move with you, reach back with an open palm for his collar to guide him up, and encourage him to move with you.

Often the reason a dog won't move while off leash is because the leash has been too tight while you trained and he has become used to the feel of the leash. Practice more, going back to using the leash, but be careful to keep the leash loosely placed over your right shoulder. Keep your hands off the leash but in place ready to use as necessary to bring Buddy back to your side with a check.

Training with your dog, spending time with each other, and working as a team is not only fun, but also it results in a dancing team. As you and Buddy heel together, you're dancing together. It's easy to see why heeling looks like dancing. When done well, you're a team working in sync — a beautiful sight.

Chapter **13**

Going to Bed and All of Its Practical Uses

Adog who knows the Go to Your Bed command is a wonderful dog and well trained (see Figure 13-1). This command is useful because it teaches your dog a place to hang out for long periods of time, such as when you're hosting guests. Another wonderful use for this command is to teach your dog where you want him to go when someone comes to the door or when you come home instead of jumping up on you or your guests. It can even become a default behavior for the door bell ringing.

One of the uses of the Go command is to teach Buddy the Go to Your Bed command. We explain the Go command in Chapter 10.

Your dog needs to understand when you say "Go to Your Bed," you mean one of three things:

>> Get on the bed when commanded "Go to Your Bed."

>> Don't *get off* the bed until given the release word or say "Okay."

>> Find your bed in the face of distractions or from anywhere in the house.

FIGURE 13-1:
A well-trained dog showing off his good manners.

© John Wiley & Sons, Inc.

REMEMBER

Your dog having a useful understanding of the Go To Bed command doesn't mean Buddy can't simply choose to get on his bed at will. The difference between being commanded to "Go to your bed" and your dog getting on his bed himself is how and when he can get off the bed. If you say "Go to your bed," he can't get off the bed until you release him with Okay. This is crucially important. When he chooses to go to the bed on his own, he can come and go at will. Your command is what makes the difference of how long he remains on the bed.

This chapter explains the importance of having a bed for your dog and what steps you can take to teach Buddy how to use the Go to Your Bed command.

Selecting a Bed for Your Dog

Before you teach your dog the Go to Your Bed command, you need to choose the bed you want to use for Buddy. A well-trained, mannerly dog should be able to be sent to and remain on his bed in the face of guests and when needed to deal with someone at your door.

Here are a few options:

>> **Elevated cot:** An elevated cot as in Figure 13-2a makes a good choice because it has an actual border to clearly define being on the bed or off the bed. Elevated beds or cots can be found all over the Internet and are often made from PVC pipe as the framework. These beds come in all price ranges and all sizes as in Figure 13-2b. Look around and find one that works for your dog and wallet.

» **Foam mattress:** A covered foam mattress as in Figure 13-2c is wonderful for older dog's joints. These beds can offer more warmth as well and definitely more cushioning. They can come with removable covers which make for easy washing.

» **Pads:** Any type of pad can make a nice bed that is easy to take along is you travel as Figure 13-2d shows. A pad can be sponge or throw rugs or old blanket.

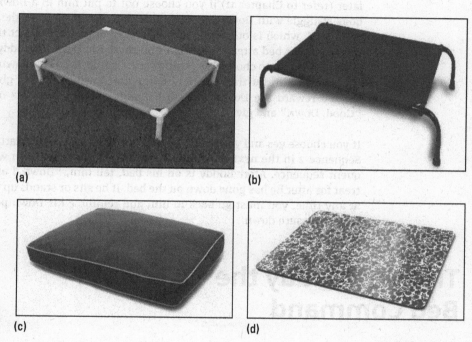

FIGURE 13-2:
Different types
of dog beds.

(a) (b) (c) (d)

© John Wiley & Sons Inc.

An elevated bed isn't mandatory; you can use any dog bed or blanket or towel, even a mouse pad or place mat to signify your dog's place, spot or bed.

Deciphering How You Want to Use the Command

You need to answer this important question before using the Go to Your Bed command: Should you command Buddy to lie down while he is on his bed?

>> If Buddy knows to lie down on his bed each time he gets on his bed, it will add one more layer of stability to the Go to Your Bed command. If so, the answer is yes.

>> If Buddy can choose his own position on the bed, it adds a freedom to Buddy to move around on his bed as long as he remains there. If so, this choice is no.

Choosing one option is a decision you need to make. The option you select is a personal one and depends on you, the owner. You can add the Down command later (refer to Chapter 11) if you choose not to put him in a Down to start. Some dogs struggle with Down and that struggle takes away from the Go to Your Bed command, which is otherwise relatively easy to teach. The fact that Buddy must remain on his bed after you've sent him there is crucial for Buddy to understand. If you allow him to choose his position, that's fine. If he lays down on his own and you reward him for that position, without a Down command given, that's okay too. To reward the Down position if Buddy chooses it on his own, simply say "Good, Down" and give him a treat.

If you choose yes and you want Buddy to lie down each time, start this behavior at Sequence 2 in the next section and continue getting the Down with each subsequent sequence. After Buddy is on his bed, tell him, "Down," and give him the treat for after he has gone down on the bed. If he sits or stands up while on the bed at any time, you must go back to him and reinforce his Down position by using collar pressure down.

Training Buddy the Go to Your Bed Command

Set up the dog bed in the location you want to use it. Ideally it's a place where Buddy can still see you hanging out with guests or still see the front door if you're going to use it as the default behavior for answering the front door. You may need to have two beds, one in the foyer and one in the family room.

Sequence 1: Starting with the Bed command

In these steps you begin with the command and use a food lure to encourage your dog onto the chosen bed:

1. **Put the bed in a logical spot in your house, conveniently out of the way yet easy to access.**

   Have plenty of small but visible treats in your pocket.

2. **Use a cookie in your hand, show Buddy the cookie, lure Buddy onto the surface of the bed, and say "Bed."**

3. **Feed him and then say "Okay" and move to the side, so your dog can get off the bed.**

   You're teaching Buddy to not only get on the bed, but also to not get off of the bed until you release him. He needs to understand these two things.

   REMEMBER

   Feed him while he's on the bed, not after he has gotten off the bed. You want his reward to be for getting on the bed, not for getting off of the bed.

4. **Practice Sequence 1 until he easily is lured onto the bed for his treat.**

Sequence 2: Adding the Go, Bed command

This sequence teaches Buddy to willingly get on the bed by using the Go command (refer to Chapter 10). Follow these steps:

1. **Place a treat on the bed while holding Buddy back a few inches from the bed and then let go of his collar and signal with your closest arm to Buddy and say "Go, Bed."**

   Use these two commands rather than the whole phrase of "Go to Your Bed" to start. Buddy knows the Go command, and you're teaching him the Bed command, so you now want these two words to stand out to him.

   TIP

   If Buddy can reach onto the bed to eat the treat without actually getting on the bed, turn the bed to be long ways on his approach and put the cookie at the far end, making it necessary for him to step onto the bed to get to the treat.

2. **Block his exit from the bed by stepping in front of him if he goes to get off without permission.**

   Then release him with Okay to get off of the bed. Praise him, but don't give him a treat for getting off.

3. **Practice Sequence 2 until he is readily going to the bed on his own and not getting off until you release him.**

   Even if you're still body blocking him, that's fine. If he gets off the bed by accident without being released, take him by the collar and gently return him to the bed by walking back to the surface of the bed with him.

Sequence 3: Increasing your distance from the bed

In the first two sequences you and Buddy are close to the bed. Now step back a foot and follow these steps:

1. **Load a cookie onto the bed as if it were a target and you and Buddy move back a foot and then signal and say "Go to your bed."**

Don't step forward with him, but let him move toward the bed on his own. (We discuss using a target in Chapter 10 when you teach the Go command.)

WARNING

Stepping forward with your dog as you want him to move away from you is called *bowling* with your dog. Don't bowl with your dog. Be aware that moving with your dog is unintentionally teaching him that you'll both be going together all of the time. In actuality you want your dog to move forward alone. Watch that your dog independently moves on without you.

2. **As you load the bed with a target piece of food, walk away with Buddy while holding onto his collar.**

As the distance increases, move back a step until you are both across the room from the bed when you send Buddy to bed with the Go to Your Bed command.

Sequence 4: Foregoing the food lure

In these steps, rather than preloading the bed with a treat, you keep the treat in your pocket and then give it to him after he obeys your command:

1. **Starting close to the bed again without putting a treat on the bed, signal with the arm closest to your dog and say "Go to your bed."**

2. **After Buddy steps onto the bed, go to him and give him a treat from your pocket.**

This change relies on Buddy learning the command, not just going for the food.

Make sure the treat isn't in your hand to start before you command him. If it is, Buddy won't want to leave you and the treat. Instead, put the treat in your pocket or on a dish near the bed on a table that Buddy can't reach. Go to Buddy while he's on the bed and give him the treat from your hand. Body block him so he doesn't get off until you release him.

REMEMBER

If your dog is snatching food from your fingers, head to Chapter 9 to discover how to stop your dog from biting at your fingers for food.

Work this way until you successfully get across the room again as in the previous sequence.

Having the bed not loaded is very different from preloading the bed as a target. Buddy will be getting the treat from you for doing what you just asked him to do. The difference is that Buddy is now working without a lure or target and working for you instead of getting a treat.

3. **While you're working on distance, randomly make the time spent on the bed change from a few seconds to 10 or 20 seconds before the release.**

   Don't give a treat for getting off the bed when asked. Say "Okay" to release and praise him only, no food. Give the treat only while he's still on the bed.

REMEMBER

Sequence 5: Increasing the time spent on the bed

Now that Buddy is getting really good at getting on his bed, you want to instill in him that he must remain there until you release him. You have already been consistent with this point but only for short amounts of time (less than a minute.) In these steps, you boost the amount of time your dog stays on the bed before you release him:

1. **Send him to his bed, rewarding him with a treat, and body blocking him from getting off the bed.**

   While you stand close, keep him on his bed for a full minute. Praise him quietly while he's on the bed. You can repeat the treat during this minute. If Buddy lies down, definitely reward the behavior of choosing to lie down on his own with a treat. After a minute, say "Okay" to release and step aside to allow Buddy to get off, but make sure the release word is what prompts him to gets off the bed, not your body language of moving to the side. Praise and pet him for getting off, no food.

2. **Increase the time on the bed to 90 seconds, 2 minutes, and so on.**

   He should be able to work up to 30 minutes on his bed with you nearby.

TIP

   If he gets off the bed, take him gently and quietly by the collar and replace him by guiding him onto the bed. After he's back on the bed, start to praise him again. Don't repeat the Go to Your Bed command because he got off without permission. By Buddy's getting off without you saying Okay, he has ended the command, not you, so replace him without a command. By not using the command again, it lets Buddy know he did an oops. If you repeat the command at this point, he'll think you're starting over again, and there was no oops on his part, which will only add confusion for him because he won't learn that you and only you end his work with Okay.

3. **Practice until he remains on the bed with no mistakes for as much as 30 minutes.**

Sequence 6: Moving around while he's on the bed

In these steps you start moving away from the bed after you reward him for getting on the bed.

1. **From a distance, say "Go to your bed."**

2. **After he leaves you and gets on the bed, go to him and give him a treat.**

By slowly moving around him, moving away from the bed, and then stepping back to the bed, you're making your location not important for Buddy while he's on his bed.

3. **Work up to being able to step to the other side of the room to mill around but to continue keeping a close eye on Buddy while he's on his bed.**

Always stop him from getting off his bed or return him to his bed if he should get off it. Stay in sight of Buddy at this sequence.

4. **Sit down in a chair and keep an eye on him.**

As you sit down, he'll be tempted to get off and come to you. Immediately get back up and gently guide him back to his bed if that happens.

Sequence 7: Adding distractions

Adding distractions are fun to do with any behavior; however, don't add distractions until you feel your dog understands his job without distractions. Keep the distractions sequential and refer to the different degrees of distractions in Chapter 10.

For the Go to Your Bed command, you can add distractions in two different places:

>> **He's on the bed, and the distractions might pull him off the bed.** As you work on these distractions, you can put a leash on Buddy to help guide him back to the bed. Some examples of distractions are other people coming and going from the room and joining you, you sitting down, eating food, dropping food, throwing a toy, shaking hands with someone who enters the room, a knock on the door, the doorbell ringing, and so on. All of these distractions are appropriate for Buddy to learn to remain on his bed.

>> **You haven't given Buddy the Go to Your Bed command yet.** For example, you alone go outside and then you come into your house and say "Go to your bed" to Buddy. Or someone else is assigned to come to your door and ring or knock on the door, and then you send Buddy to his bed with "Go to your bed."

Having a leash on his collar while you practice these distractions can be helpful. The leash allows you to better control him and help guide him to his bed while you're standing. Furthermore, with a leash you don't need to catch Buddy while he's so distracted.

Don't practice these distractions until Buddy has become successful in remaining on his bed and finding his bed from a distance. Don't rush into distractions until Buddy is ready to deal with them. That's why adding distractions is Sequence 7.

REMEMBER

Distraction training is meant to build your dog's confidence. You need to know Buddy completely understands this command before you work the command under distracted conditions.

Sequence 8: Finding the bed from another room

Teaching your dog to find a specific bed from anywhere in the house may not be something you need. The bed by the front door and the bed in the family room may not be the same bed; therefore, which bed you mean might be confusing to Buddy. As long as he finds a bed that you have trained him to go to, he can go to either bed. For example, if you need to corral Buddy for whatever reason, you can use the Go to Your Bed command. In such a situation, you may want to use the Get in for the crate command from Chapter 14.

Calling your dog to you or sending your dog to his bed or crate are choices you have, and your dog should be well versed in all commands.

To practice this sequence, stick to these steps. Always remember to follow through with the reward and release before trying another suggested location to send Buddy from:

1. **Go to the doorway or arch of the room your dog's bed is in and say "Go to your bed."**

   If Buddy needs help, you may need more practice with earlier sequences.

2. **As Buddy is successful, move farther into the next room and send him from there.**

   Always follow him without bowling him. Let him leave you before you move to follow.

   This sequence is fun because Buddy gets to run to his bed. Running is fun for dogs plus he gets a food reward after he's there.

3. Move from room to room as you vary the location from which you send Buddy.

Also vary the time of day you practice this command. Simply stand up from somewhere in the house and say "Go to your bed" to Buddy. You may not have been training him at this time, but surprise him.

By varying the times and the locations, Buddy will become well versed in watching you and listening to you at any and all times. Remember in the relationship you have with Buddy, you are the coach and he is the player. Making training fun is great, but adding training into any part of the day really keeps Buddy waiting and watching for a command from you.

WHEN THE DOORBELL RINGS, USE THE GO TO YOUR BED COMMAND

If you want Buddy to always go to his bed when the doorbell rings, you can make this his default behavior for the bell ringing. To do this, get another person to help you. Have this person outside and text her to ring the bell when you want it to ring.

Start with Sequence 1, but add the doorbell ringing first and then lure Buddy onto the bed. Then train Sequence 2, 3, and so on. If Buddy goes crazy for the doorbell, you need to do this step on leash. You should do the doorbell as a default Go to Your Bed command only after you've already taught all of the sequences in the "Training Buddy to Go to Your Bed" section. Don't start with the doorbell as your command if you haven't already taught the Go to Your Bed command.

> » Focusing on Buddy to get on and get off

> » Dashing your dog's dashing habits by teaching him door and stair manners

Chapter **14**

Getting In, Out, On, and Off and Mastering Door and Stairs Manners

Almost as annoying as unrestrained greeting behavior, but far more dangerous, is a dog's habit of dashing through doors just because they're open, or racing up and down stairs — ahead of or behind you — or jumping in and out of the car without permission. These behaviors are dangerous to your dog because he may find himself in the middle of the road and get hit. These behaviors also are dangerous to *you* because Buddy may knock you over going down the stairs or through the door.

REMEMBER

You can prevent such potential accidents by teaching Buddy not to go through a door and to wait until you tell him it's okay to go out. For the exercises in this chapter, Buddy doesn't need to sit, but many dogs will do so on their own after a few repetitions.

Getting In and Out

Get In is an extremely useful command when you're training Buddy. You can say "Get in" for the crate, the car, the door, the gate, to name a few helpful uses. Other variations are just as important. The Move Ahead of Me command is the basic concept, which is similar to the Go command (see Chapter 10 for more information). Go means move on, go with someone else, or go without me. The difference is that the Get In command means getting in a smaller opening or confined space.

Starting with a crate is an easy way to begin teaching the Get In command. (Chapter 6 mentions crates and the benefits of their use.) Even if you already use a crate, there is an ownership of the door opening that is important to teach to Buddy. You, the leader, owns the opening and gives permission for him to exit. He should enter when you tell him and not exit until you tell him. Bolting out of the crate isn't acceptable, plus he should never avoid getting in.

To teach the Get In and Get Out commands, break them down into these sequences and steps:

Sequence 1: Eating the reward

The steps in the first sequence motivate Buddy with a cookie to go inside his crate:

1. **Go to the crate and open it and hold onto Buddy's collar.**
2. **Open the crate door, toss a cookie inside, and say, "Get in."**
3. **Let go of Buddy's collar, allowing him to go in and eat it without any rules of remaining inside at this point, and leave the door open while he eats his treat.**

   He can bring the treat out or stay in and eat it. No rule yet. Repeat several times until Buddy is excited to get inside for the treat.

Sequence 2: Making Buddy wait for his treat

The steps in this sequence make Buddy wait for his reward:

1. **Say, "Get in," and release Buddy's collar to allow him to move inside.**
2. **Hand Buddy the treat through the door opening for getting inside.**

   He can eat the treat and leave because you're not yet making any rules about remaining inside.

Sequence 3: The rules of the exit begin

Now you're reading for Buddy to exit only on command. Follow these steps:

1. Say, "Get in," and go back to tossing a treat into the crate.

2. After Buddy is inside, swing the crate door shut while he eats his treat, no need to latch it, simply hold it closed.

3. When he's finished eating, make eye contact with Buddy, say, "Okay," open the door, and let him out.

If he won't look at you, make a kissy sound to encourage him to look up at you.

4. Repeat Step 1 and start controlling the door with your hand by only opening it slightly and then immediately swinging it shut again if Buddy goes to exit.

You have not said "Okay" yet, so he has no permission to exit the crate.

The action of the door swinging shut will put visual pressure on Buddy, and he'll move back inside. Remember you haven't said the release work yet.

Repeat swinging the door shut until Buddy doesn't try to exit while the door is ajar. At that point, with the door ajar, wait for him to look at you and then say, "Okay," and have a big party outside the crate.

REMEMBER

These rules remain throughout his life. He should never bolt out of a crate without your permission. If Buddy is crated in a public place, you should be able to reach in and leash him before you release him from his crate.

As Buddy gets better about entering and exiting his crate on command, he next needs to find his crate on your command.

5. Move a bit away from the crate and practice his running into his crate on command for his cookie from a slight distance.

He should then turn around, but wait for you to either close the door behind him or release him from the crate.

These distance reviews give you an opportunity to keep practicing this sequence. Initially you were right outside the crate, now 2 feet away, then 4 feet, and so on. He should get into his crate when you say, "Get in," from any distance, even from another room. Then walk up to the crate and review the exit by saying "Okay."

Well done. Review each and every day and each and every time you put him in the crate. These are life-long rules of living with your dog. Never allow him to exit the crate without controlled permission and always say, "Get in," on your command.

Getting On and Off

As you live with Buddy, you'll find the need for him to move off of the sofa, off of your lap, off of a piece of furniture, out of the car's back seat, and so on. The Get Off command is useful in all instances. When you say "Get off," Buddy should jump immediately off of what he is on. You can work on both the Get On and Get Off commands together using a sofa or big foot stool or garden wall, something that has a big upper surface that Buddy would love to get up on but can easily and safely get off of when you ask.

REMEMBER

Get On and Get Off are two commands that should bring immediate response to Buddy's actions. Your body language and immediate movement will impress this on him each and every time you give the commands. Use your body language each time, moving toward the object for when you say, "On," and turning and moving away from the object for when you say, "Off."

These two commands are especially useful when getting in and out of the back of the car. Take your lessons to the car and get Buddy jumping in and out of the car on command. Remember your part in making this go well, turning your back and moving away for getting off and stepping toward the elevated surface for getting on.

Sequence 1: Getting Buddy on something

Follow these steps to teach Buddy how to get on something like a sofa:

1. **Put Buddy on a leash and bring him to the sofa or surface you'll be using and have some good treats, small and easy to eat, with you.**

   Treats should always be small when training multiple repetitions.

2. **Offer him a treat on the edge, pat the sofa, and say a happy "Yes," allowing him to eat the treat.**

   Yes means you're perfectly doing the command at the moment of perfection, the moment he starts performing.

3. **Repeat, moving the treat a few more inches back away from the edge, pat the surface, and say, "Yes," when he reaches for the treat to eat it.**

   If Buddy willingly jumps up on the sofa, great, praise him; if not, then put your hand gently in his collar and use the treat in your other hand to encourage him closer to the sofa.

4. **Place the treat on the sofa and say, "Get on."**

If he needs help, use your body language and turn and walk along the front edge of the sofa to help bring him up and on the sofa. Gently bring Buddy up onto the sofa and let him eat his treat. Say, "Yes," when he steps up and praise him while he eats. Keep him on the sofa.

Sequence 2: Getting Buddy off something

These steps help you train Buddy get off something like the sofa:

1. **With Buddy on the sofa, on leash, turn your back to him, say, "Get off," and step forward or away from the sofa.**

The most important thing is for you to turn your back to Buddy while you say, "Get off," and walk a step away from the sofa with a slight tug on the leash. Say, "Yes," for stepping off and play with him and praise him on the floor.

2. **While you're still a step away from the sofa, say, "Get on," and step toward the sofa and give him his treat while on the sofa.**

3. **Say, "Yes," pet him while he is up, and body block him from getting off until you command him to do so; then turn away and step away and say, "Get off."**

When he does, say, "Yes," and party together on the floor.

REMEMBER

Turning your back to Buddy for the Get Off command is important. Stepping toward the elevated surface is critical for Buddy as well, especially in the early stages.

4. **Review until you no longer need to move with Buddy — until your words are the only command needed to get Buddy to move up and on and off.**

Training Door Manners

Teaching door manners doesn't require any prior training and is a good introductory exercise. This exercise is fun to teach because you can see the wheels in Buddy's brain turning. Your dog learns quickly that the only way out of the door is the release word, such as Okay. This command is meant for doors to the outside: front door, back door, gate in the fence, and so on.

REMEMBER

You don't use a verbal command for this training; the door is always there, so the threshold becomes the living command. You're teaching Buddy never to cross the threshold without permission.

Sequence 1: Opening the door

Training Buddy door manners should be a breeze. Here's what to do:

1. **With Buddy on leash and at your side, hold the leash so it's loose with no pressure on the collar.**

   The leash should have some slack, but not so much that when Buddy starts to bolt out the door, you can smoothly "check" him from stepping over the threshold (see Figure 14-1).

FIGURE 14-1:
Practicing door manners.

© John Wiley & Sons, Inc.

Choose a door that opens to the outside (or your front door that opens into a hall like in an apartment or condo) and approach it right up to the threshold.

2. **With your free hand, open the door a crack; when Buddy moves, close the door quickly.**

3. **Praise him for stepping backward when the door moves toward him as you close it.**

4. **Start over; open the door a little, and, when he moves, close it. Praise him again for stepping backward.**

If you have an overly enthusiastic dog, you may need to apply a little backward tension on the leash to keep him from moving forward. After several tries, Buddy may look at you as if to say, "Exactly what are we doing here?" The little wheels are turning. Try again, and this time he shouldn't move toward the door. When he stands still, close the door and verbally praise him with "Good dog."

5. **Repeat this process several times, each time opening the door a little wider before closing it again.**

The entire sequence take three to five minutes. You can end the session here and pick it up again at another time (after practicing this sequence), or, if your dog is still interested, continue with the next sequence.

Sequence 2: Adding some outside distraction

Distraction outside adds a new layer of enticement to Buddy going through the door. Follow these steps when Buddy is distracted:

1. **When Buddy is distracted, apply a little leash pressure in the form of a *check* (a snappy, crisp jerk back) if Buddy goes to cross the threshold.**

The action of the door has been enough to stop Buddy from crossing the threshold without distractions. In the presence of a distraction there must be a consequence should he step over the threshold without your permission.

TIP

If you're holding Buddy back from moving through the door opening, he'll never learn this exercise. The pressure of the leash is keeping him from making a mistake. He needs to control himself. Giving Buddy a verbal command such as Wait or Stay or Sit may be tempting, but he must learn to respect the open door as an invisible command and wait until you've given permission to exit for his safety.

2. **If Buddy steps toward the threshold, check him back and show no negative reaction.**

The doorway caused the check back, not you, or that's what you want Buddy to think. Praise him for stepping back when the check occurs though. He's correct when he steps back away from the door.

3. **Release him through the open door with the Okay permission command.**

With the door open and Buddy on the inside of the house, look at Buddy and say, "Okay." Step through with him and make sure you party on the outside.

4. **Repeat coming back inside and use Steps 2 and 3 to come back inside.**

Wait to release Buddy only after he has looked at you before you release him through the door. This is the leadership part of this exercise. The opening belongs to you — the leader of the pack. Waiting for him to look at you before you release may take seconds or much longer. If it's taking longer than you want, make a kissy sound to encourage Buddy to look your way. Then smile, praise, and say, "Okay."

Sequence 3: Leaving Buddy behind at the door

Buddy shouldn't follow you through a door just because you're going out. Only with the permission word should he go through the opening. Follow these steps to teach that concept to Buddy:

1. **Open the door and step over the threshold leaving Buddy behind inside; prepare the leash in Sequence 2 and be ready to check him back.**

When or if Buddy moves, check him back with the leash, close the door, and start over. When he's committed to wait on the inside of the door, step over the threshold again. If he moves, step back, close the door, and try again.

As you step over the threshold, you need to let out enough leash so you don't inadvertently pull on it, thereby causing Buddy to follow. Remember to praise for every correct response.

When Buddy holds his position after you've crossed the threshold, praise, pause, and release him with "Okay," and then let him exit. Remember, praise isn't an invitation to move! Only Okay is his release command.

2. **Approach the door, exit, and close the door behind you.**

You decide when Buddy can follow or when he has to stay. After that, your success depends on consistency on your part. After Buddy has become solid at this exercise, review the entire sequence off leash.

3. **Move to the gate in a fence and repeat the preceding steps for the gate in the fence.**

It takes a little time to teach Buddy that all openings to the outside are active openings and he must respect them because you own all openings. Put a sticky note on the door frame to remind everyone that you're teaching Buddy door manners. Everyone needs to be consistent in Buddy's training.

REMEMBER

4. **Repeat them for the door into a retail store you allow Buddy to visit.**

He should always look to you for permission to enter and exit.

The time invested in teaching door manners is well worth it, considering the exercise's application of other situations, such as stairs and a gate. The exercise also applies to entering the house. It makes no difference whether you prefer to go through the doorway first or whether you want the dog to go through first, as long as he waits until you release him. Practice going through doors your dog uses regularly.

WARNING

Motion means more to dogs than words, so make sure you stand still when releasing your dog. You don't want him to associate your moving with the release. Also, be aware that dogs have an acute sense of time. Say you usually wait for two seconds before you release him. He then starts to anticipate and releases himself after one second, defeating the purpose of the exercise. You need to vary the length of time between opening the door and the release so he learns to wait for you to release him.

Teaching Stairs Manners

If you have stairs, start teaching Buddy to stay at the bottom while you go up. First tell him "Stay." (See Chapter 11 to teach Stay.) When he tries to follow, put him back and start again. Practice until you can go all the way up the stairs with him waiting at the bottom before you release him to follow. Repeat the same procedure for going down the stairs.

Practice on a short flight of stairs first, just a couple of steps. Then move to a whole flight of stairs. Starting with a short flight makes it easier for Buddy to understand this command.

After Buddy has been trained to wait at one end of the stairs, you'll discover that he'll anticipate the release. He'll jump the gun and get up just as you're thinking about releasing him. Before long, he'll stay only briefly and then release himself. Put him back and start all over. Few things are more irritating, and potentially dangerous, than the dog's rushing past you as you are descending stairs, especially if you're carrying something.

REMEMBER

Teaching stair manners sounds like a lot of work and exercise for you. In the beginning, it does take a little time, but you'll be surprised by how quickly the routine becomes a habit for Buddy. The best part is that you're teaching him to look to you for direction. Also, we think it's important that each member of the family is consistent in following the directions. Doing so makes it easier for Buddy to understand if each family member enforces the same rules. To help remind everyone to use the training commands, add a sticky note on the staircase. Consistency is important for Buddy and for people, too.

Chapter **15**

Dealing with Common Doggie Don'ts

D oes your dog have what you think is a behavior problem? Does Buddy bark incessantly, but otherwise behave like a model dog? Does he jump on people when he first meets them, but is perfectly well behaved the rest of the time? Does Buddy chew on your favorite possessions when left unattended?

The first line of defense is some basic training (see Chapter 9). So-called "behavior problems" are more difficult in isolation than they are when Buddy knows basic commands. You'll find dealing with undesired behaviors easier to handle after you've established a line of communication with Buddy.

If you haven't done the Long-Down exercise, you may want to start there. The purpose of the Long-Down exercise is to teach Buddy in a clear way that you're in charge. For this reason, the Long Down is the foundation of all further training. Training your dog is next to impossible unless he accepts that you're the one who makes decisions. It takes four weeks to get the Long Down established as a routine. But, as soon as you've accomplished the Long Down, it can go a long way toward helping you establish your role as the leader. Teaching Buddy the Long Down shows Buddy that you decide what he does, where he does it, when he does it, and for how long he does it. In other words, you're the leader of the team.

The majority of doggy don'ts are relationship problems rather than behavior problems. These behaviors often are the result of insufficient exercise, time spent with the dog, or training. In this chapter, we discuss some of the most common doggie don'ts and provide you with some workable solutions.

REMEMBER

Behavior problems don't arise overnight. Working toward a solution may take time, patience, and training, but it's well worth it.

Preventing Bad Habits — The Five General Prescriptions for Good Behavior

Many dogs form bad habits or behavior problems that possess a common cause or a combination of causes. In order of importance, they include the following:

>> Boredom and frustration due to insufficient exercise

>> Mental stagnation due to insufficient quality time working and training with you

>> Loneliness caused by too much isolation from human companionship

>> Nutrition and health-related problems

REMEMBER

Loneliness is perhaps the most difficult problem to overcome. By necessity, many dogs are left alone at home anywhere from eight to ten hours a day with absolutely nothing to do except get into mischief. Fortunately, in addition to spending quality time with your dog, you can do some things to help him overcome his loneliness.

The following sections point out five general prescriptions for good behavior you can use as a guide for Buddy.

Good exercise

Exercise needs vary depending on the size and energy level of your dog. Many dogs need a great deal more exercise than their owners realize. Working dogs are a good example. If the owner of a working breed (Shepherds, Border Collies, Retrievers, and Terriers to name a few) lives in an apartment in a large city and the dog doesn't get enough free-running exercise, he's bound to develop behavior problems. These behaviors can range from tail spinning, which is a neurotic behavior, to ripping up furniture and destruction. This kind of dog would show none of these behaviors if he lived in a household where adequate exercise, both mental and physical, were provided. The dog determines what is enough exercise, not the owner. For example, a Bassett may be satisfied with a short walk every day, but a Border Collie needs a real job: running, chasing, and getting exhausted daily to be content.

REMEMBER

The dog trainer's maxim is: "Tired dogs have happy owners." After all, dogs that get adequate exercise and can expend their energy through running, retrieving, playing, and training rarely show objectionable behaviors. Dogs denied those simple needs frequently redirect their energy into unacceptable behaviors. Figure 15-1 shows a well-exercised pet.

FIGURE 15-1:
Tired dogs have happy owners.

© John Wiley & Sons, Inc.

When your dog engages in behaviors that you consider objectionable, the problem can be vexing. Sometimes the behavior is instinctive, such as digging. Sometimes it occurs out of boredom. However, it's never because the dog is ornery. Before you attempt to deal with the behavior, you need to find out the cause. The easiest way to stop a behavior is by addressing the need that brought it about in the first place rather than by trying to correct the behavior itself. And if there's one single cause for behavior problems, it's the lack of adequate exercise.

Good company

The *single-dog syndrome* refers to the behavior problems that develop because a dog doesn't get enough social interactions. These dogs can run away from their owners more frequently than those dogs living in multidog households. They might growl around their food bowls, be picky eaters, be possessive about toys, and be much more unruly than dogs living in homes with other dogs. In other words, dog ownership may be easier if you owned two dogs. Dogs are social animals and need companionship. If not from you, then from another dog.

If you can't bear the thought of being a two-dog household, good company is even more important. *Good company* means not only that you act as a companion to your dog but also that your dog shares the company of other dogs as frequently as possible. Some possibilities include taking regular walks in parks where he can meet other dogs, joining a dog club where dog activities are offered, or putting your puppy into doggie daycare several days a week. Socialization of your pet is a continuing process. If you're able, get another dog to be Buddy's companion. Dogs are pack animals and thrive in the company of other dogs. If you aren't able to get another dog, give yourself to your dog and be his friend by playing more and being together more. The simple act of moving your dog into your bedroom counts as quality time together. Your dog will be aware of your presence, your scent, and your breathing.

Good health

Keeping Buddy in good health isn't nearly as easy as it was 50 years ago. It seems that with the advance of science in so many dog-related fields, dogs should be healthier than ever, but this isn't the case. Too often through poor breeding practices, poor nutrition, and overvaccination, a dog's health has been threatened like never before.

REMEMBER

Owning a dog that has constant health problems — from minor conditions like skin irritations, fleas, smelly coat, and ear infections to more serious conditions that affect his internal organs, such as the kidneys, heart, liver, and thyroid — is no fun! Not feeling well can cause your dog to develop behavior problems. Health-related conditions often are confused with behavior problems. Buddy may ingest something that upsets his stomach, causing a house-soiling accident. He may develop a musculoskeletal disorder, making changes of position painful and causing irritability and sometimes snapping. These concerns obviously aren't amenable to training solutions — and certainly not to discipline. For more on your dog's health, see Chapter 4.

A dog in pain can become aggressive as a means of protecting his own space. If your dog starts to show aggressive behaviors that he has never shown before, take your dog to the vet for a complete physical done first before doing any behavior modifications. Treat the hidden condition first because without treatment his behavior won't improve.

Good nutrition

The saying "You are what you eat" applies equally to dogs as it does to people. Properly feeding your dog makes the difference between sickness and health, and it has a profound effect on his behavior. With the abundance of dog foods on the market, figuring out what's best for your pet can be difficult. Chapter 4 discusses in greater detail the ways you can correctly feed your dog and the importance of sound nutrition.

Good training

Behavior problems don't arise because your dog is ornery or spiteful, and discipline is rarely the answer. Instead, mental stagnation often can be a cause of unwanted behavior. Training your dog on a regular basis, or having him do something for you, makes your dog feel useful and provides the mental stimulation he needs. (To get started with basic training, see Chapters 9 and 10.)

REMEMBER

Use your imagination to get your dog to help around the house. You'll be surprised by how useful he can become. If you've taught Buddy to retrieve, he can help you bring in groceries from the car. He can carry a package of frozen food, a cereal box, or whatever you think he can hold in his mouth. Encourage him to take it into the kitchen. You can use Buddy to take the dirty laundry to the washing machine. He can carry his leash out to the car. (Chapter 16 shows how to teach a dog to retrieve.) Retrieving and carrying is regarded by Buddy as a reward — he loves to work — so giving him a treat each time isn't necessary. Remember to give him lavish praise, however.

Handling Your Dog's Objectionable Behavior

Like beauty, objectionable behavior is in the eye of the beholder. Playful nipping or biting may be acceptable to some and not to others. Moreover, different degrees of objectionable behavior exist. After all, getting on the couch in your absence isn't nearly as serious an offense as destroying it.

Dogs like to please, and most behaviors can be changed with a little good training. Knowing a dog's Personality Profile (see Chapter 2) helps you understand why your dog does the seemingly irritating things that he does. What's objectionable, however, is when you visit friends and their untrained dogs jump up and scratch in the process. Other critical negative behavior patterns include dogs who

>> Doesn't come when called, which is dangerous (see Chapter 10 for more on the Come command)

>> Doesn't stay when told (head to Chapter 11 to find out how to teach Stay)

>> Chases cats, squirrels, joggers, bicyclists, or worse yet, cars (see how to manage prey-drive behaviors in Chapter 20)

>> Barks incessantly (refer to the section, "Quieting the Incessant Barker," later in this chapter)

By investing a mere ten minutes a day, five times a week for about four weeks you can eliminate all these irritating behaviors. After that, brush-ups several times a week in different locations for the rest of the dog's life keep the behaviors you want sharp. Training is a lifetime process. Training takes such a small amount of time and energy to get a wonderful dog for which you can be proud. Trained dogs are free dogs — you can take them anywhere, and they're always welcome.

REMEMBER

When you believe your dog has a behavior problem, consider the following options:

>> You can tolerate the behavior or manage it, for example, by crating him when guests come over.

>> You can train your dog to change the behavior.

>> You can find a new home for the dog, one which may be more suited for his needs.

>> You can take your dog to the shelter, but do know that this could be a one-way trip for him.

We discuss each of these topics in the following sections.

Tolerating your dog's behavior problems

Considering the amount of time and energy that may be required to turn Buddy into the pet you always wanted, you may decide it's easier to live with his annoying antics than it is to try to change him. You tolerate him the way he is, because you don't have the time, the energy, or the inclination to put in the required effort to change him.

TIP

One tool that aids in tolerating any kind of inappropriate behavior is a crate. Leaving Buddy in a crate when you're at work saves you from worrying about house-training, chewing, and digging. When properly trained to stay in a crate, Buddy will think of it as his den or bedroom. He'll always be safe (and feel safe) in his crate. With a crate, he can go anywhere with you, from the car to a friend's house. Today lightweight crates can be bought for even the largest of dogs. You can even take him on vacation with you. He'll also be comfortable any time you must leave him at the vet, where dogs are kept in crates during treatment. (See Chapter 14 for more on training with a crate.)

GOING DIRECTLY TO THE SOURCE

If you want to stop a negative or annoying behavior, you must deal with the need that brought it about in the first place. When your dog goes through teething, for example, you need to provide him with suitable chew toys. When your dog has an accident in the house, ask yourself whether you left him inside too long or whether the dog is ill (and in that case, a trip to the vet is in order). If your dog is left alone in the yard and continuously barks out of boredom, don't leave him out there. When your dog needs more exercise than you can give him, consider a dog-walker or daycare.

Every behavior has a time frame and a certain amount of energy attached to it. This energy needs to be expended in a normal and natural way. By trying to suppress this energy, or not giving it enough time to dissipate, you help cause a majority of behavior problems.

By using the Personality Profile in Chapter 2, you can find out where your dog's energies lie. For example, is he high in prey drive? These dogs need more exercise than dogs in other drives. They're attracted to anything that moves quickly and want to chase it. Finding an outlet for these behaviors, such as playing ball, throwing sticks, or hiding toys and having Buddy find them, goes a long way to exhausting the energies of this drive.

WARNING

Behaviors you shouldn't tolerate are those that threaten your safety or the safety of others, such as biting people or aggression. True aggression is defined as unpredictable — without warning — and unprovoked biting (see Chapter 20 for more). You also shouldn't tolerate behaviors that threaten the safety of your dog, such as chasing cars or stealing and gulping your possessions (check out the later section "Contending with Chewing — The Nonfood Variety" to curb this behavior).

Trying to solve your dog's behavior problems

You've decided that you can't live with your dog's irritating behaviors and that you're going to work with him so he'll be the pet you expected and always wanted. You understand that doing so will require an investment of time (at least ten minutes a day, five times a week), effort, and perhaps even expert help. But you're willing to work to achieve your goal — a long-lasting, mutually rewarding relationship. Good for you! This book can help.

Obedience training, in and of itself, isn't necessarily the answer to your problems. Still, when you train your dog, you're spending meaningful time with him, which in many cases is half the battle. Much depends on the cause of the problem (refer to the earlier section "Preventing Bad Habits — The Five General Prescriptions for Good Behavior" for more information).

When all else fails: Finding a new home for your dog

Sometimes a dog's temperament may be unsuitable to an owner's lifestyle. For example, a shy dog or a dog with physical limitations may never develop into a great playmate for active children. A dog that doesn't like to be left alone isn't suitable for someone who's gone all day. A dog may require a great deal more exercise than the owner is able to give him and, as a result, is developing behavior problems. Although some behaviors can be modified with training, others can't — the effort required would simply be too stressful for the dog and/or the owner.

In instances like these, the dog and the owner are mismatched, and they need to move on to live a happier existence. Whatever the reason, under some circumstances, placement into a new home where the dog's needs can be met is advisable and is in the best interest of both the dog and the owner. This isn't a failure but rather an acceptable outcome to an unacceptable situation.

For example, Wendy recalls an incident involving an English Bull Terrier who was left alone too much and started tail spinning. The behavior escalated to the point that the dog became completely neurotic. At that point, Wendy and her husband suggested a new home and found one for the dog on a farm. The dog now had unlimited daily exercise, and within a few weeks the tail-spinning behavior had completely disappeared.

If all reclamation efforts fail — you can't live with this dog, and he can't be placed elsewhere — your final option is to take him to a shelter or to the veterinarian to put him to sleep. This option isn't to be considered lightly, and you should only follow through if you've really tried to work it out and truly see no other alternatives. If you choose to take him to a shelter, don't kid yourself; most shelters are overwhelmed by the number of unwanted dogs and are able to find new homes for only a small percentage of those homeless pets. But this unhappy fact doesn't mean that you must live an unhappy life and your dog live an anxiety-ridden one as well. There is no fault here, there is no burden that you should live with if the match was completely wrong.

Teaching Buddy to Keep All Four on the Floor

In many instances, dogs are systematically rewarded for jumping on people. When a dog was a cute puppy, for example, he received much oohing and awing; everyone was petting him and getting him all excited. Naturally he would jump up to get all that attention. As Buddy got older, relatives and friends would reinforce the behavior with lively petting, especially on top of the head, causing the dog to jump up. He quickly learned to anticipate this greeting ritual and to jump on anybody and everybody that came through the door. Figure 15-2 shows a dog jumping for attention.

FIGURE 15-2:
Does your dog jump on people?

© John Wiley & Sons, Inc.

Now that he's a 50-pound (or more!) energetic and enthusiastic 1-year-old, these assaults are no longer acceptable. Establishing a line of meaningful communication with the dog is your first approach. However, if the behavior has become severely habituated, you need to take the lead. It's never too late to do so. You can use the following two commands to prevent Buddy from jumping on your guests.

Greeting people — Using the Hello command

When someone greets Buddy out and about or at your door, she usually bends forward over him, reaches out to pet him, and says "Hello." You can train this action as the cue for Buddy to sit and be still for the petting. The Hello command and the bending forward are the dual command. Refer to Chapter 9 for specifics about teaching this command.

Using Sit and Stay as an alternative to jumping up

A more formal approach is to teach Buddy to sit on command and follow with the Stay exercise (see Chapter 11). After he's reliable with the Sit and Stay, enlist a helper and follow these steps:

1. **Before your helper comes to the door, instruct her to avoid eye contact with Buddy and to ignore him when the door is opened.**

2. **Ask the helper to ring the doorbell or knock.**

3. **Leash Buddy, tell him to "Sit" and then say "Stay" before you open the door.**

   Chances are, Buddy will get up to greet your helper. Reinforce the Stay command by checking (lifting straight up on the leash) to make Buddy sit again. If he doesn't respond, review the training equipment you're using (see Chapter 5).

   Buddy's response to a check with the leash depends on the extent to which he's distracted and his discomfort threshold. (See Chapter 3 for more information.)

REMEMBER

4. **Keep practicing.**

   Repeat the preceding steps until Buddy holds the Stay position on a loose leash when you open the door, which may take several repetitions. As soon as he's successful, stop the session.

5. **Add distractions such as the doorbell or knocking on the door.**

   Other distractions can be the person who arrives is wearing a hat or carrying a box. Before the next session, remind your helper to ignore Buddy and to avoid making eye contact with him. Review the steps from the beginning and invite your helper into the house.

   When Buddy stays, quietly tell him what a good boy he is and end the session. If he doesn't stay, reinforce the Sit with a check up on the leash putting him back into the sitting position.

You need to continue this routine until Buddy sits politely when someone comes to the door. When he reliably sits and stays, you can try the exercise off leash. His response will tell you whether he needs more training. If Buddy gets up out of his stay while off leash, you must reach in for his collar and replace him into the sitting position again. No command is necessary, but praise him quietly when he is indeed sitting again. Remember: Training is often a matter of who's more persistent: you or your dog.

Putting an End to Counter Surfing — Leave It

Buddy is *counter surfing* when he puts his nose on the counter to sniff out anything edible within reach (refer to Figure 15-3). Utilize one of the following or a combination thereof to stop this behavior when he's thinking of sniffing the counter's edge or jumping on the counter.

FIGURE 15-3: A puppy showing early signs of counter surfing.

© John Wiley & Sons, Inc.

Here is a list of some additional things you can put into practice when working on counter surfing issues.

>> **Teach Buddy the Leave It command.** This is the most important thing you can do. Refer to Chapter 9 for the how-to specifics. Buddy must know that sniffing the counter's edge isn't acceptable, so as your first step, teach him the Leave It command.

>> **Physically remove him by taking his collar and moving him away from the counter.** Set him up with food hanging half off the counter or extending off of the edge of the counter, while you're nearby. He'll know you're there, but he needs to first learn what is wrong before you can teach him from a distance without you being in the room.

>> **Use the startle response of a penny shake or an airhorn as a deterrent.** Just as Buddy sniffs at the counter's edge or the food hanging off the edge, shake the penny can or blow the air horn and the noise should interrupt and stop him in his tracks. Remember to use the noise *as* Buddy moves toward

the counter and sniffs, not after he has done so or grabbed the food. If it's after he sniffs, the response is too late because Buddy already enjoyed his stolen reward.

>> **Practice on a lower surface such as the coffee table in the family room.** Buddy should leave all snacks alone on that table even though it's in easy reach. You shouldn't need to put away to-go containers, pizza boxes, chip bowls, and so on just because Buddy is in the room with you. Practice Leave It there as well. You need to police the table and his actions, but this work will result in a dog you can trust around food that isn't his.

>> **Place a fly swatter at an angle on the counter so that when Buddy makes his ascent, it falls off and (hopefully) startles him.** Even though this tactic is successful with some dogs, others simply ignore the falling swatter. You need to remember to put the fly swatter on the counter, but this method only works if you've already trained the previous lessons while you were present.

TIP

One little trick that helps Buddy think you're psychic, and to reinforce your Leave It command, is to place a mirror in such a way that you can see the counter from another room. You can bait the countertop with something very tasty, go into the other room, and wait for Buddy to sniff. When you say "Leave it," Buddy will be amazed at your ability to catch him in the act. And for the persistent and dedicated counter surfer, you may consider an indoor containment system to solve the problem (see Chapter 5).

Quieting the Incessant Barker

On the one hand, few things are more reassuring than knowing that your dog will sound the alarm when a stranger approaches. On the other hand, few things are more nerve racking than a dog's incessant barking. Dogs bark for three reasons:

>> In response to a stimulus or distraction

>> Because they're bored and want attention — any attention — even if that attention involves the owner's being nasty to the dog (scolding or physically punishing)

>> When someone comes to the door

Therein lies the dilemma: You want the dog to bark, but only when you think he should. We cover each of these situations in the following sections.

Here are a couple general ways to get your dog to stop barking incessantly:

>> **Use a remote bark collar or a citronella collar.** The remote bark collar causes a slight stimulus be it a shock, vibration, or tone every time he barks, whereas a citronella collar sprays some citronella in the direction of the dog's nose when he barks.

These tools work well in a single-dog household. (See Chapter 5 for more info on these collars.) When the dog barks, the collar goes off. Some collars reset to a lower level if the dog is quiet for a length of time and may increase if he keeps barking continually. Buddy needs to learn how to shut the collar off by being quiet. You must help him when you initially put the collar on, especially if he barks again because the collar has startled him. When he is quiet, it will stop vibrating or emitting citronella. You can praise him for his silence.

>> **Use a command.** Some good ones include Quiet, Shhh!, or That's enough. The best time to give the command is when you're with the dog and you can say your command and immediately put your fingers into the collar and turn him around, away from the visual distraction. Praise if he stops barking. If you start commanding from a distance, Buddy will think you're barking, too. If you're too far away from him, your command will be meaningless. He'll think you're in agreement and barking along with him.

Barking as a response to a stimulus or distraction

Your dog is outside in the yard, and some people walk by, perhaps with a dog on leash, so Buddy barks. Barking is a natural response of defending his territory. After the potential intruders pass, he's quiet again. People and dogs passing are the stimulus that cause barking, and after they're removed, your dog stops. The problem here is Buddy will think his barking moved the people away, which rewards his perception of the barking having worked.

If the people had stopped by the fence for a conversation, your dog would continue to bark. To get him to stop, remove the stimulus from the dog or the dog from the stimulus. If you live in a busy area where people pass by frequently, you may need to change your dog's environment. In other words, you may not be able to leave him in the yard for prolonged periods. Putting up a privacy fence is one alternative, if you want your dog to be outside, or putting him in a crate in the house can successfully remove him from the stimulus. You also can use a remote bark collar in this situation, but first you must train him to the collar on how it works. The collar will come with a how-to manual.

Barking for attention

Sometimes it's as if your dog is barking for no apparent reason. However, even though the motivation isn't apparent to you, your dog always has a reason for barking. It can be due to any or all of the following:

>> Anxiety

>> Boredom

>> Attention seeking because he's lonely

Although Buddy's barking may be unacceptable to you, to him it's the only way he can express his unhappiness and frustration. Using a doggie daycare service a few times a week can help with his loneliness and boredom. Starting a new training hobby with him, including agility, obedience, and retrieving, is helpful. If your dog knows that an activity will occur every day at around the same time, he will stress less knowing you'll attend to his social and mental stimulation needs.

REMEMBER

Theoretically, none of the preceding reasons is difficult to overcome if you work to eliminate the potential causes. Spend more time exercising your dog. Spend more time training your dog. Don't leave your dog alone so long, and don't leave him alone so often.

As a practical matter, however, overcoming these reasons isn't that easy. Most people work for a living and must leave their dogs at home alone for prolonged periods. If you live in an apartment, your dog certainly can't bark all day. The stress on the dog is horrendous, not to mention the fact that your neighbors will soon begin to despise you and your noisy dog. Remember your dog has needs and spending quality time with you is one of them. (Chapter 21 can help if you suspect that your dog's barking is due to separation anxiety.)

Barking when someone comes to the door

Most dogs bark when someone comes to the door. While you may appreciate being alerted that someone has comes to the door, you probably want Buddy to stop when you tell him "Thank you. I've got it from here." Some dogs don't stop, however.

Take control of the situation. Training your dog at the front door is necessary, but you must do the preliminary work first before you apply the distraction of someone at the door. Keep a leash and collar near the door as a helpful tool to aid you especially in the beginning of your training. Use your Quiet command, turn your dog away from the door, and give him a command to sit and stay before you open the door.

You may also consider training Buddy by using a clicker to stop the barking, which is similar to a clicker you may have had as a child. Here's how to:

1. **Acclimate Buddy to the clicker.**

   With plenty of small treats at hand, make yourself comfortable in your favorite chair with Buddy just hanging out. Click and give Buddy a treat. Repeat several times until he associates the click with getting a treat. Because the clicker is a novel sound, he'll hear it over the distraction of someone at the door.

   The timing of the click is important — it needs to come when he's quiet, followed by the treat.

REMEMBER

2. **Recruit a helper to come to the door.**

3. **When your helper comes to the door and Buddy starts barking, listen for the brief intervals when he stops barking.**

   The instant he stops, say "Thank you," "Shh," or "Quiet," whatever command you want to use, click, and give him a treat.

   Continue until Buddy realizes that being quiet is more rewarding than barking. Stop the session here.

4. **Repeat the process over the course of several sessions until Buddy reliably responds to the command you chose.**

TIP

For more information on clicker training, see Karen Pryor's books *Reaching the Animal Mind: Clicker Training and What It Teaches Us about All Animals* (Scribner) and *Click! Dog Training System* (Barnes & Noble).

Contending with Chewing — The Nonfood Variety

The main reasons that dogs chew are physiological and psychological. The first is understandable; it could be that a puppy is teething. The second isn't so understandable. Both are a nuisance. In the following sections, we explain both reasons and provide some guidance if you're having problems with chewing.

Dogs that chew objects can be showing a nutritional deficiency, so you may want to change his diet and perhaps visit the vet for some bloodwork. Nutrition plays a key role in your dog's behavior. After changing to a properly balanced natural diet (see Chapter 4), some dogs will become nutritionally satisfied and will show no interest in chewing again. Never rule out nutrition as a step in training.

I'm teething! Examining the physiological need to chew

As part of the teething process, puppies need to chew. They can't help it. To get through this period, provide your dog with a soft and a hard chew toy as well as a canvas field dummy, which is quite chew resistant. Real bones (soup bones are ideal) are great hard toys. You can get them at the butcher; ask them to cut the ends off the long bones because the ends can break off bits and be swallowed. You can also purchase smoked long bones from vendors on the internet. These are less messy than bones from the butcher but just as popular among dogs.

Hard rubber Kong toys (www.kongcompany.com) with some peanut butter (make sure the peanut butter doesn't contain sweeteners) inserted into the center also will keep a dog amused for a long time. Don't give him anything he can destroy or ingest unless they're food items. Carrots, apples, dog biscuits, or ice cubes are great to relieve the monotony; otherwise, he may select other interesting things to chew on, such as those new shoes you left lying around or the rugs.

REMEMBER

When your dog is going through his period of physiological chewing, make sure he doesn't have access to your personal articles, such as shoes, socks, and towels. Think of it as good training for you not to leave things lying around the house. And don't forget that a lonely dog may chew up anything in his path. So make sure your dog gets enough attention from you — and that he gets some strong chew toys! When you can't supervise him, crate him (see Chapter 6.)

I'm bored! Recognizing the psychological reasons that dogs chew

Chewing that takes place after a dog has gone through teething is usually a manifestation of anxiety, boredom, or loneliness. This oral habit has nothing to do with being spiteful. If your dog attacks the furniture, baseboards, and walls, tips over the garbage can, or engages in other destructive chewing activities, don't become angry. Instead, recognize that you probably aren't providing him the stimulation he needs and give him some solid chew toys.

Use a crate to confine Buddy when you can't supervise him. Confining him saves you lots of money, and you won't lose your temper and get mad at the poor fellow. Even more important, he can't get into things that are a potential danger to him. (See Chapter 6 where we discuss crates in detail.)

REMEMBER

Confinement is a problem-solving approach of last resort. Ideally, the dog isn't left alone so long and so often that he feels the need to chew in order to relieve his boredom. Your dog doesn't need you to entertain him all the time, but extended periods of being alone can make your pet neurotic. Crating is one of the many tools you need to use to solve behavior problems. Refer to the "Preventing Bad Habits — The Five General Prescriptions for Good Behavior" section earlier in this chapter. Good nutrition, exercise, training, socialization, and health are all part of the solution. The crate can be viewed as a babysitter when you aren't around, but it shouldn't be the only solution you apply to your dog.

Dealing with a Digger

One of the favorite pastimes of many breeds such as Dachshunds is digging, or *landscaping*. They engage in this activity at every opportunity and with great zest. Because Dachshunds were bred to go after badgers that burrow into hillsides, this behavior is instinctive. Does that mean you must put up with a yard that looks like a minefield? Not at all, but you do need to assume the responsibility for

>> Expending the digging energy, which involves exercising Buddy

>> Providing an outlet for it, which means giving your dog a place where he can dig to his heart's content

>> Supervising your dog to make sure he doesn't get into trouble

REMEMBER

The good news is that most behavior problems are under your direct control, but you need to get involved. The cure to digging is rather simple. Don't leave your dog unattended in the yard for lengthy periods.

Recognize that digging is part of prey drive (see Chapter 2 for more on the drives). Because it's part of prey drive, all the tips we give you about exhausting the behavior apply here. You can't make a dog dig until he's exhausted, but you can tire out your dog by playing ball or running with him so that he's too tired to dig!

TIP

Here are a few other suggestions to help curb his digging:

>> Put up a small fenced area for him where he can dig. You can supply sand if that helps. Bury things for Buddy to find.

>> Give your dog interactive toys with food inside that he must roll around to find the treat to drop out and eat.

>> Take your dog for hikes in the woods, on a farm, or in the park. Let him dig at the dog park where can find search for critters.

>> Exercise your dog.

UNDERSTANDING THE REASONS FOR DIGGING

Although some breeds, such as the small terriers, have a true propensity for digging, all dogs do it to some extent at one time or another. Take a look at some of the more common reasons for digging:

- To participate in mimicking behavior. In training, this practice is useful, but it may spell trouble for your gardening efforts. You plant, your dog digs. If this is the case, don't garden with your dog present. Put him in the house or close the gate to your garden.

- To make nests for real or imaginary puppies. This reason applies to female dogs.

- To bury or dig up a bone.

- To see what's there, because it's fun, or to find a cool spot to lie down.

- To relieve boredom, isolation, or frustration.

If you think you have a championship digger who's digging for mice, moles, or other vermin in the ground, consider getting him involved in Barn Hunts, which we explain in Chapter 25.

Managing Marking Behavior

Marking is a way for your dog to leave his calling card by depositing a small amount of urine in a particular spot, marking it as his territory. The frequency with which dogs can accomplish marking never ceases to amaze. Male dogs invariably prefer vertical surfaces, hence the fire hydrant. Males tend to engage in this behavior with more determination than females though both can and do mark.

Behaviorists explain that marking is a dog's way of establishing his territory, and it provides a means to find his way back home. They also claim that dogs are able to tell the rank order, gender, and age — puppy or adult dog — by smelling the urine of another dog.

Those people who take their dogs for regular walks through the neighborhood quickly discover that marking is a ritual, with favorite spots that must be watered. It's a way for the dog to maintain his rank in the order of the pack, which consists of all the other dogs in the neighborhood or territory that come across his route.

Adult male dogs lift a leg, as do some females. For the male dog, the object is to leave his calling card higher than the previous calling card. This can lead to some comical results, as when a Dachshund or a Yorkshire Terrier tries to cover the calling card of an Irish Wolfhound or Great Dane. It's a contest.

When this behavior is expressed inside the house, it becomes a problem. Fortunately, this behavior is rare, but it does happen. Here are the circumstances requiring special vigilance:

» When you get a new dog or a cat

» When taking Buddy to a friend's or relative's house for a visit, especially if that individual also has a dog or a cat

» When you've redecorated the house with new furniture or curtains

» When you've moved to a new house

TIP

Distract your dog if you see that he's about to mark in an inappropriate spot. Call his name and take him to a place where he can eliminate. When you take Buddy to someone else's home, keep an eye on him or keep him leashed until he settles into his new surroundings. At the slightest sign that he's even thinking about lifting a leg, interrupt his thought by clapping your hands and calling him to you. Take him outside and wait until he's had a chance to relieve himself. If this behavior persists, you need to go back to basic housetraining principles, such as the crate or X-pen, until you can trust him again. (See Chapter 8 for more on housetraining.)

4

Taking Training to the Next Level

Play fetch with your dog, which is one of the greatest forms of exercise that leads to so much more. Discover how to play retrieve step by step.

Make your dog the star of the party by teaching him to perform trick after trick for fun or for an audience.

Put the finishing touches on your dog's training with obedience competitions and find a new hobby,

Chapter 16

Retrieving: Time to Fetch

P laying fetch is a fabulous exercise for you and your dog. If you have a natural retriever, then you already know. A natural retriever is a dog that was born retrieving — a dog that retrieves for the joy of the chase. Every dog needs an exercise outlet — some more than others. Retrieving is a good and easy way to entertain and burn off all of that energy, tiring your dog. Even on a rainy day you can throw the toy down the hall or down the stairs. Remember our motto: A tired dog has a happy owner.

REMEMBER

Play retrieve for as long as your dog is having fun. End the game while your dog still wants to play a bit longer, so he doesn't get tired of the game. For a lot of dogs, this isn't an issue, but keep in mind, you never want to call and call your dog back to you as he wanders off. Doing so is unintentional training and it backfires. Unintentional training is when you accidently teach something you don't want to teach your dog, such as calling your dog over and over again and not reinforcing the fact your dog must come to you when called. Retrieving is fun and you want your dog to love it.

This chapter looks at all of the different elements of retrieving for you and your dog. Whether your dog is a natural retriever or not, teaching all of these elements is important as you play this game with your dog. What are the rules of the game and what are you going to call the different parts of the game. Think it through then go play.

Introducing the Common Retrieving Commands to Your Natural Retriever

The main task about a trained retrieve is for your dog to bring the item back to you and actually give it to you. Here are the three retrieving commands and elements of the retrieve:

>> **Take It:** If you have a natural retriever, whether he brings it back or not, you need to have a command for him to chase the toy. We recommend Take It. (You may prefer a different command such as Get It or Fetch. Choose one and stick with it.) Say this command to mean, "Go after what I just threw." Eventually the command will mean, "Bring it back and give it to me," but until it does, here are the other two basic commands:

>> **Bring It to Me:** If your dog chases the toy, but doesn't return it to you, then the Bring It to Me command is perfect.

>> **Give:** If you have a natural retriever, then trading the toy for a treat is an easy way to get him to give it back. Just exchange a small treat you have in one hand as you reach with the other hand to get the toy. Repeating "Give" this way every time will teach the dog to release the toy.

If you have a natural retriever, a dog who willingly wants to get the toy, incorporate these three commands to the game of retrieve:

1. **Using a long leash or long rope, toss the toy a shorter distance than the line is long and say "Take it."**

   You don't want the leash to tighten up as your dog chases the toy.

2. **When your dog has the toy, praise and gently pull the line into you as you praise your dog and say "Bring it to me."**

3. **As your dog gets to you, offer a treat in exchange for reaching for the toy and say "Give."**

REMEMBER

The timing on the treat being offered should ideally have you reaching and getting the toy as the treat goes toward Buddy. In a perfect world Buddy doesn't drop the toy for you to then pick up.

Explaining the Basics of Retrieving

If your dog is a natural to retrieving — you throw a ball and he loves getting it — then teaching these steps will be easy. If you don't have a natural retrieving dog, you can still teach your dog how to fetch. It just takes patience and practice. Plus, it takes a really wonderful, special treat that you use only for retrieving. As you teach the retrieve, you'll want to also teach the Hold command because the dog must hold onto the dumbbell as part of the retrieve. He has to hold it while walking with the dumbbell in his mouth.

Here's what you need to start teaching your dog to retrieve:

» **A small can of cat food or dog food, something different and yummy:** Deliver the canned food on a spoon because it helps with the canned treat.

» **A spoon:** With a spoon you're teaching your dog to open his mouth so you can then place a foreign object (the spoon now, but the dumbbell next) into his mouth. More than likely, he'll accept the spoon with food.

» **Dumbbell:** A *dumbbell* is a wooden or plastic article used in obedience. It looks like a dumbbell, thus the name, and it has two ends that bell out, held together by a dowel in the center. The dowel should be a comfortable length for your dog to pick up behind his canine teeth without squashing his whiskers. Dumbbells are readily available online, in pet stores, and at other training outlets.

» **Chair:** Put everything (dumbbell, food, and spoon) on a nearby chair, so it's handy and Buddy can see it.

The following sections go through the steps to teach a retrieve to any dog, regardless if he is a natural retriever or not. Have fun with the different steps. Do a few repetitions each evening until you have the whole list done. Retrieving is worth the time because it's a great way to have fun and exercise with your dog.

Sequence 1: Starting with Take It

The Take It command teaches your dog to open his mouth for food. These steps introduce the Take It command easy.

1. **Preload the spoon with a pea size bit of cat food that is ready to give quickly.**

2. **Offer the preloaded spoon and say "Take it."**

   Give your dog the spoon end with the food, and you hold onto the handle.

3. **Praise effusively and make a big fuss.**

4. **Repeat this over and over again at least ten times until your dog anxiously awaits the command and reward of food off the spoon.**

Sequence 2: Working on the Hold It and Give command

Now you're ready to use the dumbbell. Going from food to a dumbbell is a bit of a transition, so be patient. Watch your body language and never bend over your dog because doing so causes your dog to feel threatened. Bending over is a defense-drive posture, and your dog won't be able to focus on the prey-drive training of retrieve if he's switched into defense drive. Keep your shoulders back and upright. (We discuss drives in Chapter 2.)

Here are the steps for introducing the Hold It and Give commands:

1. **With your dog sitting at your left side, facing the chair, put your left palm lightly on top of his muzzle and place your left index finger behind his left canine tooth.**

TIP

Place small dogs on a table for this exercise. Doing so helps you from having to lean over and create a hovering posture. It also saves your back!

2. **Gently open his mouth with your left hand by using your left index finger behind the canine teeth as in Figure 16-1 and with your right hand place the dumbbell in his mouth and say "Take it."**

Hold the dumbbell by the bell so you can easily put the bar in his mouth.

3. **Gently rest the thumb of your right hand on top of his muzzle, fingers under his chin, and cup his mouth shut as in Figure 16-2.**

REMEMBER

Make sure Buddy's holding his muzzle parallel to the ground. Then use your left hand to pet behind his head to keep his head still and straight while you hold the dumbbell in his mouth.

The goal of this progression is for your dog to accept the dumbbell in his mouth voluntarily. It's only an introduction, so you don't want to close his mouth over the dumbbell for longer than one second.

4. **Praise enthusiastically, immediately say "Give" and take the dumbbell out of his mouth.**

5. **Reward with the cat food on the spoon right away, enthusiastically praising to keep up your dog's motivation for the game.**

6. **Repeat this process ten times and then take a break.**

If Buddy is motivated, do another ten repetitions before another break or you can leave it until the next day. After your dog readily accepts the dumbbell consistently, you can go on to the exercise in the next sequence.

FIGURE 16-1:
Gently opening
your dog's
mouth.

© John Wiley & Sons, Inc.

FIGURE 16-2:
Putting the
dumbbell in your
dog's mouth.

© John Wiley & Sons, Inc.

REMEMBER

When teaching your dog to retrieve, practice this exercise once a day every day and keep it fun with special treats and lots of praise. If you're the ambitious type, you can practice more than once a day, as long as your dog remains interested and will actively work for the treat. However, practicing sporadically or less often than daily isn't a good idea because your dog will forget what he has learned during the last session, and you basically have to start all over.

Sequence 3: Helping your dog retrieve on command

After Buddy has become accustomed to having the dumbbell in his mouth in Sequence 2, you're ready to tackle the next step. The goal is for Buddy to take the dumbbell voluntarily in his mouth when you give the command. Here's how to do it:

1. **With Buddy sitting at your left side, have the chair with cat food in place, and put two fingers of your left hand through his collar, back to front, palm facing you, at the side of his neck.**

2. **With your right hand, place the bar of the dumbbell directly in front of his mouth, touching the small whiskers on his upper lip.**

    This step is different from the previous sequence where you opened his mouth and placed the dumbbell into it. Now you want him to open his own mouth and accept the dumbbell to be placed inside.

3. **Say "Take it," and when he takes it, briefly cup his mouth shut and tell him how clever he is.**

4. **Say "Give," take out the dumbbell, and reward with the cat food on the preloaded spoon.**

    At this point in the training, your dog may not yet take the dumbbell but will open his mouth. In that case, just put the dumbbell in his mouth, cup his mouth shut, and so on.

If he sits there with his mouth clamped shut, watch for signs of intention behavior. *Intention behaviors* are those actions that tell you what the dog is thinking. They range from the subtle, such as bringing the whiskers forward, to the overt, such as sniffing the dowel, licking his lips, or intently staring at the dumbbell. Buddy is thinking about taking the dumbbell but isn't quite sure he can.

When you see intention behavior from your dog, take your hand out of the collar, open his mouth, put the dumbbell in, and briefly cup his mouth shut. Praise, remove the dumbbell from his mouth, and reward with food. Repeat this process until Buddy readily opens his mouth and accepts the dumbbell on command. Praising him while he has the dumbbell in his mouth is important.

TIP

Be patient. Sometimes it can take several minutes before your dog makes a move. If absolutely nothing happens and the little wheels have come to a grinding halt, practice the preceding process five times and then try again. Some dogs appear to be particularly unwilling about taking the dumbbell voluntarily on command, but with enough repetitions, they'll get it. Keep it fun with enthusiastic praise.

Sequence 4: Helping Buddy learn to hold and reach for the object

Before you proceed with the retrieve part of this exercise, you need to teach Buddy what you want him to do with the dumbbell after he has it in his mouth. You want him to hold the dumbbell in his mouth and not drop it before the Give command. You may think this concept is obvious, but it's not evident to Buddy until you teach it to him.

Your goal is to have Buddy firmly hold the dumbbell until you say "Give." Follow these steps:

1. **Start in the usual position as in previous sequences, with Buddy at your left side and the cat food on the chair.**

2. **Put the dumbbell into his mouth and say "Hold it."**

   To prevent him from mouthing the dumbbell with his back teeth, make sure his head is parallel to the ground. Keep the upper part of your body straight so you don't hover or lean over him.

3. **Hold the back of your right hand under his chin as in Figure 16-3.**

   If Buddy decides to drop the dumbbell at this point, he'll open his mouth by dropping his bottom jaw. Keeping the back of your hand under his mouth stops this from happening. If you hold the palm of your hand under his chin, Buddy may construe it as an invitation to drop the dumbbell.

4. **Smile and count to five.**

5. **Praise, remove the dumbbell, and reward him with food on the spoon.**

6. **Repeat these steps 20 times, gradually increasing the time you have him hold the dumbbell in 5-second increments up to 30 seconds.**

TIP

If Buddy starts rolling the dumbbell around in his mouth or looks as though he'll open his mouth to drop it, give him a *gentle* tap or lift under the chin with "Hold it." Then remove the dumbbell by saying, "Give," praise, and reward.

FIGURE 16-3: Holding the back of your hand under the dog's chin.

© John Wiley & Sons, Inc.

Sequence 4: Teaching Buddy to reach for it

As soon as Buddy understands that he has to hold the dumbbell, this sequence trains your dog to reach for it. Use these steps:

1. **With two fingers of your left hand through his collar at the side of his neck, back to front with the palm facing you, hold his dumbbell 2 inches in front of his mouth.**

2. **Say "Take it."**

3. **If he does, cup his mouth shut by saying "Hold it," count to five, praise, remove the dumbbell with "Give," and reward with food.**

4. **If he doesn't take the dumbbell, gently bring his head forward by the collar toward the dumbbell until he reaches for and takes it and then cup his mouth shut by saying "Hold it," count to five, praise, remove the dumbbell with "Give" and reward with food.**

5. **Repeat Steps 1 and 2 until your dog voluntarily reaches for and takes the dumbbell.**

   Increase the distance Buddy needs to reach for the dumbbell in 2-inch increments to arm's length.

Sequence 6: Walking while holding the dumbbell

The next sequence in the retrieve is teaching Buddy to walk while holding the dumbbell in his mouth. At this point in the training, the majority of dogs understand the concept and can hold the dumbbell in their mouths and walk at the same time. If your dog does it, you can skip this sequence. Still, some dogs can't make this transition from holding the dumbbell to walking with it at the same time. They have to be taught to do so. When this approach was devised to teach retrieving, we included the walking while holding sequence just to make sure that all eventualities were covered.

Here are the steps to follow to teach Buddy to walk while holding the dumbbell:

1. **With Buddy sitting at your left side, facing the chair with the cat food and spoon from about 6 feet away, put the dumbbell in his mouth and say "Take it" followed by "Hold it."**

   Encourage him to walk toward the chair.

2. **To give Buddy confidence, put your right hand under his chin when he starts to move.**

   Your hand stops Buddy from dropping his bottom jaw as he walks, keeps his mouth closed around the dumbbell, and helps him succeed.

3. **When he gets to the chair, praise, remove the dumbbell from his mouth, say "Give," and reward him.**

4. **Repeat until Buddy walks with the dumbbell without you holding your hand under his chin.**

   Gradually increase the distance to 20 steps in five-step increments.

Sequence 7: Training Buddy for the pick-up

You and Buddy are getting close to the final progression of teaching him to retrieve. Right now you're ready for the pick-up. Resist the temptation to just throw the dumbbell and expect Buddy to pick it up and bring it back. He may actually do it, but he also may not. He may just chase it and then stand over it, not knowing what to do next. In the long run, make sure that he knows what you expect by teaching him. Here's what to do:

1. **With Buddy sitting at your left side, place the chair with the cat food and spoon behind you.**

2. **With your fingers in his collar, hold the dumbbell about 2 inches from Buddy's mouth and say "Take it."**

3. **When he does, praise enthusiastically, say "Give," remove the dumbbell from his mouth, and reward.**

   Your goal with Steps 2 and 3 is to lower the dumbbell in 2-inch increments toward the ground and have Buddy retrieve it from your hand.

4. **When you get to the ground, place one end of the bell of the dumbbell on the ground and hold the other end bell at a 45-degree angle off the ground.**

5. **Say "Take it" and when Buddy takes the dumbbell, take your hand out of the collar, say "Hold it" and back up two steps.**

   He'll quickly come to you to get his reward.

6. **Praise, remove, and reward.**

7. **Repeat until he's comfortable picking up the dumbbell with you holding it at that angle.**

Sequence 8: Bringing it back

Buddy has discovered how to go to the dumbbell and pick it up off the ground while your hand is still on it. You now progress to the stage where he'll pick it up by himself and bring it back to you. Here's how to teach this part:

1. **Place the dumbbell on the ground, but keep your hand on it.**

2. **Have Buddy retrieve the dumbbell several times while you have your hand on it.**

3. **Hold your hand first 2 inches, then 6 inches, and then 12 inches away from the dumbbell until you can place it on the ground and stand up straight.**

4. **Each time he retrieves the dumbbell, back up several steps, praise, take the dumbbell, and reward.**

5. **If your dog doesn't pick up the dumbbell from the ground, place it into his mouth and back up, praising him.**

   You don't reward Buddy when you're helping him learn; you only reward when he does something you have told him to do.

REMEMBER

   If this sequence becomes an issue and your dog continues to refuse to take the dumbbell, review the prior progressions. Make sure that you follow them religiously and that your dog masters each progression before you go on to the next.

6. **Say "Stay" and place the dumbbell 1 foot in front of your dog.**

7. **Say "Take it" and when he brings it back, praise, remove, and reward.**

8. **Repeat by then placing it 3 feet and then 6 feet in front of your dog.**

Your dog will tell you how many times in a row you can ask him to retrieve. If he has many prey-drive behaviors, you can get in quite a few repetitions. If not, he'll quickly lose enthusiasm. You're better off stopping after five repetitions and picking the game up again at the next session.

REMEMBER

For your dog, picking up a dumbbell that you placed on the ground isn't terribly exciting, and if it weren't for the reward, it would be an absolute bore. Still, this sequence is necessary because you want your dog to learn he has to do it for you and not for himself. The reward is a high value reward, canned pet food. Most likely by this time, Buddy sees you get a new can and spoon out, and he's getting really excited about your upcoming training session.

Sequence 9: Putting it all together

Now comes the fun part, where you get to throw the dumbbell and Buddy gets to chase it and bring it back. Follow these steps:

1. **Throw the dumbbell a few feet, and at the same time send your dog to the dumbbell with the command, "Take it."**

2. **As soon as he picks up the dumbbell, say "Come" or "Bring it to me" and tell him how terrific he is.**

3. **When he gets back to you, take the dumbbell with "Give" and reward him with a treat.**

TIP

Sometimes dogs get carried away by the fun of it all and don't come right back with the dumbbell. They may make a detour or just run around for the joy of it. If that happens, say "Come" as soon as he picks up the dumbbell. Then praise and reward him when he gets back to you.

4. **Gradually increase the distance you throw the dumbbell, and as he gains confidence, introduce the Sit in front with the command, "Hold it."**

When he gets back to you say "Sit" and "Hold it." Because he hasn't done this task before, you may have to hold your hand under his chin to prevent him from dropping the dumbbell. When he's successful, praise, remove, and reward. From then on make him sit and hold the dumbbell every time he gets back to you.

Congratulations! You now have a dog that retrieves on command.

TIP

You also can use the Retrieve command to have Buddy bring in the newspaper, carry his leash, and — size permitting — carry your handbag or retrieve lost keys.

Polishing and Perfecting the Retrieve

This section shows you how to put all the pieces of the retrieve together. You now introduce the Stay command when you throw the dumbbell. Slip a finger in Buddy's collar before you throw the dumbbell after saying "Stay" to guarantee that he'll indeed stay when the dumbbell is thrown. After waiting a short time, use the Take It command. Some dogs respond well to the voice command; others respond better to a hand signal given with the left hand toward the dumbbell. Practice with Buddy to see which one brings the kind of response you want.

Wait for it: Testing your dog's patience

Buddy has to learn to stay while you throw the dumbbell and until you release him to get it. Making him wait gets him even more excited about getting to his dumbbell. Trying to teach your dog patience is almost like teaching your 2-year-old child patience, but you can do it. Just follow these steps:

1. **Start with Buddy at your left side.**

2. **Put two fingers of your left hand through his collar, say "Stay" and throw the dumbbell about 15 feet.**

3. **Very, slowly let go of his collar, count to five, and say "Take it."**

4. **When he returns with the dumbbell, praise, remove, and reward.**

5. **Repeat these steps until your dog holds the stay without having to hold him by the collar.**

REMEMBER

Give the Take It command in an excited and enthusiastic tone of voice to put Buddy into prey drive. Don't use a harsh or threatening tone because that tone may put your dog in the wrong drive and make it more difficult for him to learn. You may also give a hand signal to Buddy if he's high in prey drive. It goes from the left side of your body toward the dumbbell. If at any time your dog needs motivation, throw the dumbbell and at the same time say "Take it," letting him chase after it.

Retrieving with distractions

After Buddy knows how to retrieve, he's ready for distraction training. Retrieving around distractions is so important because almost everything is a distraction to a dog. Wherever you throw the dumbbell or toy, it will land near some kind of distraction, such as a smell, a noise, other people, or other visual distraction that can keep your dog from thinking he can retrieve the item and return to you. Systematically work through made-up distractions so Buddy learns nothing can stop him from picking up the thing you threw and returning it to you.

Introduce your dog to distractions as follows (you need a helper for this sequence):

1. **Your helper stands about 2 feet from the dumbbell and assumes a friendly posture that's not threatening to the dog.**

2. **Send Buddy after the dumbbell and as soon as he picks it up, enthusiastically praise and call him back to you.**

   Look at the exercise as having been completed as soon as your dog picks up his dumbbell.

3. **As the dog gains confidence, have your helper stand a little closer and then stand over the dumbbell.**

   Also ask the helper to hide the dumbbell by standing directly in front of it with her back to the dog. You also can use a chair as a distraction by putting the dumbbell under the chair and then on the chair.

REMEMBER

Continue to use food rewards for Buddy on a random basis; that is, instead of using them every time and in a predictable pattern, use them only often enough to maintain his motivation.

During distraction training, you may see the following responses or variations thereof:

» **He hesitates and fails to retrieve.** He starts going toward the dumbbell but then backs off and fails to retrieve, meaning, "I don't have the confidence to get close enough to the helper to retrieve my dumbbell."

Without saying anything, slowly approach him, put two fingers of your left hand through the collar, back to front, palm facing you, at the side of his neck and take him to the dumbbell. If he picks up the dumbbell, back up, praise, remove the dumbbell, and reward; if he doesn't, put the dumbbell in his mouth, back up, then praise, remove, and reward. Don't repeat the command.

REMEMBER

Keep trying, and remember your dog's learning style and how many repetitions it takes before he understands. You may find that you need to help him several times before he has the confidence to do it by himself. By helping, go over and point at the dumbbell, picking it up and helping put it in his mouth if necessary. Aid in a nonconfrontational way. He isn't wrong for not picking it up. He just needs help to know he can still do it with the distraction there. As soon as he has done it on his own, stop for that session.

» **He gives up.** He leaves altogether and doesn't retrieve, saying, in effect, "I can't cope with this." In this case, use the remedy from the preceding response, helping as needed.

>> **He does nothing.** In other words, he's thinking, "If I don't do anything, maybe all of this will go away." If Buddy does nothing, use the same remedy from the first response, helping him to be successful.

>> **He becomes distracted.** He permits himself to be distracted, meaning, "I would rather visit than retrieve my dumbbell." If you experience this response, use the remedy from the first response.

>> **He takes the dumbbell to the distracter.** Slowly approach Buddy without saying anything, put the leash on the dead ring of the training collar and, with a little tension on the collar, show him exactly what he was supposed to do by guiding him to you. No extra command is given.

>> **He anticipates the retrieve without waiting to be told to do so.** In other words, he breaks the Stay and tries to retrieve without the command. He's catching on and wants to show you how clever he is.

Without saying anything, slowly approach him, take the dumbbell out of his mouth, put it down where he picked it up, go back to the starting point, and then send him. Whatever you do, don't shout "No," or do anything else that would discourage him from retrieving after you have just worked so hard to get him to pick up the dumbbell.

>> **He does it correctly.** At this point, stop training for that session.

When your dog confidently retrieves with the first level of distractions, introduce the next level. *Second-degree distractions*, which are visual and auditory, consist of having your helper crouch close to the dumbbell while trying to distract him by saying, "Here puppy, come visit for some petting." The distracter doesn't use your dog's name. After Buddy successfully works his way through the second-degree distraction, you can increase the level of difficulty to the *third-degree distractions*, which uses food or a toy. Have the helper offer Buddy a treat, a ball, or a toy about a foot away from the dumbbell. Of course, the helper never lets him have those items as in Figure 16-4. If Buddy goes to the distracter or tries to take the food, follow the preceding guidelines until Buddy does it correctly. Then stop for that training session.

TECHNICAL STUFF

Distractions add an extra dimension and take training to a higher level. Challenging Buddy to use his head with distraction training helps build your dog's confidence and teaches him to concentrate on what he's doing. This type of training is especially important for the shy dog, providing the confidence he needs to respond correctly under different conditions.

During distraction training, keep in mind that anytime you change the complexity of the exercise, it becomes a new exercise for the dog. If Buddy goes for the food, you would treat his response the same way you did when you first introduced him to distraction training. No, your dog isn't defiant, stubborn, or stupid; he's just confused as to what he should do and has to be helped again.

FIGURE 16-4:
Retrieving with third-degree distraction.

REMEMBER

When using distraction training, giving Buddy a chance to work out the situation is important. Don't be too quick to help him. Be patient and let him try to figure out on his own how to correctly handle the situation. After he does, you'll be pleasantly surprised by the intensity and reliability with which he responds. It's fascinating to watch your dog think things through with distraction training. Enjoy the process and keep it reasonable.

You're now ready to work with different objects you want Buddy to retrieve. When you do, you may have to review the first few sequences. Just because Buddy retrieves one object doesn't necessarily mean he'll retrieve others. He may need to get used to them first.

Chapter **17**

Trick Training for Fun

Every well-trained dog knows a trick or two that can impress friends and family alike. The tricks you teach your dog can be simple or complex, depending on your dog's drives and your interest. You can teach some tricks in an afternoon whereas you'll need more time for others. With your help, each trick can be a showstopper with your dog's personality shining through.

Tricks by definition are entertaining. In fact, teaching tricks is fun for both you and your dog. During the training, you'll use lots of cookies (or other tasty treats) and praise to keep the motivation going for your dog.

REMEMBER

The trick to teaching successful tricks is sequencing. *Sequencing* means breaking down what you want to teach your dog into components small enough for the dog to master, which leads up to the final product. For example, if you want to teach your dog to shake hands, start by first taking Buddy's paw in your hand with the command you want to use and then praise and reward him. The next sequence is offering your palm first instead of taking his paw, and so on to the next sequence.

You don't need to teach these tricks in any order. Choose your favorite and have fun.

TEACHING BUDDY TRICKS IS WORTH IT EVERY TIME

A new client, Martha, contacted Mary Ann a few years ago to help teach her new dog Jax the basic skills needed to become a welcome member of the family. For fun, at the end of the second lesson, I taught Jax how to shake hands. The giggle that came out of Martha was infectious. She was beside herself with joy over Jax's ability to learn the trick. By the following week, Jax was a pro at shaking hands. Martha had practiced every day, making shaking hands with Jax a stellar trick.

I like to teach tricks to my obedience clients because tricks give them a fun reason to practice. Trick training also helps teach the dog how to learn. Before long, Martha and Jax had three AKC Trick Dog Titles, and they're still going strong, doing agility and advanced obedience. Martha had no intentions of continuing to train her new dog to such a level, but with the onset of trick training, she's now doing agility and advanced obedience and scent work. They're a great team, and it all started with that laugh of joy (see the attached figure of Jax).

Shake and High Five

This trick shows you how to teach Buddy to Shake and then add a High Five for extra flair. This exercise has four sequences. Sequences 1 through 3 teach Shake and Sequence 4 adds the High Five. For the High Five, the object is to teach Buddy to raise one front paw as high as he can on command.

Needed: Treats

Command: Sit (see Chapter 11)

Command: Yes (see Chapter 9), to mark the moment of success and compliance from your dog

Sequence 1: Introducing the concept of shaking hands

Follow these steps to accustom your dog to shaking hands:

1. Sit your dog in front of you.

2. Reduce your body posture by kneeling or squatting in front of your dog so you're not leaning or hovering over him.

3. Offer him your palm at mid-chest level and say "Shake" or whatever command you want to use.

4. Take the elbow of his dominant front leg and lift it off the ground about 2 inches.

   If you don't know your dog's dominant side, he'll quickly show you.

5. Slide your hand down to the paw and gently shake as in Figure 17-1.

6. Say "Yes" and praise enthusiastically as you're shaking his paw.

7. Reward with a treat and say "Okay" to release him.

FIGURE 17-1: Help by sliding your hand from the elbow to the paw.

© John Wiley & Sons, Inc.

Sequence 2: Lifting his paw

Keep following these steps for Buddy to lift his paw:

1. **Sit your dog in front of you and reduce your body posture.**

2. **Offer your palm at mid-chest level and say "Shake."**

   You're looking for some sort of response. If nothing happens, touch his elbow and offer your palm again. Give him the chance to lift his paw.

3. **After he lifts the paw on his own, take the paw, enthusiastically praise, reward, and release.**

   If nothing happens after offering your palm and saying "Shake," take hold of his collar on the opposite side from the hand you want him to lift and tilt him slightly away from that side by pulling gently on the collar sideways. Doing so takes the weight off the leg you want to come up, and it will come off of the ground. Say "Yes," take his paw, praise, reward, and release.

REMEMBER

Stay with Sequence 2 until your dog is lifting his paw off the ground on command so you can shake it. Move on to Sequence 3 when your dog is ready.

Sequence 3: Putting his paw on your palm

When you're ready for Buddy to put his paw in your palm, keep following these steps:

1. **Sit your dog in front of you and reduce your body posture.**

2. **Offer your palm at mid-chest level and say "Shake."**

   At this point, he should put his paw on your palm. When he does, say "Yes," praise enthusiastically, reward, and release.

   If nothing happens, go back to Sequence 2.

REMEMBER

Stay with Sequence 3 until your dog readily and without hesitation puts his paw on your palm. Then, if you want to teach your dog to add an impressive high five to his shake, you can move on to the last sequence.

Sequence 4: Adding the High Five

With this trick you want your dog to raise his paw as high as he can and touch your hand rather than you shaking his paw. These steps can help:

1. **Sit your dog in front of you.**

2. **Offer your palm at his chin level and say "Shake."**

   By now your dog should readily and without hesitation put his paw on your palm with the command "Shake." When he does, say "Yes," praise, and rotate your palm to be fingers up as in a high five. Reward and release. If not, go back to Sequence 3.

3. **Raise your palm, in 2-inch increments, until you have reached your dog's limit.**

   At this point you can change the trick command to "High Five" and say "High Five" after you've said, "Shake," and gotten Buddy to lift his paw.

REMEMBER

Your hand is less like a shake-hand position and more of a high-five position with your fingers pointing up. Say "Yes" as your dog touches your palm with his paw. Praise and reward with your release. After several repetitions, your dog will stretch his paw as high as he can. Praise, reward, and release.

Find the Pea under the Right Cup

With this trick, your dog finds the right cup with the treat pea under it out of three cups. This trick is fun for both you and your dog.

Needed: Three cups: You can use plastic or paper cups from your picnic basket or small disposable flower pots that new plants come in to repot later. Kids' handbells, instead of cups, work wonders too; Just cut out the clangor because you don't need the noise from the bell. With the bells, the handles help your dog to tip the bells over during the trick.

Treats: Dry treats that scoot along the floor without leaving crumbs or residue behind, such as Os cereal or oyster crackers–type treats work best. The treat is called the *pea* in the final step.

Command: Leave It (refer to Chapter 9)

Command: Stay (check out Chapter 11)

Sequence 1: Establishing a pattern for the game

These steps in the first sequence help Buddy understand the pattern:

1. **Kneel in front of your dog on a Stay command with an ample supply of treats and your cups handy.**

2. **Put a treat on the floor and say "Leave it" and then release Buddy to the treat with "Okay."**

   If he goes before the release, simply cover the treat with your hand before he gets to the treat. This is a practice review for the "Leave It" command.

3. **Repeat the whole sequence.**

   By repeating several times you're teaching Buddy this is a game he'll want to play; he needs to get focused to play several times.

Sequence 2: Introducing the covered treat

The next steps focus on making the introduction. Buddy, meet the treat.

1. **Kneel in front of your dog on a Stay command, show him the cup, and put a treat on the edge of the upside down cup half under the cup and half showing.**

2. **Pause and then say "Leave it."**

3. **Release him to the cup and treat and praise again and again while you pet and party with him for finding the hidden treat.**

4. **Repeat until Buddy knocks over or pushes aside the cup with ease to get at the half-exposed treat.**

5. **Now completely cover the treat so Buddy can't see it.**

   Remember to enforce the Stay and Leave It commands.

6. **Release to the cup with "Okay."**

Sequence 3: Adding a second cup with no treat

You can now introduce an empty cup next to the loaded cup.

1. **Simply have two cups upside down in front of the dog on a stay as in Figure 17-2.**

2. **Lift one at a time, and then make a big deal about putting a treat under one of them.**

3. **Pause and then release and let your dog find the treat.**

   If he goes right for the correct one, or even if he doesn't, make a huge fuss of praise when he finds the treat.

FIGURE 17-2:
Two cups, one is loaded and one is empty.

© John Wiley & Sons, Inc.

Sequence 4: Moving the cups and changing their position

To keep building on this trick, follow these steps:

1. **Repeat Sequence 3, but after you've loaded one of the cups, slowly switch the cups' location by sliding them around on the floor, not lifting the cup to expose the treat.**

   Usually the dog is fascinated by this while on the Stay. Pause before releasing Buddy to the cups.

2. **Repeat this step, but slide the cups back and forth a few extra times.**

TIP

   Try to determine if your dog is simply crashing the cups over or using his nose or eyes to go to the right cup. Help him if needed by tipping over the cup.

   If your cups aren't tipping over, do this on a bit of carpet to allow for some traction. The handbells help with this because they knock over more easily because of the handles.

Sequence 5: Finishing the trick

During this sequence you add the third cup, which is when this trick really gets fun:

1. **With Buddy on a Sit-Stay, place the three cups in front of him.**

2. **Load one with a treat and allow him to watch you.**

3. **Slide the cups around in front of him and talk up the mystery of which one has the treat.**

4. **Sit back on your heels, say "Okay," and watch Buddy sniff out the correct cup (see Figure 17-3).**

One cup only has the treat. Your dog may tip them all over, but eventually most dogs get it right, going directly to the correct cup.

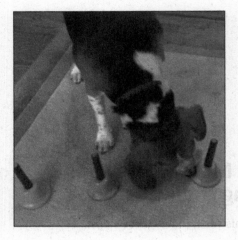

FIGURE 17-3:
Watch Buddy
sniff out the
correct cup for
the treat.

TIP

If you want to make this trick a show piece, add some drama to your voice and act as if you have a crowd in front of you. Announce and show off the Famous Buddy of the World —Buddy who can follow the cup to find the "pea" every time. "As if magic, Buddy will watch and concentrate and find the famous pea under the cups as they switch and move before his eyes. It's your show, so play it up.

Hide in a Box

With this trick, you teach your dog to get in a big box and eventually hide in it by laying down.

Needed: A cardboard box and treats

Make sure the box is big enough for your dog to get into and lay down. Save one from a delivery or visit a store that lets you take one. Close in the flaps to add stability and so the box doesn't have a top or flaps to deter your dog. Make sure the box isn't too high that your dog can't leap into it later.

Use treats easy to toss, such as cheese-flavored corn puffs, popcorn, or something special and fun. Be careful about overdoing the snacks. If you feed a kibble, you can use your dog's kibble too at meal times.

Command: Get In (refer to Chapter 14)

Command: Down (check out Chapter 11)

Sequence 1: Introducing the box on its side

The steps in this sequence help your dog get acquainted with the box:

1. **Set up your box and lay it on its side, so the opening isn't on top but rather an easy walk in.**

2. **Toss a treat into the box and say "Get it" and then release with "Okay" as Buddy eats the treat.**

3. **Repeat over and over until Buddy willingly goes in the box for the treat.**

   Turn the box if it isn't a square box, so he'll go into the box to get the treat on any side. You can move the box around the room too, so the box changing location isn't a concern for Buddy.

TIP

4. **Step behind Buddy as he goes in the box, so he doesn't just back out.**

   You want him to wait until you say "Okay."

Sequence 2: Standing the box correctly with opening on top

This sequence may take a bit of help, especially if Buddy isn't a leaper. We find helping him into the box and having him leap out helpful. Just follow these steps:

1. **Without fear or frustration, gently put Buddy into the box, lifting him up and placing him inside.**

2. **Immediately give him a treat and then say "Okay" to release him and give him another treat for leaping out.**

   The leaping out will only get a treat when you put him in the box by lifting him in. After he gets in the box himself, you'll only treat him while he's inside the box, not after he comes out. You want him to go in the box, so only reward him for going in, not for coming out.

3. **Drop a treat or two into the box and say "Get in your box."**

   If he doesn't try, lift him in so he can eat the treats inside of the box. Then say "Okay" to release him and play with him outside the box.

Dogs know when you're pleased if you let them know you're pleased. We often hear people say their dogs always repeat a behavior if they laughed at their dog for doing something because your dog reads your laughter as being pleased. Laughter is praise to a dog. Have fun with trick training.

4. **Keep practicing until Buddy gets into the box on his own. Toss treats inside and encourage him to leap inside as in Figure 17-4.**

   If you're tossing treats and he won't go and you've lifted him in a few times and he still won't do it, tilt the box over with the treats inside and have him go in for them. This shows him that the treats are there waiting for him.

REMEMBER

Get In Your Box is the command. Add it as your dog leaps inside. "Okay" is the release for your Get Out Of The Box command.

FIGURE 17-4: Buddy leaps into the box after you tossed a treat into the box.

© John Wiley & Sons, Inc.

Sequence 3: Adding the Hide command

You can wait for another day to work on this sequence. Make sure your dog is willingly getting in and out of the box on your commands before moving on to this sequence:

1. **Review your Down command outside of the box.**

   When he goes down, he'll look like he's hiding in the box.

2. **Say "Get in your box" and toss a treat inside.**

3. **Say "Down, Hide" and raise your arm as your signal.**

4. **Praise and give another treat for laying down.**

5. **Say "Okay" to release him from the box.**

6. **Praise, praise, praise.**

7. **Repeat the Down, Hide combined command until Buddy starts responding to just the Hide command alone (see Figure 17-5).**

FIGURE 17-5:
Hiding in the box
by going into the
Down position.

© John Wiley & Sons, Inc.

Sequence 4: Putting it all together

Now that you have a dog who will get in the box, wait for you to release him with "Okay" to come out, and will lay down in the box when asked, it's time to make it a performance:

1. **Have Buddy get in the box and raise your arm as you say "Hide."**

   After he hides, say "Okay" to release him to get out.

2. **You can use your imagination to make this into a bit of a celebration and show by leaving your box out and playing this trick anytime you want.**

REMEMBER

Trick training and training in general makes for a dog who is always listening to and watching you.

Pick a Hand

When it comes to showmanship, the trick in this section is a winner. You can profess that your dog can read your mind. You have both hands behind your back, one holding a treat. Then you bring them forward, and your dog noses or paws the hand that he wants you to open. If he picks the correct hand, he'll find a treat. If not, no treat. But as a "mind reader," he'll always pick the right hand, of course. (You know he's using his nose, but the audience will think Buddy is mind reading.) It's all how you play your roll of showman to your audience.

> **Needed:** Smelly treats, like beefy snaps
>
> **Command:** Touch (see Chapter 9)
>
> **Command:** Sit (see Chapter 11)

Sequence 1: Reviewing the Touch command

The steps in this sequence focus on mastering the Touch command, which requires your dog to nose your hand for a reward.

1. **Put a treat between your fingers on the palm side of your hand and offer it to your dog as you say "Touch."**

2. **Relax your fingers so your dog can eat the treat.**

3. **Practice using both the right and then the left hands.**

   Buddy should willingly nose both of your hands.

Sequence 2: Touching the back of the treat hand

The command you use isn't as important as the actions you use. Dogs learn actions and expectations first. In fact, commands are the easy part of trick training. What's important is that you're consistent with the commands you do use. These steps train Buddy to touch the back of the hand that's holding the treat.

1. **Have your dog sitting in front of you.**

   You can be sitting in a chair too.

2. **Hide a treat in your hand, between your fingers again, show it to your dog, and then turn your hand over into a fist, offering it toward his face and say "Touch, which one?"**

   When he noses your hand, say "Yes" and flip your hand over and give him the treat.

3. **Repeat this again and use either hand.**

Sequence 3: Offering both hands for dog to choose the loaded hand

The steps in this sequence work on showing both hands so Buddy can select the hand with the treat.

1. **Have your dog sitting in front of you.**

2. **Place a treat in one palm, show both palms to your dog, and then make fists and turn them over.**

3. **Say "Touch, which one?" and let him choose one with his nose (refer to Figure 17-6).**

   Open the hand he touches and give him the treat. Remember at this point, he saw the treat and saw you turn your hands, so likely he'll pick the correct one. If not, just say "Oops" and start again.

REMEMBER

You'll show the treat in the one hand, turn the hands and cup them shut, and then ask, "Which one?" If you need to still say "Touch" first, that's fine, but you'll ween off from saying it and eventually only say "Which one?"

FIGURE 17-6:
Offer both fisted hands, but only one holds a treat.

Sequence 4: Putting your hands behind your back first

After your dog has consistently had fun and success with the last sequence, it's time in these steps to put your hands behind your back before bringing them out in front, already cupped shut:

1. **Have your dog sitting in front of you.**

   This sequence requires you to be a bit animated. You want your dog to keep playing. If you simply bring your hands around and ask which one, your dog may lose interest.

2. **Play it up, show your dog the treat in front of you, and tease him a bit, but don't let him have it, and then bring your hands behind your back and put in one hand.**

3. **Bring your hands in front of you with both hands cupped shut and then offer each hand, one at a time for him to sniff, bringing the hand toward his nose, and then the other one as in Figure 17-7.**

FIGURE 17-7: Have him choose which one.

© John Wiley & Sons, Inc.

4. **Stop moving and ask, "Which one"?**

   Your dog should nose one of your hands. If he's correct, praise him and offer him the treat. You can say "Yes, Okay. What a good dog!" or something like that.

   If he touches the wrong hand, say "Oops," show him the empty hand, and that's the end of it. No treat.

5. **Start over with Steps 2 and 3.**

When you're ready, make a show of it with an audience. As you and your dog get better at this trick, you'll find what helps your dog get it right; let him sniff your hands, one at a time. Then hold them still and let him pick.

In your showmanship voice, make it fun and announce something like, "The Great Mind Reader, Buddy, traveled the world to learn this magical art. He will think and think. Could it be this hand (let him sniff) or this hand (let him sniff). Which one is it?"

Play Shy

With this trick, you teach your dog to shove his face between your knees or thighs to hide his face, acting and looking shy.

Needed: Any variety of treats

Command: Stay (refer to Chapter 11)

Command: Yes (refer to Chapter 9). Yes is the praise word that means the moment of perfection. Mark the moment he does exactly what you were wanting him to do.

Sequence 1: Putting his head between your legs

The steps in this sequence instruct Buddy to place his head between your legs:

TIP

1. **Standing up with your dog hanging around your feet, get your dog to focus on a treat in your hand.**

   Place your feet far enough apart to reach around one of your legs and get your dog to reach through your legs to get the treat in your hand. Keep your dog in front of you. If your dog comes through, that's okay, but not exactly what you want.

   Ideally he reaches through your legs to get the treat. If you have to hold him back with the other hand, initially, that's fine. Keep at it until your dog reaches through to get the treat from your hand held behind your leg.

2. **Use your Yes command the moment your dog reaches through your legs for the treat.**

Sequence 2: Holding your legs closer together

This sequence gradually gets your legs closer together until finally they're close enough that Buddy can only get his face and nose through your legs:

1. **Hold your legs closer together so your dog can reach only his head through.**

   You don't want his shoulders to go through your legs (see Figure 17-8).

2. **Start using the Shy command by saying, "Are you shy?"**

   Shy is the key word, but you can ask the whole question, emphasizing Shy.

3. **Feed from behind you, with your dog's head coming through your legs only.**

4. **Say "Yes" as you feed him.**

   Yes is the marker word. Continue to praise, and then release him from your legs.

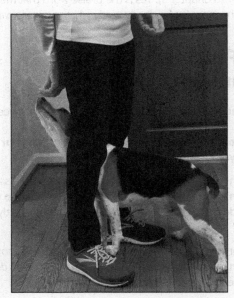

FIGURE 17-8:
Only Buddy's face should be able to push through your legs for the Shy command.

© John Wiley & Sons, Inc.

Sequence 3: Holding his head pressed between your legs

To look shy, your dog needs to keep his head pressed between your legs as if he's hiding his head. In this sequence you use the Stay command:

1. **Give the Shy command.**

   As your dog puts his head between your legs, but doesn't go through, say "Stay," which means you won't immediately give the treat. Instead, your dog should hold his head between your legs and wait for the release word to end the stay.

2. **After a few seconds, say "Okay" to release your dog and give the food reward.**

   Still give your dog the food between your legs to reinforce the position.

REMEMBER

As your dog gets more practiced on the Shy command, you won't need to put the treat behind your leg first to entice your dog's head through your legs. You may need to hold the treat with your hand hanging in a natural position, slightly around your hip, but even doing so will be less necessary as your dog learns the Shy command more solidly. Practice every day to help Buddy learn it.

TRICKS — A GREAT WAY TO ENGAGE WITH YOUR AUDIENCE

My dog and I (Mary Ann) were contracted to do a short performance every 30 minutes at a huge holiday event at a big venue. We were the entertainment as people milled around. We would do a 20-minute performance of tricks and stunts and agility and obedience. Then we would reset the stage and walk around inviting people into the auditorium for the next performance. This went on all night: Do the performance, chat up the audience, reset and walk around, repeat. After five shows, I forgot to do the Shy trick at its appropriate time during the performance, which turned out perfectly though, because for some reason, during that performance, someone in the audience, coughed quite loudly and startled my dog. He was usually stable and not sound sensitive, but that noise caused him to visibly startle and look around at the audience as if he just realized they were there.

It was amazingly perfect. I immediately jumped in and laughed and asked the dog, "What? Did you just realize people were here? Are you going to be shy now?" Bam, he stuck his head in my legs and hid his head. It brought down the house.

This is what doing a stellar trick performance is all about, talking between your dog's tricks is just as important as having a great trick dog. You are part of the act. How you keep the audience engaged is all part of your success.

Roll Over

Roll Over is always a crowd pleaser. This trick requires the dog to be on the floor and completely roll over sideways.

Needed: Yummy treats

Command: Down (see Chapter 11)

Sequence 1: Rolling over with a little help

First your dog needs to lay down, then go to his side, then roll completely over. Take each part as a complete success before moving on to the next part; really be excited with each success.

1. **Place your dog into the Down position.**

Reduce your body posture by kneeling or squatting in front of your dog so you're not leaning or hovering over him.

2. **Hold the treat in such a way that your dog has to look over his shoulder while laying on the ground.**

Keep the treat close to his nose, moving it back along his shoulder.

3. **Say "Roll over" and slowly make a small circle around his head, keeping the treat close to his nose.**

As soon as your dog moves to his side, laying on his side instead of his sternum, say "Yes" and give the treat. Even though he didn't roll over yet, he rolled to his side, which is the first big success.

4. **Repeat Step 3.**

5. **As he lays on his side, with your other hand, gently help your dog roll over completely in the direction he laid over, say "Yes," praise, and party.**

When the dog has completely rolled over, enthusiastically praise, reward, and release. Even though you helped him over, Buddy must be praised with a lot of enthusiasm. That last bit of the Roll Over is a huge deal, and you must make it a big deal with lots of praise and food.

6. **Repeat these steps until your dog is completely relaxed with you helping him roll over.**

TIP

If you're having trouble with that final roll over, move your training to a softer surface such as a bed or grass.

Sequence 2: Rolling over on his own

The steps in this sequence instructs Buddy to roll over by himself:

1. **Place your dog into the Down position.**

2. **Say "Roll over" and get him to follow the treat without any help from you.**

REMEMBER

   Move the treat around his shoulder over his back. When he does it, praise, reward, and release. If he doesn't respond or needs a lot of help, go back to Sequence 1.

3. **Repeat the steps until your dog rolls over with little to no guidance from you.**

Sequence 3: Rolling over on command

As you follow these steps to help Buddy perform the final trick, don't have a treat in your hand, but be prepared to reward immediately when you get the correct response.

1. **Say "Down" and then "Roll over."**

   The first few times you do this, you may have to use the same hand motion as though you had a treat in it. Praise, reward, and release when your dog does the trick properly.

2. **Reduce the hand motion until he does it on command alone.**

3. **Enthusiastically praise, reward, and release when he performs on command.**

REMEMBER

After your dog has mastered the trick, he'll offer this behavior anytime he wants a treat. Unfortunately, you can't reward him for that. If you did, he'd be training you to give him a treat on demand. Instead, go to random rewards when he does the trick on command.

Play Dead

Playing dead is an old favorite and a logical extension of Roll Over (see the previous section). It consists of aiming your index finger and "firing" at your dog with a command such as Bang, and your dog falls on his side or back and plays dead.

Needed: Yummy treats

Command: Down (refer to Chapter 11)

Sequence 1: Laying down on his side or back

The steps in the first sequence of this trick is to instruct your dog to lay down.

1. With a treat in your "gun" hand, use the Down command as in Figure 17-9.

2. Lean over your dog and in a deep tone of voice say "Bang" as you point your index finger at him.

Some dogs will roll on their side or back simply because of your body language and the low bang sound.

3. Praise and give him a treat while he's in that position and then release him with Okay.

If he doesn't roll on his side or back, use the treat as you did for Roll Over. Then praise, reward, and release him.

4. Repeat this sequence until your dog responds to the Bang command.

FIGURE 17-9: Load your gun (your pointed finger) with a treat in your hand.

© John Wiley & Sons, Inc.

Sequence 2: Playing dead from the sitting or standing position

After Buddy will lay over from a Down, he has to be able to "die" from any position. Follow these steps:

1. **Call you dog's name to get his attention.**
2. **Lean over your dog and in a deep tone of voice say "Bang" as you point your gun (index finger and thumb in the form of a gun) at him.**

   If he lies down and plays dead, say "Yes," praise, reward, and release. If he doesn't, show him what you want by placing him in the Dead position by giving the Down signal and moving the treat around his shoulder as described in Sequence 1 of "Roll Over." Praise, reward, and release.

3. **Repeat this sequence until your dog responds to the Bang command from the sitting or standing position.**

Sequence 3: Playing dead at a distance

To make this trick into a skit, you need to train Buddy to die to a Bang command from a slight distance:

1. **With your dog about 2 feet from you, call his name to get his attention and then give the Bang command as you point your finger gun at him.**

   If he responds, praise, go to him, reward him, and then release. If he doesn't, show him what you want and start all over.

2. **Practice this sequence as you gradually increase the distance to about 6 feet.**

Sequence 4: Presenting the trick to an audience

This sequence is our favorite and a real crowd pleaser. Put a story to it and make it for an audience. For example:

"Buddy wants to win an Academy Award one day. I've explained to him that the best way to do that is to have the perfect death scene, so Buddy is always after me to practice with me. Here we go again (with a John Wayne Western accent.) Okay, Buddy, this town ain't big enough for the two of us. It's either *you* or *me,* and I'm not going to be leaving town anytime soon. BANG! BANG!

By time you get to the BANG! BANG!, Buddy is already spinning with excitement, and he'll die immediately. As a back-up fix, should Buddy not die, you can claim a bad aim on your part or blanks loaded by mistake. Command again.

Find Mine

The Find Mine trick is one of the most impressive tricks you can teach Buddy. It combines the Retrieve with the dog's use of his nose to discriminate between different articles. It's a terrific parlor trick that will astound and amaze your friends.

REMEMBER

Needed: A leather or plastic key chain with keys on it

Using something leather or plastic makes the set of keys easier for the dog to pick up and carry.

Command: Sit-Stay (see Chapter 11)

Command: Retrieve, Take It (see Chapter 16)

Sequence 1: Retrieving something of yours

This sequence sets up this trick by teaching Buddy to retrieve an item of yours.

1. **Get your dog excited about something of yours, such as keys, and throw them a few feet in front of you and say "Find Mine."**

   If he brings them back, praise, reward, and say "Okay" to release him. If he doesn't, review the first few sequences of teaching the Retrieve in Chapter 16.

2. **Repeat this sequence until your dog readily brings back your keys.**

TECHNICAL STUFF

A dog's ability to differentiate among scents is far more acute than a person's. Dogs can be taught to identify any number of objects by scent, including underground gas leaks.

Sequence 2: Helping your dog find your item

The steps in this sequence focus on teaching Buddy to find your personal belonging, such as keys, that you've placed somewhere rather than thrown:

1. **Tell your dog to "Stay" and with him watching you, place the keys in the corner of an armchair or couch.**

   If you haven't yet taught your dog the Stay command, check out Chapter 11.

2. **Go back to your dog and send him to the keys with the Find Mine command.**

3. Praise, reward, and release him when he returns with the keys.

4. Repeat this sequence several times, each time changing the location slightly, so Buddy gets used to looking for the keys.

   Always have them visible at this point, not completely hidden. Buddy isn't ready yet, so keep it easy for him to be successful.

REMEMBER

Sequence 3: Allowing Buddy to find the keys with his nose

Now Buddy locates your keys by using his nose. This sequence is the heart of the trick and the real fun part:

1. Say "Stay" and without him watching, place the keys on the floor, just inside the doorframe of another room.

   Have him facing the other way to help him not watch where you place them.

2. Go back to your dog and send him to the keys with the Find Mine command.

   What you want him to do is to find your keys by retracing your steps and then using his nose to locate the keys.

3. Enthusiastically praise, reward, and release him when he brings you your keys.

TIP

Over the course of several sessions, make the Find Mine game increasingly difficult. For example, a fairly advanced search would involve you going into one room, coming out again, and going into another room and putting the keys behind a wastebasket. Anytime he gets stuck, help him by showing him where you placed the keys. Remember to praise and reward correct responses; however, you no longer have to reward every time.

For many years, this has been our favorite trick. Like any good trick, it's baffling if you don't understand how it's done, yet it's childishly simple for the dog. It starts with the knowledge that a dog's nose is far more powerful than a human's and that he's able to discriminate between different scents. He can certainly tell the difference between you and anybody else. Armed with this knowledge, you're ready to fleece anyone gullible enough to take on Buddy.

Sequence 4: Adding identical items and Buddy will find yours

This step requires a few identical items such as pencils, and they can all be different colors to help you remember which is which. Follow these steps:

1. **To make sure Buddy retrieves a pencil, practice by throwing the pencil a few times for Buddy to retrieve it for you.**

2. **Place a pencil on the ground that you've touched.**

   Have someone else place a pencil you haven't touched about 6 inches away from it. We refer to the pencil you haven't touched as *clean.* If you're working alone, you can use kitchen tongs to touch the clean pencil.

3. **Say "Find mine" and encourage him to pick up the scented pencil.**

   If he's correct, make a huge fuss and praise and party with him giving him a treat.

   If he seems confused and needs help, tie down the clean pencil to something like a piece of peg board or thick rug and ensure it is clean. Ask someone else to tie it down for you or do it a day in advance of your practice session (see Figure 17-10).

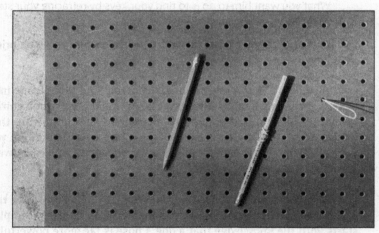

FIGURE 17-10: Tie down the unscented pencil and have your pencil loose.

Work at sending Buddy out to Find Mine with only one scented pencil untied until he always picks up your pencil and leaves the clean pencils alone. Add other clean pencils to the board, having someone else tie them down until he is perfect every time.

With the clean pencils tied down, he can only pick up the scented pencil, which will eventually click in Buddy's brain that this pencil smells differently from the pencil he can pick up. That's when you've achieved the point of this trick.

Sequence 5: Untying the clean pencils after Buddy is always finding your scented pencil

As Buddy gets better and is always picking up only your pencil, you can start having some clean pencils on the board that aren't tied down.

1. **Build on Sequence 4 and untie the pencils one at a time until they're all loose.**

2. **After you have most of the pencils loose on the board, you can start putting them on the floor as in Figure 17-11.**

   If Buddy makes a mistake at finding yours, simply go to the board and point to your pencil to help Buddy locate the pencil that has your scent on it.

   Don't rush putting too many pencils on the floor at one time. Two pencils is enough if Buddy needs more time. Make this fun for Buddy and gradually make it more challenging; no need to rush to having more pencils out there than Buddy can handle. You want him to be correct and pick up the scented pencil all of the time. Two or three unscented and clean pencils are impressive enough.

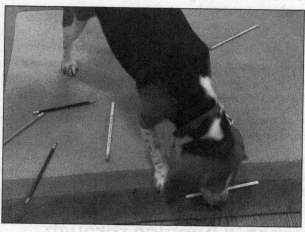

FIGURE 17-11: Use only one scented pencil.

Jump through a Hoop

A hula hoop makes a wonderful prop for this trick, which is suitable for medium- to small-sized dogs. Start by getting a hoop that's appropriate for your dog's size, and then follow the three sequences.

Needed: A yummy treat

Command: Come (see Chapter 10)

Command: Stay (see Chapter 11)

Sequence 1: Walking and jumping through a hoop

These steps teach your dog to walk first and then jump through a hoop on leash.

1. **Lay the hoop on the ground and walk your dog over to examine it.**

   Take your time with this step so Buddy thoroughly smells the hoop and isn't frightened by it.

2. **Put your dog on leash and walk him over the hoop.**

3. **Pick up the hoop and let the bottom edge rest on the ground.**

4. **Thread the leash through the hoop and encourage your dog to walk through to you by saying, "Come."**

   You can use a treat to get him to walk through the hoop. Repeat until your dog readily goes through the hoop with the Come, Jump command. Praise, reward, and release with Okay for successful attempts. By adding the Jump command immediately following the command he knows, Buddy will quickly make the association of the new command.

5. **Thread the leash through the hoop and raise it a few inches off the ground and say "Come, Jump."**

   If necessary, use a treat to get him through and then enthusiastically praise. As your dog gains confidence, begin raising the hoop in 2-inch increments until the bottom is eye level in front of him.

Sequence 2: Jumping through the hoop off Leash

The steps in this sequence train your dog to jump through the hoop off leash:

1. **Take the leash off and present the hoop in front of your dog with the bottom of the hoop no higher than the dog's knees.**

2. **Say "Come, Jump" and let the dog jump through.**

3. **Praise and reward with a treat.**

   Repeat but change the position of the hoop so that the bottom is level with the dog's elbows and then his shoulder. The maximum height you can raise the hoop depends on the size and athletic ability of your dog. Eventually you can drop saying "Come" before the Jump command.

   Keep in mind that as soon as you get to about shoulder level (the dog's, not yours), you need a surface with good traction on which the dog can take off and land safely. Wet grass and slippery floors aren't good surfaces for this trick. He may wind up injured.

WARNING

You Have Food on Your Nose

You Have Food on Your Nose is a cute trick. It involves balancing a piece of food on Buddy's nose until you give the "Okay." Some dogs even toss the food in the air and catch it on the way down. That is a natural choice the dog will add on his own, or not.

Needed: A flat treat that you can balance on a dog's nose

Command: Sit-Stay (refer to Chapter 11)

Command: Leave It (refer to Chapter 9)

Command: Hold It (refer to Chapter 16)

Sequence 1: Cupping your hand over your dog's muzzle

You need to be able to cup your hand over your dog's muzzle so you can put a piece of food on his nose. If you've taught your dog the Retrieve, he already knows to let you do this to him. If he doesn't, check out Chapter 16. Follow these steps:

1. **Sit-Stay your dog and pet him for a few seconds.**

2. **Cup your hand over his muzzle from the top, just as you do for the Retrieve as in Figure 17-12.**

FIGURE 17-12:
Cup your hand over his nose on a Sit-Stay.

© John Wiley & Sons, Inc.

3. **Kneel or squat in front of your dog and keep your upper body straight.**

4. **With your other hand hold a piece of food or a treat near your dog's nose get him to focus on the treat and say "Leave it" if Buddy keeps going for the treat without your permission.**

5. **Say "Okay" to release him and give him the treat.**

6. **Repeat until you can cup his muzzle and he sits still.**

Sequence 2: Putting the treat on your dog's nose

You need some patience in these steps as you put the treat on Buddy's nose:

1. **Gently hold his muzzle and put the treat on his nose in front of your thumb as in Figure 17-13.**

2. **Say "Stay" or "Hold It" and then release him with "Okay."**

   The treat will either fall off or get bounced into the air. Either is fine; you mainly want him to allow you to place the treat on his nose and then release him to eat it.

FIGURE 17-13:
Balance the treat
on his nose.

Sequence 3: Balancing the treat longer

The goal with these steps is to increase the amount of time you balance the treat on your dog's nose while holding his muzzle before releasing Buddy to get the treat:

1. **Start by holding his muzzle and placing the treat on his nose.**

2. **Say "Stay" and have your dog balance the treat for five seconds and then release him.**

    Use the Hold It command from Chapter 16.

3. **Repeat and increase the time to ten seconds.**

Sequence 4: Balancing the treat without your help

This sequence ends this trick by getting your dog to balance the treat without your assistance. Follow these steps:

1. **Put the treat on his muzzle and then slowly let go of his muzzle with the Stay command.**

2. **Get him to focus on your index finger by holding it in front of his nose and saying, "Hold it."**

3. **Wait a few seconds and release your dog.**

You can now gradually increase the time your dog holds the treat before you release him as well as gradually increase the distance of your finger from the dog's nose.

TIP

What if he drops or tosses the treat before you say "Okay?" Well, if you can't get to the treat before he does, reduce the time and distance until he's reliable again. Then you gradually can increase the time and distance.

Take a Bow

Performers customarily take a bow after a performance to accept the applause of the audience. This trick teaches your dog to take a bow after he has performed the tricks you've taught him.

Needed: Treats, small smelly and easily eaten

Command: Down (refer to Chapter 11)

Command: Stand (refer to Chapter 19)

Command: Stay (refer to Chapter 11)

Command: Yes marker praise word (see Chapter 9)

Sequence 1: Bowing by using a food lure

These steps get your dog to bow by using food as a treat:

1. **Stand your dog next to you.**

With a small dog, you can teach this trick on a table.

2. **Place your left hand, palm facing down, under your dog's belly with a little backward pressure against his hind legs.**

3. **With a treat in your right hand, slowly lower the cookie from your dog's nose to the ground, keeping your left hand under his belly.**

Move the treat slightly closer to his feet, not out away from the dog — from his nose toward the ground toward his elbows on the ground.

4. **Say "Take a Bow" as you move the treat and Buddy gets into the correct bow position.**

   When he does, say "Yes" and hold the treat and he's still for a few seconds before releasing and giving the treat.

   You want Buddy to lower his front end and remain standing with the rear end. When Buddy is successful, praise and say "Okay" to release.

5. **Practice this sequence until he lowers his front end on command without a treat.**

   You can use the movement of your treat hand even though it doesn't have a treat.

6. **Praise enthusiastically after each successful repetition.**

Sequence 2: Practicing until Buddy bows with little to no help

The steps in this sequence focus on practicing until Buddy bows on his own with little to no help from you:

1. **Stand next to your dog, keeping your left hand under his belly.**

2. **Say "Take a Bow" and pat the ground in front of him with your right hand.**

   When he lowers his front end, praise and release.

3. **Practice these steps several times until he responds to the command without you patting the ground.**

Sequence 3: Taking a bow on command

The final sequence in this trick teaches Buddy to take the bow when you command him to do so. Do these steps in front of an audience:

1. **Stand next to your dog, point to the ground in front of him with your left hand, and say "Take a Bow" (see Figure 17-14).**

   When he does, praise and release. If he tries to lie down, prop up his rear end with your left hand. Practice until you no longer have to prop up his rear.

2. **When he takes a bow on command, say "Stay" and release him after several seconds.**

   Be prepared for your audience's applause.

FIGURE 17-14:
Take a Bow to thundering applause.

Dog Catcher/Stranger Trick

This is by far one of the best crowd-pleasing tricks you can teach your dog. It's based on the Leave It command.

Needed: Treats

Command: Leave It (refer to Chapter 9).

1. **Practice Leave It until your dog is quite good at it.**

   Now you need to change two things to make this into the Dog Catcher trick.

2. **Reteach the Leave It command in Chapter 9 using "Dog Catcher" and also "Stranger."**

3. **Reteach the Okay command as people's names.**

   For example, "Okay, Mommy," "Okay, Joe," or "Okay Daddy." Insert any name after Okay as your release word to take the treat.

4. **Make up your story as the trick.**

Here is an example:

My dog is like my child. He's very special to me, and I want him to be safe. I've taught him to not take candy from a stranger or to go with bad people like the dog catcher. I want him to practice this safety rule regularly, and I want to remind him of the rule as often as I can. Do you mind if we practice this while you are here with us? Here goes. (Looking at your dog, say the following:) "Buddy, the world is a dangerous place. I want you to always watch out for bad people. They may try to lure you to go with them, and I don't want that to ever happen. Don't go with strangers or with the dog catcher. Only go with people you know, like Joe here or Mommy and Daddy. So let us practice. Buddy, this cookie is from the dog catcher. (Buddy should back up.) It's actually "Okay, it's from Mommy." (Buddy grabs the cookie.) This cookie is from the dog catcher. (Buddy backs up again.) It's really from a stranger. (Buddy still remains backed up.) "Okay, it's really from Joe." (Buddy grabs the cookie.)

It's a great trick. People love it, and it's great to use when you visit daycares and schools.

USING YOUR DOG'S NATURAL BEHAVIORS TO YOUR ADVANTAGE

Teaching Buddy tricks that use his natural tendencies generally makes teaching tricks easier. If your dog has a quirky habit, you may find that you can turn it into a fun trick. When you see a behavior you want to turn into a trick, tell your dog how clever he is and give him a treat.

For example, when you see Buddy sneeze and you want to turn the behavior into a trick, praise him when you see him do it and give him a treat and praise. Next, give the behavior a command, such as "Sneeze." When you see him do it, give the command, praise, and reward. It won't take long before Buddy responds to the command.

Chapter **18**

Training for Fun and Competition

I f you and Buddy enjoy working together, the sky is the limit — you can participate in many performance events. Doing so is a lot of fun, and you meet lots of nice people. Be forewarned, though: after you start, you can become addicted to these events, and your life will never be the same.

Almost every weekend of the year, you can go to some event and show off what the two of you have accomplished. Dog events are categorized as either *conformation shows*, where your dog is judged on his appearance, or as *performance trials*, where you and your dog are judged on your abilities. The shows can be held together or separately.

Different organizations have licensed shows, including those in which *designer breeds*, such as the Goldendoodle or Labradoodle, and mixed breeds can participate. This book concentrates on the shows held under the auspices of the American Kennel Club (AKC), the oldest and largest organization to license such events. To participate in an AKC–licensed performance event, such as Agility, Obedience, and Rally, your dog must be registered with the AKC. Your dog need not be a purebred dog to participate in performance events by AKC, but you do need to register your dog as a Canine Partner Listing through AKC. To do so, go to www.akc.org and search for Canine Partner Listings. If your dog is going to be accepted by AKC Partners as a mixed breed dog, he must be neutered or spayed to perform at AKC events.

The AKC awards three basic obedience titles:

>> Companion Dog, or CD, from the Novice class

>> Companion Dog Excellent, or CDX, from the Open class

>> Utility Dog, or UD, from the Utility class

The level of difficulty increases with each class, from basic control and retrieving and jumping to responding to signals and directional signals. The classes are designed so that any dog can participate successfully and earn titles. After your dog has earned a Utility Dog title, you're then eligible to compete for the special obedience titles of Obedience Trial Champion and Utility Dog Excellent.

All three classes and all levels of competition have one exercise in common: heeling. This means that you and Buddy need a firm foundation and have to practice, practice, practice. And even if you aren't planning to compete, teaching Buddy to heel is still important.

In this chapter, we take a look at the AKC Novice class and its goal, the Companion Dog title. We show you the six required exercises and the points needed to earn the title. In Chapter 19, we review the remaining exercises you and your dog need to complete the Companion Dog title.

REMEMBER

You can get your own copy of the Obedience Regulations by contacting the American Kennel Club at 5580 Centerview Drive, Suite 200, Raleigh, NC 27606-3390 (919-233-9767 or www.akc.org). Getting your own copy of the regulations is a piece of cake, so go ahead and get them. Knowing the rules is a good idea so you know what's expected from you and your dog.

Understanding the System: Your Road Map to the Companion Dog Title

If you're interested in helping your dog earn the Companion Dog title or Novice Level, you need to know the ropes on how to get started. This section provides the info you need. If you've already been to a dog show and seen a performance trial, or watched one on TV, you probably thought, "My dog could never do that." Perhaps, but remember that every one of the participants began with training their first dog.

THE RALLY CLASS

The name *rally* comes from the use of directional signs, similar to a Road Rally for cars. In the Rally class, the dog and owner complete a course following a series of 10 to 20 signs, depending on the level. Each sign, called a *station*, instructs the owner on each exercise the dog has to perform. For example, the sign may say "Forward," "About-turn," or "Halt."

After the judge has given the first Forward, the owner and dog as a team move continuously from one sign to the next on their own instead of waiting for the judge's command for each exercise (as in all the other obedience classes). Unlimited communication from owner to dog is permitted, but the owner may not touch the dog and physical guidance is penalized.

This class is fun because you can give all the extra help your dog may need in the form of commands, encouragement, and praise. It's also fast paced, because you move from one sign to the next without any interruption, which makes it very exciting for the dog.

The starting score is 100, and deductions are made for any errors on the part of the dog performing the designated exercise at a station or for not completing a required exercise. Scoring is more lenient than traditional obedience, but judges should see a sense of teamwork between you and your dog. You'll encounter approximately 40 different stations, representing all the basic obedience exercises and maneuvers. To earn an AKC Rally title, the dog must achieve three qualifying scores under at least two different judges.

The Rally class has the following different levels:

- Novice or RN: In this class, all exercises are done on leash, and there are 10 to 15 stations.

- Advanced or RA: In the Advanced class, all the exercises, which include one jump, are done off leash, and there are 12 to 17 stations.

- Excellent or RE: This class is also done off leash and includes two jumps and 15 to 20 stations.

- Rally Advanced Excellent or RAE: The Rally Advanced Excellent title requires the dog to qualify ten times in both the Rally Advanced Class and the Rally Excellent Class at the same trial.

- Masters or RM: The Masters title has only one jump and is off leash and has 15 to 20 signs.

- Rally Championship or RACH: Your dog also has the opportunity to earn a Rally Championship.

Rally gives you and your dog more opportunities for fun, exhibiting and earning more titles.

To begin in obedience, you and Buddy can enter either the Pre-Novice or the Novice class. The required exercises for both classes demonstrate the usefulness of the purebred dog as a companion, and they help you prepare for obtaining the Companion Dog title. In the following sections, we explain each of these classes and their requirements and characteristics.

You also can enter the Rally class (see the nearby sidebar "The Rally class" for more details).

Requirements for Pre-Novice

The Pre-Novice is a nonregular class, like the AKC S.T.A.R. Puppy and Canine Good Citizen programs, which are titles that you can earn before you're ready to show, and serves as an introduction to the world of obedience events. Go to www.akc.org to read more about them. (*Nonregular classes* are those in which participation doesn't earn AKC titles.) Seven nonregular classes are available: Graduate Novice, Graduate Open, Brace (two dogs handled by one person), Veterans (for dogs at least 7 years of age), Versatility, Team (four dogs and four owners), and Pre-Novice.

For the Pre-Novice class, no minimum point score is required for a qualifying score, and whoever has the highest score wins the class. Pre-Novice is ideal for people or dogs who have never participated in a dog show before.

The cornerstones of the Pre-Novice class, and of all the other obedience classes, are having a dog that does the following:

>> Pays attention to you

>> Knows how to heel

Later in this chapter, we concentrate on these two concepts.

The Pre-Novice class consists of six exercises, each with a specific point value. Your dog must respond to the first command, so you're penalized for any additional commands. All the exercises are performed on leash. Before each exercise, the judge asks, "Are you ready?" You say that you are, and the judge then gives the command, such as "Forward" for the Heel On Leash (see the later section "Let's Dance, Buddy: Heel On and Then Off Leash") and Figure 8 exercises (see the later section, "Putting a Twist on Things: Teaching the Figure 8") or "Stand your dog and leave when ready" for the Stand for Examination (see Chapter 19). These exercises are always done in the order in which they're listed in Table 18-1.

These exercises are an extension of those required for the Canine Good Citizen certificate and are a preview of those required for the Novice class, which we discuss in the upcoming section.

TABLE 18-1

The Pre-Novice Class

Required Exercises	Available Points
Heel On Leash	45
Figure 8	25
Stand for Examination	30
Recall	40
Long Sit (1 minute)	30
Long Down (3 minutes)	30
Maximum Total Score	**200**

FOR MORE INFORMATION ON DOG ORGANIZATIONS

For more information on dogs and dog competitions, check out the following organizations and their respective websites:

- **American Kennel Club** (www.akc.org): The official American Kennel Club website offers information on almost everything to do with dogs. You can get the profiles of different breeds, find out how to register your dog, and get answers to questions about registration. You can find out about dogs in competition and what titles dogs can earn. This site tells you about pedigrees and, if you have a purebred dog, how to get a three-generation pedigree from the AKC. It offers reproductions from the Dog Museum, where many famous pieces of art and old books are housed, and it has archives of articles that have appeared recently, together with information about how the AKC works.

- **United Kennel Club** (www.ukcdogs.com): The UKC is the second oldest and second largest all-breed dog registry in the United States. Founded in 1898 by Chauncey Z. Bennett, the registry has always supported the idea of the "total dog," meaning a dog that looks and performs equally well. With 250,000 registrations annually, the performance programs of the UKC include conformation shows; obedience trials; agility trials; coonhound field trials; water races; night hunts and bench shows; hunting tests for the retrieving breeds; beagle events, including hunts and bench shows; and cur, feist, squirrel, and coon events. The UKC world of dogs is a working world. That's the way Bennett designed it, and that's the way it remains today.

- **Continental Kennel Club** (www.continentalkennelclub.com): A newer and innovative kennel club that is embracing tradition while adjusting to the needs of dog owners worldwide.

The Novice class: What's expected from you and Buddy

The Novice class consists of six exercises, each with a specific point value (see Table 18-2). The six exercises are always done in the order listed in the table, and they're all pack behavior exercises. For a qualifying score, you and Buddy have to earn more than 50 percent of the available points for each exercise and a final score of more than 170 out of a possible 200.

REMEMBER

A qualifying score at an obedience trial is called a *leg.* Your dog needs three legs to earn the AKC Companion Dog title.

TABLE 18-2

The Novice Class

Required Exercises	Available Points
Exercise 1: Heel On Leash and Figure 8	40
Exercise 2: Stand for Examination	30
Exercise 3: Heel Free	40
Exercise 4: Recall	30
Exercise 5: Sit-Stay (1 minute)	30
Exercise 6: Down-Stay (3 minutes)	30
Maximum Total Score	**200**

Like the Pre-Novice class exercises, the Novice class exercises are an extension of those required for the Canine Good Citizen test. The Stand for Examination exercise, for example, is a form of temperament test similar to the "accepting a friendly stranger" and the "sitting politely for petting" exercises in the Canine Good Citizen test.

However, some important differences and additions exist in the Novice class exercises:

» Buddy has to respond to the first command.

» Walking on a loose leash is now called Heeling, and it consists of both heeling on and off leash and includes a Figure 8 on leash. (Refer to the later section "Putting a Twist on Things: Teaching the Figure 8" for more information.) It's also more exacting.

>> The temperament test requires the dog to stand and is performed off leash with you standing 6 feet in front of your dog. When you're in position, the judge will approach your dog from in front and touch Buddy's head, body, and hindquarters.

>> The Come When Called (see Chapter 10) is now referred to as the Recall. It's performed off leash and requires Buddy to stay, come on command, sit in front of you, and then go to Heel position on command.

>> The Sit and Down-Stay are done on leash for one and three minutes, respectively.

The Novice class is tailor-made for the dog who's highest in pack drive behaviors. For the dog who's highest in prey drive behaviors, this class is a little more challenging because of his distractibility around sights, sounds, and smells. (See Chapter 2 for what the different behaviors mean.)

REMEMBER

When you look at the Novice class exercises in Table 18-2, you see that 120 points depend on your dog being able to stay — for the Stand for Examination, the Recall, the Sit, and the Down-Stay. So you can see how important the Stay exercise is. (You can find out more about helping Buddy with the Stay command in Chapter 11.)

First Things First: Teaching the Ready! Command

The first exercise in either the Pre-Novice or the Novice class is the Heel On Leash, and when training to perform, it's best to teach your dog a command that tells him that the two of you are going to heel together. The Ready! command does just that. Notice that the command includes an exclamation mark and not a question mark. You say it in a quiet and yet excited tone of voice — almost a whisper.

The reason Ready! is chosen is simple: In an obedience trial, the judge asks, "Are you ready?" before she says "Forward" (or any other directive).

When the judge asks you the question, naturally you're expected to give some indication that the two of you are ready to go. By answering with "Ready!" Buddy snaps to attention and is all set to go. The judge then says "Forward," at which point you say "Buddy, Heel!" and start to move.

REMEMBER

No doubt you're wondering why all this is necessary when Buddy is supposed to respond to the Heel command and move with you when you do. The reason is that when you give the Heel command, you want to make sure that Buddy's attention is on you and not something else that may have attracted his attention. Otherwise, he may just sit there like a bump on a log, totally engrossed in what's going on in the next ring, and when you start to walk, he has to play catch-up.

To avoid this scenario, teach Buddy the Ready! command. In addition, you need to decide on your leadoff leg — the one that tells the dog when he's expected to go with you. If you're right-handed, you'll be more comfortable making your leadoff leg your right, but you can start on either leg as long as you're consistent. Experiment and see which one works better.

In the following sections, we show you how to get Buddy positioned next to you on the leash before starting the process of teaching him the Ready! command.

Using Control Position

Before you start teaching Buddy the Ready! command, you must get him positioned in such a way that helps him succeed. You need to hold the leash in *Control Position*, which makes it easier for you to remind Buddy of his responsibility to pay attention to you and stay in Heel position when he permits himself to become distracted (see Figure 18-1).

To hold the leash in Control Position, follow these steps:

1. **Attach the leash to your dog's training collar.**

2. **Position both rings of the collar under his chin.**

3. **Put the loop of the leash over the thumb of your right hand.**

4. **Neatly fold the leash, accordion-style, into your right hand, with the part going to the dog coming out from under your little finger.**

5. Place your right hand against the front of your leg, palm facing your leg.

6. With your left hand, grasp the leash in front of your left leg, palm facing your leg.

REMEMBER

Keep both hands below your waist at all times and your elbows relaxed and close to your body. Take up enough slack in the leash so that the leash snap is parallel with the ground.

Working through the sequences of the Ready! command

Most commands you teach your dog consist of several steps, called sequences. Each sequence adds to the dog's understanding of the command. The following sections show you the six sequences you use to teach the Ready! command. Each of the following sequences usually change only one small thing, but the slight change makes the Ready! command more meaningful and reliable. These sequences are meant as a training plan; do one sequence each training session, and then worry about the next sequence at the next training session.

Sequence 1: Focusing Buddy's attention on you

The goal of Sequence 1 is to systematically teach your dog to focus on you and pay attention. Here are the steps to take:

1. **Attach the leash to the training collar and sit your dog at Heel position.**

   Your dog is in *Heel position* when the area from his head to his shoulder is in line with your left hip, with both of you facing in the same direction.

2. **Hold the leash in Control Position and look at your dog, keeping your left shoulder absolutely straight.**

   Don't forget to smile and relax. (We discuss the Control Position in the previous section.)

3. **Say your dog's name, release with an enthusiastic "Okay," and take five steps forward at a trot, keeping your hands in Control Position.**

   Don't worry about what Buddy is doing; just concentrate on your part.

4. **Repeat several times.**

Sequence 2: Introducing Buddy to the Ready! command

With Sequence 2, you introduce your dog to the Ready! command. Practice the different sequences in this section over the course of several sessions.

REMEMBER

When teaching this command, hold your hands in Control Position and keep your shoulders absolutely straight. You want to use body language to communicate forward motion to your dog. Dropping your left shoulder or pointing it back communicates just the opposite and switches Buddy out of pack drive, which he needs to be in to heel well.

Follow these steps to introduce the Ready! command:

1. **Attach the leash to the training collar, and sit your dog at Heel position.**

2. **Hold the leash in Control Position and look at your dog, keeping your left shoulder absolutely straight.**

3. **Quietly and in an excited tone of voice, say "Ready!"**

4. **Say "Buddy, Heel," move out briskly for five paces at a normal speed, and then release with "Okay."**

   REMEMBER

   Wait until you finish giving the command before you move. Otherwise, you're teaching your dog to move on his name, which isn't a good idea.

5. **Repeat this sequence several times.**

Ignore what Buddy is doing in this exercise. Concentrate on your part of keeping your hands in position and starting and releasing on the leadoff leg. Be sure to keep the exercise fun and exciting for your dog.

Sequence 3: Getting Buddy to respond to Ready!

The goal of Sequence 3 is to teach your dog to respond to the Ready! command. Here's what to do:

1. **Attach the leash to the training collar, and sit your dog at Heel position.**

2. **Hold the leash in Control Position and look at your dog, keeping your left shoulder absolutely straight.**

3. **Quietly and in an excited tone of voice, say "Ready!"**

4. **Say "Buddy, Heel," start at a fast pace as quickly as you can for ten paces, and release.**

5. **Repeat several times.**

TIP

Here are a couple helpful hints for you as you do this sequence the first few times:

>> **Wait until you've finished the command before you start to run.** Taking off without having told your dog what you want would hardly be fair to him. You may feel a little tension on the leash before Buddy understands that you want him to move with you.

>> **Resist the temptation to let your left hand trail out behind you when you feel a little tension on the leash and resist the urge to let your left shoulder drop.** Hook the thumb of your left hand under your waistband and lock it in place; concentrate on keeping your left shoulder straight.

After four to five tries, you'll notice that Buddy is actually responding when you say "Ready!" and is becoming more attentive to the command.

Sequence 4: Rewarding Buddy's response

This sequence rewards dogs that respond to the Ready! Command and helps those that are a little slow to pick up on it. Check out these steps:

1. **With your dog sitting at a Heel position, neatly fold the leash into your left hand, which should be placed at your belt buckle.**

2. **Hold a treat in your right hand, placing your hand at your right side.**

3. **Look at your dog, smile, and say "Ready!"**

4. **Do one of the following:**

- If he looks at you, tell him how clever he is, give him the treat, and release.

- If he doesn't look at you, put the treat in front of his nose, and move the treat in the direction of your face. When he follows the treat, tell him how clever he is, give him the treat, and release.

5. **Repeat until your dog responds without hesitation to the Ready! command.**

Sequence 5: Reinforcing the Ready! command

Sometimes Buddy will be distracted to such an extent that he won't respond to the Ready! command. For those occasions, you need to be able to reinforce the command so he knows that when you say the magic word, he has to pay attention no matter what's out there. Perform the following Sequence 5 steps to reinforce the Ready! command:

1. **Attach the leash to the training collar, and sit your dog at Heel position.**

2. **Hold the leash in Control Position and look at your dog, keeping your left shoulder absolutely straight.**

3. **Give the Ready! command.**

4. **Do one of the following:**

- If Buddy looks up at you expectantly, praise and then release.

- If he doesn't look up at you, check the leash in the direction you want him to focus — usually up toward your face. When he looks up, praise and release.

REMEMBER

Nagging your dog with ineffective checks isn't a good training technique. Get a response the first time so you can praise and release him. If you repeatedly don't get a response, review the prior sequences.

5. **Repeat until your dog is rock solid on responding to the Ready! command.**

Sequence 6: Convincing Buddy to ignore distractions

This sequence is the review progression for the entire Ready! exercise. The goal of this sequence is to help your dog ignore distractions. During this sequence, you start working with a helper who will try to distract your dog. Your helper can be a friend or family member. The three main distractions are

» **Visual, or first degree:** Helper approaches and just stands there.

» **Auditory, or second degree:** Helper approaches and tries to distract Buddy with "Hello, puppy! Want to come and visit?" or whatever else comes to mind. Note that the name of the dog isn't used.

» **Object of attraction, or third degree:** Helper approaches and offers Buddy a toy or a treat.

When performing the following steps, practice with first degree until your dog ignores the distracter. Then move on to second degree and third degree.

1. **Neatly fold the leash into your right hand, and place your left hand around the leash directly under your right hand, as though you're holding a baseball bat.**

   Allow about 2 inches of slack in the leash and place both hands against your belt buckle.

2. **Give the Ready! command.**

3. **Have the helper approach in a nonthreatening manner.**

TIP

   When you're working on distraction training, have the helper approach your dog at a 45-degree angle and not straight on from the front or the side. Straight-on approaches are considered confrontational to some dogs. The helper starts to approach the dog from 10 feet away and stops 2 feet from the dog.

4. **Do one of the following:**

   • If your dog keeps his attention focused on you, praise and release.

   • If he permits himself to become distracted, reinforce, praise, and release.

   Review this exercise with Buddy on a regular basis.

Heeling Despite Distractions

After you've taught Buddy to pay attention to you on command, and while he's sitting at the Heel position (see the earlier section "Working through the sequences of the Ready! command"), you have to teach him to pay attention during heeling. Up to now, most of your heeling has probably been done in areas relatively free of distractions, perhaps even in the same location. The time has come to expand Buddy's horizons. You need to get him out to new places.

For Buddy, any new location is a form of distraction training. Everything looks different, and more important, everything smells different. When you take him to a new place, let him acclimate himself first — take in the sights and smells. Give him a chance to relieve himself as well. Some dogs want to leave their mark in a new place, so making sure Buddy is empty is important during a trial.

When you participate in an obedience trial, defecating or urinating in the ring is an automatic non-qualification (NQ), so you need to teach Buddy that when he's working it's not the time or place for bathroom breaks.

The following sections provide the info you need to make sure your dog is successful when heeling around distractions.

Helping your dog heel in new places

In a location new to your dog and after he has had a chance to look around a bit and relieve himself, do some heeling with particular emphasis on having your dog pay attention to you. Anytime his attention wanders — he may want to sniff the ground or just look around — remind him with a little check that he has to pay attention to you. When he does, tell him what a good boy he is, and then release him with "Okay."

Check the leash in the direction you want your dog to focus — somewhere on you. Depending on his size, this can be your ankle, lower leg, upper leg, torso, or face. Focusing on your face would be ideal, and some dogs learn it quickly; others are structurally unable to.

When you release Buddy, take five steps straight forward at a trot. Keep both hands on the leash. You want to get him excited about heeling with you. If he gets too excited and starts to run ahead, release him with somewhat less enthusiasm. After any check to refocus the dog's attention on you, release him. Doing so makes it fun for your dog to watch you.

Using a distracter while you're heeling

The purpose of heeling with distractions is for your dog to ignore them, concentrate on what he's supposed to do, and focus his attention on you. Exactly how he accomplishes this goal isn't important, so long as he does. Dogs have excellent peripheral vision and can heel perfectly well without directly looking at you.

You now need a helper to assist you. Heel your dog past your helper, who can be standing, sitting, or squatting while smiling invitingly at your dog. If your dog permits himself to become distracted, check him to refocus his attention on you. When he does refocus on you, praise and release with "Okay." Repeat until your dog ignores your helper and instead pays attention to you as you pass the distracter.

After your dog has learned to ignore your helper, have the distracter talk to your dog (the dog's name isn't used) and then eventually offer him a treat. You want to teach your dog to ignore such distractions and remain attentive to you. When he does, be sure to praise and release him. After Buddy has caught on to the concept that he has to pay attention to you no matter what, use the release less frequently.

Let's Dance, Buddy: Heel On and Then Off Leash

Heeling is like dancing with your dog. And *you* have to lead. If you know anything about dancing, you know that you have the tougher job. The dog will follow only your lead, so you need to give him the necessary cues to change direction or pace. *Remember*: The Heel On Leash is a requirement for both Pre-Novice and Novice classes (refer to the earlier section "Understanding the System: Your Road Map to the Companion Dog Title" for more on these classes).

TIP

Heeling is a pack-drive exercise (see Chapter 2). Before giving the command to heel, put your dog into pack drive by smiling at him and gently touching him on the side of his face. In an obedience trial, you can do this before you respond to the judge that you're ready, but not after.

In the earlier section "Heeling Despite Distractions," you discover how to teach Buddy to heel around distractions. In order to master the Heel On Leash, you need to review that exercise on a frequent basis. In addition, you need to work on perfecting turns and changes of pace. In the Automatic Sit section, we discuss how to work turns and changes of pace.

Under the AKC Obedience Regulations, the judge of an obedience trial will call a heeling pattern for you. The pattern has to include — in addition to normal pace — a fast pace, a slow pace, and a right, left, and about-turn. That pattern is the bare minimum. A simple heeling pattern may look something like this: forward, fast, normal, left turn, about-turn, halt, forward, right turn, slow, normal, about-turn, halt.

If you have your dog's attention, and if you don't accidentally confuse him with incorrect cues, your obedience trial should go reasonably well. Still, you need to look at each of the maneuvers in this section as separate exercises that you and Buddy have to practice — sort of like the steps of a particular dance.

REMEMBER

If you need to check your dog, release with "Okay" after the check. And when your dog is doing something correctly, or is trying, be sure to reward him with a treat or praise.

TIP

Once a week, test your dog's understanding of heeling by doing a little pattern with him that's similar to what you'd perform in the ring. Just remember that in the ring, you're not allowed to check your dog, and you can't have any tension on the leash. The only true test is when your dog is off leash, but using the leash-in-pocket technique gives you a good idea of what you need to practice. The purpose of testing your dog's understanding of heeling is to see what you need to practice. Most of your time should be spent practicing. Test every fourth or fifth session. Refer to Chapter 19 for more about the leash-in-pocket technique.

The halt

When you *halt*, Buddy is expected to sit at Heel position without any command or signal from you. This maneuver is called the *Automatic Sit*, because the cue for the dog to sit is when you stop. Under the Obedience Regulations, you're penalized if you use a command or signal to get the dog to sit. The dog has to do it on his own.

To teach Buddy the Automatic Sit, follow these steps:

1. **Put the rings of the training collar on top of your dog's neck, but no pressure on the leash.**

2. **As you come to a halt, check with your left hand straight up with a quick snap but immediately relax the pressure.**

Be careful that you don't inadvertently check toward or across your body, because doing so will cause your dog to sit with his rear end away from you and not in a straight line. As a result, you and your dog will be penalized.

REMEMBER

3. **Practice two or three Automatic Sits with a check, and then try one without a check.**

Your dog will immediately tell you where you stand with that exercise.

Changes of pace and turns

For the changes of pace and turns, your dog will take his cue from your leadoff leg. Here are the three techniques in teaching this concept:

>> The release

>> An object of attraction, which can be a treat or favorite toy

>> A check

Changing pace

This section contains a changing pace example. Suppose you want to teach your dog to stay with you as you change pace from slow to normal. Perform these steps:

1. **Release your dog with "Okay" from a slow pace on your leadoff leg.**

   The idea of this step is to get your dog all excited about accelerating with you from slow to normal pace.

2. **As you go from slow to normal, use a treat to draw the dog forward as the leadoff leg makes the transition.**

   Hold the leash in your left hand and the treat in your right. Show the dog the treat just as you're about to make the change and draw him forward with the treat in your right hand as the leadoff leg accelerates into normal pace.

3. **Hold the leash in Control Position and occasionally, and only when necessary, give a little check straight forward at the same time the leadoff leg makes the transition.**

   The check teaches your dog that ultimately it's his responsibility, on or off leash, to accelerate when you change pace. You can read more about the Control Position in the earlier section "Using Control Position."

REMEMBER

Most of your repetitions of any of the heeling components should include the release or a treat.

Making turns

Your dog needs to learn three different turns: right turn, left turn, and about-turn. When making any of these turns, try to keep your feet close together so your dog can keep up with you. Don't make a wide turn by shuffling your feet, but rather as you keep your legs close together, make several small steps making the correct turn: right, left, or about.

For the right and about-turns, Buddy needs to learn to accelerate and stay close to your side as you make the turns. You can teach him by using these techniques:

>> The release as you come out of the turn

>> A treat to guide him around the turn

>> A little check coming out of the turn, if necessary

When you use a treat, do the following:

>> Neatly fold the leash into your left hand and place it against your right hip. Doing so keeps your shoulder facing in the proper direction.

>> Hold the treat in your right hand at your side.

>> Just before you make the turn, show your dog the treat, and use it to guide him around the turn.

>> Hold the treat as close to your left leg as you can so your dog learns to make nice, tight turns.

For the left turn, Buddy first needs to slow down (so you don't trip over him) and then accelerate again. Draw back on the leash just before you make the turn, and then use the same techniques that you use for the right and about-turns.

REMEMBER You don't have to practice these maneuvers in succession as long as you do two or three of each during a training session.

Putting a Twist on Things: Teaching the Figure 8

The *Figure 8* is a fun exercise. In the ring, it's done around two people, called *stewards*, who stand 8 feet apart and act as posts. You and your dog start equidistant from the two posts and walk twice completely around and between them. In practice, you can use chairs as posts. In order to stay in Heel position, your dog has to speed up on the outside turn and slow down on the inside turn, while you maintain an even brisk pace throughout.

TIP One lament frequently heard is, "He does fine at home, but take him anywhere and forget it!" To solve this problem, make a point to seek out new locations for training, at first without distractions and then with distractions, to see how Buddy does. A dog is only truly trained when he can perform anywhere you take him, not just at home.

REMEMBER Until your dog masters this exercise, he'll have a tendency to forge or crowd on the inside turn and to lag or go wide on the outside turn. When teaching the exercise, use your body as your main communication tool. By rotating the upper part of your body back toward your dog, or forward away from your dog, you cause him to slow down or speed up respectively. Your left shoulder will be the cue for your dog, indicating what you want him to do. When the left shoulder points back, your dog will slow down; when it points forward, he'll speed up. Just as dogs communicate with each other through body language, so can you.

Go ahead and try it. It's almost the same motion as the twist, only from the waist up. Rotate the upper part of your body first to the left and then to the right. You'll use this motion to control your dog's momentum.

In the following sections, we introduce a set of sequences to show how to get started on training Buddy for a successful Figure 8 exercise. *Remember:* The Figure 8 is a requirement for both Pre-Novice and Novice classes (refer to the earlier section "Understanding the System: Your Road Map to the Companion Dog Title" for more on these classes).

Sequence 1: Preparing Buddy for the Figure 8

The Figure 8 is an exercise where you and Buddy heel around two people or posts in a figure 8 pattern. Before you begin practicing going around posts, use the steps in this first sequence to teach Buddy that he has to speed up his pace when you circle to the right and slow down when you circle to the left.

For the inside turn in which you circle to the left, follow these steps:

1. **Start with your dog sitting at the Heel position, with your leash in Control Position.**

You can read more about Control Position in the earlier section "Using Control Position."

2. **Say "Buddy, Heel" and walk a circle to the left, about 4 feet in diameter, at a slow pace.**

3. **Twist your shoulders and torso to the left as you walk.**

4. **Release your dog with "Okay" after you've completed the circle.**

TIP

After two or three tries, you'll notice how your dog responds to your body cues. If nothing happens, exaggerate your body motion.

For the outside turn in which you circle to the right, use the following steps:

1. **Start with your dog sitting at Heel position with the leash neatly folded into your left hand.**

2. **Put your left hand against your right hip.**

Doing so keeps your left shoulder facing forward.

3. Have a treat in your right hand.

4. Say "Buddy, Heel" and walk in a circle to the right, about 4 feet in diameter, at your normal brisk pace.

5. Use the treat, which is held just in front of his nose with your right hand, to guide your dog around; give him the treat after you've completed the circle.

The Obedience Regulations are quite specific about the position of your hands. For the Heel On Leash, you can hold the leash in either hand or in both, as long as they're in a natural position. For the Heel Off Leash, your arms can swing naturally at your side or you can swing your right arm naturally at your side and place your left hand against your belt buckle.

When making the outside turn, you're looking for a visible effort on the part of your dog to accelerate. Repeat these steps several times so you become comfortable with the maneuver. Then try going at a trot.

Sequence 2: Introducing Buddy to the actual Figure 8

The goal of the second sequence is to teach your dog the Figure 8. Following is the review progression for this exercise:

1. Place two chairs about 12 feet apart.

2. Start with your dog sitting at Heel position, 2 feet from the centerline, equidistant between the chairs.

3. Neatly fold the leash into your left hand and place it against your belt buckle; hold a treat in your right hand.

4. Say "Buddy, Heel" and start to walk at a slow pace around the chair on your left, rotating the upper part of your body to the left.

5. When you get to the center between the two chairs, show your dog the treat in your right hand and guide him around the chair on your right at a trot, keeping your left shoulder facing forward.

6. Stop at the center and sit your dog; then praise and release with "Okay" and be sure to give him the treat.

Buddy should now be sitting without a command or correction.

Hold the treat at your right side and out of Buddy's sight until you get to the center and want him to speed up. Then hold it as close as you can to your left leg so he learns to stay close to your side. Don't show the treat to him on the inside turn, or he'll try to get to the treat instead of slowing down. Your success in keeping Buddy at Heel position without crowding or lagging depends on how well you use your shoulders, twisting your torso, to communicate with him. Dogs follow your shoulder while heeling. Twist your left shoulder forward to circle right and twist your left shoulder backwards to circle left.

Sequence 3: Doing the perfect Figure 8

This sequence's goal is the perfect Figure 8 — the way you have to execute it in an obedience trial. Figure 18-2 shows a dog working a Figure 8. Here's how to do it:

1. **Practice the review progression (see the preceding section), making two complete Figure 8s.**

2. **Start from the center and complete one Figure 8 at normal pace, using your shoulders to cue your dog.**

   Stop in the center. Buddy should now sit on his own without any further help from you. Repeat the review progression often to maintain your dog's enthusiasm.

3. **Over the course of several sessions, put the chairs closer together in 1-foot increments until they're 8 feet apart.**

FIGURE 18-2: The perfect Figure 8.

© John Wiley & Sons, Inc.

4. **Practice a Figure 8 with the leash-in-pocket technique, concentrating on the direction of your shoulders.**

5. **Try a Figure 8 off leash.**

    Although the Figure 8 is done on leash in the Novice class, practicing it off leash is a good test. You'll quickly see where your dog needs more practice.

TIP

At one point or another, you may have to use a little check going into the outside turn to impress on Buddy how important it is to you that he speed up.

Your Dog Isn't an Elephant: Reinforcing Training

True or false? After my dog is trained, I'll never have to practice his lessons again.

Answer: False.

Your dog doesn't have the memory of an elephant, so you need to review his lessons on a regular basis. For example, if you've used the Recall Game (see Chapter 10) to teach Buddy to come when called, you need to reward him with a treat on a variable schedule when he responds to your call and comes to you. If you get lax, the association between the command and the reward will weaken. You can tell when this begins to happen: First, Buddy doesn't come immediately. He may take a detour or lift his leg just one more time. Then, you have to call him again. Finally, he ignores you when you implore him to come.

TECHNICAL STUFF

The principle of *successive nonreinforced repetitions* sounds more complicated than it is. These repetitions are responses to a command without any reinforcement, such as not giving your dog a treat when he comes to you after you've called him.

Every time your dog responds to a command without reinforcement, which can be a reward or a check, depending on how you have taught the dog the command, it's a nonreinforced repetition. The number of successful repetitions without reinforcement is finite and depends on the extent to which the behavior is in harmony with the dog's instincts or drives. After a Labrador Retriever has been trained to retrieve, he'll happily fetch almost indefinitely without any reinforcement. An Afghan Hound, on the other hand, will probably retrieve only a few times without reinforcement. The Labrador was bred to retrieve; the Afghan wasn't.

REMEMBER

Every command you've taught your dog needs to be reinforced on a random basis, or the association between the command and the reinforcement weakens.

Several years ago, we had an excellent demonstration of this principle when we visited friends in Newfoundland, who have two delightful Whippets. Every morning, our friends took a short ride to the local park for their own daily walk and to let the dogs run. Naturally, we joined them.

The park covers about 100 acres with wonderful walking trails, plenty of wildlife, and a large pond inhabited by a variety of fowl. After we were inside the park, much to our surprise, our friends let the dogs loose. When we say surprised, it's because Whippets are sight hounds — they're extremely high in prey drive and love to chase anything that moves. They're also incredibly fast and can cover great distances in seconds. We were wondering how our friends would get these dogs back.

To make a long story short, when the dogs ranged a little too far or started chasing something, our friends called them back. To our amazement, the dogs came instantly every time, and every time they got a treat. The response was reinforced!

TIP

Any taught response needs to be reinforced. You needn't worry about the exact number of nonreinforced repetitions your dog will retain of a given behavior. All you need to know is that they're finite. To keep him sharp, randomly reinforce — whether you think he needs it or not.

Making excuses and blaming the dog is easy, but your dog isn't an elephant and needs occasional reminders.

Chapter **19**

Completing the Companion Dog Title

hapter 18 introduces the American Kennel Club (AKC) Novice class and its goal — the Companion Dog Title. That chapter is an overview of the six required exercises for the title and the points needed to earn that title. It also provides the nitty-gritty details for successfully completing the first exercise — heeling on and off leash. This chapter covers the remainder of the exercises for the Companion Dog title, putting the final touches on the commands that you have already taught Buddy:

>> Stand for Examination

>> Heeling Off Leash

>> Recall

>> Group Stay Exercises

- Long Sit-Stay

- Long Down-Stay

The benefits of earning the Companion Dog title are knowing that you have a well-trained dog, that the two of you can work together as a team, and that you are spending quality time together. It's also a great feeling of accomplishment.

If you don't know if you want to compete in obedience with their dog, this chapter does put the final touches on the basic commands you've already taught Buddy. Continuing to work with Buddy and making yourself a more consistent trainer is a win-win situation: you get a bond with Buddy and you have a better trained dog in front of your friends and out in public.

During a training session, practice different exercises, and vary the order. Start with some brisk heeling as a warm-up, including fast starts and changes of pace. Keep training interesting and fun for both of you.

WARNING

Dog shows are held indoors and outdoors in all kinds of weather conditions. If the dog show that you're attending is outdoors and it's raining, the judge will have on rain gear, which may include a big, floppy hat or poncho — something your dog may not have experienced before. Don't be caught unprepared: practice under those unpleasant conditions and wear different items your dog may see.

You're Getting a Check-Up: Preparing for the Stand for Examination

The *Stand for Exam*, in other words the Stand and Stay exercise is a requirement for the Novice class, but it's also a practical and useful command to teach your dog in general. (We discuss Stand here and the Stay command in Chapter 11.) Brushing, grooming, and wiping feet, as well as visiting the vet, are certainly a lot easier with a dog who has been trained to stand still than with one who's in perpetual motion or worse yet, flipping upside down under your chair in the veterinary office.

In the ring, the Stand for Examination looks something like this:

1. You give your leash to the steward, and the judge says, "Stand your dog and leave when ready."

2. You stand your dog in Heel position on your left side, say "Stay," walk 6 feet straight forward in front of your dog, turn around, and stand facing the dog.

3. The judge approaches your dog from in front and touches your dog's shoulders, body, and hindquarters with one hand. The judge then says, "Back to your dog."

4. You walk around behind your dog and return to the Heel position.

REMEMBER

When you begin teaching this exercise to your dog, you can stand, kneel on your right knee or both knees, or place your dog on a table, depending on his size. You want to avoid leaning over him, because if you do, he'll want to move away from you — especially if he's low in defense-fight behaviors (see Chapter 2 for more on personality).

To prepare Buddy for the Stand for Exam exercise, you need to teach him a number of sequences. First, you need to teach him to stand on command, although you may physically place him into a Stand. Then you need to teach him to stand still, and finally you teach him to allow you or someone else to touch him while he stands still. We review each of the sequences in the following sections.

Sequence 1: Introducing the Stand command and Stand Stay

Your goal is to teach your dog the Stand-Stay command. Here is how to get started:

1. Start with Buddy sitting at your left side, off leash, with both of you facing the same direction.

2. Put the thumb of your right hand in the collar under his chin, fingers pointing to the floor, palm open and flat against his chest.

3. Apply a little downward pressure on the collar, say "Stand," and at the same time, apply backward pressure on his *stifles* (the joint of the hind leg between the thigh and the dog's knees) with the back of your left hand.

4. Keep both hands still and in place — the right hand through the collar and the left hand against his stifles — and count to ten.

5. Praise and release with "Okay."

6. Gradually work up to 30 seconds standing still while you hold him in place.

Repeat this exercise three to five times per training session over the course of several sessions.

Sequence 2: Showing Buddy how to stand still without holding him in position

Now your goal is to get Buddy to stand still without holding him in position. Check out these steps:

1. **Place Buddy into a Stand, and keep your right hand in his collar to steady him.**

2. **Take your left hand away from his stifles after you have him standing as we mention in Sequence 1.**

3. **Count to 30, and reposition him if he moves.**

4. **Praise and then release.**

REMEMBER

   Praise is a verbal thing — not a petting thing. When you praise Buddy, be sure that he remains in position. Praise tells him he's doing something correctly, and it's not an invitation to move. Don't confuse verbal praise with the release word "Okay."

5. **When he's steady without you holding onto him with your left hand in Step 3, take your right hand out of the collar on the next repetition.**

   It will take Buddy several sessions to master standing still without you holding him still.

Sequence 3: Working on the Stand-Stay command

The next goal is to teach Buddy the Stand–Stay. Here's how to do it:

1. **Stand your dog as described in the earlier section "Sequence 1: Introducing the Stand command and Standing Still."**

2. **Take both hands off your dog and stand up, keeping your shoulders square.**

3. **Say "Stay."**

4. **Count to 30, praise, and release.**

5. **Practice until you can stand next to him for one minute without Buddy moving a paw.**

   At any point that he moves, reposition him back into the standing position without repeating the command.

TIP Learning the Stand-Stay command (or Sit or Down-Stay) isn't exciting for your dog, so follow the exercise with something he enjoys. After the release, play ball or throw a stick. Give him something to look forward to.

Sequence 4: Leaving Buddy in a Stand-Stay

Progress to leaving Buddy in a Stand-Stay position. These steps show you how:

1. **Stand in Heel position next to your sitting dog.**

2. **Put the thumb of your right hand through the collar as in Sequence 1.**

   Depending on the size of your dog, you may need to bend at the knees to avoid leaning over him.

TIP

3. **With a little downward pressure on the collar, say "Stand."**

   He should now stand without needing you to touch his stifles. If he doesn't, physically assist him by placing your left hand against his stifles.

4. **Take your right hand out of the collar and stand up straight.**

5. **Say "Stay" and step directly in front of him slowly.**

6. **Count to 30, step back to Heel position, praise, and release.**

   Reposition Buddy if he moves.

7. **Gradually increase the distance you leave him to 6 feet in front.**

8. **From now on when you leave him, go 6 feet straight forward, turn and face him (do not back away from him), count to 30, go back, praise, and release.**

Sequence 5: Getting Buddy familiar with the Return

After you leave Buddy in a Stand-Stay, you, of course, need to return to him and go to Heel position. When you return to Buddy, walk around and behind him to Heel position. Introducing the Return is this sequence's goal. The following steps can help:

1. **Stand your dog and go 6 feet in front of him (see the preceding section).**

2. **Go back to your dog, put two fingers of your left hand on his withers (the highest part of the back between the shoulder blades) to steady him, and walk around behind him to the Heel position.**

Usually a dog will move the first time you walk around behind him because he worries you're leaving him. Therefore, touching him on his shoulders helps to steady him while you move around behind him.

3. **Pause, making sure he doesn't move, and then praise and release.**

4. **When he understands that you're going to come around behind him, avoid touching him as you return to the Heel position.**

In an obedience trial you aren't allowed to touch the dog upon your return.

Sequence 6: Preparing Buddy for the actual examination

Your final goal is to teach Buddy the examination part of the exercise. For this sequence, you need a helper, which can be a family member. Eventually, however, a stranger needs to examine Buddy, and because the judge may be either male or female, you need to practice with both men and women.

To introduce your dog to this exercise, start with the Sit for Examination, which is almost identical to the Sit for Greeting or Hello Command in Chapter 9. Do the following:

1. **Put the rings of the training collar on top of your dog's neck.**

2. **Attach your leash to the collar.**

3. **Sit your dog in Heel position, next to your left leg, facing the same direction as you're facing.**

   Do the exam in a sitting position before you try the Stand for Exam position.

4. **Neatly fold the leash into your left hand, hold it above his head, with a little slack in the leash, and say "Stay."**

5. **Signal your helper to approach and offer your dog the palm of his or her hand.**

TIP

   If Buddy tries to say get up and visit the helper, reinforce the Stay command with a check straight up, which is a quick tightening of the leash and immediately slacken the leash again.

6. **Signal your helper to lightly touch Buddy's head and back.**

7. **Praise and release with "Okay."**

8. **Repeat Steps 1 through 7 until he readily permits the examination by another person.**

   Practice the examination over the course of several sessions.

9. Repeat the steps off leash with your dog standing at Heel position, then with you standing directly in front, then 3 feet in front, and finally 6 feet in front.

Figure 19-1 shows a dog being examined on a Stand for Examination.

REMEMBER

If, while off leash, Buddy moves when the helper touches his head, you must gently reposition him back into the Stand by putting one hand under the collar below Buddy's chin and your other hand in front of his knees. Buddy needs to know that you want him to remain in the Stand position. Signal your helper to examine Buddy again while you hold Buddy in the Stand position the next try and praise him for being still even though you're holding him in position.

FIGURE 19-1:
This well-behaved pooch stands for examination.

© John Wiley & Sons, Inc.

Before every exercise, the judge asks, "Are you ready?" You answer with "Ready!" for the heeling exercises and "Yes" for everything else, including the Stand for Examination. (Check out Chapter 18 for how to prepare your dog for the Ready! command.)

Heeling Off Leash

Heeling Off Leash is really only an extension of Heeling On Leash, but it isn't quite the same. Buddy knows when he's on leash and when he's off leash. When he's on leash, he may give you the impression that he's perfect. Then you take the leash off, and he acts as though he has no idea what the exercise is all about. The reason is simple — he knows he's off leash.

If this situation happens to you, review Heeling On Leash and reinforce the Heel command with a treat or a check when he needs help. For normal pace, he usually doesn't need any reinforcement, but he probably does for changes of pace and turns.

Remember that Heeling Off Leash is the ultimate test of your training. With a little practice, Buddy will get the hang of it. To make sure he understands, 90 percent of your practicing should be done on leash so you can remind him what you expect from him.

TIP

You can remind your dog of his responsibility to remain in Heel position by taking him by the collar as you do when heeling with the "leash in Pocket" technique (see the following section).

Transitioning to Heeling Off Leash

To make the transition from Heeling On Leash (which we discuss in Chapter 12) to Heeling Off Leash, we use a technique called the *leash-in-pocket technique*. This maneuver lets you and your dog experience the feeling of Heeling Off Leash while he's still attached.

The leash-in-pocket technique, which we show in Figure 19-2, teaches your dog that it's his responsibility to remain in Heel position. Unless he learns to accept that responsibility, he won't be reliable off leash. You can help the process by being consistent in reminding him of that responsibility. Anytime you make a move to bring him back to Heel position, you must follow through. If Buddy deviates and you reach for the collar, but he corrects himself and you do nothing or you don't follow through by touching his collar and bringing him back to you, Buddy won't learn anything.

Here's how this technique works:

1. **With your dog sitting in the Heel position and the leash attached to the collar, take the leash and fold the excess up and put it into your left hip pocket.**

2. **Put your left hand against your belt buckle, and let your right hand swing naturally at your side.**

FIGURE 19-2:
Using the
leash-in-pocket
technique.

© John Wiley & Sons, Inc.

3. **Say "Buddy, Heel" and start to walk your normal brisk pace.**

   If your dog deviates from Heel position, *slowly* reach for the collar. Put two fingers of your left hand through the collar, palm facing you, at the side of his neck, and bring him back to Heel position. Keep walking, let go of the collar, and tell him what a good dog he is.

REMEMBER

When you reach for your dog, be sure you do it slowly and deliberately so as not to frighten him. Remember, he's still on leash and can't go anywhere. If you start snatching at him, he'll become apprehensive and try to bolt. For Buddy, this lesson is important. He must learn to accept you reaching for the collar so you can do it when he's actually off leash.

TIP

If you've difficulty getting two fingers through the collar — because your dog is small or has lots of hair around his neck — use the leash snap to bring him back to Heel position. When you get to the off-leash part, put a little hang tag on his collar that you can easily grasp.

At first, keep the time and distance short, so you have a better chance of maintaining your dog's interest and attention. As you train with the leash-in-pocket technique, gradually increase the number of steps, make a right turn, take another ten steps, halt, praise, and release. Remember to say your dog's name before you make the turn. Start over and incorporate an about-turn, using his name before the turn. Also incorporate changes of pace.

As you and your dog's proficiency increases, add distractions in the order you did in Chapter 10. You also need to gradually increase the time and distance that you heel your dog before a halt. How much total time should you spend on this exercise? After a two-minute warm-up of heeling in Control Position in a large circle or straight line with plenty of releases, you should spend no more than one to two minutes per training session.

Successfully getting off leash

Whenever you feel like you and Buddy are ready for Heeling Off Leash, get started. If you have any doubt about what Buddy will do, practice in a safe area, such as your fenced backyard. Here are the steps to follow:

1. **Start with a two-minute warm-up in Control Position (see Chapter 18).**

   Walk in a large circle or a straight line. Forget about turns, and concentrate on keeping his attention on you. Now is the time to remind him to pay attention to you. If you need to, check and then praise and release with "Okay."

2. **Set up for the leash-in-pocket technique, heel for 10 to 15 steps, and release.**

   Set up again and heel for about the same distance and halt.

3. **As you halt, put your right hand against his chest, place him into a Sit, and stand up.**

4. **Unclip the leash from his collar and put the snap into your left pocket so a loop dangles on your side (see Figure 19-3).**

5. **Say "Buddy, Heel" and start at a brisk pace.**

   If you need to reinforce, very slowly reach for his collar, bring him back, let go of the collar, and praise.

6. **Halt after ten steps and sit your dog.**

7. **Put the leash back on your dog and release him.**

8. **Go on to another exercise or end your session.**

REMEMBER

Proficiency comes in small increments and not all at once. Add something new to your off-leash heeling each session, such as a turn (use his name) or a change of pace. Keep it short and snappy and make it exciting and fun. Over the course of several sessions, both you and Buddy will become increasingly confident and begin to work as a team. Resist the temptation to go beyond his ability to be successful.

FIGURE 19-3:
Leash-in-pocket technique with the snap looped in your pocket.

© John Wiley & Sons, Inc.

When you and your dog are comfortable doing this exercise in an area relatively free of distractions, you can go on to Heeling Off Leash with distractions. Use the same order as you do when Heeling On Leash — that is, making it incrementally more difficult as you progress.

Mastering the Recall

The *Recall* exercise is different from the traditional Come command where you're only concerned about the dog coming to you (see Chapter 10). The Recall consists of these four components, which we discuss in the following sections:

>> Stay

>> Come

>> Front

>> Finish

The Recall is performed from one end of the ring to the other. The judge tells you to leave your dog in a Sit–Stay and to go to the other side of the ring. She then tells you to call your dog. You give the Come command, Buddy comes, and he's expected to sit directly in front of you. The judge then says "Finish," and you say "Buddy, Heel," and Buddy goes to the Heel position.

Stay

The first part of the Recall exercise requires your dog to master the Stay command. Chapter 11 covers the basics of this command. We cover training your dog to stay with distraction in "Training for the Group Stay Exercises" section later in this chapter.

Come with distractions

Even though Buddy already knows the Come command, you still need to work on distraction training — for which you need a helper. Leave Buddy in a Sit-Stay and go 20 feet in front of him. With your helper positioned equidistant between you and Buddy — about 2 feet from Buddy's anticipated line of travel and facing Buddy — the helper crouches and smiles.

Call your dog, and as he passes the distracter, you say "Okay" and release backward. To *release backward*, throw your hands up invitingly and take a few steps back with an enthusiastic "Okay!" Then give him a treat when he gets to you. If he goes to the distracter, smile and very slowly approach Buddy. Put the leash on the dead ring of the training collar and, with a little tension on the leash, show him exactly what he should've done by trotting backward to the spot where you called him. (To find out which ring is the dead ring on your dog's training collar, visit Chapter 5.) Praise and release backward when you and the dog get to the spot where you called him. You may need to show him a few times until he catches on. After he's successful, stop for that session. Figure 19-4 shows a dog coming with distractions.

TIP

If your dog veers from the distracter, use two distracters, separated by about 10 feet, and teach your dog to come between them. As Buddy progresses in his training, work your way through second and third degree distractions (which we discuss in Chapter 10).

REMEMBER

The purpose of distraction training is to build your and your dog's confidence that he can do it. It also teaches him to concentrate on what he's supposed to do. If at any time you feel the exercise is too much for him, stop. Come back to it at another session.

Front

The object of both the Front and the Finish (see the following section) is to teach the dog a position, and you can practice both exercises indoors in the form of a game. The Front is similar to the Automatic Sit at Heel (see Chapter 18) in that the dog is supposed to come to you and sit in front without a command to sit. Using a chute to teach the dog exactly where you want him to sit when he comes to you teaches Buddy exactly where you want him to sit. For a chute, use plastic rain gutters that are appropriately placed for the size of the dog. They should be cut to lengths about as long as your dog. Place them on the ground, just far enough apart so your dog can sit comfortably in between.

FIGURE 19-4: Coming with distractions.

© John Wiley & Sons, Inc.

TIP

When practicing the Front, keep the upper part of your body erect. If you lean over or toward your dog, he won't come in close enough. If you need to get down to his level, bend at the knees.

The following sections provide a set of sequences that help you teach your dog the Front using a chute. First you familiarize him with the chute and then you coax him into it.

Sequence 1: Getting Buddy used to the chute

Sequence 1's goal is to get Buddy familiar with the chute. Making sure he's used to the chute is important because it teaches him to sit straight in front of you. Here's the best way to familiarize Buddy with the chute:

1. **Place the chute pieces on the ground 2 feet apart.**

2. **Walk your dog through the chute a few times.**

3. Heel your dog into the chute and encourage him to sit.

4. Repeat Steps 1 through 3 until he readily sits in the chute.

If Buddy is uncomfortable going into the chute, widen it.

Sequence 2: Teaching Buddy to come into the chute and Front

Sequence 2's goal is to teach your dog to come into the chute and perform a straight Front (see Figure 19-5). Try these steps:

1. Heel your dog up to the chute and tell him to stay.

2. Walk through the chute and face your dog.

3. Hold a treat in both hands below your waist and stand straight up.

4. Call your dog and, as he comes, bring your hands to your waist, using the treat to make him sit directly in front of you.

You want to teach Buddy to sit as close as possible in front of you without touching you. Using treats helps lure him in. Only give him the treat when he sits straight, however. If he doesn't sit straight, say "Oops" and try again.

FIGURE 19-5: Using chutes to teach a straight front.

© John Wiley & Sons, Inc.

5. Give him the treat, praise, and release backward.

See the section "Come with distractions" earlier in this chapter for info on the Release Backward.

6. Practice Steps 1 through 5 about five times.

7. When your dog masters Steps 1 through 5, leave him in a Stay 3 feet from the entrance of the chute and call him to you for a Front.

8. Increase in 2-foot increments the distance that you leave him facing the entrance of the chute, until he's 35 feet from the entrance.

After he's comfortable with it, you can use treats to practice this sequence without the chute.

REMEMBER

In the ring, you aren't allowed to carry food or give second commands. You can give either a command or a signal but not both. The exception is the Stay command, which can be accompanied by a signal.

Ultimately, Buddy needs to sit in front of you with your hands hanging naturally at your side, so you need to wean him from seeing you with your hands in front of you.

Finish

After your dog comes to you and sits in front, the judge says "Finish." You say "Buddy, Heel," and your dog goes to Heel position. He can either go directly to Heel position to the left, or go to the right and walk behind you to Heel position. Eventually teach both directions, to keep your dog's attention.

REMEMBER

For both finishes, you can use either a command or a signal. A signal is preferred for most dogs because the dog more readily understands a signal than a command, and it more clearly indicates to the dog the way you want him to go. Here's a list of the commands and the signals you can use for each Finish:

>> **Finish to the left:** You can use the Heel command, and for the signal you can use your left hand to indicate the direction you want Buddy to go.

>> **Finish to the right:** You can use the Place command, and your right hand to indicate which direction to go.

TIP

Your dog's response to the Finish to the right or left tells you which direction is better for him. As a general rule, a long-bodied dog does better going to the right.

In the following sections, we show you the sequences to teach Buddy to Finish on command or signal from either the left or the right.

Sequence 1: Introducing a Finish to the left and right

Your Sequence 1 goal is to introduce Buddy to the Finish to the left. Here are the steps:

1. **Sit your dog at Heel position, say "Stay" and step directly in front of him.**

2. **Say "Buddy, Heel" and then take a step back on your left leg, keeping the right leg firmly planted in place as you guide him with a treat held in your left hand in a semicircle into Heel position.**

   Make the semicircle large enough so that he winds up in the correct position.

3. **Give him the treat, praise, and release with "Okay."**

4. **Repeat Steps 1 through 3 until he enthusiastically and briskly goes to Heel position.**

You'll quickly see that the guidance of your left hand becomes his signal to go to heel.

The Finish to the right uses the same progressions as the Finish to the left, except that you step back on the right leg and guide Buddy around behind you into Heel position and say "Buddy, Place." When you're using a treat, switch it behind your back from the right hand into the left. The same applies to the leash.

Sequence 2: Teaching a Finish on command or signal

Your Sequence 2 goal is to teach Buddy to Finish on the left on command or on signal. Here are the steps:

1. **Put the leash on the training collar.**

2. **Neatly fold the leash into your left hand.**

3. **Step in front, say "Buddy, Heel," and step back on your left leg, using the leash to guide him into Heel position.**

   The signal is the same guiding motion you use in Sequence 1 (see the preceding section).

4. **Reward him with a treat from your pocket, praise, and release.**

5. **Practice Steps 1 through 4 until he goes to Heel position without any tension on the leash.**

6. **Eliminate the step back on the left leg and experiment by using either the command or signal.**

Training for the Group Stay Exercises

The group exercises are the last part of the Novice class test for the Companion Dog title. They consist of a Long Sit and a Long Down for one and three minutes, respectively, and they're done on leash in a group or line of several dogs and people. The number of dog/handler teams in a group depends on the number of exhibitors competing in the class and the size of the ring. Here's how the group exercises work:

1. The judge tells the teams to line up on one side of the ring.

2. He or she instructs the handlers to sit their dogs and leave their dogs, whereupon the handlers go to the opposite side of the ring, turn, and face their dogs.

3. After a minute the judge gives the order to return and the handlers go back to their dogs, walking around behind the dogs to Heel position. (See the earlier section "Sequence 5: Getting Buddy familiar with the Return" for more on teaching the Return.)

The same procedure is followed for the three-minute Down. A dog that lies down during the Long Sit, sits during the Long Down, or moves out of position, receives a nonqualifying score.

REMEMBER

When you're training your dog, increase only one variable at a time. When teaching any type of Stay, for example, increase the distance or the time or duration but not both together. Increase the length of the Stay, the duration, and then increase the distance from each other when Buddy is steady. (You can read more about the Stay command in Chapter 11.)

Look at the Stay exercises from the perspective of duration and distance. Teach Buddy to stay in place for a specific period of time with you about 3 feet in front. Then the first time you increase the distance from your dog, decrease the time you're away from him.

TIP

Although you can give a command and/or signal for any Stay exercise, your dog's Personality Profile (see Chapter 2) influences whether you want to use a signal. Any Stay is a pack-drive exercise, so you want your dog in pack drive. For dogs low in defense-fight behaviors, a Stay signal puts them into defense drive where they're uncomfortable. Using a Stay signal may cause the dog to break the Stay and come to you — or to whine and fidget. The Stay hand signal causes you to drop your shoulder and move your signal hand in front of your dog's face. Both of these movements can and will put your dog into defense drive and switch him out of pack drive. Instead, smile and say "Stay" with no hand signal.

Because he's competing for the Companion Dog title, Buddy already knows the basics of the Sit and Down–Stay (if not, check out Chapter 11). You just need to fill in the missing pieces. In other words, you need to practice. Even though when you compete in Novice the Stays are done on leash, we recommend you practice your Stay commands off leash at this point in your training to have a better trained dog. Train to achieve the level of training you want on your dog. Remember you get the dog your train, so train for the dog you want. You just need to fill in the missing pieces. In other words, you need to practice

>> With distractions

>> Off leash

>> At the right distance

>> For the requisite length of time plus one minute

>> At different locations and on different surfaces

Setting up self-generated distractions

To introduce *self-generated distractions* (meaning those you create), put the leash on your dog's training collar with the rings under his chin. Then say "Stay" and step 3 feet in front of him. Place your left hand against your belt buckle and hold your right hand ready to reinforce. Jump up and down in place and then to the right, the middle, the left, the middle, forward, and backward. Any time Buddy wants to move, reinforce the Stay by checking upward with the leash in your right hand, putting him back into the sitting position. How vigorously you do these distractions depends on Buddy's Personality Profile (refer to Chapter 2). As he learns, add clapping and cheering. And periodically review these distractions in your training. Remember you're trying to make Buddy think about the Stay command in the face of distractions, building his confidence level. You aren't trying to cause Buddy to stress. Use distractions sensibly.

Increasing the level of difficulty

Practice with self-generated distractions off leash from about 3 feet and then 6 feet in front of Buddy to increase the level of difficulty of the Sit–Stay and Down–Stay. When Buddy is off leash and you need to reinforce the Stay, slowly approach him and put him back by placing two fingers of each hand through the collar at the side of his neck. If he's coming to you, put him back from in front — that is, guide him back to the spot where you left him in such a way that you're facing him when you reinforce the Stay. Don't repeat the command but simply replace him into position. If you repeat the command, it will appear to Buddy that you're starting over again instead of reinforcing the error of breaking the Stay command.

REMEMBER

Whenever you approach your dog, do so in a nonthreatening manner so he doesn't become anxious. You never want your dog to become frightened when you approach him.

Gradually increase the time to two minutes for the Sit-Stay and four minutes for the Down-Stay. Although practical, these exercises are boring for both you and your dog. You usually don't need to practice them every session. Once or twice a week suffices. Afterward, reward your dog with something he enjoys, like throwing a Frisbee or a stick.

When Buddy stays for the requisite length of time, gradually increase the distance you're away from him to 35 feet. Increasing the distance should go quickly, because this exercise isn't new for him. Be sure also to practice in different locations and on different surfaces.

TIP

Because Buddy must remain sitting or down until the judge releases the group, it isn't unusual for dogs to anticipate breaking the Sit or Down as soon as the owner returns. A good way to head off this behavior is occasionally to return and then without stopping continue back to your distant position. Buddy should always wait for his release word before leaving his Stay position.

OOPS: PLAYING THE YO-YO GAME

Some handlers have unintentionally taught their dogs, or the dog has taught them, what we call the yo-yo game. The scenario goes something like this:

1. Buddy is in a Sit-Stay with his handler standing 30 feet away.

2. Buddy lies down, and the handler approaches to reinforce the Sit-Stay.

3. Buddy sits up by himself, and the handler retreats.

This scenario can, and often does, deteriorate into the yo-yo game. Buddy lies down, the handler approaches, Buddy sits up, and the handler retreats, with Buddy not having learned to stay in position on a Stay command.

Moral of the story? When you make any move to reinforce any command, you *must* follow through, even if Buddy corrects himself before you've had a chance to reinforce the command. After you've started toward him, slowly continue without saying a word. When you get to him, touch his collar, and apply slight pressure in the correct direction to enforce the position. Let go of the collar, turn around, and leave, and always do it with a smile.

5 Handling Special Situations

Understand what aggression is, where it comes from, and how to defuse it if you dog is aggressive.

Be prepared and know how to handle unique situations like thunderstorms and stressful situations before you see them to keep a step ahead of life with your dog.

Keep your old dog's life full and fun. Learning what keeps your older young is as easy for him as it is for you.

Know when you need to look for professional help. Don't do so blindly. Know what to ask and what to look for when you do.

Chapter **20**

Addressing Aggression

Aggression: Be not afraid. Aggression can be considered a normal behavior, not to be feared. You can manage it using basic commands and leadership as well as patience and observations. Don't wait and watch for aggressive behaviors to manifest. Instead be proactive and directive to your dog. After all, *you* are the coach of the team. Be in charge and manage through obedience and training. This chapter discusses recognizing aggression, understanding what it arises from and how to manage it, and therefore training to avoid it.

Understanding Aggression

The term *aggression* means different things to different people. For example, a passerby may consider a dog as being furiously aggressive when he runs along the fence in a yard while barking and snarling. But if he's your dog, you may consider the behavior to be a perfectly normal reaction. The dog is protecting his territory, which is what you expect from him.

REMEMBER

Of the many behaviors a dog expresses, perhaps the most misunderstood is aggression. With aggression goes health, self-confidence, survival, a good work ethic, ability to handle stress, a greater capability of bonding, and the ability to breed. Here we discuss the connection between aggression and your dog's drive and some causes for aggression.

Examining the link between aggression and drives

Aggression in Buddy can rise from any drive. Consider the following to help you grasp how aggression can show up in Buddy (Chapter 2 explains the different drives in greater detail):

>> **Prey drive:** This drive is considered the "killing" drive because the hunting of prey stimulates it. Although people see chasing and attacking as aggression, these behaviors are actually normal prey drive. We discuss how to manage prey drive later in the "Managing a Dog's Aggression — Prey, Pack, Defense Drives" section.

>> **Defense drive:** Aggression rises from defense drive, both fight and flight, because defense drive is all about protecting oneself. For example, if while walking your dog, a stranger approaches and your dog starts growling, he may be afraid about the unknown person, and the growl or aggression is referred to as *defense flight*. Conversely if your dog wants to protect himself or you and he's willing to fight, the growl is referred to as *defense-fight*. In either case, it's now your job to manage the situation correctly.

TIP

Managing the environment and the dog is a great way to stop aggressive behavior. You can choose to cross the street, turn around and go the other way, or command your dog to "Heel" and pass the stranger, keeping yourself between the stranger and your dog. Basic training exercises such as Heel and heeling in a circle with the dog on the inside circle can help you manage the dog by giving him something on which to focus his attention: you. If your dog is on your left, circle to the left as if you're inside a hula-hoop. Doing so forces your dog to look up at you, because you're coming into his space by circling with him and into him. If he's looking up at you, he won't be looking at the thing that's causing him to be aggressive. Under no circumstances should you make any effort to calm your dog by reassuringly petting him and telling him in a soothing voice, "There, there, it's perfectly okay." Buddy will misinterpret your soothing as praise.

>> **Pack drive:** Aggression rising out of pack drive is due to the hierarchy of those involved: possibly between you and your dog or between two dogs. When the aggressive behavior is directed toward you, ask whether you and Buddy have previously resolved this question of rank order: "Who is top dog?" Usually it hasn't been, and Buddy is convinced that he is top dog or can become top dog. He isn't a bad dog; he's just a pack animal and is looking desperately for leadership. If you don't provide that leadership, he'll fill the vacuum. Dogs are quite happy and content when they know their rank order.

If the aggression is between two dogs of your household, you need to support the more dominant dog such as passing out treats and meals to the *alpha dog* (top dog) first. The more dominant dog is top dog; it may not be your favorite and often not the first dog in the household. Alpha depends on which dog wants to be top dog more, who is monitoring doorways, which one is pushing past the other dogs, which dog is territorial about the best dog bed, which dog always wants the best of everything. That dog needs your support by letting him have the first of everything while you hold back the other dog. If you don't support the top dog by allowing him the rights of the top dog, then he'll become more adamant and pushy and therefore potentially harm a dog who is taking away his rightful place or due. By supporting the true top dog, you're sending a message to the other dog that indeed the other dog isn't top dog. Above all, you are leader of the pack.

If the aggression is between your dog and another dog, you need to manage your dog by putting him under command and don't allow him to make wrong choices on his own. You should command him to "Heel" and get your dog to focus on you. See Chapters 9 and 11 for leadership exercises and basic obedience commands.

Looking at the causes of aggression

Many factors, including environment, poor health, or heredity, can cause aggressive behavior, such as biting and growling. Keep reading to see how each can cause aggression.

REMEMBER

Aggression is a natural and even necessary phenomenon. In the case of unwanted aggression, human mistakes or misunderstandings are the usual cause. The owner may be unintentionally rewarding the undesired behavior, causing it to occur again and again, or the owner may not have socialized the dog properly. Only when you're unable to manage aggression or don't understand its origin, does it become a problem.

Environmental causes

The most common cause for dog bites is environmental — the result of a misunderstanding or outright mismanagement of the dog. A misunderstanding can occur when a puppy or dog nips at the owner's hand during play or when the dog is playing retrieve and accidentally bites the hand when his owner tries to get the stick. Most dog owners can recognize when a bite occurred due to a misunderstanding — in this case, the dog will likely be just as horrified as the owner.

Bites occurring because of mismanagement are a different matter. For example, say the kids are playing with Buddy and he has had enough, so he retreats under the bed. When one of the children crawls after Buddy and tries to drag him out, Buddy snaps at the child's hand and may even make contact. This scenario isn't uncommon, and it's coming out of defense-flight drive. Even though the dog may not have provided any warning, his behavior was predictable — the fact that Buddy retreated should have told the children that he'd had enough, that he's trying to flee. Similarly, when you stick your hand in the crate of a dog that isn't yours and he growls at you, you should know that you need to remove your hand. The dog is acting out in defense-flight drive. If you persist, he has given you ample warning that he may bite.

One scenario frequently encountered is the dog when told to get off the couch or bed growls at the owner. When the owner is asked whether the dog has had any basic training, the answer invariably is "not much" or "none." In this case, the first order of business should be teaching the dog the basic impulse control exercises — Sit and Stay and the Leave It commands, along with door and stair manners. All are considered leadership exercises. See Chapters 14 about getting on and off the furniture, Chapter 9 for Leave It, and Chapter 1 for the beginner exercise.

Lack of socialization

Lack of socialization as a puppy to different people, to other animals, and to different environments in the first weeks of your owning him can cause aggression around strangers, so it's crucial that your puppy from 8 weeks on, get out and meet people. The human socialization period is from 7 to 12 weeks of age, and dogs must meet people during this time.

WARNING

Keeping your dog at home until he has had all his vaccinations at 6 months of age prevents proper socialization with people and other dogs and the lack of proper socialization can be a cause for aggression. During the critical socialization period, up to 7 weeks of age and early puppyhood, Buddy learns dog language from other dogs allowing him to behave appropriately around them. After Buddy has had his first set of vaccines (for parvovirus and distemper), it's safe to take him out and about. The benefit of early socialization far out weights any risk. It's critical that Buddy be taken different places in puppyhood so he learns to accept different environments. Chapter 7 talks about the human socialization period, also which is up to 12 weeks of age. Training in different areas is helpful to the puppy because he discovers that his training is enforced not just at home but also wherever he finds himself. (Refer to the nearby sidebar "Socializing your pup when he's young" for more information.)

Poor training plan on the owner's part

Inappropriate punishment can also cause aggression. Pulling a dog into a crate, pulling him through doors, treating him roughly, or punishing him for house-breaking errors can all cause high states of anxiety. Remember, a puppy is just a baby that hasn't been taught what you expect from him. Be patient, be kind, and have compassion. Take your puppy to local puppy training classes and learn how to treat him appropriately. Accidents are reflections on your inability to read your dog. It isn't his fault. Look to changing your behavior.

Poor health causes

If a dog is in poor health, he can become irritable and aggressive. If a dog who never has shown any aggressive tendencies before all of a sudden is growling or snapping, the first thing you must look into is a veterinary exam. If a dog is in pain, he is going to protect his surroundings and he will watch out for someone who might bump into him or touch him. Pain is a big cause of aggressive behavior. It you don't pinpoint the problem physiologically you will never fix the aggression behaviorally.

In these cases, the dog's action isn't a behavioral problem but a health problem. If you've never seen aggression in a dog who is several years old and suddenly he's becoming irritable, have a health check and bloodwork done at your veterinarian's office.

SOCIALIZING YOUR PUP WHEN HE'S YOUNG

A few years ago, it was brought to Wendy's attention that a number of Rottweilers had bitten their veterinarians when taken for their six-month checkups in England. Apparently, the situation had gotten so bad that many vets didn't want these dogs as clients anymore. At that point, the Rottweiler Club of England consulted Wendy. What she discovered was that the same veterinary community that didn't want these dogs as clients anymore had advised the dog's owners not to let the dogs out in public before they had all their vaccinations — that is, until they were 6 months of age. Those owners who followed this advice ended up with completely unsocialized dogs.

This example is a classic case of aggression on a grand scale caused by a lack of understanding of behavior. Socialization is a continuing necessity throughout your dog's life. If you don't socialize Buddy, you'll have problems as he grows. Take this advice seriously and get Buddy into a good puppy class as soon as you can. Also continue to take him out so he can mix with other dogs as he continues to mature. (Check out Chapter 6 for more.)

Hereditary causes

Hereditary aggression, unless selectively bred for, is relatively rare, because it contradicts the whole concept of domestication. Dogs who are high in one drive over another produce offspring who are more likely going to be similar in their personalities or drives. Meet the parents of a puppy before you choose a puppy from a specific litter.

Managing a Dog's Aggression — Prey, Pack, Defense Drives

This section examines the triggers of aggression in the context of the three drives — prey, pack, and defense (which includes fight and flight drives). The triggers are different in each drive, and so is the management. Your dog's Personality Profile (see Chapter 2) tells you the likely triggers so you can predict what Buddy will do under certain circumstances. Discovering how to anticipate your dog's reaction under certain situations is part of managing his behavior.

Other than ignoring or putting up with the behavior, you have three basic options:

>> **Expending the energy:** Each behavior has a time frame, or energy, and you can manage it by expending that energy, which means exercise specifically focused on that energy. The exercise can be playing ball (prey drive), jogging (pack drive), playing tug-of-war games (defense drive), or any game. Basic training is always essential for all drives.

>> **Suppressing the energy:** This option means that the dog isn't given an outlet for the energy. Suppression can be an effective temporary solution, provided that the dog has periodic opportunities to expend the energy.

WARNING

Total suppression can be dangerous. Liken it to a bottle of soda that's shaken vigorously. When you take the top off, it explodes. So a dog who has been bred to run (for example, a Greyhound or Whippet) but suppressed will run for a long time and may not come back when the dog finally gets loose. Working dogs that come from generations of dogs who have worked for a living don't make good pets when their natural behaviors are suppressed. Unless they have an outlet for their intelligence, they can become grumpy, irritable, and obsessive over toys. Some even indulge in self-mutilation. Training and working these dogs regularly is a necessity.

For example, a Malinois dog, which is bred to work, lived in a home as a pet with no job and only got to walk around the block two times a day, not nearly enough mental stimulation or release of prey drive or exercise. This dog had bitten its owners and also kept running off. The solution was a job: obedience training and an outlet for prey drive. The trainer on the case walked around the perimeter of a fenced field and showed the dog where he had previously hidden a lot of toys. He brought the dog back to the entrance to the field and told her to find a toy. It took about 20 minutes for the dog to find them all, but the activity had expended the energy and mental stimulation she needed and she was calm and happy for the rest of the day. She never showed any tendencies to bite when she was given the opportunity to work. Plus the owners and the dog did basic obedience, which gave the dog even more of an outlet and leadership with the owner.

» **Switching the drive:** When Buddy growls at another dog, for example, he's in defense drive. To manage the situation, switch him into pack drive. Give him a command such as "Come," check the leash with a quick snap in your direction if necessary to turn the dog toward you, and then lavish on calm praise for having come. Doing so should switch him into pack drive.

Depending on the situation, you're going to use a combination of the three options in your management program. In the following sections, we look at the triggers and management for aggression caused by the three different drives.

Dealing with aggression from dogs high in prey drive

You shouldn't be surprised that *prey behaviors*, those associated with chasing and killing prey, are one of the leading causes for aggression. In a sense, aggression coming from this drive is the most dangerous, because so many different stimuli can trigger it. Dogs high in prey drive are stimulated by sounds, smells, and moving objects. Chapter 2 can help you further recognize a dog that is high in this drive.

Triggers for prey drive

Anything that moves can trigger prey behaviors. Dogs high in prey drive chase cars, bicycles, joggers, cats, other dogs, squirrels, bunnies, you name it. And if they catch up with whatever they're chasing, that's when the problem becomes real. Running after a car for example can get your dog killed. Running after a cat can be dangerous if the cat stops, turns, and attacks your dog. He can lose an eye that way. Running after squirrels and other critters also needs to be stopped. Imagine that you're traveling with Buddy and stop at a rest stop that has trees, squirrels, and picnic tables with families enjoying an outing. If Buddy gets loose and chases the squirrel, you can run into trouble. If you're lucky, the squirrel goes up a tree and Buddy doesn't catch it. But the act of chasing can terrify the families and also can lead Buddy to keep going out onto the highway.

Prey drive can be triggered in a training class situation when dogs are moving in the class such as during the Heel exercise. Some beginner dogs get overly excited and start barking at the other dogs. This behavior makes it impossible for the instructor to guide the students, and it makes the other dogs in the class nervous and excited, too. Barking can be common in under-socialized dogs. To diffuse this situation, it's wise for the instructor to instruct the owner and dog to do a circle left, heeling in a tight circle, about the size of a hula hoop during the moving exercises and have them work a bit away from the group. If you're the student in this situation, it's a good idea either to work on the sidelines or put your dog into the car if you can't manage him. Practice at home until the dog has become more confident and can rejoin the class.

Management

Play retrieve games on a regular basis, and make sure your dog gets plenty of exercise. When you take him for a walk and he spots a cat or squirrel, distract him, redirect his attention on you by doing a circle left, heeling in a small circle together, or turn and go in the opposite direction. The Leave It command (see Chapter 9) may be sufficient, or you may need to give him a check on the leash to refocus his attention on you. Basic training is a must to control this kind of behavior in the long term like Figure 20-1 shows.

© John Wiley & Sons, Inc.

FIGURE 20-1:
Releasing energy from prey drive.

REMEMBER

If he doesn't reliably respond to the Come command, don't let Buddy loose in situations where he may take off after something. Better yet, train him to come reliably on command. Whatever you do, don't let Buddy chase cars, joggers, or cyclists.

Handling aggression from dogs high in defense drive

Survival and self-preservation govern defense drive, which consists of both fight and flight behaviors. Defense drive is more complex than pack or prey because the same stimulus that can cause aggression (fight) also can elicit avoidance (flight) behaviors. *Cornered flight drive,* where the dog thinks he has no escape, can even be more dangerous than fight drive because the dog feels he has nothing to lose, so he'll fight to the death.

After some basic training, dogs with high fight drive are terrific companions and protectors, great competition and show dogs, and a joy to own. As young dogs, they may start bucking for a promotion. You may see signs of aggression toward you when you want the dog to get off the furniture or in similar situations when he doesn't want to do what you tell him.

REMEMBER

If a puppy is allowed to grow up doing anything he likes and isn't given parameters for what he can and can't do, he likely won't make a satisfactory pet. After all, he'll develop a sense that he can do anything he pleases.

Full-fledged signs of aggression don't just suddenly occur. He'll start off by giving many warnings, from growling to lip lifting to staring at you. If you condone these behaviors and avoid dealing with them, your dog is on his way to becoming aggressive.

Buddy also may be aggressive toward other dogs. When meeting another dog, he'll try to lord it over the other dog. The classic sign is putting his head over the shoulder of the other dog. The dog of lesser rank lowers his body posture, signaling that he recognizes the other dog's rank. When two dogs perceive each other as equal in rank is when a fight may ensue. Left to their own devices (that is, off leash), chances are they'll decide that discretion is the better part of valor. Both know that there are no percentages to fighting. They slowly separate and go their own ways.

A true dogfight is a harrowing and horrifying experience, and most people prefer not to take the chance that it'll occur. Discover how to read the signs and take the necessary precautions by keeping the dogs apart. Dogs are no different from people: not all of them get along. Refer to the sidebar in this chapter about being attacked by another dog.

WARNING

Some owners inadvertently cause dogfights by maintaining a tight leash on the dog. A tight leash alters your dog's body posture, thereby giving an unintended aggression signal to the other dog. Maintain a loose leash when meeting another dog so you don't distort Buddy's body posture. And at the slightest sign of trouble, such as a hard stare from the other dog, a growl, or a snarl, happily call your dog to you and walk away. *Happily* calling is important because you want to defuse the situation and not aggravate it by getting excited. You want to switch the dog from fight drive into pack drive.

A female dog is entitled to tell off a male dog who's making unwanted advances. She may lift her lip, a signal for the male dog to back off. If the male doesn't take the hint, she may growl or snap at him. This behavior isn't aggression but perfectly normal dog behavior.

Triggers for defense drive

Aggressive behaviors can be set off in a dog with defense drive (fight and flight) by a variety of triggers. Some of the more common ones are

>> Approaching the dog in a threatening manner or walking directly at a dog

>> Hovering or looming over the dog (bending at your waist is a very threatening posture)

>> Staring at the dog

>> Teasing the dog

>> Telling him to get off the couch or bed, which is a prime location

>> Trying to remove something from his mouth (see the sidebar, "Taking something out of Buddy's mouth")

You can avoid some of these triggers altogether — like teasing him, staring at him, or hovering over him. Just don't do them. Other triggers, though, you need to deal with.

TAKING SOMETHING OUT OF BUDDY'S MOUTH

At some point during your dog ownership, you'll need to remove something from Buddy's mouth. It could be a chicken bone from the garbage, your shoe, or anything else inappropriate. Don't yell at him or chase him. He'll redouble his efforts to eat whatever it is. Try the Leave It command (see Chapter 9). If that doesn't work, try a trade. Offer him a fair trade, such as a piece of cheese or a treat. As he reaches for it, of course, the chicken bone (or whatever you're after) will drop out of his mouth. Remember, never chase Buddy and corner him. Doing so destroys the very relationship you've been working so hard to achieve.

Management

If you've identified that your dog's aggression is triggered by defense drive, management is your solution. The following sections explains some ways you can manage your dog out of the defense drive.

PROVIDE EXERCISE AND TRAINING

One way to manage aggressive behavior is to provide plenty of exercise and training. Exercise physically tires the body, and training tires the brain. If there is a lack of mental stimulation, the dog will get into trouble. Aim for two training sessions a day, each at least ten minutes long. If you keep to the same time schedule, you'll have a happy puppy or dog.

REMEMBER

Training doesn't stop just because Buddy grows up. He loves to use his brain all the way into old age. Using his brain helps keep him young. Be inventive in your teaching. Get him to help you around the house — teach him to retrieve the newspaper or trash from the yard. He'll love the challenge. Periodically review door and stair manners, getting in and out of the car, and his recall. A short obedience routine is always enjoyed, and teaching him tricks can be fun. (See Chapter 17 for tricks and games you can practice with Buddy.)

PLAY TUG OF WAR

Another way to manage aggression is to expend the energy in the fight drive by playing a good game of tug of war. This game allows your dog to use his time frame of wanting to growl, tug, and bite. Instead of trying to suppress the behavior, dissipate its energy. The absence of an outlet for that energy, or efforts to suppress it, only makes matters worse. Figure 20-2 shows a game of tug of war.

FIGURE 20-2:
The tug-of-war game.

© John Wiley & Sons, Inc.

Put aside ten minutes several times a week to play tug of war at the same time every day. A routine helps the dog learn to expect an energy outlet at the same time every day, which helps manage his excitability. Here's what you do:

1. **Get a pull toy, a piece of sacking, or a knotted sock to use for the game.**

2. **Allow your dog to growl and bite the object and shake it while you're holding it.**

   After a satisfying tug, let Buddy have the toy.

WARNING

   Be careful not to tug too hard toward you; you could injure Buddy's mouth or loosen a tooth.

3. **Let him bring the object back to you to play again.**

4. **Be sure to let him win each time by letting him carry it to his bed or wherever he wants to go.**

   Some people object to the approach of letting the dog "win." Win exactly what? You started the game, you ended the game. You made all the decisions.

5. **When you've had enough, walk away from this session with the dog in possession of the toy.**

   Remember that everything belongs to you, especially the affection, attention, and time he seeks from you. If your dog comes after you for more playtime, then simply turn your back on him and ignore him.

A TUG-OF-WAR CASE IN POINT

Historically tug of war has been a taboo to play with your dog. The misconception was that the dog shouldn't be allowed to win and challenge you for the toy. Instead, what's really happening is that when the dog wins, he inevitably shoves the toy back at you to keep playing the game. When proving that the tug of war is a good concept, we were teaching a class of students who were very advanced in their training. Many of them were training their second or third dogs, and all were experienced handlers. They had chosen dogs with a relatively high fight drive because they knew how well those dogs trained and how well the bonding is with high drive dogs, but they had to live with the dog's tendency toward aggressive behavior and always had needed to be careful in a class or when the dog was around other dogs.

For the entire eight-week session, the owners were told to put time aside daily to play tug of war with their dogs. By the third week, we noticed a big difference in the dog's temperaments. When together in class, the dogs became friendly toward each other, played more, trained better, and were perfectly well behaved when away from home.

REMEMBER

The game effectively discharges the energy and the time frame in that drive. Remove the game from regular training sessions and do it only when you and your dog are alone with no distractions. It's his time and his only. You'll be amazed at how satisfying the game is to your dog and at the calming effect it has on him. Refer to the nearby sidebar, "A tug-of-war case in point" for more about using this game.

PRACTICE THE LONG DOWN

A third way to manage high-fight-drive aggression is with the Long Down (see Chapter 11). We can't emphasize the importance of this exercise enough. The Long Down is a benign exercise and establishes quite clearly who is in charge (that would be you) in a non-punitive way. For dogs who express any kind of aggressive behavior, go back to this exercise and do a 30-minute Down. Make this the last thing you do at night, and do it two or three times a week.

USE A MUZZLE

If your situation has reached the point that you're afraid of your dog, he tries to bite you, or you can't get him into the Down position, use a muzzle. You also may require professional training help (see Chapter 23).

When you're nervous or anxious about what your dog may do when encountering another dog or person, your emotions go straight down the leash, which can cause your dog to react in an aggressive manner. In a sense, your worries become a self-fulfilling prophecy. You can solve this dilemma with the use of a muzzle.

REMEMBER

Using a muzzle is a simple solution to a complex problem. It allows you to go out in public with your dog without needing to worry about him. A strange thing happens to a dog while wearing a muzzle. After you've taken away his option to bite, he doesn't even try. It's almost as if he's relieved that the decision has been taken away from him. Even better, it gives you peace of mind and allows you to relax. On the other hand, although your dog acts differently, so will people you encounter; a muzzled dog might make people apprehensive, although other people might relax seeing a muzzle because it shows that the owner is taking responsibility for what the dog might do. A muzzle can be a good tool as you work toward training a high fight-drive dog. But a muzzle isn't a substitute for seeking professional help.

Training to a muzzle should be done slowly and gently because at first many dogs panic from having something around their faces. But with diligence, common sense, and some compassion for the dog, you can train him quite easily to accept it. Here's what you need to do:

1. **Drop a treat into the muzzle and allow your dog to fish it out with his nose and tongue.**

2. **Repeat the treat in the muzzle and the put the muzzle on your dog for a few seconds and then take it off again.**

3. **Give him a treat and tell him what a good boy he is.**

4. **Repeat Steps 1 and 2 over the course of several days, gradually increasing the length of time your dog wears the muzzle.**

5. **When he's comfortable wearing the muzzle at home, you can use it when you take him out in public.**

In some European cities, ordinances require certain breeds to wear muzzles in public. Many of these dogs happily accompany their owners on walks. They're well behaved and seem to be quite comfortable with their muzzles.

REMEMBER

Many owners are reluctant to use a muzzle because of the perceived stigma attached to it. You need to make a choice: stigma or peace of mind? Something else to think about: suppose that your dog actually bites someone. When you have such a simple solution, why take the chance?

Controlling aggression in dogs high in pack drive

Pack drive consists of behaviors associated with reproduction and being part of a group. Believing that a dog high in pack behaviors could be aggressive may be difficult to grasp, but you must accept the fact. This type of dog may

>> Show signs of aggression toward people

>> Attack other dogs with no apparent reason

>> Not stop the attack when the other dog submits

Triggers for pack drive

The problem with aggression stemming from pack drive is that few obvious triggers seem to exist. Aggressive behavior is frequently observed in dogs that are taken away from their litters and mothers before 7 weeks of age. Between 5 and 7 weeks of age, a puppy learns to inhibit his biting (see Chapter 7). He also learns canine body language at this time. In short, your puppy learns he's a dog. Puppies that haven't learned these lessons tend to be overly protective of their owners and may be aggressive to other people and dogs. They can't interpret body language and haven't learned bite inhibition, which is learning not to bite down hard when a dog is mouthing someone or another dog.

WARNING

In a household with more than one dog, when one dog is being petted and the other is seeking your attention at the same time, the dog being petted may aggress toward the other dog. This overpossessiveness is common from dogs who were taken away from a litter too earlier, before the canine socialization period.

Lack of adequate socialization with people and other dogs prior to 6 months of age also can cause subsequent aggressive behaviors. The owner and the dog haven't worked out leadership when partners of the owner can't show affection to each other in front of the dog. When growling occurs when one partner hugs his or her partner, it shows the dog is taking ownership of the one person instead of seeing the people as leader of the pack. At this point, you must do the Long Sit and Long Down exercises regularly, focus on basic obedience such as heeling and quick compliance to all commands, and work with your dog every day.

Management

You can solve a lack of socialization with other people by gradually getting the dog used to accepting another person. As always, the job is made easier when the dog has had some basic training and knows simple commands like Sit and Stay (which we describe in Chapter 11). A trained dog is a free dog. Train your dog, and he'll be welcome to go with you in public.

Aggression toward other dogs, especially if the aggressor has had a few successes in his career, isn't so simple to resolve. Prevention is the best cure here. Keep your dog on leash and don't give him a chance to bite another dog when you're away from home.

TIP

A holistic approach to calm dogs with aggressive tendencies is to get some essential oil of lavender from a health food store. Put just a couple drops on a small cloth and wipe them onto your dog's muzzle and around his nose. Lavender has a calming effect and helps in class situations where one dog aggresses at another dog. The lavender scent enables the dog to concentrate on his work. You can also use the oil in a spray bottle (four drops of oil to 8 ounces of water) and spray the room before the dogs come in. It really works wonders with the dogs and even calms the owners. Students who have been in agility competition and have dogs that couldn't concentrate because of the number of dogs and people around them have found that wiping their dogs' muzzles and noses with the oil has made a dramatic improvement in their performances.

Coping with Aggression around the Food Bowl

Your dog may growl when you get close to his food bowl. From his point of view, he's guarding his food — an instinctive and not uncommon reaction. The question is this: should you try to do anything about it? And if the answer is yes, what do you do?

Some owners unwittingly exacerbate the behavior by trying to take the dog's food bowl from him while he's eating. Doing so definitely isn't a good idea. Why create unnecessary problems? Don't attempt the practice of taking food away from him and then putting it back. Imagine how you'd feel if someone kept taking away your dinner plate and putting it back. In no time at all, you'd become paranoid at the dinner table. Removing food for no reason repeatedly creates apprehension and makes the guarding and growling worse.

Instead, put the empty food bowl down and add some food into the bowl a scoop or spoonful at a time, which will make your presence near the bowl more welcome because you're adding food to the bowl. For the first few times, allow him to eat the amount in the bowl before adding more. Then work up to adding more as he's still eating what you recently added.

REMEMBER

You can also change the environment. Make sure Buddy is fed in a place where the children or other dogs can't get to his food. A good place to feed him is in his crate. Give him his food and bones in his crate and allow him to eat his food and treats in peace and quiet. And make sure that when he's in there, everyone leaves him alone. Chapter 8 explains how to train your dog to a crate. Follow the directions and the food bowl aggression problem will be solved.

A lot of conflicting advice is available about the subject of feeding Buddy. But one bit of advice that is always true is to leave Buddy alone when you feed him. Give him a place where he can be quiet and enjoy — and more importantly — digest his food, without the stress of kids, people, or other animals around his food bowl. Respect his space. If you insist on taking his food away, you'll train your dog to be neurotic. It will destroy the very relationship you're trying to build, and doing so is one of the first steps in teaching Buddy to become aggressive.

Dealing with Fear-Biters

The term aggression for fear-biters is actually a misnomer. These dogs in defense-flight drive don't aggress; they only defend themselves. When they do bite, it's out of fear; hence they're called *fear-biters*. Anytime this type of dog feels he's cornered and unable to escape, he may bite. Biting to him is an act of last resort. He'd much rather get away from the situation.

REMEMBER

Avoid putting this type of dog in a position where he thinks he has to bite. Use a similar approach to the one we describe in Chapter 21 for submissive wetting. Fear-biters are most comfortable when they know what's expected of them, as in training. Timid behavior can resurface when they're left to their own devices and not given clear instructions on how to behave.

Dogs high in flight drive can appear shy around strangers, other dogs, or new situations. They may hide behind their owners and need space. Keep them a good distance away from people and other dogs, and don't corner them for any reason. Use your body to reassure these dogs; squat down to their level, bending your knees and not hovering over them, and coax them to you with some food. Be patient to gain their confidence and never ever grab for them.

TIP

A dog high in flight drive needs confidence building. Training with quiet insistence and encouragement is one way to achieve a more comfortable dog. To get the dog used to people and other dogs, enroll him in an obedience class. Be patient with this dog and figure out how to go slowly. If you try to force an issue, you may wipe out whatever advances you've made.

GETTING ATTACKED BY ANOTHER DOG

What do you do when you're walking your dog down the street on leash and another dog comes out of nowhere and attacks your dog? You do this:

- No matter what, don't yell or scream. Remember, prey drive is stimulated by sound — especially high-pitched sounds. Screaming just escalates the intensity of a dogfight. Try to keep calm at all times.

- While your dog is on leash and you hold the leash, your dog is at the mercy of the loose dog approaching. Let go of the leash if a fight is about to start so your dog can either retreat or fend for himself.

- For your own safety, don't try to separate the dogs, or you may get bitten. In the vast majority of incidents like this, one dog gives up, and the other one walks away.

- Canvass the neighborhood to find out who the loose dog belongs to. Then visit the person in a friendly way and make her aware that her dog is running loose and scaring (or harming) your dog. Perhaps times can be worked out so that when you walk your dog, the other dog is confined. Under no circumstances should you try to see whether the dog has a collar or tag. You would lean over the dog to do this, which would trigger more aggression. If talking to the owner doesn't work, consider walking in a different location.

A high flight-drive dog needs a structured and predictable environment. Walk, feed, and play at certain times of the day so the dog knows what's coming. Dogs have a phenomenal biological clock, and deviations from the time of walking and feeding can make undesirable behaviors resurface.

Handling Aggression in Different Circumstances

Aggression can happen to even the best-behaved dogs. Put dogs in a situation that triggers aggression and they can get into a fight. Be in charge and manage through obedience and training. Buddy may have demonstrated aggression in these situations. In these sections we explain how you can deal with that behavior.

Aggression in a multi-dog household

If you have several dogs in your household, you may encounter aggression. To avoid it, separate them when you feed them or give them high value treats such as real bones that are fresh from the butcher. Make note of what triggers the aggressive behavior you see and try to avoid putting the dogs in those situations again. Aggression also can happen over toys, so be vigilant.

Doorways are a common place for fights to break out because dogs often see the doorway as a rite of passage with the top dog going first. If one of the dogs wants to push through the door while another dog does also, a fight can erupt. To avoid these fights, award and control aggression in multi-dog households when dogs are going through doors into the yard or out the door. Use the door manners we discuss in Chapter 14 to control the door. Teach each dog door manners separately, then two at a time, and then all of them together. After all, you own the door, not the dogs. Leadership exercises, basic obedience, and door manners are all necessary when you have multiple dogs who are all vying for status by going through the door first.

Dogs also get excited about going out either into the yard or on a walk, and the level of excitement builds and one dog can jump on the other. If that happens, go back to training the Stay command (refer to Chapter 11) and release the dogs individually by name to go through the door. If one dog breaks its Stay and runs toward the door, simply close the door on the dog, guide it back to its Stay location, wait a few seconds, and try again. Door manners takes constant practice, time, and patience, but they're worthwhile and bring peace to the household.

Aggression while grooming

We strongly recommend grooming a dog on a table. Any table will do — just put a towel on it so the dog doesn't slip. Clipping toenails, cleaning ears, and removing hair mats in your dog's coat are so much easier on both you and Buddy if you don't lean over him. Keep a handful of small treats in your pocket; each time you do something, such as cut out a mat or clip a toenail, give a reward. You soon will have a dog that looks forward to his weekly grooming instead of you both dreading it. If you start grooming Buddy as a puppy, you shouldn't have any problems. See Chapter 6 about grooming your puppy early.

Aggression at the veterinarian

If you know that your dog has had unpleasant or painful procedures done at the veterinarian in the past, chances are he won't be happy to be in that veterinarian's office again. If you have any doubts about your dog being aggressive when his blood is drawn or when he's having a physical examination, suggest to the vet that the dog be muzzled, thus providing peace of mind for all concerned. Also make sure that you take your dog in your car to places that have a positive influence — like a nice walk, obedience classes, hiking, vacation, and so on. That way he'll never know when it's time for the veterinary visit and he'll be much less anxious in the car.

Chapter **21**

Helping Buddy Handle Special Situations

Dogs can have a variety of phobias and other problems — some that are related to training and others that aren't. Depending on the severity, these problems can be solved with your help. In this chapter, we list some of the more common ones and the approaches that have worked to solve them.

Reacting to Loud Noises and Thunder

Some dogs have keener senses of hearing than others, to the point where loud noises literally hurt their ears. Some dogs leave the room when the family starts yelling or someone is simply telling a story with a loud voice. Some dogs do the same thing — leave the room completely — because the TV has been turned on. Fear of thunder also can be the result of this type of sound sensitivity.

Under ordinary circumstances sound sensitivity isn't a problem, but it can affect a dog's ability to concentrate in the presence of moderate to loud noises. A car backfiring causes this dog to jump out of his skin, whereas it only elicits a curious expression from another dog.

Dogs that experience fear of thunder and lightning become agitated and apprehensive when they sense an approaching storm. They may try to get out of the house, hide under the bed, engage in destructive behaviors, or exhibit other neurotic signs. Attempts to console the dog only reinforce his fears.

TIP

One product that claims an 85 percent success rate in controlling these symptoms is the Thundershirt — a pressure wrap that applies a gentle, constant pressure on a dog's torso. For more information, see www.thundershirt.com. The security that the Thundershirt gives helps dogs cope in the face of stress caused by noise. The sensation is similar to the security that the den or crate gives to a puppy or dog. When the Thundershirt works, it's amazing. Dogs who usually pant and drool and leave the room remain with the family and can cope with the family's help. Playing and distracting a worried dog that is also wearing the Thundershirt is a great combo to get through the fear. The homeopathic remedy Aconite is helpful for some dogs as well. (Chapter 4 provides more information on homeopathic remedies.)

Coping with Separation Anxiety

With *separation-related behaviors*, also called *separation anxiety*, your dog becomes anxious and stressed when you leave him. He's emotionally responding to being physically separated from the person to whom he's attached. Dogs that experience separation anxiety usually are high in pack drive and low in defense (fight) drive. (See Chapter 2 for more information on the many drives your dog may have.)

The most frequent inquiries about separation anxiety come from individuals who have just adopted a rescue dog. With these dogs, a certain amount of anxiety on the dog's part is understandable. Everything is new, including the people, surroundings, and routine. Giving the dog a week or two to settle in and establishing a routine before becoming overly concerned is the first avenue of prevention. Start training and bonding with the new dog immediately.

In some cases, having an overly solicitous owner makes the problem worse. As the owner prepares to leave the house, he or she makes a big fuss over the dog: "Now don't worry. Mommy/Daddy will be back soon, but I have to go to work for now. You be a good boy while I'm gone, and I'll bring you a nice treat." Such reassurances only increase the dog's anxiety at the expectation of being left alone.

The owner then makes an equally big fuss upon his or her return: "Poor boy. Did you miss me while I was gone? I missed you too. Were you a good boy?" These utterances increase the dog's excitement in anticipation of the owner's return.

TIP

The best way to leave the house and to return is to make your departure benign and with little fanfare. Put a special treat in the crate with your dog and leave. On your return, open the crate door quietly and head out to the yard for a potty break. No big party or greeting, simply push past your dog and head outside to go potty. The transition from being alone to not being alone for the dog needs to be less starkly different.

The most typical and obvious signs of separation anxiety are destructive behaviors (destructive chewing, scratching, and in severe cases, self-mutilation), vocalizations (whining, barking, or howling), house soiling, pacing, and excessive drooling.

TIP

One solution to Buddy's boredom and loneliness is to get another dog. They can keep each other amused, and two dogs are more than twice the fun of one dog. But be warned that two dogs can also mean double trouble.

If you don't want to get another dog, try the approaches we discuss in the following sections. One of these may be just the trick to getting Buddy more comfortable at home without you.

Testing the desensitizing approach

People are just as much creatures of habit as dogs are, and they tend to follow a specific pattern before leaving the house. This pattern becomes the dog's cue that you're about to depart. Make a list showing your customary routine before leaving the house. For example, you may pick up your bag or briefcase, grab the car keys, put on your coat, turn off the lights, and then reassure and pet the dog.

TIP

At odd intervals, several times during the day, go through your routine exactly as you would prior to leaving, and then sit in a chair and read the paper or watch TV, or just putter around the house. By following this procedure, you'll begin to desensitize the dog to the cues that you're about to leave.

When your dog ignores the cues, leave the house without paying any attention to the dog. Leave for about five minutes and then return. When you return, don't pay any attention to him for about five minutes. After that, interact in a normal fashion with your dog.

Repeat this process over the course of several days, staying out for progressively longer periods. Turning on the radio or TV and providing suitable toys for your dog also may help. Whatever you do, make sure to ignore the dog for five minutes after your return. With this process, you want to take the emotional element out of your going and coming so your dog will view the separation as a normal part of a day and not as a reason to become apprehensive.

Trying the DAP approach

Another way to cope with separation anxiety is to use DAP — Dog Appeasing Pheromone — a product developed by vets that mimics the properties of the natural pheromones of the lactating female. After giving birth, a mother dog generates pheromones that give her puppies a sense of well-being and reassurance.

DAP is an electrical plug-in diffuser that dispenses the pheromone, which the dog's sense of smell detects. See Figure 21-1 to take a look at a DAP dispenser. The pheromone reminds the dog of the well-being he felt as a puppy. In clinical trials, DAP was effective in about 75 percent of cases in improving separation-related behaviors. To be effective, the diffuser must be plugged in 24 hours a day. DAP, which is odorless to people, is available at pet stores and from pet product catalogs.

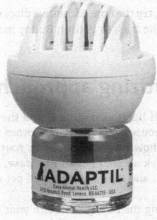

FIGURE 21-1:
A DAP dispenser.

© John Wiley & Sons, Inc.

Looking at some other options

Consider enrolling your dog in a doggie daycare facility where he can meet and play with other dogs while you're away. It may take his mind off wondering where you are. For more on your dog's social needs and the pros and cons of doggie daycare, flip to Chapter 3.

For relatively mild cases of separation anxiety, a visit from a pet sitter during the time he's left alone may be enough to allay his anxiety.

Soiling the House

House soiling that occurs after you've housetrained your dog and that isn't marking behavior can have a variety of causes other than separation anxiety. Its usual causes are one or more of the following:

» **You've left your dog too long without giving him a chance to relieve himself.** As the saying goes, accidents happen, and that's just what it was — an accident. You know your dog's endurance and schedule, so don't blame the dog when for some reason you were unable to adhere to his needs. You may have had to work late, or some other unforeseen event prevented you from getting home on time. As long as it doesn't become a regular occurrence on your part, the behavior won't be a continuing problem. If it becomes a frequent occurrence, consider getting a dogwalker to walk your dog at lunch and perhaps in the evening if you're going to be extra late.

» **Your dog may have an upset stomach.** Abrupt dietary changes, such as changing dog foods, are the most common cause for an upset tummy. Any time you change your dog's diet, do so gradually by mixing the new food with his old food over a period of several days so his system can get used to the new food.

Another cause of upset stomach may be from something he ate that didn't agree with him. Giving treats at holiday times that your dog ordinarily doesn't get, such as turkey and gravy or pizza, can create havoc with his digestive system.

» **Your dog may have *cystitis*, or a bladder infection.** This condition is more common among female dogs than male dogs and may cause dribbling. Cystitis is an inflammation of the bladder wall that can be caused by a bacterial infection. It makes Buddy feel as if there's constant pressure on his bladder, and he'll think he has to urinate all the time, even after just relieving himself. When he does urinate, it can burn, which in turn causes him to spend a lot of time cleaning himself.

REMEMBER

Although not dangerous in and of itself, cystitis can cause all sorts of problems if left unattended, because the bacteria can spread up into the kidneys. If you see any of the preceding symptoms, a trip to your vet is a must. A short course of the appropriate antibiotics cures this inflammation quickly.

» **If your dog is older, he may have developed urinary incontinence.** The slackening of the sphincter muscles that holds the urine in the bladder can cause incontinence, which often happens as your dog ages. So many dogs are put to sleep for this perceived problem, which although not easy to live with, can be solved in several ways, including being treated with medication and homeopathic remedies.

Acupuncture, which we discuss in Chapter 4, is probably the best treatment and is very effective. If you can find a vet trained in acupuncture, have your dog go through a series of treatments to solve the problem. Many vets today are trained in acupuncture, and finding one who can help isn't difficult. A change in diet to a more natural diet also can often solve this problem (see Chapter 4). Finally, you can find many herbal and homeopathic remedies on the market specifically targeted at the kidney and bladder of older dogs. A good holistic vet can help you make the best choice for your dog.

>> **Your dog may be stressed.** Lifestyle changes, moving into a different house, work schedules changing, long-term company, or high levels of emotion in the household can all change a dog's routine to the point that anxiety causes changes for the dog. Be sensitive to the pets in your life. As your life changes, so does theirs. Stress is as real to dogs as it is to people. Give the dog what he needs: exercise, mental stimulation, social time, and so on. Most behavior problems can be isolated to a change for the dog or a need not being met.

TIP

While you're finding a vet to help you, you still have to live with the soiling problem. Put a tablecloth that's plastic on one side and soft on the other under your dog's blanket or bed. Doing so saves the furniture or floor, and both are easy to wash. You also can consider diapers, but only as a last resort because the urine may burn his skin. Don't give up on your dog friend — explore the alternatives and see how you can support Buddy. Chapter 22 provides more information on caring for your older dog.

Dribbling and Submissive Wetting

Dogs that are high in defense flight and low in defense fight drives are notorious for submissive wetting behavior. (See Chapter 2 for more on your dog's drives.) This behavior usually occurs upon first greeting the dog. He will either squat or roll over on his back and dribble, dating back to his days as a puppy when his mother cleaned him.

REMEMBER

When Buddy dribbles urine, don't scold him, because it reinforces the submissive behavior and makes it worse. By scolding him, you only make him act even more submissively, which brings on the wetting. Also, don't stand or lean over your dog or try to pick him up, because that, too, makes him act submissively and causes wetting.

Fortunately, submissive wetting isn't difficult to solve. Follow these steps:

1. **When you come home, ignore your dog.**

   Don't approach Buddy; let him come to you instead. Go outside together and greet in the yard instead of inside the home.

2. **Greet your dog without making eye contact and by offering the palm of your hand.**

   This step is important. The back of the hand transmits negative energy, and the palm of the hand transmits positive energy.

REMEMBER

3. **Be quiet, and let him sniff your palm.**

4. **Gently pet him under the chin, not on top of the head.**

   Be sure to pet under the chin rather than on top of the head, because dogs generally don't like being patted on the head. To them, it's much like a child being pinched on the cheeks.

5. **Don't reach for or try to grab the dog.**

   Reaching for or trying to grab him causes him to be afraid of you, creating anxiety and worsening the problem.

TIP

When friends visit you, they also can help you manage your dog's wetting behavior. Tell your visitors when they arrive to ignore the dog and let him come to them. Instruct them about offering the palm of the hand and about not trying to pet the dog.

Taking Buddy on the Road

Whenever possible, take your dog with you when you travel. Traveling with a well-trained dog is a real pleasure because you know he'll behave himself around people and other dogs.

When you travel with your dog, you need to ensure that Buddy has the opportunity to stretch his legs every few hours, just as you do. The same rules of housetraining apply when you're traveling. If he's still a puppy, be prepared to stop about every two hours. An older dog can last much longer.

In the car, crate Buddy for his and your safety. For reasons not entirely clear to us, many people drive with their dog loose in the car. The problem with this situation occurs when you have to make an emergency stop — Buddy can be thrown, causing injury to him and possibly you and your passengers. If you drive a sedan that can't accommodate a crate appropriate for the size of your dog, at least get a barrier to install behind the first row of seats.

Start with a review of teaching Buddy door manners (see Chapter 14). After that, apply the same progressions teaching Buddy to enter and exit the car with particular emphasis on exiting.

WARNING

When given a chance, many dogs love to ride in the car and stick their head out of the window. Don't allow them to do this — it's dangerous! He may get hit by a pebble or stone thrown up by a car in front of you. He also can injure his eyes with flying debris.

TIP

When traveling with your dog, make a point to keep to his feeding schedule and exercising routine as closely as possible. Sticking to customary daily rhythm prevents digestive upsets that can lead to accidents.

Getting used to entering the vehicle

First, practice entering the car in the driveway or garage. Put Buddy's training collar on him and attach the leash to the live ring (refer to Chapter 5) to determine which is the live ring. Have him Sit and Stay, and then open the car door. If he moves, reinforce the Stay command. (By now Buddy should sit on command; if he doesn't, head to Chapter 11.) Count to five and then tell him to get into the car with whatever command you have chosen — Get In for example. After he's in the car, take off the leash, and close the door. If you're using a crate and he has been trained to get into the crate in the car, follow the same procedure except direct him to jump into his crate. Just remember to close the crate door so it doesn't interfere with closing the car door.

REMEMBER

At first, some dogs may be reluctant to jump into the car or crate, in which case you have to lift them in. With several repetitions (and provided Buddy is physically able to jump into the car or crate), he'll do it on his own. Some dogs are too small to jump into the car without help. Ramps are great for those dogs who can't physically jump into the car or crate.

Staying put before exiting the vehicle

When taking Buddy on the road, an especially important exercise is teaching him to stay in the vehicle when you open the door from the outside. That way you can leash him before letting him out. Your dog should never exit the car or crate without your permission word. See Chapter 14 for door manners and getting out of a crate. An open door isn't an invitation for your dog to leap out. Put on Buddy's leash before giving him the Okay exit command.

TIP

If Buddy tries to make a move to get out of the car, close the door (being careful you don't slam his tail or any of his limbs in the door!). Repeat opening and closing the door until he stays so you can attach the leash to his training collar. Then count to five and release him with "Okay" to exit the car.

REMEMBER

Review these sequences over several sessions until both of you are comfortable with the procedure and the rules. When Buddy reliably remains in the car, you need to practice around distractions. On a weekend, go to the local park when it's busy with people and dogs. Exit the car, crack open the door through which he'll exit, and close it again, open a crack, close it again, repeating until he remembers his job isn't to leave without permission. Then open the door all the way, and he'll tell you whether he needs more training.

Getting ready for your road trip

In preparation for your road trip, you need to train Buddy to ride in the car and to get in and out of it as we describe in the preceding sections. You don't want to be in a position of having to take Buddy out of the car at a busy interstate rest stop for a potty break and have him get loose.

If Buddy is used to relieving himself off leash, you may want to teach him to eliminate on leash on command. (A good phrase is the "Hurry up and go potty. Hurry up.") After all, when you stop during your trip at a busy rest stop and are looking for a few blades of grass, you certainly can't have Buddy off leash. Dogs need to practice going potty on leash if they're used to relieving themselves in a fenced yard.

REMEMBER

Make sure you also pack all his possessions needed for the trip, such as his collar and leash, water and food, blankets, bowls, toys, towels to dry him off in case he gets wet, clean-up material if he throws up or has an accident, baggies for multi-purpose cleanup and disposal, and any medications. You may want to make a list so you don't forget anything. Buddy needs his own suitcase or bag to store everything.

If you're planning to visit relatives or friends and Buddy is going to stay in their home, about a week before the trip start reviewing his basic exercises — Sit and Stay (no jumping up on people), Down, Come (you can use the Touch command), and Leave It. (You can read about all these exercises in Chapters 9 and 10.) Your hosts will be impressed with (and appreciative of) how well behaved Buddy is.

When you arrive at your destination and are finished with the hugs and hellos, immediately take Buddy to an area where he can relieve himself. If necessary, clean up after him. Above all, try to stick to Buddy's daily routine as much as possible, especially his feeding and elimination schedule. It would be most embarrassing if he had an accident in the house.

Easing carsickness

Some dogs get carsick, which manifests itself in excessive drooling or vomiting, and can be attributed to

» True motion sickness

» A negative association with riding in a car

Dogs that have a tendency to get carsick usually aren't taken for rides very often. And when they're taken for a ride, it's usually to the vet. You can compare his reaction to that of a child who, every time it gets in the car, goes to the doctor for a shot. It doesn't take many repetitions before your dog makes an unpleasant association with your car.

Some dogs get sick in vans because they *can't* see out of the window, and others get sick in cars because they *can* see out of the window. In the latter case, covering the crate may solve the problem.

REMEMBER

Whatever the reason for the dog's reaction, you can create a pleasant association with the car. By working with your dog to make car rides a positive experience, you can tell how well he's taking to the car and how much time you need to spend at each sequence.

Throughout the following remedial exercise, maintain a light and happy attitude. Avoid a solicitous tone of voice and phrases such as, "It's all right. Don't worry. Nothing is going to happen to you." These reassurances validate the dog's concerns and reinforce his phobia about the car. Buddy will think you're praising him for his anxiety. Here's what to do:

1. Open all the car doors and, with the engine off, lure or put Buddy in his crate (see Chapter 14 for crate training), which is in the car.

You also can feed him in his crate. After he's in the crate (no matter how he got there), give him a treat, tell him how proud you are of him, and immediately let him out again. Repeat this step until he's comfortable in his crate.

2. When Buddy is confident getting into the crate, close the doors on one side of the car, with the engine still shut off.

3. When he's comfortable with Step 2, tell your dog to get in the crate, give him a treat, and close all the doors.

Let him out again and give him a treat. Repeat until he readily goes into the crate, and you can close all the doors for up to one minute.

4. **Tell your dog to get into the crate, close all the doors, get into the car with him, and start the engine.**

   Give your dog a treat. Turn off the engine and let him out.

5. **Now it's time for a short drive — no more than once around the block or out the driveway and back in.**

   Increase the length of the rides, always starting and ending with a treat or a game he loves.

When Buddy is comfortable riding in the car, make it a point to take him for a ride on a regular basis. You want the ride to be a pleasant experience for him, like going for a walk in the park — not just the annual trip to the vet.

WARNING

You need to be careful about leaving Buddy unattended in the car for more than 10 minutes when the outside temperature is greater than 60 degrees Fahrenheit and the sun is shining. The temperature inside a car, even with the windows partially open, rises quickly.

TIP

If you discover that he truly has motion sickness, give Buddy a ginger cookie when you start your journey in the car — the ginger will help to calm his stomach.

Going to Doggie Daycare

Doggie daycare has become almost as popular as daycare for children and with good reason. The dog isn't left alone at home alone for the entire day with nothing to do (except possibly get into mischief). At doggie daycare he gets to play with other dogs and have a good time for most of the day (Figure 21-2 is a great example). When his owners pick up Buddy in the afternoon, he's sufficiently tired and doesn't make any other demands on them except dinner.

Dogs don't have to be trained for daycare, but most likely they'll be evaluated beforehand. For their own convenience in handling the dogs, the staff may train the dogs to understand at least the Sit and Stay commands. The environments that daycare facilities offer vary enormously; they may be spa-like or spartan. Most have an indoor facility, but many also have an outdoor area. Some offer grooming, bathing, and training as well. Some even have swimming pools. Check ones in your area to see if you like how the staff interacts with the dogs and how much exercise your dog will be getting.

FIGURE 21-2:
Dogs getting the exercise and social interactions that they need and want.

© John Wiley & Sons, Inc.

REMEMBER

Before committing to a daycare facility, you should have a chance to evaluate the facility and its program, and the facility will have the opportunity to evaluate Buddy. For you, things to look for are cleanliness, supervision, the number of dogs in a given space, indoor and outdoor areas, ratio of staff to the number of dogs, appropriate rest times for the dogs, and how they're housed during this time (they're usually crated). Rest breaks between play sessions are also important. Don't forget to ask about rest for your dog during the day. You and Buddy both have to be comfortable with your choice, but his opinion is particularly important. Does he look forward to going to that facility, or does he balk? Pay attention to how *he* feels.

Minding Your Manners at the Dog Park

Many communities have dog parks — designated areas where dogs can run and play off leash. Some parks are fenced, and some aren't. Some municipalities make the park available to the community; other parks are privately operated. Both may restrict entry, either by residency requirements or fees. All dog parks have rules, which are posted at the entrance (if the park is fenced).

REMEMBER

The two main rules require you to pick up after your dog and to control him at all times. Unfortunately, both rules often are ignored. It never ceases to amaze how many so-called "conscientious" dog owners seem to be oblivious to these rules. One of the main reason for the nation's growing anti-dog sentiment stems from the fact that so many dog owners don't clean up after their dogs and don't keep them under control. The gyrations some owners go through to get their dogs to come to them when it's time to go home are prime-time comedy.

Before you ever take Buddy to a dog park, make sure you have distraction-trained him to come when called. And keep in mind that when you take him to the dog park for the first time, it's best to take off the leash; the vast majority of dogfights occur when one or both dogs are leashed. The "regulars" at the park will have formed a pack, which will rush up to Buddy, the newcomer, to investigate. While perfectly normal, the experience can be overwhelming for Buddy. Fortunately, it rarely results in an altercation as long as everyone stays calm. After the initial greeting ceremony is over, everyone will go his own way. Promise Buddy and yourself that you won't enter a dog park if you think too many unruly dogs are inside. Stand outside of your car for a minute and watch what's going on inside. Go back home if you don't feel comfortable.

Almost every park has a bully, so it's your responsibility to keep your eye on Buddy to intervene, if necessary. The owner of the bully is usually singularly oblivious to what his or her dog is doing — and much less interested in correcting the undesired behavior. Because bullies "teach" other dogs bullying behaviors, the owner needs to correct the bully's behavior.

WARNING

Even under the best of circumstances, dog parks contain some hazards. After visiting a dog park you should thoroughly clean your shoes or take them off before you go into the house. (You can even reserve one pair just for the dog park.) Before letting your dog into the house, thoroughly clean his feet (consult your vet for a safe disinfectant). Moreover, if you regularly visit a dog park, you should get biannual fecal examinations for your dog from your vet.

Keeping Your Canine Calm at the Vet's Office

Most dogs don't like to go to the vet's office, whether it's something serious or just for the semiannual or annual checkup. People experience similar feelings about their own annual physicals.

For the untrained dog, the anxiety level of going to the vet is increased by the owner, who's fidgeting with the dog, telling him not to do this, to quit doing that, to behave himself, to calm down, to sit still, to not visit, and on and on. Because the dog hasn't been trained, he doesn't have a clue what his owner wants, so he has an increase in apprehension.

For the trained dog, the owner's message is reassuring — "Sit," "Down," "Stay," and "Good dog!" are all commands he's used to. Instead of hearing "Don't do whatever you're doing," he hears "Good dog." (See Chapter 11 for basic training.) And keep in mind that the trip in the car to the vet's office also often is traumatic if the dog isn't used to the car. To avoid this problem, check out the earlier section "Taking Buddy on the Road."

Being Patient with the Rescue Dog

The main problem with rescues isn't that they're inherently different from a puppy you may get from a reputable breeder; the issue is that you don't know their background. Many dogs are brought to the shelter for no other reason than that they've outgrown that cute puppy stage. Others are turned in because they've become unmanageable — read this to mean they suffer from a "lack of basic training." The reasons vary, some legitimate though most not.

The majority of rescue dogs turn out to be fine pets with training and good health. After several weeks of getting used to their new homes, most are happy to be where they are. Even so, some come with behavioral baggage of unknown causes. The most common is separation anxiety, ranging from mild to severe. (You can read more about this behavioral issue in the earlier section "Coping with Separation Anxiety.") Another one is unexplained aggressive-appearing behavior (see Chapter 20). Many of the quirks of rescues can be solved, but it starts with basic training.

Chapter **22**

Keeping Your Senior Dog Young: Teaching an Old Dog New Tricks

Old dogs are wonderful to have around. They have known you for so long, have shared so many memories with you, have been there for you through good times and bad, and know your every move. They're precious resources and loving family members, and they deserve the best you can give them. Some good souls also adopt older dogs; these dogs can be wonderful pets as well. Older dogs require less exercise as a rule and are often trained to a certain degree.

In this chapter, we discuss the best ways to train these senior citizens so they stay healthy, happy, and young at heart. We also provide some reminders about the importance of keeping your older dog well groomed. If you want to introduce a young canine friend to your senior dog, we provide tips on the best ways to do that as well.

Older dogs thrive on knowing their daily routines. They wake up at a certain hour and go to the door to be let out for their morning or evening walk. They like to eat at set meal times. In fact, you often can set your clock by their habits. Adhering to Buddy's customary routine is extra important if he's losing his sight and/or hearing. If he's becoming deaf, remember that he can't hear you when you approach. To avoid startling him, make sure you gently touch him to let him know you're nearby, especially when approaching him from the rear. Old dogs startle quickly and may get irritable if they're woken up abruptly. Changing Buddy's routine can cause needless anxiety to your old friend.

Old Gray Muzzle: Exploring the Signs of Aging in Dog Years

What does "old" really mean? In the case of dogs, old is breed-specific; the aging process is related to the size of the dog. The life expectancy of giant breeds, such as Mastiffs or Newfoundlands, is often only 7 to 8 years, whereas smaller dogs live older than 15 years. Medium to large dogs live 10 to 13 years. If these dogs have been fed a species-appropriate diet (raw food), they then become old much later — giant breeds around 12, medium size dogs around 14, and small or toy dogs around 16 to 18. See Chapter 4 for Wendy's advice on feeding healthy.

A number of factors affect life expectancy in dogs. At the top of the list is diet, which shouldn't come as a surprise. A dog's muzzle doesn't have to turn completely gray with age unless there's a genetic component. He'll have some white hairs for sure, but if you feed and supplement Buddy correctly, he can age without looking old at all. (The later section "Taking Care of Your Older Dog's Health and Nutrition Needs" provides some pointers.)

Another factor is spaying and neutering. Recent studies show that spayed females lived longest of dogs dying of all causes, whereas nonspayed females lived longest of dogs dying of natural causes. Although neutering protects your male dog against testicular cancer, neutered males have the shortest lifespan, probably as a result of prostate cancer.

Depending on the breed of your dog, you may see the signs of aging beginning from 7 years on and sometimes even before. Signs are graying of the muzzle, loss of hearing and vision, arthritis, and an inability to get around as well, weight gain, and decreased energy. Some of these changes can be delayed by following the simple preventative steps that we suggest in this chapter.

TIP

For more information on how to take care of your older pet, see *Senior Dogs For Dummies* by Susan McCullough (John Wiley & Sons, Inc.).

Teaching Exercises to Keep Buddy's Mind and Body Sharp

The value of exercise as your dog ages can't be overemphasized. Just as humans have less energy, less muscle mass, and less ability and endurance as they age, dogs experience the same things. Humans can enroll in classes at the gym to keep themselves supple, but your dog relies on you for help.

In the following sections, we show you some exercises for your dog that involve the use of most of Buddy's muscles, tendons, and ligaments. Remember that muscles keep bones in place. So keeping Buddy's muscles flexible will strengthen his skeletal system as well as his heart and lungs, improve his circulation, and help to keep his immune system strong. We also make suggestions to keep his mind sharp. Training your old friend can be fun for you and your dog, and it can add years to his life.

REMEMBER

Do be careful that you don't ask too much from Buddy. If you find him stressing or unable to do a certain exercise because it's painful for him, have your veterinarian check him out.

TIP

Many of these exercises require you to use treats as motivation. Treats should be small and not too hard and should provide very few calories. Look for treats that have only three or four ingredients in them or whole food treats like dehydrated liver or jerky treats. Stay away from food made in China because there is no assurance that what is listed in the ingredients in the treats is actually true. Plus, treats made in China have no quality control and have been recalled many times, causing sickness and even death.

Begging

The balancing act in this exercise makes use of most of the muscles along his back as well as stomach and side muscles. Balancing strengthens Buddy's *core*, or center body muscles. How your dog is built determines whether he's able to achieve perfect balance without help or whether you may have to assist him by holding his front paws. Strong core muscles allow Buddy to run and turn more easily. Here's what to do:

1. **With your dog sitting in front of you, hold a treat about an inch above his nose.**

   You can find out more about the Sit command in Chapter 11.

2. **As he stretches his neck to reach the treat, slowly elevate the treat until Buddy is sitting on his haunches.**

   Getting himself balanced takes a while, so be patient. After he balances himself, give him the treat.

3. **Increase the time that Buddy holds the begging position until he can hold it for about 15 seconds.**

   Repeat four times each session.

Crawling

Crawling stretches the back and neck muscles, which helps Buddy to remain limber and able to look up, down, and to the right and left. Practice this exercise on a soft surface so Buddy doesn't graze his elbows or stifle (knee) joints. Nearly all breeds of dogs can do this exercise. Follow these steps to help your dog do the crawling exercise:

1. **With a treat in your right hand, have Buddy sit at your left side.**

2. **Put your left-hand palm down on Buddy's shoulders and slowly lower the treat between his front paws.**

   As Buddy follows the treat, slowly, an inch at a time, pull the treat forward with your right hand.

3. **As he lowers his body, keep your left hand on Buddy's shoulders so he can't get up; he should start to crawl toward the treat.**

REMEMBER

Be careful not to apply too much pressure on his back, because doing so will stop his ability to crawl forward and it may hurt him.

Aim for four crawls and then reward him. Repeat four times during a session, each time starting from the sitting position. As Buddy gets the hang of this exercise, you can increase the number of crawls before rewarding him.

Walking backward

Walking backward strengthens the muscles of Buddy's back legs. As mentioned earlier, muscles keep bones in place. With older dogs, their hips and back legs often become arthritic (especially those spayed or neutered at a very young age). *Arthritis* occurs when bone grinds on bone and inflammation appears, causing pain and discomfort. To help Buddy if he already has some arthritis, or to help prevent it, keeping his back leg muscles in shape is a good idea. (You also may want to check with your veterinarian about getting monthly Adequan shots, which are excellent for relieving arthritis in dogs. Or consider using Myristin, which is an arthritis supplement.) The muscles and nerves in this part of the body control the bladder and rectum. Keeping them strong helps Buddy to avoid incontinence in old age. Try these steps to teach Buddy to walk backward:

1. **With Buddy standing in front of you, take a treat and hold it at his nose level.**

   If you need help with the Stand command, check out Chapter 19.

2. **Slowly take tiny steps toward him, and when he steps backward, reward him.**

   Do it again, aiming for two steps. Reward each increment. Your goal is to reach 25 steps per training session before rewarding. Build up to 100 steps, rewarding every 25 steps. Be careful to keep your hands still and in the same position.

When Wendy's vet first recommended this exercise for her Lab, Annabelle, she thought "Wow, that's a lot of steps!" But after Annabelle caught on, it took less than five minutes to complete the 100 steps with dramatic improvement of her mobility. She was rewarded every 25 steps. See Figure 22-1 to see Annabelle in action.

Doing neck and head stretches

The following head and neck stretching exercises helps keep Buddy's muscles in his head and neck region supple. The nerves to the eyes, ears, and mouth are all contained in this area of the body, so keeping the muscles along his cervical spine stretched will keep his head, neck, mouth, teeth, and gums in good shape. If you start these exercises around the age of 8, they can go a long way to preventing loss of hearing and sight as Buddy ages. If your dog is older than 12 when you start these exercises, he'll probably be stiff in the beginning, so go slowly. If you're persistent and do these exercises with Buddy daily, you'll be surprised at how quickly the flexibility comes back.

FIGURE 22-1:
Twelve-year-old
Annabelle
walking
backward.

Here's how to do it:

1. **With Buddy sitting in front of you, take a treat and slowly lower it between his front legs.**

   Don't let him lie down, but allow him to stretch his neck far enough down to reach the treat. Reward him when he reaches the treat.

2. **Take another treat and slowly move it past his shoulder, first to the right and then to the left, having Buddy stretch his neck as far as he can.**

   Reward each stretch. See Figure 22-2 to see this step in action.

3. **Take the treat and hold it just above his head so he stretches upward.**

   Reward him when he stretches for the treat.

Using the coffee table stretch

The coffee table stretch is an important one to do because it helps stretch Buddy's spine. When his spine is in good shape, he'll move around much more freely and easily. Follow these steps:

1. **Tell Buddy to lie down just a few inches in front of a coffee table.**

   To find out more about the Down command, head to Chapter 11.

FIGURE 22-2:
Neck stretches
to keep Buddy
in shape.

© John Wiley & Sons, Inc.

2. **Put a treat on the edge of the table and tell Buddy to stand and stretch forward for the treat.**

Be careful not to put the treat too far from him. You don't want him to walk toward it; rather you want him to stand up from the Down position and stretch. This exercise goes slowly in the beginning because Buddy has to figure out what to do, but be patient.

WARNING

Walking, sitting, and downing

Walking, sitting, and downing are all great for keeping Buddy in shape. Simple as these activities seem, they go a long way to exercise all the muscles in Buddy's body. You can do them inside around the house, but it's better if you can take him for a ten-minute walk and practice them daily. It makes his daily walks more fun, and it's good for you too. Have a pocketful of treats before you leave! Here are the steps to take:

1. **With Buddy on leash at your left side, walk ten steps forward and say "Sit."**

If Buddy doesn't sit, use a treat to make him sit. See Chapter 11 for details.

2. **Go ten steps and say "Down."**

If he doesn't, head to Chapter 11 to see how to teach Buddy the Down command. Each session you can alternate between a Sit and a Down, two times each. Make sure you make a big fuss of him and reward him by giving him a treat when he's successful.

Swimming

One of the best exercises for Buddy is swimming. It allows him to use his entire body without putting pressure on his aging joints. More and more facilities now have hydrotherapy pools for dogs. These pools have a current that can be adjusted. (Figure 22-3 shows a senior dog enjoying a swim.) If Buddy doesn't know how to swim, look for a facility where a qualified instructor is in the pool with your dog. Start slowly, building up Buddy's stamina to 20 minutes, two to three times per week. Most of swimming facilities insist that Buddy wear a life jacket, and they have a selection for you to choose from that will fit him. This is a good safety requirement.

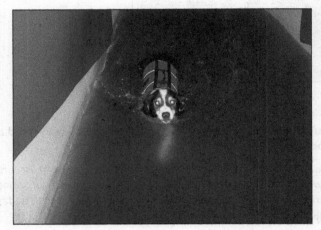

FIGURE 22-3:
Swimming is a great activity for your senior dog.

© John Wiley & Sons, Inc.

REMEMBER

You can find facilities close to you by using your favorite browser to search for hydrotherapy pools for dogs. Be sure to enter your town and state in the keywords. Visit the facility before you book an appointment for Buddy to swim. You want to make sure that the facility is clean and that a qualified person will be swimming with your dog. Avoid pools that are dirty or where dogs are left to swim around by themselves. Also avoid those where the dogs are tethered across the pool to make them swim in place. This setup is only used at pools in veterinary facilities where qualified instructors are supervising the swimming and monitoring the heart rate of the dogs.

Another possibility is taking Buddy to a local lake or pond, but do due diligence. Check the body of water thoroughly before you allow Buddy to swim in it though. Many ponds and lakes are in rural areas and serve as a runoff for farm fields or contain deadly algae. These farm fields are heavily fertilized, and the runoff goes into the pond or lake. Also, the bacterial count in most ponds is very high, especially around the muddy edges. If you find that Buddy is scratching and he gets runny eyes after swimming in one of these areas, don't take him back. Bathe him immediately and take him to your veterinarian to determine whether he has picked up a staph infection.

If you have your own swimming pool, and it has steps where Buddy can get in and out, let him have the occasional swim. However, be aware that the chlorine in the pool can irritate his eyes, making them red and runny. Too much swimming in a chlorinated pool can dry out his coat, so you may have to add extra oil to his food. (See www.volharddognutrition for the oil we recommend.) Also, keep in mind that dogs not used to swimming can tear the liner of the pool.

Applying mental stimulation

Treat dispensers are a great way to keep any dog amused and mentally sharp. These toys range from puzzles to simple rubber toys with holes for treats. Most rely on the concept of putting a treat in the toy and letting the dog figure out how to get the treat out of the toy. Whether pushing around the toys with their noses or using their paws, these toys can be great fun for dogs. Our only objection to some of them is that they can be really noisy when pushed around on a hardwood floor.

Buster Cubes, which you can read more about at www.bustercubes.com, are popular for this type of play. You can find more complex interactive toys and puzzles on Amazon.

Playing games indoors also can be helpful for stimulating your dog mentally. In the winter, you may not be able to exercise Buddy outside, so having several games and toys that can be played indoors is necessary to keep Buddy exercised both physically and mentally.

TIP

To exercise your dog's mind, play the Find It game, which is really easy to do. Follow these steps:

1. **Show your dog his favorite toy, leave him on a Sit-Stay, and place the toy close to the door of the room.**

   To read about the Sit-Stay, check out Chapter 11.

2. **Return to your dog and point to the toy with your hand closest to your dog while telling him to "Find It" and bring it back to you.**

   After he has learned Find It, start placing the toy around the corner and send him to fetch it. Gradually increase the level of difficulty by putting the toy in different places around the house. Dogs love this game, and it keeps them mentally stimulated.

Last, but not least, take Buddy to a new area to walk once a week. Make sure it's safe to let him off leash and to do all the normal doggie things like smelling and wandering around. If you have a friend who has a dog that's a friend of Buddy's, make a date so the dogs can walk together. These weekly walks will give Buddy something to look forward to, and both dogs will be content. Being mentally stimulated and being allowed to be a dog are two of the kindest things you can do for your old friend.

Taking Care of Your Older Dog's Health and Nutrition Needs

To understand why good nutrition is vital to the health and well-being of your dog (which in turn affects his ability to learn and your ability to train him), you need to think of Buddy's body as a machine that has an engine. For the engine to work correctly, all the component parts of the engine must be in good order. It must be given the correct fuel (think food), for example; if the fuel given is of the wrong blend, the engine may splutter and lose power. If the fuel is totally incorrect, the engine may stop working altogether. As your dog ages, his engine needs to be given the very best fuel you can afford. In the following sections, we provide you with information regarding feeding your senior pup and keeping him healthy with supplements.

WARNING

In many instances, older dogs take a lower dose of medication than is indicated by their weight. If your senior friend has to be put on medication for any reason, watch for side effects. If you notice adverse reactions, your vet will either reduce the dose or change the medication.

Maintaining Buddy's slim and trim figure with a satisfying diet

How much and what kind of food you feed Buddy as he ages depends on you. You're in charge of how much and what Buddy eats. Keeping him slim to the point you can feel his ribs (but not see them) is your contribution to keeping him healthy. Studies show that a decrease in caloric intake can add years to Buddy's life. Vets report that more than 50 percent of all older dogs they see are grossly overweight. Just as obesity in humans creates all sorts of health hazards, the same applies to Buddy. Heart disease, diabetes, cancer, and joint problems are all associated with Buddy being overweight.

Buddy has an uncanny knowledge of what's good for him and what isn't. If he becomes a picky eater on the food you're currently feeding, head to Chapter 4 and review some healthy alternatives. If Buddy isn't getting the exercise he needs and he's overweight, you need to cut down the amount of food you're feeding. Try decreasing his food by about 10 percent for a week and see if that helps. Add in some fresh raw foods to satisfy his hunger. If he maintains weight, you're putting in more calories than he's burning on a daily basis. Cut back 25 percent and see whether that decrease doesn't trim him down.

REMEMBER

Be careful not to give high-calorie treats. Use fresh vegetables like pieces of carrot, cucumber, or broccoli instead. Raw fruits can be used in moderation. Apples are favorites with many dogs, but peel them first to remove the skin, which harbors the insecticide sprays used in growing them.

Here's one of our favorite sayings: "If your dog is overweight, *you're* not getting enough exercise." Get your dog moving to help keep his weight in check. Take him for walks and play games with him. Refer to the earlier section "Teaching Exercises to Keep Buddy's Mind and Body Sharp" for some tips.

If you haven't switched to a balanced, raw food, or supplemented commercial diet, now may be the time to do so. In terms of prolonging Buddy's life, a balanced, raw food diet is the best you can feed. Raw food is easy to digest, and you control Buddy's caloric intake with this type of diet. It provides all the nutrients needed in old age and breaks down and converts to energy.

The diet we recommend is called NDF2. All you have to do is to add water and the meat your dog likes best. In fact, this diet is used by a lot of the top-winning show and working dogs in the country. If you watch the Westminster Dog Show, you'll see many dogs that are fed this way. Chapter 4 provides information on all these diet options.

WARNING

According to a study by Tufts University of 100 commercially available foods, so-called "lite" or weight-management dog foods for older dogs have shown a wide variance of calories recommended to maintain a dog. In fact, many of them recommend more calories than an older dog requires. With most of these foods, pets would actually gain weight were the owners to adhere to the feeding directions on the labels. These foods generally are full of indigestible grains. These make Buddy's body work harder to break down the food in his stomach that doesn't give him energy. And often poor Buddy experiences gas when on these foods. Not what we recommend for your old friend.

If you must use a dry kibble for your dog, at least add some fresh foods and supplements so his digestion works better and he feels better. If you feed Buddy correctly, he'll feel like a puppy again.

Making life easier with supplements

As Buddy ages, he'll need some supplements so he can digest and break down his food and medications. For example, chances are high that he'll need a supplement to support his aging joints. You'll also want to use supplements to boost his immune system and improve his cognitive abilities.

The $5 billion a year supplement industry produces thousands of products. It's overwhelming to the average dog owner and almost impossible to make an informed choice. We've made the job easier by listing in the following sections the supplements we have used successfully over the years. Unless otherwise noted, these products are available through www.volharddognutrition.com.

Digestive enzymes

To readily absorb food and utilize it, senior dogs (those older than 8) need to be supplemented with digestive enzymes. Enzymes help practically all body systems function better. Digestive enzymes specifically break down food particles for storage in the liver or muscles and are used when the body needs them. They're naturally secreted along the digestive tract and help the nutrients in food to be absorbed into the bloodstream.

REMEMBER

As Buddy ages, the production of these enzymes slows down and the food he eats isn't as well absorbed and turned into energy. Supplemental digestive enzymes are particularly useful for dogs who experience digestive upsets, such as vomiting and diarrhea, and who have gas and have problems with weight control. Digestive enzymes also help older dogs that are on medication; they make it easier to absorb and cause it to work better.

Immune booster

To rebuild the immune system, the Immune Booster supplement is a vitamin/mineral mix that contains colostrum. *Colostrum* is the yellowish fluid that's secreted by the mammary glands of mammals after they've given birth. It contains high levels of proteins and immune factors that help to protect the newborn from infection. Sources used in supplements generally come from either cows or pigs. Colostrum boosts the body's immune system, burns fat, and builds lean muscle. It's especially useful in healing the body, so you can use it for any dog who has experienced surgery, illness, or trauma of any kind. It also can be used before and after vaccination. Colostrum works quickly, and we recommend its use for only three weeks. Too much colostrum can make your dog very itchy. Look on Amazon for this type of supplement.

CAUTION: OLD DOGS CAN EASILY BE OVERDOSED

Evo, Wendy's Newfoundland, had stubbed his toe. He was 13 years old and getting frail. Her holistic veterinarian suggested an antibiotic plus the homeopathic remedy Nat Sulph, which is specific for nail beds. For the first couple of days Evo was fine, but then he stopped eating, was lethargic, and was constantly rubbing his head with his paws. He looked close to death's door. In reading the instructions on the antibiotic, Wendy noticed the side effects included the symptoms Evo displayed. She reduced the dose, and he immediately improved. She continued with the homeopathic remedy, and the situation resolved itself.

Was this anyone's fault? Was Evo allergic to the antibiotic? Probably not. It was simply that he was frail, old, and didn't have the kind of energy to deal with such a high dose of antibiotics.

Myristin (arthritis formula)

Cetyl myristoleate is a unique fatty acid ester incorporated into the fat layers of cell membranes. It's often referred to as the WD-40 for joints because of its lubricating qualities. Myristin helps to reduce pain and inflammation caused by bone grinding against bone. It helps over a period of a month or so to rebuild the synovial fluid that stops bones rubbing together. We recommend this arthritis formula for dogs with weak rear ends, dogs who limp, and all older dogs experiencing arthritis. Wendy has used it for close to 25 years and finds it to be the best of its kind on the market.

System Saver

The System Saver supplement is an herbal anti-inflammatory that contains frankincense, green tea, turmeric, and orange peel flavonoids. It's effective for use with hip dysplasia, arthritis, tendonitis, dermatitis, autoimmune and degenerative disorders, and inflammatory bowel and respiratory diseases that haven't responded to traditional medications. It has shown amazing results in skin problems that have genetic tendencies and that are impossible to cure otherwise.

RNA

Ribonucleic acid (RNA) is one of the substances used successfully for aging and degenerative diseases. By taking a capsule twice a day, RNA has been found to increase skin elasticity and to energize the body. It's antiviral and has cognitive enhancing effects. Wendy has used RNA for many years with her older dogs and has found that their ability to heal is enhanced, their cognitive abilities don't diminish with age, and they don't lose their hearing or sight. The idea behind using RNA is that you provide the cells with an abundance of their basic building materials to repair any damage caused by aging. Look for it on Amazon.

Keeping Up with Grooming

Grooming Buddy as he gets older is critical to his well-being. If he feels well, he'll be easier to train. Simple things like keeping his nails short, his coat brushed out, and his ears and teeth clean make him feel good.

REMEMBER

As Buddy ages, it's not as easy as it was for him to take part in self-grooming. Older dogs aren't as flexible as they used to be. So reaching their rear ends or tummies to clean may not be possible for some dogs, especially if they're overweight. As a result, their fur can get matted easily. Look under Buddy's arms to make sure that his freedom of movement isn't curtailed by mats.

In addition to your normal grooming for Buddy, here's a rundown of the things you should get in the habit of doing for him every week when he's older:

» **Put some time aside to give him a really good brush (and wash) from top to toe.** Brushing stimulates the skin by bringing blood to the surface and keeps it healthy by removing dead fur. Just because you have a smooth-haired dog or one that goes to the groomer every six weeks doesn't mean that a weekly brush isn't necessary. Pay particular attention to the rear, the underside of the tail, and the back of the hind legs. Look for any discharge from the genitals and any fur mats that may make it uncomfortable for your older dog to get up and down easily. He may get some feces stuck on the fur around his rectum or urine on his back legs, but frequent washing of this part of his body will prevent skin burns. We suggest using a coconut oil shampoo, which is gentle and doesn't take the oil out of his coat. Trimming the hair around these areas makes it easier to keep clean for both of you.

» **Check Buddy's ears for any odor and clean them.** If they have a musty odor, Buddy may have a yeast infection, which can be painful. And if it isn't treated, it can cause deafness. If you see black discharge, he may have ear mites. Talk to your vet about what she recommends to clear the infection. As a weekly cleanser you can use apple cider vinegar and water (half and half) on a cotton ball and wipe out the ears. Or, as long as Buddy has no sore spots, rubbing alcohol on a cotton ball does a great job for overall cleansing.

Be sure not to poke around too far in the ear — just clean the part you can easily see. Avoid using cotton swabs and sticking your finger into the ear canal. Not only is this painful for Buddy but you also can damage the ear.

» **Trim his nails regularly.** Buddy's nails don't get the wear and tear they did when he was young, so they don't wear down as easily. Allowing nails on the front feet to get too long forces the dog to walk on his nails and pushes his weight onto his shoulders, weakening them. As a general rule, when you can hear your dog's nails clicking along the floor when he walks, they're too long. If you feel you can't trim his nails by yourself, take your dog to the groomer or your vet for a trim on a regular basis. (See Chapter 6 for tips on getting a dog used to this practice.) Figure 22-4 shows a well-groomed set of nails. You'll notice that it's difficult to see the nails on this dog's foot. If you can see the nails sticking out, they're likely too long.

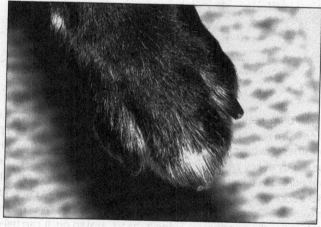

FIGURE 22-4:
Keeping your senior's nails short is a must.

© John Wiley & Sons, Inc.

» **Check Buddy's teeth.** Buddy's mouth is the gateway to his overall health. When his teeth get coated with tartar, his gums will become inflamed. Gum disease produces bacteria, which drains into his stomach and has been implicated in heart attacks, strokes, and some cancers. To clean his teeth, you can use a toothbrush and some doggie toothpaste. Both are available at any pet store. An effective tartar remover is a gel called Petzlife (available at petzlife.com), which you rub onto Buddy's teeth daily. Petzlife also puts out an oral mist that you spray on his teeth. Both products work to dissolve the tartar in one month. This product is a good alternative to putting

Buddy under anesthesia at the veterinarian for a teeth cleaning. With the correct diet and raw appropriate bones twice a week, Buddy's teeth should stay clean throughout his life (see Figure 22-5).

FIGURE 22-5: Clean teeth keep your old dog healthy.

REMEMBER

If your dog's teeth are badly stained and his gums are inflamed, the only alternative is to take your dog to the veterinarian and have him put under anesthesia to have his teeth professionally cleaned. Anesthesia is a risk for Buddy at any age, but he could have an adverse reaction if he's older. Sometimes you just can't avoid a professional veterinary teeth cleaning. Make sure that Buddy's blood panel is taken before he's put under the anesthesia. This panel indicates the health of his liver (which has to metabolize the anesthesia), kidneys, heart, and so on. It can tell you whether it's safe for Buddy to have this procedure done. After his teeth are cleaned, use oral brushing or gel products on a regular basis.

» **Keep Buddy's eyes clear and clean.** A good choice to clean eyes is homeopathic eye drops for Buddy when his eyes get watery or weep liquid. This can happen when running him in a different park or out in the country and can be a sign of allergies. We use Similasan Allergy Eye Relief, available at any large drug store. Even eye saline available where you buy contact supplies is a great flush for cleaning and rinsing out Buddy's eyes.

WARNING

Yellow or greenish discharge in Buddy's eyes usually indicates an infection and a trip to your veterinarian may be necessary. Don't let this go thinking it will resolve itself. It could lead to a more dangerous condition.

Bringing Home a Puppy to Help Rejuvenate Buddy

Raising a young dog and teaching him life's lessons in the presence of your older dog can help Buddy stay young. Plus, puppies brought up with older dogs are easy to train because they usually mimic the older dog's behavior.

Don't wait too long to introduce a puppy to Buddy. Bring him in when your older dog is young enough to enjoy him. If your dog has been fed, trained, and exercised well, he really won't age that much until he's 11 or 12. Before Buddy is having trouble getting around is an ideal time to bring in the puppy. Buddy can still get around okay, teach the puppy manners, and enjoy his new companion's company. If your dog is showing signs of aging at 8 or so, don't wait any longer. Do it now, because the older dog, if he isn't feeling well, won't enjoy a puppy under foot.

REMEMBER

You can introduce a puppy into a household that has an older dog by following our suggestions in Chapter 6. The main thing to remember is that it's Buddy's house, and he has to invite the youngster to come in. Introductions are best done on neutral territory, such as the front lawn, the sidewalk, or somewhere away from the house. Let both dogs sniff each other all over. Buddy knows by smelling the puppy that he isn't a small grown dog but rather something tiny that needs help in learning to be a dog. Then tell Buddy to take the puppy home. Let Buddy in the house first and have puppy follow him in. Make sure you always feed, brush, and train Buddy before the puppy. Buddy is number one, and peace will reign if he's treated that way.

Using a crate with the puppy is the best way to stop the puppy from jumping all over Buddy when he's taking his nap. When Buddy is teaching the puppy manners, it's normal for him to growl at times, just leave him alone to teach the lesson. However, don't let puppy take liberties with Buddy, and crate him when it becomes obvious that Buddy dislikes the attention.

For example, Fritz, a Dachshund puppy, came to Wendy when Annabelle, her Labrador, was 11 years old and beginning to age. Teaching Fritz took years off Annabelle's life — she got a lot more exercise trying to keep up with puppy and looks years younger than her chronological age. Figure 22-6 shows Annabelle with another 6-month-old puppy friend named Felix. Teaching puppies is what Annabelle likes to do, and it keeps her mentally alert and happy.

FIGURE 22-6:
Playing with
a puppy keeps
an older dog
feeling young.

Looking Into Dog Beds, Ramps, Wheelchairs, and Carts

As Buddy ages, you need to provide a soft bed for him to sleep on so his elbows, knees, and other joints are protected from hard surfaces. A soft bed is especially important if he's becoming arthritic. And if his back legs get weak and he has difficulty getting up and walking, you may need to purchase a product to help him maneuver higher places or simply stay mobile. In the following sections, we provide some information on products that we and our students have used over the years.

Making Buddy cozy: Beds

With a plethora of beds to choose from, you may find it difficult to determine which one is the best one for Buddy. The right one is mostly dependent on his size. Make sure it's soft to protect his joints. When you have dog beds all over the house, you'll find at different times of the day the dogs will be stretched out on them enjoying their naps. Buy beds with washable outer covers. In the dog crates for traveling, a great idea is to use sheepskin-topped beds that are filled with either a microfiber pad or sponge in a waterproof casing that can be washed.

TIP

You'll find an enormous price difference in beds from different sources. Search the Internet to comparison shop before investing in new beds. See Chapter 13 for other dog bed ideas.

The detergent you use to wash your dog beds is also important. Many of the popular brands contain chemicals that can cause contact allergies on the skin around the joints of older dogs. As Buddy age, he sleeps more than he did as a younger dog and spends more time on his bed. So if your dog gets a red rash where his body contacts the bed, changing your detergent may be in order. Look for hypoallergenic detergents, which should keep your dogs from experiencing any contact allergies.

Making heights more manageable with ramps

Ramps aren't as important for smaller dogs as they are for dogs weighing more than 50 pounds. Small dogs can be lifted onto the couch or bed, into the car, or into the bathtub. However, the larger the dog, the stronger your back has to be. With the giant breeds, it's next to impossible to move them if you're alone.

TIP

We advise using a ramp while Buddy is still firm on his feet. Introduce it to him when he reaches 8 or so. Train large dogs to use the ramp for getting into the vehicle and into the bathtub. Doing so is much less stressful for Buddy (and you) than trying to get him to jump up with his front legs so you can lift up the rear.

Look for a ramp that is lightweight and telescopes down to a third of its size. These features make it easy to pack on top of or next to the crates in the car. One place to look is www.dogramp.com. Dog ramps usually are priced around $200.

Helping the handicapped dog: Wheelchairs and carts

Having your beloved dog become paralyzed in the rear and unable to move is heartbreaking. Disease, trauma, or old age can cause the paralysis. However, paralysis doesn't mean the end of life for your pet. A number of companies have designed wheelchairs or carts with wheels to support the rear end of your pet.

Wendy once had an old German Shepherd who became paralyzed at age 14. She never gave up on her, and it was her first introduction to using carts with wheels. The cart was made to her measurements. The dog lived two more years using her cart and had a very happy life.

Your handicapped dog also can be fitted with a cart made to measure by an orthopedic veterinarian. Check out www.k9-carts.com to find their products. At this company's website you can see a video of how dogs manage to retrieve, run, and go for long walks in their carts, enjoying every moment.

A TRAINED DOG EQUALS A GREATER BOND

The house seems empty. I (Mary Ann) lost my dog to cancer. The heartache is a pain that many understand, yet some don't, because they've chosen to live without a pet. I don't really understand people who don't live with pets in their lives. Of course, owning a pet is a true lifestyle change; I do understand that. Having no pets and losing out on the love you get from them, no matter how short lived, is something I would never choose. My husband and I lost one of my dogs, my show dog, an obedience, agility, rally, trick dog — a dog that went with me to schools to meet children and be an ambassador of her kind, a good, well-trained dog, my beloved, Australian Shepherd, Benna (refer to the photo). Training a dog completes the bond you can have with a dog. After you've trained a dog, she is yours forever. My life's goal is to share the knowledge of training with everyone I can so they too can know the love of a well-trained dog.

© John Wiley & Sons, Inc.

Benna came into my life while I still had my last show dog working and doing well in his field. I didn't realize it, but Benna would be held at bay by him until I began to think she was a bit of a loner. When we lost him though, Benna blossomed into her own. It's not that she wasn't there by my side before he died. It was just that she occupied his place next to me after he left it, which was nice. She was special, beautiful, and loving. And she was a big presence, too. She was a guard dog, protecting us from the daily postal carrier, the neighbor's driveway usage, and every stray squirrel that dared enter her domain. And now that presence is gone.

I don't have that sidekick, that 50-pound hunk of gorgeous hair nestled by my desk. She wasn't ready to go; she was in perfect health, or so I thought. But silent cancer crept in and yanked her from me while I was traveling abroad. It was hemangiosarcoma, which is the silent cancer because with it, the dog feels just fine, until the day she didn't. And that was the day we lost her. I'm glad to think she felt fine until that day, but I'm sad that I wasn't with her the day she didn't. She wasn't alone though. Others were there and that's what matters. The choice was made during emergency surgery, which was the right and only decision. My friend was keeping her during our travels, and she immediately noticed the change in Benna's attitude. Benna was rushed into surgery and was cared for all the way. But now the house is empty.

We have other dogs, but they're small and comfortable on the couch. My Aussies didn't care about their own comfort as long as they were near me. That's the difference I feel — palpable with the emptiness in my heart and at my feet.

I can't imagine living without her presence. Sure, the house is cleaner without a dog, and the house is quieter and my guests are easier to host without managing the dog as well. But my heart is emptier, and it's not just the house. My life is emptier, my office is emptier, my day is quieter. How long can I let this go on? I need to miss Benna. I need to mourn the quiet. Then I will look around and find another heart dog. I can't live without my partner in life. I feel doing so is a tribute to the dog I loved and lost, to not ever want to live without the love of a dog in my life. My husband feels the same way about his dog and knows how I'm feeling without mine. We're a perfect match.

My previous dogs, the ones that came before Benna, each hold a special place in my memories, filling my life with stories and laughter. I choose life with a trained dog, and I suffer the loss without her. It hurts, but having the moments of loss are worth it because I had the moments of joy. The time spent training your dog will give you the joy of dog ownership. Every training moment is part of that journey. My motto is and always will be: Know dog, know joy; no dog, no joy!

Chapter **23**

Supplementing Your Training Efforts with Expert Help

You have a number of choices when it comes to Buddy's education. You've obviously chosen to train out of a book (good choice!), but a time may come when you need expert help. This chapter outlines your options, including attending obedience training classes, hiring a private trainer, and sending Buddy to be trained, such as a board and train. Each choice has pros and cons, and your own personality and lifestyle determine your preference.

No matter what decision you make, keep in mind that there are enormous quality differences not only in terms of training effectiveness, but also in how the dogs are treated. Dog training is a completely unregulated area, and anyone — yes, anyone — can proclaim himself a trainer. And keep in mind that teaching skills aren't the same as training skills. To teach people how to train their dogs, an instructor needs good communication and people skills along with a thorough knowledge of dog training.

REMEMBER

When you attempt to make a rational choice, remember that many paths lead to a well-trained dog. Beware of experts who say only their way is the right way. Successful dog training depends not so much on the how, as on the why. Dogs aren't a homogeneous commodity, and the approach to training has to take into account the dog's Personality Profile (see Chapter 2) as well as your own personality.

Going to Obedience Training Class

If you find you need outside help, we recommend an obedience training class where you're instructed how to train your dog. Having taught obedience training classes for more than 40 years, we're naturally biased in favor of this choice. A basic class usually addresses your most immediate concerns, such as not pulling on the leash, teaching the Sit and Down-Stay commands, and mastering Come. You also can find classes devoted to puppy training and advanced training for performance events when you and Buddy are ready.

REMEMBER

When you go to an obedience training class, don't expect the instructor to train your dog. That isn't her job. The purpose of the class is to show you what to do, have you try it a few times to make sure you've got it right, and then send you home to practice. Be prepared to attend class at least once a week and practice at home at least five times a week.

We think taking Buddy to school is perhaps one of the best things you can do for the both of you. Here's why:

>> Classes get you out of the house into an atmosphere where you can spend quality time together and strengthen the bond between you and your dog.

>> Both of you have fun while learning useful things that make living together that much easier.

>> Classes are excellent way for you to meet similar people and for Buddy to socialize with other dogs.

>> Classes usually are economical and keep your training on track with weekly sessions.

>> A knowledgeable individual tells you what you may be doing wrong and can help you succeed.

>> Classes automatically provide a distracted environment for you to work on communicating with your dog while he's distracted.

WARNING

Here are a few drawbacks to consider:

>> Most classes are sequential in nature. So, if you miss a class, you'll fall behind and may have a difficult time catching up. Falling behind is discouraging and may cause you to drop out.

>> The schedule and location may be inconvenient.

>> The instructor dictates how, what, and when.

>> The training method may not be right for you or your dog.

>> A group class is full of distractions, which can be frustrating at first.

The following sections help you find the right training class for you and your dog.

Good obedience training class criteria

Obedience training classes are offered in almost every community. Until fairly recently, obedience and kennel clubs conducted the majority of classes. Today, however, schools or private individuals also teach classes. The difference has nothing to do with the quality of the training; it relates solely to profit motive. Clubs are nonprofit organizations, and the instructors — usually members who have trained and shown their own dogs — generally volunteer their services. Training schools and individuals who hang out their shingles are for-profit organizations. Some of the large pet chain stores also offer obedience training classes.

To locate a class, ask people you know for referrals, such as your veterinary office, groomer, and friends who own well-mannered dogs. You also can use your favorite Internet browser to search for local dog obedience training classes. You'll likely have several choices.

TIP

Call one of the organizations listed to find out where and when the class meets. Ask whether you can observe a beginner class. Most organizations will allow you to observe a class, but if you aren't allowed to observe a class, forget that organization. When you do go to observe, leave Buddy at home so he doesn't interfere with the class and you aren't distracted.

When you're at the session, ask yourself a few questions about the class you're observing:

>> **What is your first impression of the class?** You're looking for a friendly, pleasant, quiet, and positive atmosphere. The training area should be clean.

>> **Do the dogs seem to have a good time?** You can quickly tell whether the dogs are enjoying themselves or whether they'd rather not be there.

>> **How does the instructor deal with the class participants?** You want the instructor to be encouraging and helpful, especially to anyone who seems to be struggling.

>> **How does the instructor deal with the dogs?** You want the instructor to be nice to the dogs, not to yell at them or create anxiety or fear.

>> **Does the instructor appear knowledgeable?** As a student, you aren't likely to be able to tell whether the instructor actually is knowledgeable, but at least he needs to give the appearance of being so.

>> **What is the ratio of instructors to students?** We always aim for a one-to-five ratio, with a limit of 15 students for one instructor with two assistants (see Figure 23-1).

>> **Is the space adequate for the number of dogs?** Insufficient space can cause aggression and frustration in a class situation.

FIGURE 23-1:
A group class of dogs showing off a beautiful Sit-Stay in line.

© John Wiley & Sons, Inc.

If you don't like what you see and hear, find another organization. If you feel satisfied with what you're seeing, it may be the right class for you and Buddy. But while you're visiting, you need to find out a few more bits of information:

>> **The cost of the class and what is included:** For example, our basic training courses — or Level 1, as we call it — consist of six hour-long sessions and include a training collar and leash and weekly homework sheets. What a particular organization includes in its fee varies. At the very least, you should get a homework sheet as a reminder of what was covered in class and what you need to work on during the upcoming week.

>> **The goal of the program:** What can you expect from your dog after completing the class? What do they teach in the class? Does it match what you're hoping to learn? Often the instructor teaches more in class than what you realized you needed, which can be a good thing. Your main goal after all should be to discover how to train your dog.

Puppy classes

Taking Buddy to a puppy obedience training class is the best investment you can make in his future. The benefit of taking a puppy to class is that he can socialize with other young dogs and have fun, yet learn manners and the proper way to interact with his own kind. Buddy's brain at this point in his young life is like a sponge, and he'll remember nearly everything you teach him now for the rest of his life. He'll learn all those lessons that will make him an ideal pet.

TIP

Look for an organization that offers puppy classes, preferably one that teaches basic control instead of just socialization and games. Nothing is wrong with socialization and games; both are necessary, but at the right time and in the right context. Look for a class where the people are having fun with their dogs and where the instructor is pleasant and professional to the students. Above all, you want to see happy dogs.

You want Buddy to view meeting other dogs as a pleasant but controlled experience, not one of playing and being rowdy. As he grows older, playing and being rowdy is no longer cute and will make him difficult to manage around other dogs.

The ideal puppy class allows the puppies to interact with each other for up to three minutes before the class starts for the first two classes only. After the second week, the puppies should be allowed to play for three minutes after class. By delaying playtime, Buddy learns that he must be obedient to you first and that the reward of playing comes after he has worked. This practice will help develop a lifetime habit that you want to instill while he's young.

WARNING

Stay away from classes where you're told that Buddy is too young to learn obedience exercises. This type of organization shows a lack of knowledge of dog behavior.

You can expect your puppy to learn Sit, Down, Stand, Come, and Stay, all on command; he'll also learn to walk on a loose leash. An excellent program, with well-trained instructors, also will train Buddy to do the same exercises off leash as well as on signal. For Buddy, these exercises are easy stuff.

Advanced classes

Most people who go on to advanced training start training their dogs in a beginner class. They then discover that the organization offers more advanced training as well as different activities. For example, you may find that in addition to obedience training the organization offers other types of training such as Rally or Agility (which we discuss more in Chapter 25). Or you may discover that some of the members have therapy dogs and so on. You may enjoy training and wish to broaden Buddy's horizons. If you and Buddy enjoy what you're doing, go for it.

TIP

To train for participation in performance events, join an organization that offers training at that level. The organization's instructors can coach you and your dog in the intricacies of the various requirements.

Hiring a Private Trainer

You may have serious time constraints that keep you from going to classes with your dog, so you may be considering a private trainer. Private trainers can be expensive, but using their services is better than not training at all.

You can take private lessons from an instructor, either at your house or at some other location. Under such an arrangement, the instructor may customize the lessons to you and your goals. In terms of time and effort, private lessons can be one of the more efficient arrangements.

TIP

In selecting a private trainer, be choosy. This individual has a great impact on shaping your dog's skills. Ask for references — and call them. You also want to inquire into the trainer's experience. Make sure the trainer's teaching method is one you want to practice with your dog. For instance, you want to steer clear of abusive training methods.

REMEMBER

Anyone can declare himself a dog trainer! Look for someone who belongs to one of the following groups:

>> The IACP, or International Association of Canine Professionals (www.dogpro.org)

>> The APDT, or Association of Pet Dog Trainers (www.apdt.com)

>> The NADOI, or The National Association of Dog Obedience Instructors (www.nadoi.org)

These national organizations provide continuing education for their members. These organizations don't condone abusive methods of training. Ask how many conferences the trainer has attended and whether he's certified by that organization. Avoid trainers who have just begun training dogs. Chances are they haven't had enough experience with different dogs to be helpful.

When you've found a trainer you're comfortable with, find out whether the training will take place at your residence. Most trainers go to the dog's home, which is an advantage because the trainer gets to see where and how Buddy lives, allowing him to tailor a program to meet your special needs. But before you sign on the dotted line, watch how the trainer interacts with Buddy and especially how he works him. Before committing to a long-term arrangement, ask the trainer whether he'll work with Buddy first. If you like what you see, then you can commit to further training sessions.

Sending Buddy to a Board and Train

If your trainer takes Buddy with him to train at his location for a period of time, called a *board and train,* you'll still have to become involved and learn both the various commands Buddy has learned and how to reinforce these commands. After all, the object is for Buddy to obey you, not just the trainer. You'll be expected to work Buddy under the trainer's direction so you can learn what and how he was taught.

You should be allowed to see where Buddy will live. Often you'll need to provide certain things for Buddy while he's gone, specifically his regular diet. It's much easier on Buddy's system if he stays on his own food.

Being away from you can be stressful. It's ideal if Buddy has the opportunity for play and exercise while he's away. Ask as many questions as you want until you're sure you'll be comfortable leaving Buddy with his trainer at the board and train.

After Buddy returns you'll still need to take lessons and do the work with him. After all, there's no such thing as a finished product when it comes to dog training. You'll need to continue to practice and review his lessons, but doing so should be easier at this point because someone has trained Buddy; now it's your turn.

6

The Part of Tens

Discover how training your dog is fun when you have a plan and know how to identify certain traps you want to avoid falling into.

Identify ten fun and exciting sporting activities you can do with your dog if you want to take your training to the next level.

Find out why dogs do some of the silly things they do.

Chapter **24**

Ten Training Traps and How to Avoid Them

O ne of the definitions of *trap* is "a trick by which someone is misled into acting contrary to their own interest or intentions." This definition pertains to human-to-human interaction and human-to-dog interaction. In the realm of dog training, dog owners lay some of these traps themselves, and others the dog lays for them. Sometimes the occurrence of traps doesn't really matter, but all too often it does. So, in this chapter, we explore these training traps, how to recognize them, and how to avoid them.

Procrastinating on Basic Training

As soon as you get your puppy or older dog, you need to start immediately training him. Often owners can think of all kinds of reasons to put off basic training. When it's a puppy, he's too young, cute, or small to begin training. We still hear the old refrain, "Let him have his puppyhood." But, in reality, training doesn't interfere with puppyhood — if anything else, it enhances it. Did your parents wait until you were a teenager before starting any schooling? Of course not. If it helps, think of it this way: Your puppy will start to train you from the day he steps into the house. The same applies when you acquire an older dog. So don't be bashful about training him. Get into the habit of looking at your interactions with Buddy as teaching opportunities.

In addition to housetraining, you can start with crate training, leash training, name recognition, the Long Down exercise, and the Touch command. (You can get more info on housetraining and crate training in Chapter 8. Check out the other chapters in Part 1 for information on these other topics.) *Remember:* All these exercises should be taught in an area free of distractions. No other people or dogs should be present. When Buddy understands a command, you can begin to add distractions.

Buying into Attention-Seeking Behavior

Barking for attention is the most annoying form of attention-seeking behavior. The same applies to jumping up on people. The dilemma is that in your efforts to get the dog to stop, you're giving him the attention he seeks. For a dog, negative attention — such as yelling at the dog to stop — is still attention.

When dealing with attention-seeking behavior, remember that everything belongs to *you*, including your attention. You decide when to dispense it and when to withhold it. The first rule is to ignore the dog — turn your back on him and walk away. This approach requires a bit of patience, but most dogs realize quickly that their way doesn't produce the desired results and they will stop. As you walk away, wait for and notice the quiet, the end to the barking, and then praise and interact with your dog.

REMEMBER

This advice doesn't mean that you should neglect your dog. Just the opposite — give him plenty of attention by stepping up your basic training regimen. The difference is that you decide when to initiate the interaction and when to end it, not Buddy. And don't forget to determine whether Buddy is barking or jumping up for another reason, such as needing to go out.

Forgetting to Release Your Dog from a Stay

The quickest way to undermine your efforts to teach and maintain a reliable Stay is to overlook releasing your dog. You release a dog by saying "Okay." When you forget to release Buddy, he'll begin to release himself, which isn't acceptable. You're the decision-maker, and you decide when he can move, not the other way around.

TIP

During the day you have several opportunities to reinforce the Stay command. For example, reinforce Stay when you feed your dog and when entering doorways. (Chapter 11 provides more info on teaching Stay.)

Eliminating Rewards Too Soon

During the teaching of various exercises, most dog owners use rewards like treats and verbal praise. Oftentimes, however, owners stop using treats as the dog masters commands, and then the dog stops obeying those commands. To avoid this behavior, after the dog is familiar with a command, begin to reward correct responses on a random basis so he won't know when he's going to be rewarded. Random rewards are powerful motivators because they rely on the principle of "hope springs eternal." Always carry treats in your pocket to reinforce desired behavior.

We like to use random rewards for the life of the dog. Compare it to your paycheck — would you continue working if you didn't get paid?

Using Your Dog's Name as a Command

Your dog's name is used to focus his attention on you and is followed by a command, such as "Buddy, Come." His name isn't an all-purpose command to control or direct his behavior. If you're repeatedly yelling his name in frantic and varying tones of voice without getting a response, it means that you have to get back to basics. It also teaches your dog to ignore you.

REMEMBER

When you call your dog's name, ask yourself, "Exactly what am I trying to communicate?" Do you want him to stop doing what he's doing? Do you want him to come to you? Be specific and use a command. For example, use the Come command if you want your dog to come to you. Use the Down command if you want your dog to lie down. A command should follow your dog's name.

Having to Repeat Commands Away from Home

When you give a command and nothing happens, you probably repeat it and hope it will produce the desired result. Repeating commands, however, isn't a good training practice. More often than not, you're systematically teaching your dogs to tune you out. He's telling you in no uncertain terms that he has gaps in his education.

We frequently hear, "Well, he always does it at home," and he probably does. Whatever the command involved, chances are it was taught at home, a location familiar to the dog and usually without distractions. His obeying at home doesn't mean that Buddy will generalize the learned behavior to new and different locations with serious distractions.

To avoid this training trap, you need to review in new locations those commands you've taught him at home. After that, you must review the commands around distractions, such as other dogs. One of the built-in benefits of obedience classes is that they provide a different place with plenty of other dogs as distractions. (Chapter 23 provides more information on obedience training classes.) Buddy will learn to focus on you and to ignore the distractions that come with class.

REMEMBER

Are you home free after teaching Buddy in obedience school? Not quite, but training will become much easier. After the first class, the location is familiar to Buddy, and after several classes the other dogs will be too, so you still need to practice in new locations with new distractions.

Punishing Your Dog When He Comes to You

The quickest way to cause a problem with the Come command is by punishing your dog, either verbally or physically, when he comes to you. And that's one problem you don't want to create.

"Whenever your dog comes to you, be nice to him" or "Whenever your dog comes to you, don't do anything the dog perceives as unpleasant." And what your dog perceives as unpleasant may be entirely different from what you think he perceives as unpleasant. Some dogs don't like to be bathed, in which case you wouldn't call your dog to you to give him a bath. Instead, you simply go get him, clip on a leash, and using a happy tone of voice bring him to the tub. Under no circumstances, should you drag your dog to be bathed or groomed. The same applies giving medications.

WARNING

The absolute worst thing you can do is to verbally or physically punish your dog when he comes to you after having enjoyed a romp around the neighborhood. No matter how mad or upset you may be, welcome him home with lots of praise. The last thing your dog does is what you're punishing him or praising him for. Allowing himself to be touched or caught while running loose is what he did last. Praise him profusely because you always want him to come to you when he is loose outside.

Running After Your Dog

If you want your dog to come to you, chasing after him is counterproductive to your goal. Instead of chasing after your dog, consider some common situations and the solutions:

>> If your dog is chasing a rabbit (or anything else), you need to review teaching your dog to come when called.

>> If your dog is running from you because he's not bonded to you, play the Recall Game that we explain in Chapter 10.

>> If your dog is running from you because he thinks it's a game of chase, run the other way and have him chase you. As soon as he does, stop with your back to him and intently examine the ground as though you've found something of particular interest. Dogs are curious creatures, so he'll want to see what you've found. At that point, slowly take him by the collar and attach the leash. If you try to snatch him too quickly, he'll just bolt again.

WARNING

Under no circumstances should you ever verbally or physically punish your dog when you finally corral him.

Expecting Too Much Too Quickly

Many dog owners become frustrated with training because they feel the dog isn't progressing quickly enough. But keep in mind that dogs learn the same way that everybody else does — through experience, clear and concise instructions, and repetition. What the novice trainer has to realize is that she's learning as well and that her aptitude for the task will influence how quickly the dog learns.

Experienced trainers, for example, can train a dog in a fraction of the time that it takes a beginner. In an obedience class, the budding trainer is guided step by step, so basic training is usually accomplished within several weeks. Consistently applying the techniques in this book will yield similar results. The key is patience, persistence, and, above all, never blaming the dog — he's trying just as hard as you are.

Ignoring the Principle of Consistency

When training your dog, consistency counts, so don't ignore the principle; otherwise, you'll end up with a poorly trained dog. A maxim that trainers use says, "Don't give a command unless you're able to reinforce it." For example, if you tell Buddy to sit and he ignores you, you need to reinforce the command. Show him exactly what you want him to do by placing him into a sit. Failure to do so will result in unreliable responses to the command in the future.

Of course, you'll encounter times when you don't or can't follow that maxim, such as when you're in the shower. Just make a mental note that you need to review Buddy's response to the command.

Consistency results in a pattern of behavior that becomes habitual. Consider the following examples:

>> After Buddy has grasped the concept that he has to wait to eat his meal until you've released him (see Chapter 1), he'll dutifully wait until you release him. In fact, after a while, you won't even have to tell him to wait.

>> After you've introduced door manners to Buddy (see Chapter 14), you'll see the same results as with waiting for his food. As you approach the door, he'll stay, again without having to be told, when you open the door and leave.

These results can be achieved in several training sessions through consistency. The behaviors are easy to teach because most dogs are quick studies and quickly figure out what is to their advantage. They think, "I don't get to eat/go out unless I stay first."

Chapter **25**

Ten Fun and Exciting Sporting Activities

I n addition to obedience competition (see Chapters 17 and 18), you and your dog can participate in numerous other performance events. Many are conducted under the auspices of the American Kennel Club (AKC), and some, such as Schutzhund trials, aren't. The AKC awards more than 50 different performance titles in eight different categories. And other organizations have an almost equal number of titles. In this chapter we discuss the AKC competitions and more, including Flyball competitions and Schutzhund trials. We also include a section on service dogs who work for a living.

Agility Events

Agility is an exciting and exhilarating sport for both owner and dog. The popularity of agility competitions has experienced phenomenal growth since 1994 when it became a titling sport in the AKC, and with good reason: Dogs love it, human participants love it, and it has enormous spectator appeal. Agility competitions began in England and were then introduced in the United States. You may have seen agility competitions on television on one of the channels that specialize in televising dog events and on primetime channels as well. Figure 25-1 shows a dog competing in an agility trial.

FIGURE 25-1:
A dog in
action during
an agility trial.

In agility competition, the dogs, under the direction of their owners, negotiate a complex obstacle course that includes walking over a teeter, a 5-foot high A-frame, and a 4-foot high plank with ramps; weaving in and out between a series of poles; jumping over and through objects; and going through tunnels. To compensate for the size differences among dogs and to make the competition fair, seven height divisions exist.

As with obedience, the level of difficulty increases with each higher class as does the number of obstacles. Other than the exercises themselves, some significant differences exist between agility trials and obedience trials. We outline the differences in Table 25-1.

TABLE 25-1

Differences between Agility and Obedience Trials

Agility	Obedience
Your dog must be able to work on both your right and left side.	Your dog works on your left side.
You have minimum time limits during which you and your dog have to complete the course.	There is no time limit (within reason).
The obstacles and the order in which the obstacles are to be negotiated vary.	The exercises and the order of the exercises are always the same.
Continuous communication with your dog is encouraged.	During your dog's performance of an exercise, you can't talk to your dog and can give only one command.

No doubt, part of the appeal of agility competition is its seeming simplicity. Almost any dog in reasonably good physical condition quickly learns the rudiments of the various obstacles. And, almost any owner who's also in reasonably good physical condition can compete in agility. But few things are ever as simple as they appear.

REMEMBER

Beginning agility is deceptively simple, but it's not as easy as it looks. Because the courses you and your dog have to negotiate are never the same, your ability to communicate with your dog is important. Any lapses in communication invariably result in Buddy's failure to complete the course correctly. You're also competing against the clock and have to make split-second decisions. In addition, you need to memorize the course before you and your dog compete.

Agility is wonderful for dogs with both high prey drive and pack drive and teaches your dog to work with you as a team, turning it into a pack drive game (Chapter 2 describes pack drive in more detail). Dogs that belong to the Herding, Working, Sporting, Toy, and Nonsporting groups all do well in agility. One of the fastest dogs is the Border Collie.

You can see what makes agility so exciting. The two of you really need to work as a team and to keep your wits about you. We highly recommend that you try it. You'll be amazed how your dog will take to it. We aren't suggesting that you try to set up an agility course in your backyard — few people have the wherewithal to do that. Find out from your local dog organizations where agility trials are being held and then take a look. Most communities have a group or an individual who holds classes that meet on a regular basis where you and Buddy can get started. Even if you aren't interested in competing, agility courses are good mental stimulation for Buddy as well as good exercise for both of you.

Tracking Titles

The dog's incredible ability to use his nose and follow a scent is the basis for tracking events. Any dog can participate, and if you enjoy tromping through the great outdoors in solitude with your dog, tracking is for you. Tracking also is potentially the most useful activity you can teach your dog. Many a tracking dog has found a lost person or lost article. Dogs that like to use their noses do well in this sport such as Beagles, Bloodhounds, and German Shepherds, though almost all dogs can be taught to track.

Your dog's sense of smell is almost infallible. Local law enforcement often uses dogs to sniff out bombs, drugs, and other contraband. Researchers are even using them to detect cancer in a person.

Buddy can earn three tracking titles:

» **Tracking Dog (TD):** The track has to be at least 440 yards, but not more than 500 yards in length. A person lays the track 30 minutes to 2 hours before the event, and it has three to five turns. It doesn't have any cross tracks or obstacles.

» **Tracking Dog Excellent (TDX):** The track has to be at least 800 yards, but not more than 1,000 yards in length. The track has to be not less than three hours and not more than five hours old. It has to have five to seven turns. It must have two cross tracks and two obstacles, such as a different surface or a stream.

» **Variable Surface Tracking (VST):** The track has to be at least 600 yards, but not more than 800 yards in length. Age of track is the same as for the TDX. It has to have four to eight turns. It has to have a minimum of three different surfaces, such as concrete, asphalt, gravel or sand, and vegetation.

The principal differences between the classes are the age of the track and the surface. Your dog has to complete only one track successfully to earn its title, unlike obedience or agility titles, for which three qualifying performances are required.

REMEMBER

The basic idea of successful tracking is the dog's ability to follow the track layer's footsteps from beginning to end. A dog that veers too far away from the track and has obviously lost the scent is whistled off and doesn't qualify on that particular occasion.

Barn Hunt AKC

Barn Hunt grew out of the dog's natural instinct for hunting rats and mice in barns and in the country. This sport requires teamwork between you and your dog. The dog must indicate when he has located a rat inside of mountains of hay bales. Rats are contained in safe cages so they don't come into direct contact with the dogs hunting them. Therefore, no rats are harmed.

High prey-drive dogs are best suited for this category, but any dog that can get into a tunnel of straw that is 18 inches wide and the height of a bale of straw can give it a try. The Barn Hunt association claims that a "Barn Hunt tests the nose, speed, agility, and surefootedness of dogs that have a history of above-ground vermin hunting."

An instinct test for beginners at most Barn Hunt competitions is pass or fail. Several levels and titles are available, and with each level the number of hidden rats increases with other distractions and diversions.

Lure Coursing

Another event that relies on your dog's desire to chase moving objects is Lure Coursing. Instead of running behind a living prey such as a rabbit, the lure is a mechanized white plastic bag on a laid-out string that is motorized and zigzags around the course. A remote controls this machine so that the plastic bag stays just out of the dog's reach, and yet the dog can catch it at the end for the dog to pretend kill, catch, and shake in order to keep up the dog's motivation.

Lure Coursing can be so fun for dogs with plenty of prey drive. It keeps Buddy happy and fit while you provide an outlet for his extra energy. A group, club, or even an individual can purchase the Lure Coursing machines that move the mechanical bag. Lure Coursing is a great way to burn off that prey drive energy and to meet people and their dogs, too.

Schutzhund Training

The word Schutzhund means "protection dog." Schutzhund training, which is one of the oldest organized competition, originated in Germany in the 1900s and is the precursor to obedience exercises, tracking, and agility. In fact, many of its exercises have been incorporated into today's performance events.

Schutzhund training all began when the German Shepherd came to be used as a police dog. German Shepherds were thought of as being the only true multipurpose dog and were expected to guard and protect, herd, track, be a guide dog for the blind, and, of course, be good with children.

As a police dog, a dog's main responsibility is to protect his handler. He also has to be able to pursue, capture, or track down suspects. Searches require great agility, perhaps jumping into windows and negotiating stairs and even ladders. Naturally, he has to know all the obedience exercises. It wasn't long before competitions began among police units to see who had the most talented and best-trained dog. Dog owners became interested and the sport of Schutzhund was born.

Schutzhund training consists of three parts: protection, obedience, and tracking. To qualify for a title, the dog must pass all three parts. When obedience and tracking were introduced in this country, they were patterned after the Schutzhund dog. Agility competitions derived in part from the Schutzhund obedience exercises, which include walking over the A-frame as well as different jumps.

Schutzhund training, which is rigorous and highly athletic and one of the most time consuming of all dog sports, isn't limited to German Shepherds. Other dogs of the guarding, working, and herding breeds, which have the aptitude such as Rottweilers and Belgian Malinois, can participate. Even some of the nonguarding breeds can do it, although you won't see them at the upper levels of competition.

Flyball Competitions

Flyball is a relay race consisting of two teams with four dogs on a team. The course consists of two sets of four hurdles, set up side by side and spaced 10 feet apart. At the end of each set of hurdles sits a box that holds a tennis ball. At the same time, each team sends the first dog to retrieve the ball. The dogs jump the hurdles, retrieve the ball, and return over the hurdles. When the first dog crosses the finish line, the next dog starts and retrieves the ball until all four dogs on each team have completed the course. The team with the fastest time wins, provided no errors were made, such as a dog going around one or more of the hurdles, either coming or going. For information, visit the North American Flyball Association's website at www.flyball.org. Dogs high in prey drive do well in Flyball.

Freestyle Performances

Canine Freestyle is a choreographed musical program performed by a dog/owner team, sort of like figure skating for pairs. The object is to display the team in a creative, innovative, and original dance. In Freestyle, the performance of every team is different, although the various performances often share basic obedience maneuvers and are put to music.

Started in the early 1990s as a way to bring some levity to obedience training, Freestyle has caught on like a house afire. Chances are you have seen it on one of the TV shows featuring dog activities. Freestyle is fun to watch and fun to train. Any dog high in pack drive will do well. In competition you see almost all breeds competing. For more information, visit The World Canine Freestyle Organization's website at www.worldcaninefreestyle.org.

Dock Diving Dogs

If Buddy is a retrieving fanatic and loves to swim and jump into water, then Dock Diving Dogs is for him (see Figure 25-2).

FIGURE 25-2:
A Dock
Diving dog.

Photograph by Diana Rockwell

Here are the basic rules: You throw your dog's favorite toy off a dock. On your command, Buddy runs and jumps into the water and retrieves his toy. The goal is to match your throw and Buddy's jump so his launch is as long as possible before he lands in the water. Dogs can also compete for height and distance.

Detection Dogs or Scent Work

After man discovered the dog's incredible scenting ability, the detection dog was born. Humans have approximately 10 million olfactory cells compared to dog's 200 million olfactory cells.

Because of their keen senses, dogs are now routinely used to detect drugs and explosives and search for victims buried in the rubble of collapsed buildings and avalanches. The dog has even replaced the pig to hunt for truffles, probably because he isn't as inclined as the pig to eat the truffles he finds.

AKC Scent Work is a titling sport where detection dogs locate a specific scent and then indicate that he has found the scent. This new sport has become quite popular because nearly any dog can do it. With practice you discover how to read your dog as he locates the hidden scent in a room or outside in a searchable area. Your dog is judged by how he lets you know precisely where the scent is located.

AKC Scent Work uses anise, birch, clove, and cypress. You can easily find all as essential oils and they're easy to use. The oil typically is used on a *hide*, which is a cotton swab hidden for your dog to find. Buddy must indicate to you that he has found the scent by sitting, pawing, barking, or showing a similar type response. As the levels get more difficult, Buddy has to find more hides. The scent can be buried or placed high above his head.

Working as a Service Dog

The term "service dog" was first used to describe police dogs and dates back to the beginning of the 20th century. Training for this job started in Germany with the German Shepherd. Over the years, the tasks of service dogs have multiplied to an astonishing degree. You now can find seizure-detection dogs, cancer-detection dogs, and blood sugar-level-monitoring dogs, as well as assistance dogs such as emotional support dogs. The following section describe two of the most common service dogs and their duties.

Assistance dogs

Assistance dogs are used to help individuals in need. (See Figure 25-3 for a look at a working assistance dog.) The following list includes the main types of assistance dogs:

>> **Guide dogs for the blind:** The use of dogs to assist blind individuals dates back to 1930, when the first training centers were started in England. Guide dog organizations tend to have their own breeding programs in order to cement the physical and behavioral traits necessary to become a reliable guide dog. Guide dogs undergo the most extensive training of any of the assistance dogs.

>> **Dogs for the deaf and hearing impaired:** These dogs are trained to react to certain noises and to alert their masters. For example, a dog may jump on the bed when the alarm clock goes off, tug at his owner's leg when someone is at the door, or take his owner's hand to alert him to the presence of an unexpected guest.

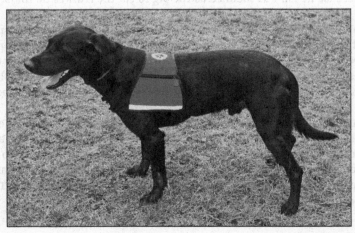

FIGURE 25-3: You can recognize assistance dogs by their jackets.

© John Wiley & Sons, Inc.

>> **Dogs to assist the physically handicapped:** A good assistance dog for the handicapped can respond to about 50 different commands, such as retrieving objects that are out of reach or have been dropped, opening and closing doors, pulling wheelchairs, or turning light switches on and off. Excellent retrieving skills are a must for assistance dogs for the handicapped.

>> **Therapy dogs:** The main purpose of the therapy dog and his handler is to provide comfort and companionship to patients in hospitals, nursing homes, and other institutions. The training is based on the Canine Good Citizen program with some added requirements. Any well-trained dog with good social behavior skills can become a therapy dog.

In addition to their specialized skills, all assistance dogs play an important therapeutic role for their owners, especially children who have impairments that can cause them to become physically or emotionally withdrawn from society. Each type of assistance dog has trusted organizations that provide training and/or dogs to help people — children, adults, therapy, blind, deaf, and so on. Search online for more specifics to suit your needs that an assistance dog can aid.

Companions

Every year a new sport or competition trends for you and your dog to try. You'll always need the basics in obedience to enjoy a wonderful relationship between you and your dog. From reading assistance dogs at the local library where kids read to dogs to competitions that title your dog to great heights, a trained dog is capable of almost anything. A favorite motto to adopt is "A trained dog is a free dog." So keep training!

More than likely, you have a dog that serves as a pet and companion, a living being that's devoted to you. Your dog is always happy to see you and doesn't argue or complain.

Chapter **26**

Ten Reasons Dogs Do What They Do

W ho knows why your dog does some of the things that he does? Or more important, who *wants* to know why your dog does some of the things that he does? Well, if you're curious, this chapter offers answers to a few of these questions.

Why Do Dogs Insist on Jumping on People?

The behavior of dogs jumping on people goes back to the weaning process. As puppies grow, the mother dog begins to feed them standing up so puppies have to stand on their hind legs to feed. Then, as her milk decreases, the puppies jump up to lick at the corner of her mouth, trying to get her to regurgitate her semi-digested meal. When she does, it's the puppies' first introduction to solid food.

As dogs grow, jumping becomes more of a greeting behavior, as in, "Hi, good to see you," much like people shake hands when they meet someone. Because the behavior is so instinctive, modifying it is sometimes difficult. Although you're probably pleased that your dog is happy to see you, you'd also probably prefer a more sedate greeting, especially if Buddy is a large dog. Because jumping on people is a friendly gesture from the dog's point of view, we suggest modifying the behavior in a positive way by teaching a reliable Sit command (see Chapter 11) and petting only when Buddy is sitting.

Why Do Dogs Sniff Parts of Your Anatomy That You'd Prefer They Didn't?

When two dogs meet each other for the first time, they often go through what looks like a choreographed ritual. After some preliminaries, they sniff each other's respective rear ends and genitals. Dogs "see" with their noses and gather important information in this way. They can identify another dog's gender, age, and rank order, information that dictates how they interact with one another.

When meeting a new person, a dog wants to know that same information. Some are confirmed "crotch sniffers," but others are more subtle. Although embarrassing for the owner and the "sniffee," the behavior is harmless enough and easily remedied with the Sit command. (Head to Chapter 11 for information on teaching Buddy to sit on command.)

Why Do Male Dogs Lift Their Legs So Often?

All dogs *mark* their territory by leaving small amounts of urine — the male more so than the female. You can liken the behavior to putting up a sign or billboard; it lets other dogs in the neighborhood know he has been there. The scent enables dogs to identify the age, gender, and rank order of every dog that has marked that spot.

When you take Buddy for a walk, he intently investigates various spots and then lifts his leg to deposit a few drops of urine to cover the area, thereby reclaiming his territory. Male dogs have a special fondness for vertical surfaces, such as a tree or the side of a building. Corners of buildings are a special treat. Height of a particular marking is important because it establishes rank. Comical contortions can be the result, such as when a Yorkshire Terrier tries to cover the mark of a Great Dane. Females don't seem to have that need, which explains why they can do their business in a fraction of the time it takes a male. Both males and females also may scratch at the ground and kick the dirt after urinating to spread their scent, thereby claiming a larger amount of territory.

REMEMBER

If your male dog starts to mark things in your house, it may be because something new is introduced into the household. The regression in this housetraining may occur when a baby or another pet is added to the family, or even when a new piece of furniture or drapes are added to the household. If this happens to you, refer to Chapter 8 and follow the instructions for potty training.

Why Do Dogs Mount Each Other?

Both female and male dogs can display mounting behavior. Even though this behavior is more normally associated with males trying to flirt or breed with a female, it also can be seen male to male, female to female, and female to male. Most people think it's only related to sex, but it also can be a dominance display with dogs of the same gender — the one on top reminding the other who is in charge — or it can be a behavior that's displayed when dogs that know each other well have been separated for some time. The behavior is then a form of bonding, like a hug, meaning, "I missed you."

Instead of discouraging this behavior, we have found it better to leave the dogs alone; they work things out well between themselves. They have to, because they're pack animals and know exactly the message they're trying to convey, usually to bring harmony back to the household or situation. However, if this behavior goes on too long, distract with food or a squeaky toy or take Buddy for a walk.

REMEMBER

The time mounting behavior can be construed as abnormal is if a female has some vaginal discharge indicating some sort of infection, which smells as if she's in season. In that case, other dogs won't leave her alone, and a visit to the vet is the appropriate remedy.

Why Do Dogs Like to Chase Things?

Dogs chase things for a variety of different reasons:

>> To chase intruders, be it people or other animals, off their property

>> To chase a potential meal, such as a bird, rabbit, squirrel, or chipmunk

>> To chase just because the object is moving, such as cars, bicycles, or joggers

>> To chase because it's fun

Whatever the reason, chasing usually isn't a good idea because it can endanger the safety of people and the dog. Unless you're prepared to keep Buddy on leash under circumstances where he's likely to chase, you need to train him to come when called, especially around strong distractions. (Chapter 10 provides tips on how to successfully teach the Come command.)

Why Do Dogs Roll in Disgusting Things?

Dogs delight in rolling in the most disgusting stuff, such as dead fish, deer or rabbit droppings, and similar decaying debris. To make matters worse, the urge to roll seems strongest just after Buddy has had a bath. Do dogs *like* to smell putrid?

Behaviorists believe that because the dog is a pack animal, he's merely bringing back to the pack the scent of possible food sources. The pack can then track down a meal. The behavior is instinctive. Most dogs roll at one point or another, some to a greater extent than others. It's just part of being a dog. If you have taught a reliable Leave It command (Chapter 9) and/or Come command (Chapter 10), you can interrupt the behavior. But another solution if you have a constant roller: Keep several bottles of shampoo handy.

Why Do Dogs Eat Weeds or Grass?

Dogs come with many instinctive behaviors. One of those behaviors is the incredible knowledge of what weeds to eat and when. One reason a dog eats grass is to induce vomiting. He may have eaten something that disagrees with him, and the grass goes into the stomach and binds whatever it contains, which is then expelled. It's an adaptive behavior that protects the dog against indigestion and food poisoning. As a result, dogs that have access to the right kinds of grasses, those with wide, serrated edges, rarely get food poisoning. New grass is also sweet and tasty to dogs. Dogs eat it as a treat, and it won't make them throw up in those cases.

Dogs have an infallible knowledge of which weeds to eat. These weeds often are the very same that are found in capsules in the health food store to boost immune and other body systems. Should you stop your dog from eating weeds? Absolutely not! He knows much better what he needs than you do. Just make sure you don't expose your dog to areas that have been sprayed with chemicals. If your dog insists on eating a plant that you know is not good for him, use the Leave It command (see Chapter 9).

Why Do Dogs Hump Humans' Legs?

Some believe that humping humans' legs is a sign of dominance, but this is doubtful. Puppies often hump their littermates, a behavior believed to be practice for future sexual encounters. Many dogs continue humping humans' legs or other dogs even after they're spayed or neutered. The explanation is probably as simple as they have learned the behavior feels good. Distract with either food or a squeaky toy to change the behavior.

Why Do Dogs Scoot on Their Rear Ends?

Once in a while, your dog may appear to be sitting and then will suddenly drag himself around on his front paws, with his rear end on the floor. It looks as if he's trying to clean (or scratch!) his rear. This behavior can mean that his anal glands — small scent sacks just inside the rectum — are full and need emptying. When they need emptied, you need to take him to your vet so she can express the glands. With some breeds, these small glands have to be emptied a couple of times a month. With other breeds, you never see this behavior.

Another reason for this behavior is tapeworms. The segments of these worms are pushed out through the rectum and irritate the dog. To rid himself of the segment, he'll scrape his rectum on the carpet or on the grass outside. If you think your dog has worms, visit your vet with a small fecal sample and let her make a diagnosis.

Why Do Dogs Circle Before Lying Down?

In the wild, dogs had to trample down the grass to make a bed for the night. Even though this tamping down is no longer necessary, the behavior is instinctive. You can still see when your dog makes small circles stomping on his bed. The behavior is harmless — let him be a dog.

REMEMBER

You may have to intervene when he's tearing up your bedspread or your couch. If that should happen, you need to deny him access to the bed or couch, or consider covering them with something that you don't mind being destroyed.

Index

J

K

L

triggers
  for defense drive, 378
  for pack drive, 382–383
  for prey drive, 375–376
trimming
  nails, 140
  nails on senior dogs, 417
trustworthiness, housetraining and, 167
tug of war, 379–381
turns, making, 338, 340

U

UD (Utility Dog), 324
ultrasonic handheld devices, 118
United Kennel Club (UKC), 327
upset stomach, 393
urinary incontinence, 393–394
Utility Dog (UD), 324

V

vaccinations
  about, 89–90
  for boarding, 92
  flea and tick medications, 92–93
  overvaccinating, 90–92
  for schooling, 92
Variable Surface Tracking (VST), 444
vegetables, adding to dry kibble, 81–82
vehicles
  entering, 396
  exiting, 396–397
veterinarian visits
  about, 88
  aggression during, 387
  managing visits to, 401–402
vibration collars, 115
visual stimuli, responses to, 48–49
vitamins, 76–77
Volhard, Wendy (author)
  Holistic Guide for a Healthy Dog, 2nd Edition, 66, 84
volharddognutrition (website), 66, 84, 88, 109, 127, 411, 414
Volhards' Canine Personality Profile, 31–35
VST (Variable Surface Tracking), 444

W

walking
  about, 219
  adding distractions, 226–229
  collars for, 219–221
  heeling, 224–226
  leashes for, 219–221
  pleasure, 221–224
  for training, 18
Walking Backward exercise, for senior dogs, 407
Walking exercise, for senior dogs, 409
Warning icon, 3
washing
  puppies, 138–140
  senior dogs, 416
water, for drinking, 77–78, 168
water-soluble vitamins, 77
weavers, 49
web leashes, for walking, 220
websites
  Amazon, 115, 116
  American Holistic Veterinary Medical Association, 96, 97
  American Kennel Club (AKC), 18, 324, 326, 327
  Animal Poison Control center, 98
  Assistance Dogs International, Inc., 20
  Assistance Dogs of America, Inc., 20
  Association of Pet Dog Trainers (APDT), 430
  Buster Cubes, 411
  Canine Assistants, 20
  Canine Companions for Independence, 20
  Cheat Sheet, 4
  chiropractic veterinarians, 137
  Continental Kennel Club, 327
  dogfoodadvisor, 68
  dogramp, 421
  Dogs for the Deaf, 20
  Dr. B's Longevity food, 83
  Guiding Eyes for the Blind, 20
  gundogsonline, 115
  Handcraft Collars, 101
  International Association of Canine Professionals (IACP), 430
  k9-carts, 421
  Kong toys, 151, 266

About the Authors

Wendy Volhard and her late husband Jack have been best-selling authors of many dog training books, which have been translated into ten languages. They co-authored the first three editions of *Dog Training For Dummies* and also produced a two-set DVD called "Living with Your Dog," which shows the Volhard method of developing a mutually inspiring relationship with man's best friend. Jack died in 2016, but Wendy carries on with the legacy and has joined with her colleague and friend, Mary Ann Zeigenfuse, LVT, to produce this fourth edition.

Wendy is the recipient of four awards from the DWAA. She wrote numerous articles, was a regular columnist for the *American Kennel Gazette*, and co-authored many books, including the *Canine Good Citizen: Every Dog Can Be One*, which was named Best Care and Training Book for 1995 by the DWAA, and *The Holistic Guide for a Healthy Dog*, which is now in its second edition.

Wendy, whose expertise extends to helping owners gain a better understanding of why their pets do what they do, developed the Canine Personality Profile, and her two-part series, "Drives — A New Look at an Old Concept," was named Best Article in a specialty magazine for 1991 by the DWAA. She also developed the most widely used system for evaluating and selecting puppies, and her film, *Puppy Aptitude Testing*, was named Best Film on Dogs for 1980 by the DWAA.

Wendy specializes in behavior, nutrition, and alternative sources of healthcare for dogs, such as acupuncture and homeopathy, and she has formulated a balanced homemade diet for dogs that is now available at www.volharddognutrition.com. The February/March 2010 issue of *Bark Magazine* included Wendy in its list of Best and Brightest 100 for developing the Puppy Aptitude Test and the Drives Profile.

Wendy shares her home with two Labrador Retrievers, two Standard Wirehaired Dachshunds, and two cats. The dogs are more or less well trained, and the cats do their own thing. All are allowed on the furniture, but they do get off when told. Wendy is a true practitioner — she has obtained dozens of conformation and performance titles with her German Shepherds, Labrador Retrievers, Landseer Newfoundlands, Wirehaired Dachshunds, and Yorkshire Terriers.

Through the classes, lectures, seminars, and training camps in the United States, Bermuda, Canada, England, and Puerto Rico, the Volhards and Mary Ann Zeigenfuse have taught countless owners how to communicate more effectively with their pets. Individuals from almost every state and 15 countries have attended their training camps that still continue to this day run by Theresa Richmond and Mary Ann. Check out www.mahoganyridge.net for more information.

Internationally recognized as "trainers of trainers," Jack and Wendy were inducted into the Hall of Fame of the International Association of Canine Professionals in 2006. Visit their website at www.volharddognutrition.com/ and look under the Resources tab for information on the Drives profile and Puppy Testing.

Mary Ann Zeigenfuse, LVT, has had her life go completely to the dogs. When she was a child the one thing she wanted more than anything else was a dog, but she was never allowed to own one. There was one short period when the family had a dog, but it was short lived and it only cemented her desire to acquire her life-long "best friend" one day. Because of that denial, her life is now filled with dogs. She went to college to be a veterinary technician and practiced veterinary medicine as a licensed technician for more than 40 years. She worked in an emergency practice followed by a humane society and then a 24-hour practice where she ultimately became the head technician in a six-doctor practice. Also, during that time she was on the board of the humane society and started her own dog training business after being the training director of a different dog training school.

In addition to owning her own dogs and showing them in performance sports, she boarded dogs in her home and helped others train their dogs while giving classes and lessons almost daily.

During her study of dog training, she became involved in the Volhard Motivational Method of dog training where she ultimately met Jack and Wendy Volhard. They became her mentors and eventually they worked together, giving seminars around the country and teaching at their week-long training camps where she taught people how to become dog trainers as well as helping them train their own dogs. Her life has been full of dogs, hers and others.

She wrote her first book: *Dog Tricks, Step by Step,* (Macmillan Publishing) and tech edited an earlier version of *Dog Training For Dummies,* so when she was asked to work on this edition as a rewrite, she enthusiastically said yes.

As a dog trainer, every dog teaches her something. Every dog trainer she meet shows her something even if it's only how they communicate with the dogs with which they work. Communication is the key to all dog training. Without communication, no training can take place. Dogs need to understand what his owner wants, they need to know when his owner is pleased, and they need to know when the owner is finished and moving on. Play is a big part of training a dog. After all, training can be viewed as play as well as work, enjoyable either way.

Her goal in writing this book was to show how communication works and how a dog owner must communicate to his dog for both the dog and owner to learn the game of dog training.